Networking Linux®
A Practical Guide
to TCP/IP

New Riders Professional Library

Networking Linux®
A Practical Guide
to TCP/IP

New Riders

201 West 103rd Street,
Indianapolis, Indiana 46290

Pat Eyler

Networking Linux: A Practical Guide to TCP/IP

International Standard Book Number: 0-7357-1031-7

Library of Congress Catalog Card Number: *00-103791*

05 04 03 02 01   7 6 5 4 3 2 1

Interpretation of the printing code: The rightmost double-digit number is the year of the book's printing; the rightmost single-digit number is the number of the book's printing. For example, the printing code 01-1 shows that the first printing of the book occurred in 2001.

Composed in Bembo and MCPdigital by New Riders Publishing

Printed in the United States of America

Trademarks

Warning and Disclaimer

Publisher
David Dwyer

Associate Publisher
Al Valvano

Executive Editor
Stephanie Wall

Managing Editor
Gina Brown

Product Marketing Manager
Stephanie Layton

Publicity Manager
Susan Petro Nixon

Senior Development Editor
Lisa M. Thibault

Project Editor
Elise Walter

Copy Editor
Krista Hansing

Indexer
Chris Morris

Manufacturing Coordinator
Jim Conway

Book Designer
Louisa Klucznik

Cover Designer
Brainstorm Design

Proofreader
Sarah Cisco

Composition
Ron Wise

About the Author

Pat Eyler has been working with TCP/IP and UNIX since 1988 and with Linux since 1993. He has worked as a network analyst, administrator, and engineer for Boeing and Ameritech. He has also spent time as a systems administrator for Philips and Fidelity. He has taught courses on systems administration and networking for American Research Group and the U.S. Army. More recently he has been involved in supporting e-commerce and Web development for various 'clicks and mortar' and 'dot com' companies.

Pat has also written material for companies, user groups, and the general public on Linux/Unix, shell scripting, and networking. Some of his best work has appeared in the *Linux Gazette*.

Pat has designed and managed LANs and WANs supporting everything from small/home offices to multiple campus networks. His favorite network is at home, where he is busily teaching his home-schooled kids to use Linux instead of that other OS.

Pat spends his non-technical time with his family. They enjoy traveling, reading, and cooking. He and his family are active members of the Church of Jesus Christ of Latter-day Saints.

About the Technical Reviewers

These reviewers contributed their considerable hands-on expertise to the entire development process for *Networking Linux: A Practical Guide to TCP/IP*. As the book was being written, these dedicated professionals reviewed all the material for technical content, organization, and flow. Their feedback was critical to ensuring that *Networking Linux: A Practical Guide to TCP/IP* fits our readers' need for the highest quality technical information.

Ivan McDonagh been programming for almost 20 years and is entirely self taught. He first fell in love with computers at school and learned to program in BASIC using punch cards. Ivan subsequently had many opportunities to work in real-time using both PDP and VAX mini-computers, and his interest in UNIX-like operating systems has remained since that time.

Ivan's interest in programming, particularly systems programming, lead inevitably to GNU/Linux about 4 years ago and he has avidly used, programmed and promoted GNU/Linux at every opportunity since then. Ivan currently works full-time as a salesman in the tobacco industry and part-time as a Linux books technical reviewer.

Ivan currently uses the Debian/GNU Linux distribution and has used Red Hat and Caldera, among others. Recently the Linux from Scratch (`www.linuxfromscratch.org`) idea caught Ivan's attention and he will be migrating to that as soon as possible.

Brad Harris attended Stanford University while a member of the National Security Agency's prestigious Undergraduate Training Program. He continued under the auspices of the NSA to develop advanced biometric techniques before joining the System Security Analysis and Testing division as a penetration tester. He is now employed as a senior software engineer for Affiliated Computer Systems, Inc., where he performs penetration testing and software development.

Acknowledgments

I could not have written this book without the great sacrifice and support of my wife and kids. They've been behind me for more effort than we ever imagined at the outset of this project. Polly, Eliza, and Michael—We made it!

In addition, I'd like to thank the many reviewers from PASA (the Portland Area Systems Administrators), Seth Arnold, Lucas Sheehan, Doug Munsinger, Allen Supynuk, Philip Jacob, and members of the support mailing lists for mon, ipchains, and Ethereal. To all of you—Thanks for the ideas, the encouragement, and the occasional harrassment.

I'm sure there are others whom I've forgotten. To them I owe my thanks as well. If your name should be here, please drop me an email at pate@gnu.org, and I'll make sure your name shows up on the Web site.

This book is all about open standards and free software. Far too many people wrote code, RFCs, or documentation for me to ever begin thanking them all. I hope that I got names right where I used them, and that I didn't forget to mention any names that belong in these pages.

In addition to all of this, I'd like to thank my editors at New Riders Publishing. If this is a book worth reading, it is in large part their fault. Brad, Ivan, Stephanie, John, and Lisa—Thanks for putting up with me.

Finally, I can't send this book out to the world without giving thanks to the Lord. "With God, all things are possible." Without Him, this book certainly would not have been.

Although many people have helped make this book better, any errors are solely my own.

Tell Us What You Think

As the reader of this book, you are the most important critic and commentator. We value your opinion and want to know what we're doing right, what we could do better, what areas you'd like to see us publish in, and any other words of wisdom you're willing to pass our way.

As the Executive Editor on this book, I welcome your comments. You can fax, email, or write me directly to let me know what you did or didn't like about this book—as well as what we can do to make our books stronger.

Please note that I cannot help you with technical problems related to the topic of this book, and that due to the high volume of mail I receive, I might not be able to reply to every message.

When you write, please be sure to include this book's title and author as well as your name and phone or fax number. I will carefully review your comments and share them with the author and editors who worked on the book.

Fax: 317-581-4663
Email: stephanie.wall@newriders.com
Mail: Stephanie Wall
          Executive Editor
          New Riders Publishing
          201 West 103rd Street
          Indianapolis, IN 46290 USA

Introduction

Welcome to *Networking Linux: A Practical Guide to TCP/IP*. I hope you learn as much by reading this book as I did by writing it. I found out a lot of things—about networking, about writing, and about myself. To help you get as much from this book as possible, I'd like to share the following ideas about what you'll find between the covers, and how to best make use of it.

Enjoy!

Organization of this Book

This book is divided into three parts, with an initial chapter (Chapter 1) that is not included in the parts. Chapter 1, "Prelude to a Practical Guide," gives an overview of the terminology and technology used through the rest of the book. Included in the appendixes are some important RFCs. While these documents are available on the 'Net, having them bound with this book, and indexed too, should be a real win.

Part I of this book, "The Protocols," provides a layer-by-layer look at the protocols. It reviews the use of these protocols, details the structure of the packets that make them up, and explains how they interoperate to make networks work.

Part II, "Using the Protocols Effectively," covers network administration from a hands-on point of view. Most of the emphasis is on troubleshooting, with a chapter detailing a problem-solving pattern, and another giving case studies of network problems. This part also includes a chapter covering network baselining.

Part III, "Tools for your Toolkit," provides an introduction to a number of free tools that will make your networking life easier. These introductions cover the installation and use of tools for network troubleshooting, network monitoring, and network security. Part III is covered by the *Open Publication License* (OPL), so it's free software! The most recent version of this section is online at the book's Web site (http://www.networkinglinuxbook.com). The DocBook source is available, and you're invited to help make it the best guide to free networking software available.

If you're new to networking, start out with Chapter 1, then read Part I. After you have a handle on how networks work, you can read Parts II and III in bits and pieces. The order you read these in is more interest-based than anything else.

If you've already been working with networks for a while, skim through Chapter 1. If you find anything new, follow up in the appropriate chapter in Part I. You'll probably want to refer back to Part I occasionally as you work through the rest of the book. Parts II and III are aimed at you. Read Part II, and add the ideas contained therein to you bag of networking tricks. Then read through Part III in whatever order interests you. The applications listed there are a great set of tools for any networking professional. Hopefully you'll find a shiny new toy to keep you occupied.

Other Resources

There are three kinds of resources that will make this book more useful:

- The book's Web site
- Mailing lists
- Your network

As mentioned in the previous section, I maintain a Web site for this book. It contains information about mailing lists related to this book (questions, errata, and announcements about new editions). It has all the known errata online, and a system for submitting errata. I've tried to build a good section of links to tools and other information that is also maintained there. The Web site also has the full text of Chapters 9, 10, and 11 (these are built frequently from the source, so they are more up-to-date than the book).

In addition to the mailing list I maintain for this book, there are many other mailing lists pertaining to TCP/IP, networking, and Linux. Some of them are linked to from the book's Web page. Get involved—You'll learn a lot.

Probably the best resource, though, is your own network. Grab Ethereal (see Chapter 10, "Monitoring Tools") and start watching the traffic. Read a chapter of the book, then fire up Ethereal and watch the traffic in real life. There's no teacher like experience.

How This Book Was Written

This book was written in DocBook and compiled to pdf for the technical reviewers and rtf for the publisher. I used emacs (with psgml mode) to compose the Docbook. The source code was kept in cvs. All the actual writing occurred on an IBM Thinkpad 240 running Red Hat Linux 6.2 (with a few extras). This book would never have been possible without the rich tools made available by the wonderful world of free software.

Prelude to a Practical Guide

THE *TRANSMISSION CONTROL PROTOCOL/INTERNET PROTOCOL* (TCP/IP) suite, sometimes called TCP or IP, is often viewed as a maze of acronyms and jargon. Although I don't have a magic wand to make the terminology disappear, I hope to provide you with the tools that you need to understand what's going on behind the curtain. To help minimize confusion, I'll *italicize* the first occurrence of new terms.

Before diving into a detailed look at the protocols, tools, and applications that make up TCP/IP, we'll walk through some background information to help provide context for the later chapters. The rest of this chapter introduces layered protocols, describes TCP/IP in brief, gives an example of TCP/IP at work, discusses the organizations and methods involved in specifying TCP/IP, provides some information about the development of the TCP/IP protocol on Linux, and discusses physical-layer issues.

Note from the Author

If you've already got a handle on these, you may want to just skim this chapter on your way to Chapter 2, "Link-Layer Protocols." If you want to cut to the chase but really aren't that familiar with how layered protocols work, you would probably benefit from reading the section "TCP/IP in Action: A Narrative," later in this chapter, before moving on. In fact, if you ever get lost in the protocol stack, referring to that section can help put things back into perspective for you.

Layered Protocols: A Description and History

In the beginning, custom written communications programs allowed one computer to talk to another[1]. If you wanted to talk to a different computer, you had to write a new program to do so.

This approach could not scale past a very few computers. A similar situation occurred in the early days of European trains. Individual regions built their own rail systems without trying to match track sizes (called gauges) with neighboring systems. If you wanted to ship cargo or travel between two regions, you had to stop at one or more regional boundaries and change trains because the one you were on couldn't use the tracks for the new region.

The first attempts to overcome this problem were proprietary *protocols* allowing computers from the same manufacturer to talk to one another. None of these protocols is in wide use today, but *Unix-to-Unix Copy Program* (UUCP) is similar in concept: a monolithic protocol that can be used only with another computer that understands UUCP. Fortunately, UUCP is widely available instead of being locked up as a vendor-specific protocol. (Even more fortunately, UUCP is rarely used anymore and is implemented on top of TCP in most cases where it is used.)

The next stage of the protocol evolution was the layered protocol. In this model, the protocol is broken into layers arranged in a stack (rather like dishes in a cupboard). Each of these layers is comprised of one or more protocols, an unfortunate duplication of terminology. Every layer is meant to pass information vertically within the stack. Non-TCP/IP examples of layered protocols include *eXtensible Name Service* (XNS, the ancestor of the Novell protocol stack) and *System Network Architecture* (SNA, the IBM communications protocol).

Typically, layered protocols are discussed in terms of the *OSI seven-layer model*. Each layer is responsible for certain functions within the network (for example, the network layer addresses and routes packets, and the presentation layer encrypts and compresses data).

These different layers (and potentially different protocols at each layer) can be thought of like a set of several different games. Some of the games use the same kinds of things (such as laminated playing cards). Of all the games using cards, some use the same kind of deck (a standard 52-card deck, for example). Even those using a standard deck make up a wide variety of games (for example, poker, gin rummy, and solitaire), and you can't really mix the rules between them.

The data at any given layer is organized in much the same way as the data at any other layer. A *packet* (a generic term for a blob of data at any layer) is composed of two parts, a header and a payload (or data), as shown in Figures 1.1 and 1.2.

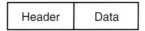

Figure 1.1   The basic organization of a packet.

Each layer encapsulates those above it.

Figure 1.2   A packet encapsulating a higher-level packet.

This process adds some overhead to the amount of data transferred,[2] and this is one of the complaints against layered protocols. In light of the benefits, however, the cost seems minimal.

The two big wins with this model are that it is easy to implement and easy to extend. Implementing the protocol means that any given hardware vendor can utilize a protocol stack so that its equipment can communicate with any other vendors' equipment (assuming that the specifics of the protocol are open and that the other vendor has also implemented it). Extending a protocol means adding functionality to it.

In the case of TCP/IP, the protocol specifications are wide open, and *Requests for Comments* (RFCs), which are described later in this chapter, give precise details about the various protocols in the TCP/IP suite. Not only are the RFCs available, but several reference implementations also can be used by anybody wanting to do so.

Extending TCP/IP by adding a new application-layer service typically requires only implementing a protocol at one layer of the model while making use of the existing layers for the rest of the work. For example, if you wanted to implement a protocol to allow all your networked hosts to exchange uptimes, you could rely on IP and the *User Datagram Protocol* (UDP) to deliver the data, and concentrate on how to format and use the information in the application-layer protocol that you develop.

TCP/IP

TCP/IP was developed to provide a vendor-neutral layered protocol for the Department of Defense. The fact that it is now the *lingua franca* of the Internet speaks not only to its own design, but also to the benefits of layered protocols.

TCP/IP breaks from the OSI model in that it has only four layers: a *link layer*, a *network layer*, a *transport layer*, and an *application layer*. Some authors add a fifth layer, the *physical layer*, beneath the link layer (see Figure 1.3). I think this is inappropriate, however, because the TCP/IP specifications don't deal with the differences between physical-layer implementations of link-layer protocols (for example, there is no real difference in the way TCP/IP treats Ethernet frames from a 10BaseT source or a 100BaseTx source). I will provide a brief overview of physical-layer issues at the end of this chapter.

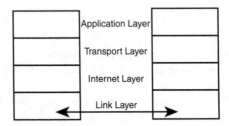

Figure 1.3   The TCP/IP protocol stack.

We'll talk about each of these in a lot more detail in the remainder of this section, but let's run through them quickly right now. As can be expected, there are a number of minor variations of and exceptions to the following descriptions.

Link Layer

The link layer sits at the bottom of the stack. It is responsible for transmitting and receiving chunks of information (often called *frames* or packets). Examples of protocols at this layer are *Ethernet* and the *Point-to-Point Protocol* (PPP).

Network Layer

The network layer sits above the link layer. It is responsible for routing and addressing chunks of data. At the Internet layer, these chunks are termed *datagrams*. For our purposes, the major protocol at this level is the *Internet Protocol* (IP).

Transport Layer

The transport layer sits above the network layer. It is responsible for ensuring that data comes from and goes to the right processes on a host. Data is handled in units often called *segments* (but sometimes also called datagrams[3]). TCP and UDP are the main protocols at this layer.

Application Layer

The application layer sits at the top of the stack and is often implemented in user applications such as Telnet or Netscape. Data in the application layer is handled in units generally called *messages*. Many protocols (and associated programs) are part of this layer.

TCP/IP in Action: A Narrative

To try to put all this (and everything that follows) into perspective, let's watch some email being sent to a remote host. Be forewarned that this is a bit of an oversimplification, but it should provide all the meat we need for now. Although TCP/IP is often explained from the link layer up, I'll turn things upside-down for this example and walk from the application layer down.

For our example, I'm logged into cherry and will be sending an email to my wife on mango. (A diagram of the hosts and the network that connects them is shown in Figure 1.4.)

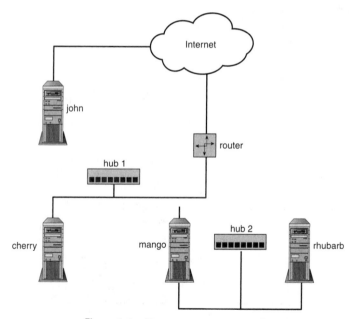

Figure 1.4   Two systems on a network.

Because we are dealing with the protocols, it really doesn't matter which program sends the mail as long as it implements the *Simple Mail Transfer Protocol* (SMTP). Often multiple programs implement the same protocol—sendmail, qmail, and postfix are just a few *mail transfer agents* (MTAs) that implement SMTP. A user doesn't generally use an MTA directly; instead, the user uses a *mail user agent* (MUA), such as pine, balsa, or evolution.

After I've finished writing the email message in my MUA, it is handed to the MTA for delivery. The MTA first determines mango's address and then sends the message and mango's address to TCP for handling at the transport layer (see Figure 1.5).

Figure 1.5   An email message in a TCP segment.

TCP then initiates a session with mango, and after the session is set up (courtesy of the lower layers), it sends a series of segments containing the email message down to IP at the network layer. Each segment in the session contains enough information to identify the unique process on each machine and what part of the application-layer message it carries (see Figure 1.6).

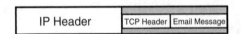

Figure 1.6   A TCP segment in an IP datagram.

IP uses the initial segments (the request to set up the session) and determines where to send its datagrams. If the destination is not on the local network, IP must determine the appropriate *gateway* to send them. In this case, cherry and mango are on the same network, so no routing is required. IP then passes its datagrams down to the Ethernet device handler on the link layer for delivery (see Figure 1.7).

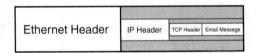

Figure 1.7   An IP datagram in an Ethernet packet.

The Ethernet system must map the IP address of the destination (or gateway) to a hardware address using the *Address Resolution Protocol* (ARP) or by looking in the machine's ARP cache,[4] if there is an entry for that address. In this case, cherry has the following ARP cache:

```
[root@cherry /root]# arp -a
? (192.168.1.1) at 00:A0:D2:1C:64:E8 [ether] on eth0
? (192.168.1.11) at 00:C0:F0:26:B1:EC [ether] on eth0
[root@cherry /root]#
```

After the address has been mapped, the IP datagram (which carries a TCP segment, which in turn carries a portion of an SMTP message) is wrapped in an Ethernet packet and sent to its destination (see Figure 1.8).

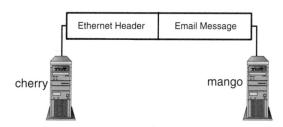

Figure 1.8   An Ethernet packet carrying email between hosts.

On mango, the Ethernet packet is received and inspected. If the host determines that it is for local delivery, it determines where to deliver its contents.[5] In this case, the packet contains an IP datagram that is passed to the IP stack.[6]

The IP stack inspects the datagram and finds that it carries a TCP segment, which is passed to the TCP stack. The IP stack may need to take some special action before passing the segment up to the TCP stack, reassembling a segment from a series of datagrams for example.

TCP inspects the datagram that it has received and passes the SMTP message to the local MTA, at the application layer, for delivery to an end user.

RFCs

TCP/IP is controlled by the *Internet Engineering Task Force* (IETF), a volunteer standards body with an open admission policy. RFCs are used to develop and maintain the various TCP/IP-related standards. These documents are freely distributed by the IETF.

RFCs 1122 and 1123 are the host requirements RFCs. (RFC 1009 is the router requirements RFC.) These three documents form a basis for much of the discussion in the rest of the book. The accompanying sidebar excerpt from RFC 2400 helps to explain some of the terminology used in and about RFCs.

Explanation of Terms

There are two independent categorizations of protocols. The first is the maturity level or state of standardization, one of standard, draft standard, proposed standard, experimental, informational, or historic. The second is the requirement level or status of this protocol, one of required, recommended, elective, limited use, or not recommended.

The status or requirement level is difficult to portray in a one-word label. These status labels should be considered only as an indication, and a further description, or applicability statement, should be consulted.

When a protocol is advanced to proposed standard or draft standard, it is labeled with a current status.

What Is a "System"?

Some protocols are particular to hosts, and some are particular to gateways; a few protocols are used in both. The definitions of the terms will refer to a "system" that is either a host or a gateway (or both). It should be clear from the context of the particular protocol which types of systems are intended.

4.1 Definitions of Protocol State

Every protocol listed in this document is assigned to a maturity level or state of standardization: standard, draft standard, proposed standard, experimental, or historic.

■ **4.1.1 Standard protocol**—The IESG has established this as an official standard protocol for the Internet. These are assigned STD numbers (see RFC 1311). These are separated into two groups: IP protocol and above, protocols that apply to the whole Internet; and network-specific protocols, generally specifications of how to do IP on particular types of networks.

■ **4.1.2 Draft standard protocol**—The IESG is actively considering this protocol as a possible standard protocol. Substantial and widespread testing and comment are desired. Comments and test results should be submitted to the IESG. There is a possibility that changes will be made in a draft standard protocol before it becomes a standard protocol.

■ **4.1.3 Proposed standard protocol**—These are protocol proposals that may be considered by the IESG for standardization in the future. Implementation and testing by several groups is desirable. Revision of the protocol specification is likely.

■ **4.1.4 Experimental protocol**—A system should not implement an experimental protocol unless it is participating in the experiment and has coordinated its use of the protocol with the developer of the protocol.

Tag	Tag Name	Meaning and Value
0x0105	Vendor-Specific	This tag may be used to pass vendor proprietary information. The contents of the Tag Value field begin with a 4-byte vendor ID, which is 0x00, followed by the 3-byte vendor portion of the Ethernet MAC address. Use of this tag is not recommended and may be legally ignored by any implementation.
0x0201	Service Name Error	This tag typically has a tag length of 0x00 and indicates that the requested service cannot be honored. If there is data in the Tag Value field, it must contain a printable explanation of the service request denial.

PPPoE Active Discovery Initiation

The discovery stage begins with the client sending a *PPPoE Active Discovery Initiation* (PADI) packet to the Ethernet broadcast address. The Code field is set to 0x09. The Session ID is set to 0x0000. The PADI packet must carry a service name tag and can carry no other tags.

PPPoE Active Discovery Offer

Any access concentrators on the local network may respond with a *PPPoE Active Discovery Offer* (PADO) packet if it is capable of serving the request. In a PADO packet, the Code field is set to 0x09, and the Session ID is set to 0x0000.

The PADO packet must carry a service nametag matching the one found in the PADI packet and an AC name tag containing its own unique name. It may also contain any number of service name tags indicating services offered by the access concentrator.

PPPoE Active Discovery Request

Having received one or more PADO packets, the client selects one and replies to it with a *PPPoE Active Discovery Request* (PADR) packet. The Code field is set to 0x19, and the Session ID is set to 0x0000. The PADR packet must contain a service name tag that indicates the service being requested by the client. It can also contain other tags.

PPPoE Active Discovery Session Confirmation

The server responds to a PADR packet with a *PPPoE Active Discovery Session-confirmation* (PADS) packet. The Code field is set to 0x65, and the Session ID is set to a 2-byte value uniquely identifying this session.

The PADS packet must contain a service name tag and can contain other tags. If it cannot accept the service name in the PADR, it must reply with a PADS containing a service name error tag. The Session ID is set to 0x0000.

When the PADS packet has been sent, the PPPoE session has been started and the PPP session stage begins.

PPPoE Active Discovery Terminate

Either host involved in the PPPoE session may shut down the session by sending a *PPPoE Active Discovery Terminate* (PADT) packet. The PADT packet has a Code field of 0xa7 and a Session ID matching the sessions unique identifier. No tags are required in a PADT packet.

No further traffic can be sent over a PPPoE session after a PADT packet has been received. Normal PPP shutdown should be completed before the PADT is sent.

PPP Session Stage

When the Discovery Stage has been completed, normal PPP traffic can be carried within the PPPoE session. All Ethernet traffic is unicast traffic throughout the session. The PPPoE Code field is set to 0x00 for all session traffic, and the PPPoE payload is a PPP packet.

PPPoE Decoded

Figure 2.4 shows a PADI frame. The Version field is 0x1. The Type field is 0x1. The Code field is 0x09 (PADI). The Session ID is 0x0000. The Payload Length field is 0x0004. The packet has just one tag, a service name tag. The tag type is 0x0101. The tag length is 0x0000.

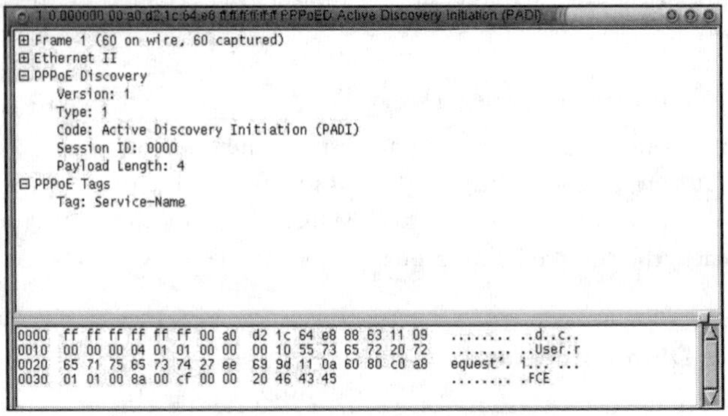

Figure 2.4   A PPPoE PADI frame.

Figure 2.5 shows a PADO frame. The Version field is set to 0x1, as is the Type field. The Code field is 0x07 (PADO). The Session ID is 0x0000. The Payload Length field is 0x002a. This frame has three tags: an access concentrator name tag, a service name tag, and a cookie tag. The access concentrator name tag has a tag type of 0x0102. Its tag length is 0x000e. It contains the 15-byte string "crashtestdummy" as its tag value.

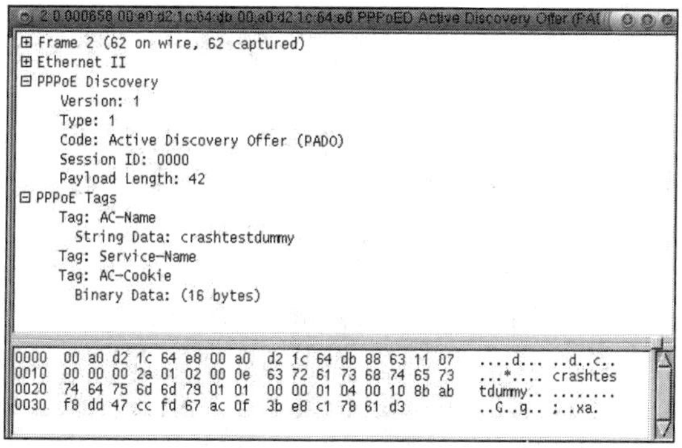

Figure 2.5   A PPPoE PADO frame.

A PADR frame is shown in Figure 2.6. In this packet, the Version and Type fields are both set to 0x1. Its Code field is 0x19 (PADR). The Session ID is still 0x0000. The Payload Length field is 0x0018. This packet carries two tags, a service name tag and a cookie tag.

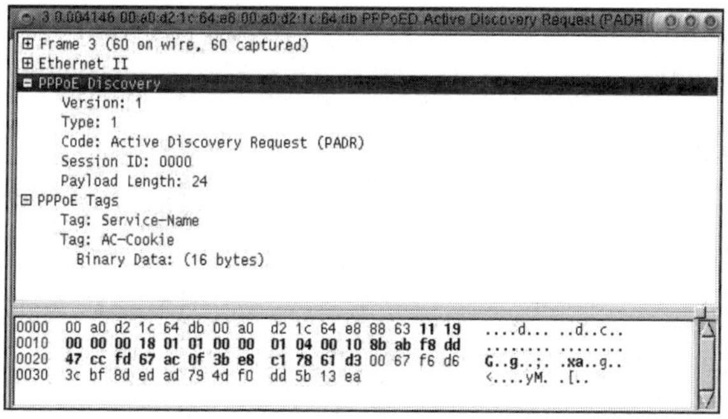

Figure 2.6   A PPPoE PADR frame.

Figure 2.7 shows a PADS frame. Its Version and Type fields are both 0x1. The Code field is set to 0x65 (PADS). The Session ID has been assigned and is 0x0001. The Payload Length is 0x0004. This packet has only one tag, the session name tag.

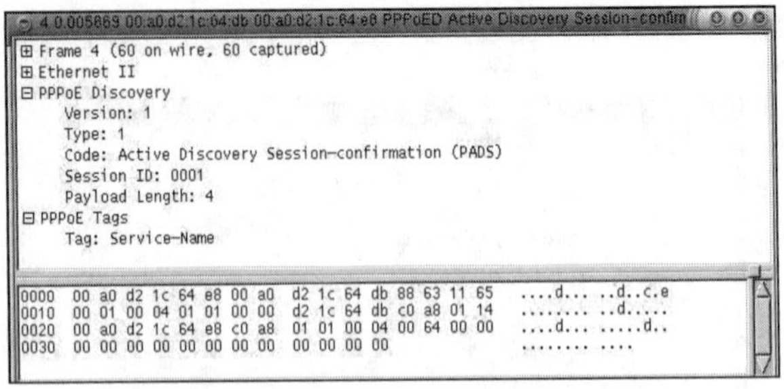

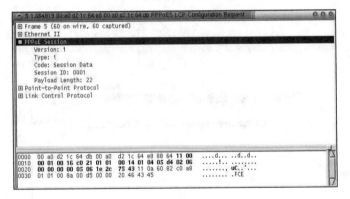

Figure 2.7   A PPPoE PADS frame.

A typical PPPoE session frame is shown in Figure 2.8. It has Version and Type fields of 0x1. Its Code field is 0x00 (Session). The Session ID is 0x0001. The Payload Length is 0x0016. The payload of this packet is a PPP LCP packet.

Figure 2.8   A PPPoE session frame.

```
○ 1 0.000000 Sun_7e:40:af ff:ff:ff:ff RARP Who is 08:00:20:74:40:af?  Tell 08:00:20:7e:40:af        ○ ○ ○
⊞ Frame 1 (64 on wire, 64 captured)
⊞ Ethernet II
⊟ Address Resolution Protocol (reverse request)
       Hardware type: Ethernet (0x0001)
       Protocol type: IP (0x0800)
       Hardware size: 6
       Protocol size: 4
       Opcode: reverse request (0x0003)
       Sender hardware address: 08:00:20:7e:40:af
       Sender protocol address: 255.255.255.255
       Target hardware address: 08:00:20:7e:40:af
       Target protocol address: 255.255.255.255


0000  ff ff ff ff ff ff 08 00  20 7e 40 af 80 35 00 01       ........  .~@..5..
0010  08 00 06 04 00 03 08 00  20 7e 40 af ff ff ff ff       ........  .~@.....
0020  08 00 20 7e 40 af ff ff  ff ff 00 00 00 00 00 00       .. ~@...  ........
0030  00 00 00 00 00 00 00 00  00 00 00 00 00 00 00 00       ........  ........
```

Figure 2.12   A RARP packet.

MTU

Each of the link-layer protocols imposes different limits on the packets that it carries. Among these restrictions is the maximum size of the packet; this is called the *maximum transmission unit* (MTU). PPP normally uses an MTU of 296, Ethernet uses an MTU of 1500, FDDI uses an MTU of 4464, and 4Mbps Token Ring uses an MTU of 4464.

Because each link layer can define a different MTU, and because a packet might traverse multiple networks en route to its final destination, a *path MTU* is defined. In Chapter 3, "Network-Layer Protocols," we'll look at IP fragmentation (a potential outcome of differing MTUs) and how to avoid it using path MTU discovery. An example of path MTU is shown in Figure 2.13.

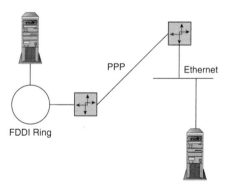

Figure 2.13   An internet with various link-layer protocols represented.

In this example, the path MTU is 296 because the PPP link sitting between the Ethernet LAN at one site and the FDDI ring at the other have negotiated a lower rate than is normally used.

Endnotes

1. April Fool's Day is the holiday of the Internet. Each year on April 1st, a number of less-than-serious RFCs are published. RFC 1149 was one of these.

2. Most modern PPP connections allow the PPP client to "discover" its IP address by querying the PPP server. This allows pools of PPP servers to provide dial-up connection to end users without forcing them to configure their IP address each time they connect.

3. Any time you see a number preceded with the 0x prefix, it is a hexidecimal number. Most of the numbers we'll deal with in TCP/IP decodes are hex.

4. Please see the "Ethereal" section in Chapter 10, "Monitoring Tools," for more information on how to read these Ethereal screenshots.

5. The RFCs provide a fairly rigid definition for what hosts *should* do and what they *must* do. I try to follow their usage of these terms. If a host "must" do something, it is not considered to have a standards-compliant implementation if it fails to do that thing. If a host "should" do something, it can still be standards-compliant even without that behavior. These terms are defined in RFC 2119.

6. In 802.3 Ethernet, bytes 13 and 14 are a Length field. This requires 802.3 packets to carry type code information in another header inside their Data field.

7. They do take up bandwidth and present a problem condition that should be corrected.

8. Although these 3 bytes are unique in theory, some circumstances break this rule. Some Ethernet cards and some OSes (including Linux) will allow you to set a different MAC address; assigning a duplicate address can cause you serious problems. In addition, some vendors have had quality control issues resulting in duplicate addresses being assigned. Fortunately, the latter case is fairly rare.

9. In today's switched networks, this is not necessarily the case. See the brief discussion of switches at the end of Chapter 1, "Prelude to a Practical Guide."

10. Because some hosts cannot properly determine their own network and ARP for addresses on remote networks, a work-around is available. Proxy ARP (or "the disgusting ARP hack") enables a router to answer ARP requests for hosts in any remote network it knows how to reach. See Chapter 3 for more information about routing.

11. RARP has been mostly superceded by the BOOTP and DHCP protocols.

cherry:
```
[pate@cherry ~]$ netstat -rn
         Kernel IP routing table
Destination      Gateway        Genmask          Flags  MSS Window  irtt Iface
192.168.1.10     0.0.0.0        255.255.255.255  UH      0 0        0 eth0
192.168.1.0      0.0.0.0        255.255.255.0    U       0 0        0 eth0
192.168.2.0      192.168.1.2    255.255.255.0    U       0 0        0 eth0
127.0.0.0        0.0.0.0        255.0.0.0        U       0 0        0 lo
0.0.0.0          192.168.1.1    0.0.0.0          UG      0 0        0 eth0
[pate@cherry ~]$ /sbin/ifconfig
         eth0     Link encap:Ethernet   HWaddr 00:E0:98:7C:95:21
                  inet addr:192.168.1.10  Bcast:192.168.1.255  Mask:255.255.255.0
                  UP BROADCAST RUNNING MULTICAST  MTU:1500  Metric:1
                  RX packets:0 errors:0 dropped:0 overruns:0 frame:0
                  TX packets:0 errors:0 dropped:0 overruns:0 carrier:0
                  collisions:0 txqueuelen:100
                  Interrupt:3 Base address:0x200
```

usps:
```
[pate@usps ~]$ netstat -rn
         Kernel IP routing table
Destination      Gateway        Genmask          Flags  MSS Window  irtt Iface
192.168.0.2      0.0.0.0        255.255.255.255  UH      0 0        0 eth0
192.168.0.0      0.0.0.0        255.255.255.0    U       0 0        0 eth0
192.168.1.1      0.0.0.0        255.255.255.255  UH      0 0        0 eth1
192.168.1.0      0.0.0.0        255.255.255.0    U       0 0        0 eth1
192.168.2.0      192.168.1.2    255.255.255.0    U       0 0        0 eth1
127.0.0.0        0.0.0.0        255.0.0.0        U       0 0        0 lo
0.0.0.0          192.168.0.1    0.0.0.0          UG      0 0        0 eth0
```

patton:
```
[pate@patton ~]$ netstat -rn
         Kernel IP routing table
Destination      Gateway        Genmask          Flags  MSS Window  irtt Iface
192.168.0.12     0.0.0.0        255.255.255.255  UH      0 0        0 eth0
192.168.0.0      0.0.0.0        255.255.255.0    U       0 0        0 eth0
192.168.1.0      192.168.0.2    255.255.255.0    U       0 0        0 eth0
192.168.2.0      192.168.0.2    255.255.255.0    U       0 0        0 eth0
127.0.0.0        0.0.0.0        255.0.0.0        U       0 0        0 lo
0.0.0.0          192.168.0.1    0.0.0.0          UG      0 0        0 eth0
```

Given this information, let's walk through some examples.

A Local Routing Example

If cherry wants to send traffic to kumquat, it first compares its own IP address with kumquat's IP address in light of its own subnet mask. 192.168.1.10 and 192.168.1.12 are in the same Class C network, and with a mask of /24, they are in the same subnet as well. Because kumquat's IP address is local, the IP datagram is addressed to kumquat and put into an Ethernet frame with kumquat's MAC address.

When kumquat receives the frame, it reads the IP address and sees that the datagram is addressed to itself. Any return traffic would go through the same steps.

A Single-Hop Routing Example

When cherry sends traffic to patton, it again compares IP addresses. In this case, 192.168.1.10 is in a different network than 192.168.0.12, so cherry will have to send its traffic via a router. Then cherry consults its routing table. There are no explicit routes for the 192.168.0.0 network, but there is a default gateway entry, usps, so cherry will route through it. The IP datagram is addressed to patton and put into an Ethernet frame with usps's MAC address.

When usps receives the Ethernet frame, it sees that the IP address is not local. Because usps is configured to forward (or route) packets, it checks its IP routing table to determine the next hop for the IP datagram. Here, patton is on a locally connected network, so the datagram is put into an Ethernet frame with patton's MAC address and is sent out through the appropriate network interface.

When patton receives the frame, it checks the IP address in the IP datagram and determines that the datagram is for local delivery.

After the IP stack has finished with the datagram and the application has returned a response, patton checks its own IP address against cherry's. It finds that cherry is not local, so patton will need to use a router to deliver the datagram carrying the response.

Next, patton checks its routing table and finds that usps is the proper router for the 192.168.1.0/24 network. The datagram is then addressed to cherry and put into an Ethernet frame addressed to usps.

Finally, usps checks the IP datagram address and sees that it is for cherry. Checking its routing table, usps finds that cherry is locally connected. The datagram is put into a new Ethernet frame addressed to cherry and is sent out through the appropriate network interface.

A Two-Hop Routing Example

When cuke wants to send an IP datagram to patton, it first compares its IP address with patton's in light of its own subnet mask. 192.168.2.51 and 192.168.0.12 are in different networks, so cuke checks its routing table for an appropriate entry. There is no explicit route entry for the 192.168.0.0 network, so cuke uses its default gateway. The IP datagram addressed to patton is put into an Ethernet frame addressed to fedex.

After receiving the Ethernet frame, fedex checks the enclosed IP datagram and sees that it is addressed to 192.168.0.12. The 192.168.0.0 network is not directly attached to fedex, so it looks in its routing table to see where to send the datagram. There is no explicit route entry, so fedex uses its default gateway, usps. The IP datagram is put into a Ethernet frame addressed to usps and is sent out through the appropriate network interface.

When usps receives the Ethernet frame, it checks the IP datagram and finds that it is addressed to 192.168.0.12. The 192.168.0.0 network is directly attached, so usps bundles the IP datagram into an Ethernet frame addressed to patton and sends it out through the proper network interface.

Then patton receives the Ethernet frame and finds that the enclosed IP datagram is addressed to itself. After handling the IP datagram, if there is a response to be sent, patton follows the same series of steps to send the response.

Tracing the return path of the IP datagram is left as an exercise.

Routing by Degrees

All routing on a host is done according to that host's own routing table. Three basic kinds of entries exist in this table, corresponding to three kinds of routing: locally attached networks (direct routing), statically assigned routes (static routing), and dynamically assigned routes (dynamic routing). Each of these is discussed separately in the next sections.

Direct Routing

When two hosts are on the same network and subnet, no router is needed to pass traffic between the two hosts. IP datagrams are sent between them using directly addressed link-layer frames.

This is the simplest form of routing available. Entries are automatically added to a hosts routing table when a new network is attached with the /sbin/ifconfig command.

Static Routing

In simple networks, or simple portions of meshed networks, routing entries can be entered into a host's routing table by hand with the /sbin/route command. This is typically done only when the route is not likely to change because any changes must also be entered by hand. The default gateway entry in a routing table is almost always a static routing entry.

Dynamic Routing

Where the routes between networks are likely to change, dynamic routing makes the most sense. This relies on an underlying routing protocol such as RIP-2, OSPF, or BGP to pass information about routes to networks between routers. RIP-2 is discussed in more detail in Chapter 5, "Application-Layer Protocols."

Dynamic routing is the key to a meshed internet's capability to survive losing connections between networks. A simple example is shown in Figure 3.4.

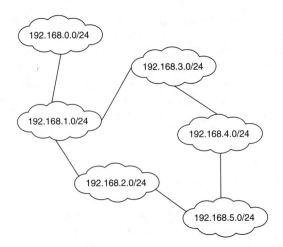

Figure 3.4   A small meshed internet.

In this internet, the 192.168.0.0/24 network can send traffic to the 192.168.5.0/24 network through either the 192.168.2.0/24 network or the 192.168.3.0/24 network (all the traffic will flow through the 192.168.1.0/24 network, though). Traffic will normally flow along this path:

192.168.0.0/24 to

192.168.1.0/24 to

192.168.2.0/24 to

192.168.5.0/24

Traffic routed through the 192.168.3.0/24 network would require an extra hop as it passes through the 192.168.4.0/24 network. This extra hop is reflected in the routing table entries passed between the routers.

If the connection between 192.168.1.0/24 and 192.168.2.0/24 went down for some reason, the routing tables would be updated to show that the new best path was as follows:

192.168.0.0/24 to

192.168.1.0/24 to

192.168.3.0/24 to

192.168.4.0/24 to

192.168.5.0/24

Although this is longer than the old path, it still works and is thus promoted to the best path. When the link between 192.168.1.0/24 and 192.168.2.0/24 recovers, the routing table will revert to the shorter path through the 192.168.2.0/24 network.

Turning Your Linux Box into a Router

All Linux boxes are capable of routing IP traffic. This capability is turned off by default on most Linux distributions. A kernel parameter called `ip_forward` controls this functionality. The following command will enable routing on your system:

```
echo 1 > /proc/sys/net/ipv4/ip_forward
```

If your box is connected to two or more IP networks, it will begin to route traffic between them. Of course, it will route only traffic that is sent to it as a router, so you should inform the hosts on its connected networks that this router is now in place. For a simple network, this is likely to mean adding your router as the default gateway on your individual hosts. For a more involved network, you will want to start the routed, gated, or zebra daemons and let them advertise your new router. For more information on these programs, see Chapters 5 and 7.

More Advanced Tricks

The 2.4 Linux kernel includes the capability to go far beyond this simple routing. Some of the advanced routing capabilities with the new kernel include routing based on type of service, rerouting traffic based on the application-layer protocol, packet filtering, network address translation, traffic shaping, and a variety of other tricks.

Packet Filtering

Packet filtering is the process of determining whether to route, accept, or deny a packet based on information in the packet header. The simplest form of packet filtering relies on a comparison of source and destination IP addresses (see Figure 3.5).

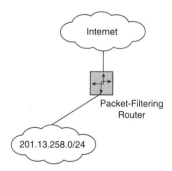

Figure 3.5   A small network.

Given a network like the one shown in Figure 3.5, the packet filter might set up rules to block traffic like this (using a simple pseudo config code explained here).

```
deny 10.0.0.0/24 201.13.25.0/8
deny 172.16.0.0/20 201.13.25.0/8
deny 192.168.0.0/16 201.13.25.0/8
deny 127.0.0.1/24 201.13.25.0/8
deny 201.13.25.0/8 201.13.25.0/8
allow 0.0.0.0/32 201.13.25.100/0
deny all
```

Each rule is of this form:

```
action source/mask destination/mask
```

The masks in these rules are not subnet masks; each bit represents a changeable bit starting from the least significant bit in the address. For example, the destination/mask combination 201.13.25.0/8 represents all addresses from 201.13.25.0 to 201.13.25.255 (any bit in the last octet can be set to any value).

The first five rules deny connections from three classes of traffic: the RFC 1918 private addresses (discussed earlier), the local loopback addresses, and the internal network (to prevent spoofed traffic). The sixth rule allows traffic from any host (not already denied) that is destined for 201.13.25.100. The final rule denies everything else.[7]

The Linux packet-filtering capabilities are provided by netfilter and iptables. These tools are described in their own section in Chapter 11.

Network Address Translation

Network Address Translation (NAT) is the method for mapping a private internal address space (normally made up of RFC 1918 addresses) to one or more routable IP addresses. This functionality can help provide security (by obscuring your internal address structure and by preventing connection to your internal hosts) and minimize IP address overhead (by using a private address space instead of having to acquire routable IP addresses from your ISP).

A common form of NAT is called *masquerading*. IP masquerading maps any internal address space to a single IP address. This is commonly used to allow several PCs in a home or small office to share a single dial-up, DSL, or cable-modem connection to the Internet.

IPv4

The Internet Protocol (IP) is defined by RFC 791. IP provides routable addressing, fragmentation and reassembly, and type of service (TOS)–based delivery options.

A Discussion of IPv4

The IPv4 header is normally 20 bytes long. It contains a 4-bit Version field (this will always be 4), a 4-bit Header Length field (this will normally be 5, indicating five words of 4 bytes each, for a total of 20 bytes), a 1-byte TOS field, a 2-byte *Total Length* (TTL) field, a 2-byte Identification field, a 3-bit Flags field, a 13-bit *Fragment Offset* field, a 1-byte *Time To Live* (TTL) field, a 1-byte Protocol field, a 2-byte Header Checksum field, a 4-byte Source Address field, and a 4-byte Destination Address field.

TOS

The TOS byte is divided into three sections. In the first section, 3 bits are used for a precedence field, which is little used today. In the second section, 4 bits are used to indicate TOS, and only one of them may be set. The four possible TOS flags are `delay`, `throughput`, `reliability`, and `cost`. If none of these bits are turned on, normal routing is to occur. The third section is a 1-bit reserved space; this bit is reserved and must be set to 0.

The TOS bits allow better control over how a packet will be routed. An interactive application such as ssh should set the delay bit, indicating that packets should be routed to minimize delay. An application transferring data should set the throughput bit to gain routing geared toward maximizing throughput. These options are explained more fully in RFC 1349. In addition to TOS routing, the 2.4 Linux kernel provides powerful tools for *shaping* network traffic based on a number of possible keys; these tools will be discussed in Chapter 11.

Total Length

The Total Length field indicates the total length of the IP datagram (including header) in bytes. IP is limited to 65535 bytes, 65515 of which can be payload. If the IP datagram is fragmented (see the section "Fragmentation Flags," which follows shortly), the Total Length field indicates the size of the fragment. In practice, TCP and UDP limit the size of their data to avoid sending extremely large packets (8192 bytes is a common ceiling).

Identification

Each datagram from a given host is uniquely identified by the 2-byte Identification field. This identification does not change between fragments of a single datagram, which allows a datagram to be reassembled at the destination.

Fragmentation Flags

The 3-bit Flags field contains two flags dealing with fragmentation and a reserved bit. The first bit is reserved and must be 0. The second bit is the Don't Fragment flag. If the Don't Fragment bit is set, it indicates that this packet should not be fragmented; instead, an *Internet Control Message Protocol* (ICMP) error message should be generated.[8] The third bit is the Last Fragment flag. This bit is set when there are no further fragments for this datagram.

Fragmentation Offset Field

If the datagram has not been fragmented, the Fragmentation Offset field will be set to all 0s. If the datagram has been fragmented, the field will indicate the number of 8-byte words this fragment is from the start of the datagram. An example of fragmentation appears in the section "IP Fragmentation."

TTL

The TTL field indicates the number of hops that the packet can make before being discarded. When a packet is created, it is given a TTL of 64. Then, each time that it passes through a router, the TTL is decremented by 1. This prevents undeliverable packets from floating around the network forever.

Protocol

The Protocol field indicates which protocol is carried in the payload of the IP datagram. We are concerned with three possible values: these are 0x06 (TCP), 0x11 (UDP), and 0x01 (ICMP). Each of these protocols is dealt with in the next chapter.

IP Checksum

The IP checksum is computed over the header data only; none of the payload is used in the computation. For the purpose of the checksum, the Checksum field is initially filled with zeroes.

Source and Destination Addresses

The Source and Destination Address fields contain the IP addresses of the sending and target hosts. These fields are not changed in the flow of IP data across a network, except in the case of source-routed datagrams (see Table 3.4). Because of security concerns, source routing is not commonly used any longer.

IP Options

IP headers will exceed 20 bytes when IP options are included. In this case, the Header Length field will be reset to the value 0xf, and the following additional fields will be made available: Copy Thru Gate (1 bit), Option Class (2 bits), and Option Number (5 bits). The Copy Thru Gate field indicates whether these IP options should be attached to each fragment of an IP packet (when set to 1) or not (when set to 0). The Option Class field has two unreserved values, 00 indicates traffic control codes, and 10 indicates measurement and debugging codes. Some of the options are shown (with brief explanations) in Table 3.4.

Table 3.4   **IP Options**

Class	Option Code	Option Name	Length	Description
00	00000	End of Option List	—	Indicates that there are no further options in the Options field.
00	00010	Security Handling	11	Defines how a packet is to be handled (in a military environment). See RFC 1108 for more details.
00	00011	Loose Source Routing	Variable	Indicates that a packet should traverse a specified set of routers. Other routers may also be traversed.
10	00100	Collect Internet Timestamps	Variable	Indicates that a packet should be stamped with the current time by each host that it traverses.
00	00111	Record Route	Variable	Indicates that a packet should be stamped with the IP address of each host that it traverses.
00	01001	Strict Source Routing	Variable	Indicates that a packet should traverse a specified set of routers. Only the routers listed may be traversed.

IP Fragmentation

IP datagrams can be much larger than the MTU of the path that the datagram follows as it is delivered. Figure 3.6 shows an example of a small network in which this might occur.

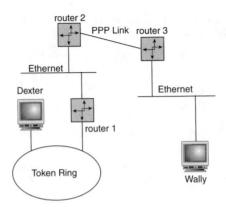

Figure 3.6   IP fragmentation in a small network.

The Token Ring network has an MTU of 4096, the Ethernet has an MTU of 1500, and the PPP connection has an MTU of 576.

If an IP datagram of 4096 bytes is sent over the Token Ring from Dexter to Wally on the remote Ethernet, it will be fragmented into three new datagrams (each with the same ID number) as it passes through router 1 onto the local Ethernet. The first two datagrams are 1500 bytes long, and the third is 1156. Remember that each of them carries an IP header, so you've added 40 bytes (for the two new IP headers) plus padding to reach the required 8-byte word length added to the overhead of the initial datagram.

As they move from the local Ethernet to the PPP link through router 2, each IP datagram is fragmented again. The first two datagrams fragment into three new datagrams each: 576, 576, and 388 bytes. The third datagram has now fragmented into three datagrams as well: 576, 576, and 44 bytes. These nine datagrams account for an additional 160 bytes of IP header and some amount of padding.

As the nine datagrams pass through router 3 onto the remote Ethernet, they are not reassembled. Reassembly of the initial datagram occurs only at the endpoint of the transmission.

The additional bandwidth used by fragmented datagrams, as well as the CPU utilization required to fragment and reassemble the packets, make initial-path MTU discovery a desirable option.

IPv4 Decoded

In the IP datagram shown in Figure 3.7, the IP version is set to 4. The header length is set to 5, which indicates that there are no headers. The Precedence and TOS flags are set to 0x00, meaning that no special-handling flags are set. (This is labeled "Differentiated Services" in the Ethereal screen capture.) The total length is set to 0x003c (or 64 bytes). The datagram ID is set to 0x0054. The Flags field is set to 010, indicating that the Don't Fragment flag is set. Because there is no fragmentation, the fragment offset is zeroed out. The TTL is 0x40 (64), showing that this datagram has not passed through any routers. The Protocol is set to 0x06 (TCP). The Checksum is 0x3c66, which is correct for this datagram. The Source Address is 127.0.0.1, and the Destination Address is 127.0.0.1. This packet was part of a TCP connection over the loopback interface of a host.

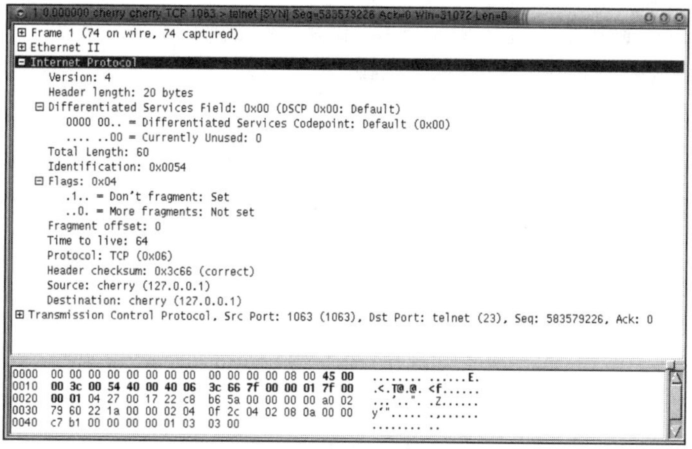

Figure 3.7   IP datagram.

Endnotes

1. More precisely, they might be blocked by a packet filter. Packet filters are often part of a firewall. This is a small but important distinction.

2. Bitwise ANDing means that each bit of the things compared are checked. If both are true (1), then the result is true. If one or both are false (0), then the result is true. If 10 (00001010) and 12 (00001100) were bitwise ANDed, the result would be 8 (00001000).

3. The host portion can be either 1, 2, or 3 bytes, depending on the class of the address.

4. In fact, every IP address uses a subnet mask. Where the mask is not given, the default mask for that class of network is assumed (24 bits for a Class C address, 16 for a Class B address, and 8 for a Class A address).

5. If you are in a network that includes BSD4.2-based systems (such as old Sun or Ultrix boxes), you should avoid using the all 0s subnet. If you don't have any such beasts in your environment, you don't need to worry.

6. Because a real understanding of subnets comes only with repeated use of them, I'll leave the completion of this cheat sheet as an exercise. There are also tools available to compute subnet masks for you. These are great time-savers, but you should know how all of this works before you start to rely on them.

7. These rules are not suitable for securing a network. They are given only as examples.

8. This makes the `Don't Fragment` bit useful for diagnostic tools.

4

Transport-Layer Protocols

THE TRANSPORT LAYER CARRIES DATA BETWEEN HOSTS for the applications above it and diagnostic information about the connections between hosts on the network. This information is carried by TCP (and the related *T/TCP*), UDP, or ICMP. These protocols are quite different in function and appearance (as you'll see in their respective sections). TCP guarantees a reliable flow of data, allowing the application implementation to ignore such details. UDP does not guarantee delivery, which forces the application to ensure reliability. ICMP does not carry data in the traditional sense, but it carries data about the network or other connections on the network. In this chapter, we'll discuss ports and sockets, TCP, UDP, and ICMP.

Ports and Sockets

At the transport layer, higher-layer protocols are referred to by their port numbers. These are 2-byte numbers that correspond to a particular application or process. Some port numbers are reserved or registered, and are recorded in RFC 1700. Access to these ports is often controlled through a *daemon* such as inetd (http at port 80 is a common exception to this rule of thumb). Other ports are assigned "on the fly" to an application (either a server or a client may *bind* to a port in this way).

inetd (and similar daemons) act as a "switchboard" for a host. This process is configured to listen on multiple ports and then spawn a server process of the appropriate type for each incoming connection. inetd is susceptible to several kinds of attacks and is often replaced or supplemented with other tools. xinetd and TCP wrappers are examples of a replacement server and a supplemental server, respectively, and are covered in Chapter 11, "Security Tools."

Reserved ports are those with a value of 1 to 1023 (inclusive). The use of these ports is restricted to processes started by root. These ports are assigned to applications by the *Internet Assigned Numbers Authority* (IANA). Because the use of these ports is controlled by a standards body, they are sometimes called "well-known ports."

Ports in the range from 1024 to 65535 (inclusive) are called *registered ports* if they are listed in RFC 1700. Although these are listed by the IANA, they are not standardized by them. A server process may be bound to any port in this range, but it is considered good practice to try to avoid widely used reserved numbers.

This range of ports is also used by client processes. For example, when a user makes a Telnet connection to a remote host, the local Telnet client is bound to a port in the unrestricted range—1027, for example. The Telnet client then tries to make a connection with the server at port 23. Because Telnet access is normally handled through inetd, it receives the incoming request and starts an in.telnetd process to deal with the Telnet session.

Commonly Used Ports

Tables 4.1, 4.2, and 4.3 (culled from the /etc/services file) represent many commonly used services. Some services are provided over both TCP and UDP; others are not.

Table 4.1 **Services Provided Internally to the IP Stack**

Port/Protocol	Name of Service
7/tcp	echo
7/udp	echo
9/tcp	discard
9/udp	discard
11/tcp	systat
13/tcp	daytime
13/udp	daytime
15/tcp	netstat
17/tcp	qotd
19/tcp	chargen
19/udp	chargen
37/tcp	time
37/udp	time

Table 4.2   **Services Provided by External Daemons on Restricted Ports**

Port/Protocol	Name of Service
20/tcp	ftp-data
21/tcp	ftp
22/tcp	ssh
22/udp	ssh
23/tcp	telnet
25/tcp	smtp
53/tcp	domain
53/udp	domain
67/tcp	bootps
67/udp	bootps
68/tcp	bootpc
68/udp	bootpc
69/udp	tftp
79/tcp	finger
80/tcp	www
80/udp	www
88/tcp	kerberos
88/udp	kerberos
98/tcp	linuxconf
110/tcp	pop3
110/udp	pop3
111/tcp	sunrpc
111/udp	sunrpc
113/tcp	auth
137/tcp	netbios-ns
137/udp	netbios-ns
138/tcp	netbios-dgm
138/udp	netbios-dgm
139/tcp	netbios-ssn
139/udp	netbios-ssn
161/udp	snmp
162/udp	snmp-trap
220/tcp	imap3
220/udp	imap3
389/tcp	ldap
389/udp	ldap
443/tcp	https
443/udp	https

continues

Table 4.2 **Continued**

Port/Protocol	Name of Service
512/tcp	exec
513/tcp	login
513/udp	who
514/tcp	shell
514/udp	syslog
520/udp	route
543/tcp	klogin
544/tcp	kshell
636/tcp	ssl-ldap
873/tcp	rsync
873/udp	rsync

Table 4.3 **Services Provided by External Daemons on Registered Ports**

Port/Protocol	Service Name
2401/tcp	cvspserver
2401/udp	cvspserver
3306/tcp	mysql
3306/udp	mysql
4559/tcp	hylafax
5308/tcp	cfengine
5308/udp	cfengine
5432/tcp	postgres
5432/udp	postgres
6667/tcp	ircd
6667/udp	ircd
10080/udp	amanda
10081/tcp	kamanda
10081/udp	kamanda
10082/tcp	amandaidx
10083/tcp	amidxtape

What Is a Socket?

Because a port number in isolation is not terribly helpful, port numbers are often kept in context as a *socket*, which is an IP address with a port number. Thus, a Telnet connection from cherry to mango might have the following sockets:

Client Side	**Server Side**
cherry socket	mango socket
192.168.1.10:1027	192.168.1.1:23

TCP

The *Transmission Control Protocol* (TCP), defined in RFC 793 and clarified in RFC 1123, is more involved than UDP, but with the added cost of running TCP comes a larger feature set and greater reliability. The sessions provided by TCP are the cause of much of the overhead of the protocol, but they provide many of the benefits of TCP.

Sessions provide a continuous connection between two processes, a mechanism for tracking the amount of data outstanding in a connection, a means for retransmitting lost data, and a method for acknowledging packets that have been received. They provide a system of congestion control without the application needing to handle it. TCP also controls the size of packets being sent and maintains an orderly flow of packets back to the application, even though it may receive packets out of order (or duplicated packets) from the IP layer.

A Discussion of TCP

In our discussion of TCP, we'll cover the structure of the TCP header, session startup and shutdown, and T/TCP. Each of these subsections builds on the information presented in the ones before it, so you'll want to read them straight through.

The Header

A TCP header is comprised of the following fields: a 2-byte Source Port number, a 2-byte Destination Port number, a 4-byte sequence number, a 4-byte Acknowledgment number, a 4-bit Header Length, a 6-bit Reserved field, a 6-bit Flag section, a 2-byte Window Size, a 2-byte TCP Checksum, a 2-byte Urgent Data Pointer, and any options.

The port numbers of the source and destination processes are carried in every TCP segment, and they define the socket on each side of the connection, as described in the previous section "Ports and Sockets."

The Sequence number identifies the first byte of data included in this segment. The bytes in a TCP stream are not counted from zero; instead, they are counted from a fairly random point agreed on in the TCP session startup. (This process is defined in the next section, "Session Startup and Shutdown.")

The Acknowledgment number is tied to the sequence of the other end of the connection. It represents the next byte that this machine is waiting for from the other machine.

The Header Length is the number of 4-byte words used for the TCP header. The header is normally 20 bytes long, giving a 4-bit value of 5. Options are often used in the TCP session startup. When options are present, the Header Length is set to 6 (24 bytes), and an Option of 0x0204XXXX is set. The XXXX is a 2-byte number corresponding to the *maximum segment size* (MSS) allowed by the sending host. If this option is not used, the MSS is set to 536 (for a total of 576 bytes, after adding 20 each for the standard IP and TCP headers). Some use is made of options to improve performance over *long fat networks* (LFNs). Other options include *Noop* 0x01 and the *end-of-option List* 0x00; each of these options is only 1 byte long.

> **TCP over LFNs**
>
> The capacity of a connection is the product of the bandwidth (in bits per second) and the round-trip time (in seconds). Because this number becomes quite large in modern WANs (in excess of 320,000 bits, or 40,000 bytes for an OC3 between New York and California), the window size is no longer capable of effectively handling flow control. Two options are provided to help circumvent this problem.
>
> The first, called *window scaling*, changes the size of the TCP window from a 2-byte value to a 4-byte value. This is done by bit shifting the window up to 14 bits. The window scale option is 0x03030X (where the *X* is the value of the bit shift to be done). Window scaling can be done only in the SYN and SYN-ACK packets of the TCP session startup.
>
> The second relies on the timestamp option (0x080aSSSSSSSSRRRRRRRR, where SSSSSSSS is the time stamp and RRRRRRRR is the timestamp reply), which helps avoid duplicate data being put in the wrong section of the buffer. Timestamping can be used throughout the TCP session.

Following the reserved bits are a series of 1-bit flags used by TCP:

- **URG**—This segment contains urgent data.
- **ACK**—The acknowledgment number contains a valid value.
- **PUSH**—This requests faster handling of the packet.
- **RST**—This requests the expedited shutdown of the remote process because the local process is going down or has gone down.
- **SYN**—This sets the initial sequence number for the host. This bit is set only during the initial startup of the TCP session.
- **FIN**—This flag requests that the connection be gracefully shut down.

The ACK, SYN, and FIN bits are discussed in the next section, "Session Startup and Shutdown."

The Window Size field is used in conjunction with the Acknowledgment number to provide flow control. It shows the amount of buffer space available on the sending host for incoming packets from this session, starting with the Acknowledgment number. It works as follows:

After the session is set up (as described in the next section), cherry has an Acknowledgment number of 0x00000020 and a Window Size of 0x0040 (64 bytes). This is an abnormally small number, but it is used for the sake of example. mango sends a packet with 17 bytes of data and a second packet of 20 bytes. Somehow, the first packet is lost on the way to cherry. When cherry sends its next packet, it still has an Acknowledgment number of 0x00000020 (because it hasn't seen the first 17 bytes of traffic from mango), but it decreases its Window Size to 0x002c.

Then mango sends a 10-byte packet to cherry, which responds with an acknowledgment number of 0x00000020 and a Window Size of 0x0022. mango then resends its first packet, and cherry replies with an Acknowledgment number of 0x00000046 (reflecting all the data that it has received) and a Window Size of 0x0040 (its full buffer is available again).

This method of flow control using a change in the window size is called the *sliding window*.

The TCP Checksum is a mandatory checksum that is computed over a pseudoheader, the TCP header, and the data carried by the packet. The pseudoheader contains fields from the IP header to verify that the packet was received by the correct host. The fields used are the 4-byte source IP address, 4-byte destination address, 4-byte padding (all 0s), 1-byte transport protocol, and 2-byte transport length. A diagram of this pseudoheader is shown in Figure 4.1.

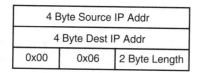

Figure 4.1   A TCP pseudoheader.

The Urgent Data Pointer is used to indicate the last byte of urgent data carried in the TCP data. This is used to allow the *inband* transmission of emergency data. If the datagram carries urgent data, it must also have the URG flag set. This urgent data often represents an interrupt in interactive traffic such as Telnet, rlogin, or FTP. For example, typing an interrupt to change your Telnet options would be done with urgent data.

Session Startup and Shutdown

Both session startup and session shutdown impose overhead on the session itself. This overhead allows the session to be properly administered when it has started, and to be closed properly when finished.

The Three-Step Handshake

TCP session startup is called the three-step handshake (or the three-way handshake). It is composed of the first three TCP segments transmitted. During the three-step handshake, initial sequence numbers are exchanged and acknowledged, and then startup options are exchanged.

The handshake starts with the client sending a datagram to the server. This datagram has the SYN flag set and the initial value for the client's sequence number. If an MSS or window scaling option will be used, those options are set in this datagram as well. This datagram is often called the SYN datagram or SYN packet.

In step 2 of the handshake, the server sends a datagram to the client. The SYN and ACK flags are both set, the client's sequence number is acknowledged (with a value of the sequence number incremented by 1), and the server's sequence number is set. Again, if the MSS or window scaling option is to be used in this session, it is set in this datagram. This datagram is called the SYN-ACK packet or datagram.

The final step of the handshake is from the client to the server. In this datagram, the client sets the ACK flag, acknowledging the server's sequence number (again with the count incremented by 1). This is called the ACK packet or datagram.

The netstat, nmap, and ethereal tools (discussed in Chapter 9, "Troubleshooting Tools," and Chapter 10, "Monitoring Tools") describe TCP sessions as being in various states. The three-step handshake moves a TCP session through several of them. The following section reviews the common steps for a client and then a server. Figure 4.2 shows all these states.

The client starts in a CLOSED state and moves directly to the SYN_SENT state as it sends a SYN packet. When it has received the server's SYN-ACK packet, it moves to an ESTABLISHED state, where it stays until session closure.

The server also starts in a CLOSED state. It normally binds to a port and waits for incoming packets; this is called the LISTEN state. After it has received the SYN packet and sent the SYN-ACK packet, it moves into the SYN_RCVD state.[1] When the server receives the client's ACK packet, it moves into the ESTABLISHED state, staying there until session closure.

Normal Session Closure

When a session is closed normally, four packets are required. Either end of the connection can request that the session be closed.

Session closure starts when one of the machines involved in the session sends a datagram with the ACK and FIN flags set. This is often called the ACK-FIN packet. The second machine responds with a datagram in which just the ACK flag is set; this is called the ACK packet. Because TCP sessions are full duplex, the second machine could continue to send data at this point, but this is uncommon.

The session closure is completed when the second machine sends a datagram with both the ACK and the FIN flags set, and receives the response from the first machine with the ACK flag set. At this point, both halves of the TCP session are closed.

During the normal session closure, the TCP session passes through several states. It follows one of two paths through these states, as described next.

The first (and more common) path through session closure is as follows: On the machine that closes its half of the TCP session first, the session starts in the ESTABLISHED state. When the ACK-FIN packet has been sent, it moves into the FIN_WAIT_1 state. When the ACK packet has been received, it moves into the FIN_WAIT_2 state. When it receives the ACK-FIN from the remote machine, it sends an ACK packet and enters the TIME_WAIT state, where it stays for an implementation-specified period (RFC 793 specifies 2 minutes, but other values are often used).

If the remote machine starts the normal TCP session closure, the local machine goes into the CLOSE_WAIT state after it has received the ACK-FIN packet and sent its own ACK packet. When the local machine has sent its ACK-FIN packet, it enters the LAST_ACK state and waits for an ACK packet from the remote host.

It is possible for some savings to be realized by closing both halves of the TCP session at once. This is called a *simultaneous close*. In this case, the first host sends an ACK-FIN packet, the second machine responds with an ACK-FIN packet, and then the first machine sends a final ACK packet. This reduces the number of datagrams required for session closure from four packets to three. This eliminates the FIN_WAIT_2 state from the first box's series of states.

Figure 4.2 shows a diagram of the states that a TCP session moves through.

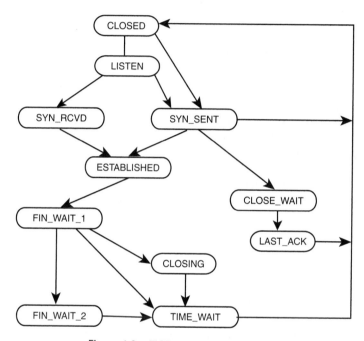

Figure 4.2   TCP session state diagram.

Session Reset

TCP sessions are normally reset (or aborted) for one of two reasons. Either the client has tried to connect to a nonexistent port, or one of the hosts involved manually aborted the session.

When the server receives the SYN packet from the client requesting a connection to a port without a process bound to it, the server responds with a datagram having the RST flag set. The client should then drop the session as though the client had attempted to create a connection to an unavailable port.

When a session is aborted by one side of the connection, it sends a datagram with the RST flag set. The other machine does not send a response; it just aborts the session and notifies the application layer that it has reset the session.

Timing Out

Keepalive timers are not part of the TCP specification, but this has not kept some TCP/IP protocol stacks from implementing them. Generally, keepalive packets are sent after a wait of two hours. When the packet is sent, three possible outcomes are possible:

- The remote host is unreachable.
- The remote host is reachable, but the connection is dead.
- The remote host is reachable and the connection is still live.

In the first case, the local host will retry keepalives nine more times, at 75-second intervals. If there is no response, it will close the connection. Note that the remote host could be unreachable because it has crashed, been turned off, or so on; this is reasonable cause to shut down a connection. The remote host could also be unreachable because of a transient network error; this is not a very good reason to shut down the connection. The local host has no way of determining why the remote host failed to respond, so it sometimes closes packets better left open.[2]
In the second case, the remote host will reply with a RST packet and the local host will close the connection. This is a special case of a port being unavailable (described earlier). In the third case, the remote host will respond with an ACK packet, and the connection will be kept alive.

T/TCP

Because TCP imposes an overhead of seven packets just for setup and shutdown of a session (and often additional packets carrying acknowledgments), it is not well suited for short, repeated traffic. A solution that allows transactional traffic is defined in RFC 1379. *Transactional TCP* (T/TCP) allows a single TCP session to carry multiple transactions. This is done by adding a 4-byte *Connection Count* (CC) field to the TCP header. Each transaction within the TCP session uses a unique CC, so each host must then keep track of the current, valid CC of the remote host in the session.

TCP Decoded

The captured packet in Figure 4.3 shows a Source Port of 0x0413 (1043) and a Destination Port of 0x1770 (6000). The source and destination ports are both in the range available for clients, but the destination is at the well-known port (or the registered port) for the X-11 system and is likely the server in this exchange. The source machine has a current Sequence number of 330802776 and is sending an Acknowledgment for byte 327043426 (the next byte that it expects to see). The Header Length is set to 0x8, representing 32 bytes of header. This is followed by the required padding and flags at 0x18 (00011000 in binary), which represent ACK and PUSH. The Window Size is set to 0x7900 (30976 bytes). The Checksum is 0x5e75.

Because the Header Length is 32 bytes, we know that there are 12 bytes of options, 32 (header length) − 20 (normal header length) = 12 (bytes of header). In this case, the options are 0x00 (a NOP), 0x00 (another NOP), and 0x010108a007b5cdb007b5cda (a timestamp with a timestamp value of 8084699 and an equivalent timestamp reply).

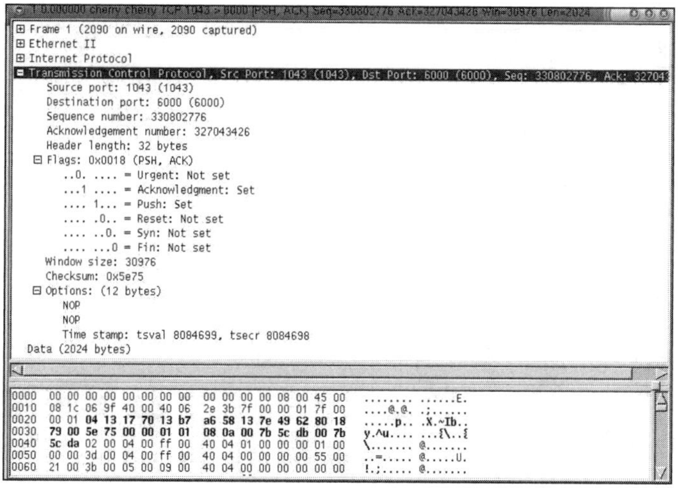

Figure 4.3   A TCP header.

In Figure 4.4, we can see the three-step handshake occurring. A user on cherry starts a Telnet session to mango, mango replies, and cherry responds to the reply. These three packets are exchanged before any Telnet data (set-up data or live data) can be passed.

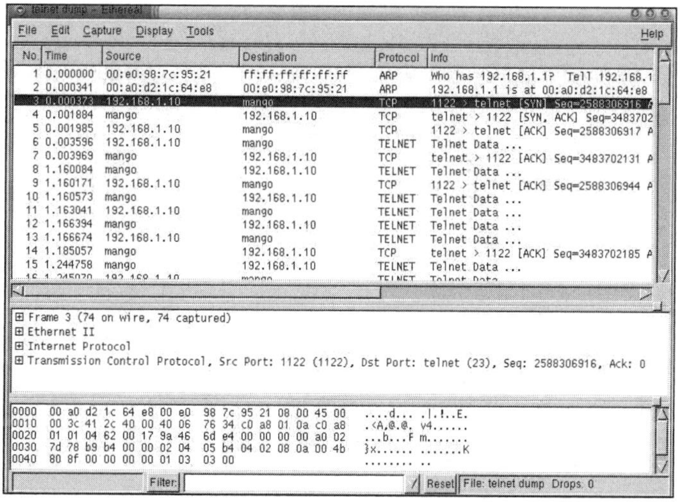

Figure 4.4   The three-step handshake.

The first packet of the three–step handshake shows cherry setting the SYN bit in the Options field, with a Sequence number of 2588306916. At this point there is no value for the Acknowledgment number. This is shown in Figure 4.5.

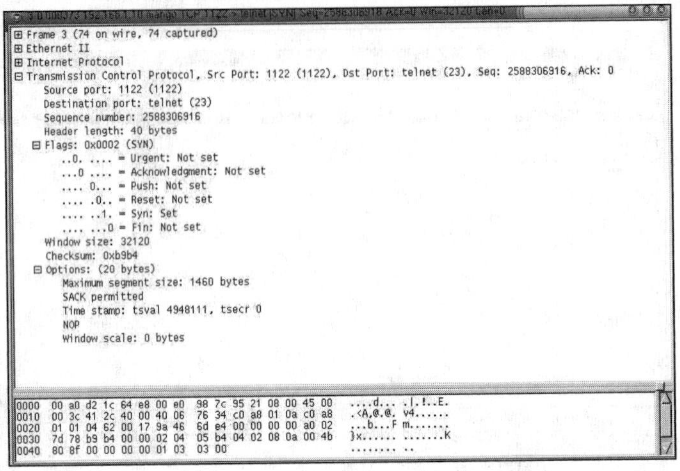

Figure 4.5   The SYN packet of the handshake.

The second packet is from mango. It has both the ACK and the SYN bits set. It has a Sequence number of 3483702130 and an Acknowledgment number of 2588306917. Notice that the sequence number has no connection to the sequence number that was used by cherry; instead, it is the acknowledgment number that reflects the remote host's sequence number. mango uses an acknowledgment number 1 byte larger than cherry's sequence number because this is the next byte that it expects to receive. Figure 4.6 shows this.

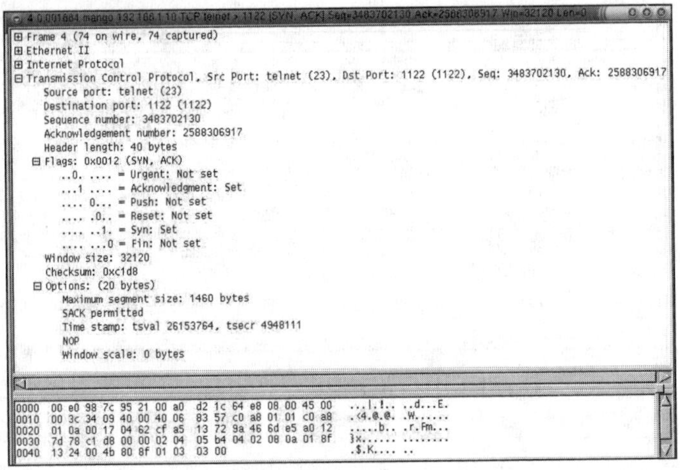

Figure 4.6   The SYN-ACK packet of the handshake.

In the final packet of the handshake (shown in Figure 4.7), cherry no longer has the SYN bit set, but it does have its ACK bit set. It has now incremented its sequence number by 1, indicating that this is the next byte of data that it will send. cherry sets its Acknowledgment number to 3483702131, one more than mango's sequence number, showing the next byte that it expects to see.

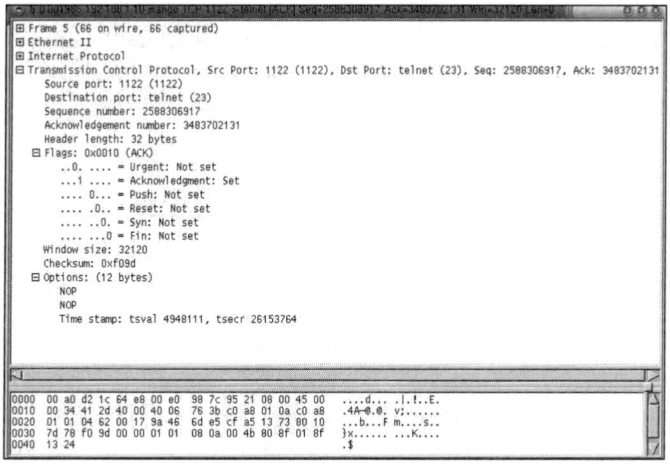

Figure 4.7   The ACK packet of the handshake.

With the three-step handshake out of the way, the application-layer data can start to be passed in the following TCP segments. This course continues through the data capture until the connection is terminated.

In Figure 4.8, showing a TCP stream, you can see the termination beginning with the highlighted packet. The shutdown starts when mango sends a packet with both the ACK and FIN bits set. cherry responds with a packet that has the ACK bit set. Then cherry sends a packet with the ACK and FIN bits set.

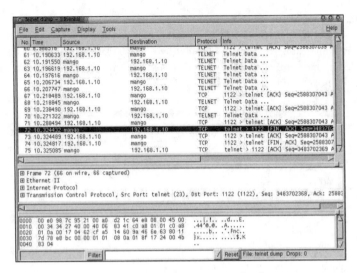

Figure 4.8 The four-step session shutdown.

Figure 4.9 shows mango's response, the final packet with just the ACK bit set. Figure 4.9 shows a view of the first packet in the shutdown. The flag bits have been highlighted in this screen capture, and you can see that the ACK and FIN bits are turned on (the 0x11 value corresponds to 010001).

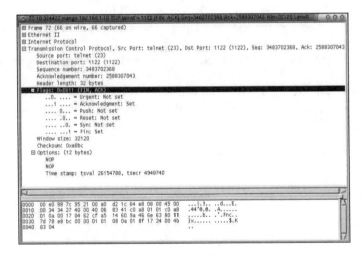

Figure 4.9 The first ACK–FIN packet.

UDP

The *User Datagram Protocol* (UDP) is defined in RFC 768. UDP provides a simple transport protocol using datagrams to carry data from the source to the destination.

UDP offers a speed advantage over TCP at the cost of some robustness. There is no UDP session, so there is no session startup and no overhead of tracking a data window. The header is half the size of a TCP header. Because UDP is not stream-oriented like TCP, each datagram carries a discrete chunk of data for the upper-level application (or the largest part of a discrete chunk of data allowed by the path MTU).

A Discussion of UDP

A UDP header is made up of four fields, each 2 bytes long: UDP Source Port, UDP Target Port, Message Length, and Checksum. The Source and Target Ports are used to indicate the process used at either end of the connection, as described earlier. The Message Length indicates the number of bytes in the UDP header and the data carried by the datagram; the minimum value is 8 bytes.

The Checksum for UDP is optional. If the Checksum is not calculated by the sender, it is sent as an all-zero field (0x0000). When used, it is computed for the data and for a pseudoheader constructed like the TCP pseudoheader discussed in the previous section. The pseudoheader is shown in Figure 4.10.

4 Byte Source IP Addr		
4 Byte Dest IP Addr		
0x00	0x11	2 Byte Length

Figure 4.10   UDP pseudoheader for checksum computation.

Padding is required in at least one (and possibly two) places in the checksummed data. There is a 1-byte pad between the destination IP address and the Protocol field. If there is an odd number of bytes in the data portion of the UDP datagram, an additional 1-byte pad is required to make the checksummed data align on a 2-byte boundary.

UDP Decoded

The UDP packet in Figure 4.11 is a DNS request. The Source Port is 0x0402 (1042), and the Destination Port is 0x0035 (53 or DNS). The Length is 0x0032 (50 bytes). The Checksum is in use and has a value of 0x590b.

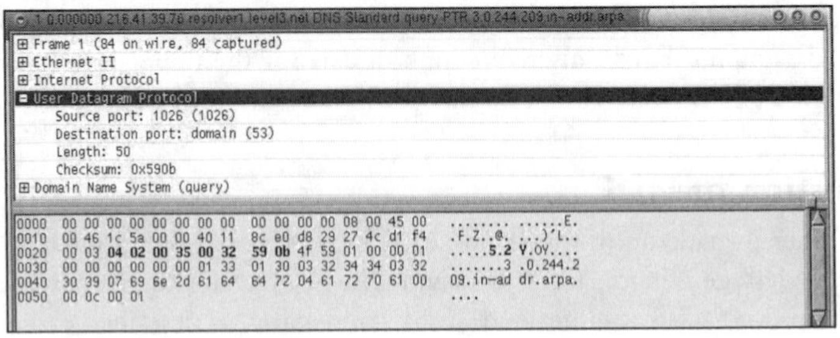

Figure 4.11   A UDP header.

Although UDP doesn't have sessions like TCP, it is possible for UDP-based applications to carry out transactions. The network trace in Figure 4.12 shows a good example of this. Note that the first packet is a generic request and receives an empty answer. The next two requests are for distinct host names and receive distinct answers.

Figure 4.12   A trace of DNS transactions over UDP.

ICMP

While TCP and UDP carry data, The *Internet Control Message Protocol* (ICMP) provides diagnostic and error reporting capabilities. Because of this functionality, ICMP becomes an important tool in understanding our networks.

Protocol Review

ICMP packets can be generated by IP hosts when certain errors are encountered, or by an application. These two causes of ICMP packet generation help us to break ICMP packets into two classes: ICMP errors and ICMP requests/responses.

ICMP errors are generally caused by a failure to deliver an IP datagram. Because IP datagrams do not follow a set path through a network, ICMP error messages are sent back only to the source host, not to any intermediate routers. (These facts enable us to build diagnostic tools like traceroute, which is discussed in Chapter 9.)

ICMP packets all follow the same basic structure: a 1-byte Type field, a 1-byte Code field, and a 2-byte Checksum field, followed by a variety of fields, depending on the type of packet. Like the checksum in the IP header, an ICMP checksum uses a value of 0x0000 for calculating the checksum. Unlike an IP checksum, which uses only the header, the entire ICMP packet is used in the calculation.

We'll look at the structure of several kinds of ICMP packets in turn. Table 4.4 shows the different kinds of ICMP packets at a glance.

Table 4.4 **ICMP Packets with Type and Code**

Type	Code(s)	Function
0/8	0	Echo request/response
3	0-15	Destination unreachable
4	0	Source quench
5	0-3	Redirect
9/10	0	Router advertisement/solicitation (not shown)
11	0-1	TTL exceeded
12	0-1	Parameter error
13/14	0	Timestamp request/response (not shown)
15/16	0	Obsolete (not shown)
17/18	0	Subnet mask request/response (not shown)

Note: Not all the ICMP messages listed in this table are described in the text. I have tried to describe only the most common and important of the ICMP messages here.

Five kinds of errors are defined not to produce ICMP messages:

- A failure involving an ICMP error message
- An IP datagram with a broadcast destination address
- A link-layer frame with a broadcast destination address
- Any fragment of an IP datagram other than the first
- Any datagram whose source address is not a unicast address

If ICMP error messages were sent in response to these kinds of errors, the result could be a heavy period of traffic called a *broadcast storm*.[3]

Echo Request/Reply

The *ICMP echo request and reply messages* are the basis of the /bin/ping command discussed in Chapter 9. The source host issues an ICMP echo request (Type 8), and the destination host sends back an ICMP echo response (Type 0).

The ICMP echo request/reply message is laid out as follows: a 1-byte Type field, a 1-byte Code field (always 0x00), a 2-byte Checksum field, a 2-byte ID Number field, a 2-byte Sequence Number field, and a variable-length Data field. The ID Number is unique to each ping command issued. The Sequence Number increments separately in each ping command. If you run a script such as the following, you will notice that each ping has a different ID Number but the same Sequence Number:

```
for count in 1 2 3; do
    /bin/ping -c1 192.168.1.1
done
```

If you run this command, you will see that each ping has the same ID Number but increasing Sequence Numbers:

```
/bin/ping -c3 192.168.1.1
```

Destination Unreachable

ICMP Destination Unreachable messages are sent when a packet cannot be delivered to its destination. Destination Unreachable messages are laid out as follows: a 1-byte Type (0x03) field, a 1-byte Code field (see Table 4.6), a 2-byte Checksum field, a 4-byte Reserved field (this field must be 0x00000000), a 20-byte Failed IP Header field, and an 8-byte Failed IP Datagram field. The 20 bytes of the Failed IP Header field give all the data required to identify the IP packet that caused the error condition to occur. The 8 bytes of the Failed IP Data field show the first 8 bytes of the transport-layer header; this provides enough information to identify the application that caused the error condition. The layout of this kind of ICMP packet is shown in Table 4.5.

Table 4.5   **ICMP Destination Unreachable Message Fields**

Size	Contents	Example Data
1 byte	Type	03
1 byte	Code	00
2 bytes	Checksum	0a7b
4 bytes	Reserved	00 00 00 00
20 bytes	Failed IP header	45 …
8 bytes	Failed IP data	05 b3 …

Table 4.6 shows the various Code values that can be sent in ICMP Destination Unreachable messages.

Table 4.6   **ICMP Destination Unreachable Codes**

Code	Meaning
0	Network is unreachable.
1	Host is unreachable.
2	Protocol is unreachable.
3	Port is unreachable.
4	Fragmentation is needed but is disallowed.
5	Source route failed.
6	Destination network is unknown.
7	Destination host is unknown.
8	Obsolete.
9	Destination network is prohibited.
10	Destination host is prohibited.
11	Network is unreachable for TOS.
12	Host is unreachable for TOS.
13	Communication is prohibited by filter.
14	Host precedence violation occurred.
15	Precedence cutoff is in effect.

Codes 0 through 3 are the most common values, although type code 4 is used when determining the path MTU of a network connection.

Source Quench

ICMP source quench messages are used when a router is nearing its buffer capacity. The router will send its message to the source host of the datagram that triggered the event. The system that receives the source quench message is supposed to reduce its transmission rate until it stops receiving source quench messages.

The source quench message contains the following fields: a 1–byte Type field (always 0x04), a 1–byte Code field, a 2–byte Checksum field, a 4–byte Reserved field (this field should be 0x00000000), a 20-byte Failed IP Header field, and an 8-byte Failed IP Data field. Table 4.7 shows a comparison of the fields in source quench messages.

Table 4.7   **ICMP Source Quench Message Fields**

Size	Contents	Example Data
1 byte	Type	04
1 byte	Code	00
2 bytes	Checksum	0a7b
4 bytes	Reserved	00 00 00 00
20 bytes	Failed IP header	45 ...
8 bytes	Failed IP data	05 b3 ...

Redirect

ICMP redirect messages are sent when a host attempts to use an inappropriate router. Figure 4.13 shows a network in which this might occur.

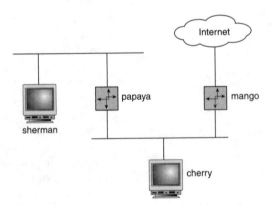

Figure 4.13   A network with two routers.

cherry uses mango as its default router, per the following routing table:

```
Kernel IP routing table
Destination     Gateway        Genmask          Flags  MSS Window  irtt Iface
192.168.1.10    0.0.0.0        255.255.255.255  UH       0 0          0 eth0
192.168.1.0     0.0.0.0        255.255.255.0    U        0 0          0 eth0
127.0.0.0       0.0.0.0        255.0.0.0        U        0 0          0 lo
0.0.0.0         192.168.1.1    0.0.0.0          UG       0 0          0 eth0
```

mango needs to send traffic to sherman (which lives on a network behind papaya). cherry sends the first packet to mango, which forwards it to papaya and sends an ICMP redirect (ICMP message Type 5 Code 0) to cherry. Then cherry should update its routing table to look like the following:

```
Kernel IP routing table
Destination     Gateway          Genmask            Flags   MSS Window   irtt Iface
192.168.1.10    0.0.0.0          255.255.255.255  UH         0 0            0 eth0
192.168.1.0     0.0.0.0          255.255.255.0    U          0 0            0 eth0
192.168.2.0     192.168.1.11     255.255.255.0    UD         0 0            0 eth0
127.0.0.0       0.0.0.0          255.0.0.0        U          0 0            0 lo
0.0.0.0         192.168.1.1      0.0.0.0          UG         0 0            0 eth0
```

All further traffic to the 192.168.2.0/24 network should now go through papaya.

An ICMP redirect message is laid out in the same way as the ICMP source quench message described earlier. The fields are a 1-byte Type field, a 1-byte Code field, a 2-byte Checksum field, a 4-byte Reserved field (this field should be 0x00000000), a 20-byte Failed IP Header field, and an 8-byte Failed IP Data field. The layout of the ICMP redirect message and the possible values of the Code field are shown in Tables 4.8 and 4.9.

Table 4.8 **ICMP Redirect Message Fields**

Size	**Contents**	**Example Data**
1 byte	Type	05
1 byte	Code	00
2 bytes	Checksum	0a7b
4 bytes	Reserved	00 00 00 00
20 bytes	Failed IP header	45 ...
8 bytes	Failed IP data	05 b3 ...

Table 4.9 **ICMP Redirect Codes**

Code	**Meaning**
0	Redirect for network
1	Redirect for host
2	Redirect for network and TOS
3	Redirect for host and TOS

TTL Exceeded

The *ICMP TTL exceeded message* is the basis for the /usr/sbin/traceroute command. It is generated when a packet's hop count exceeds its TTL. (Please note that there is a code representing a timeout while waiting for defragmentation as well.) TTL messages contain the following fields: a 1-byte Type field (always 0x011), a 1-byte Code field, a 2-byte Checksum field, a 4-byte Reserved field (this field should be 0x00000000), a 20-byte Failed IP Header field, and an 8-byte Failed IP Data field. The ICMP TTL exceeded message and valid Code values are shown in Tables 4.10 and 4.11.

Table 4.10 **ICMP TTL Exceeded Message**

Size	Contents	Example Data
1 byte	Type	0b
1 byte	Code	00
2 bytes	Checksum	0a7b
4 bytes	Reserved	00 00 00 00
20 bytes	Failed IP header	45 ...
8 bytes	Failed IP data	05 b3 ...

Table 4.11 **ICMP TTL Exceeded Codes**

Code	Meaning
0	TTL equals 0 during transit.
1	TTL equals 0 during reassembly.

Parameter Error

When an error in the IP header of a packet is detected, an *ICMP parameter error message* is sent to the originating host. This message indicates that one of the fields is either missing or incorrect. The parameter error message's layout is similar to the other ICMP error messages: a 1-byte Type field (always 0x0c), a 1-byte Code field, a 2-byte Checksum field, a 1-byte Pointer to Bad Data field, a 3-byte Reserved field (always 0x000000), a 20-byte Failed IP Header field, and an 8-byte Failed IP Data field. The message layout of an example error message is found in Table 4.12. Note that the Pointer to Bad Data field is 0 (indicating that the error is in the first byte).

Table 4.12 **ICMP Parameter Error Message**

Size	Contents	Example Data
1 byte	Type	0b
1 byte	Code	00
2 bytes	Checksum	0a7b
1 byte	Pointer to Bad Data	00
3 bytes	Reserved	00 00 00
20 bytes	Failed IP header	40 ...
8 bytes	Failed IP data	05 b3 ...

Table 4.13 shows the valid Code fields for an ICMP parameter message.

Table 4.13   **ICMP Parameter Error Codes**

Code	Meaning
0	IP header is bad.
1	Required option is missing.

Endnotes

1. During the SYN-RCVD state, the server must allocate a transmission control block. Only a small number of these structures are set aside in memory, so this presents a vulnerability for the server. Crackers trying to disable a server attack this weakness when trying to execute a SYN Flood attack.

2. This is one of the reasons that timeout is not a part of the TCP specification.

3. A broadcast storm is a period of very heavy traffic (sometimes consuming all available bandwidth), characterized by traffic sent to nonunicast addresses.

5

Application-Layer Protocols

FROM OUR START DOWN AT THE LINK LAYER in Chapter 2, "Link-Layer Protocols," we've moved our way up the protocol stack. Now we've reached the top. Here in the lofty reaches of the application layer, we see a lot more variety than at any other layers we've discussed. In this chapter, we'll discuss three protocols: RIP, TFTP, and HTTP. The first two are built on UDP; the third uses TCP.

RIP

The *Routing Information Protocol* (RIP), is used to pass routing information between networked hosts.[1] RIP was officially specified in RFC 1058, which was written several years after the protocol was originally implemented in Berkeley UNIX. Currently, the most common version of RIP in wide use is RIP version 2, or RIP-2, specified in RFC 1388. RIP-2 packets can be understood by older machines running RIP because RIP-2 uses the reserved fields of RIP to pass additional information, and RIP ignores these fields. For the remainder of this section, we'll be talking about RIP version 2—where the term *RIP* is used, it refers to RIP-2.

RIP provides only a very simple routing scheme: It relies on hop count as the only metric for determining which path to take. Each participating host broadcasts a message containing its list of known destination networks with the corresponding hop count. Because updates are broadcast only periodically (typically every 30–90 seconds), it can take a long time for routes to propagate a network. RIP has a provision to help keep this to a minimum—anything requiring more than 15 hops is considered unreachable.

Figure 5.1 shows the routers used to connect several small networks. Table 5.1 shows the interfaces and IP addresses of these routers (the name is given in the format *name.interface*). This network will be used to show the normal workings of RIP and to illustrate a shortcoming of RIP with its solution.

Table 5.1 **Routers, Interfaces, and Addresses**

Name and Interface	**IP Address and Subnet Mask**
aaron.0	192.168.1.1/24
aaron.1	192.168.2.1/24
aaron.2	192.168.3.1/24
alan.0	192.168.4.1/24
alan.1	192.168.5.1/24
alan.2	192.168.6.1/24
bob.0	192.168.6.2/24
bill.0	192.168.5.2/24
bill.1	192.168.12.1/24
bill.2	192.168.13.1/24
bruce.0	192.168.3.2/24
bruce.1	192.168.14.1
brandon.0	192.168.2.2/24
brandon.1	192.168.15.1/24
chuck.0	192.168.13.2/24
chuck.1	192.168.21.1/24
caleb.0	192.168.12.2/24
caleb.1	192.168.22.1/24
caleb.2	192.168.23.1/24
carl.0	192.168.14.2/24
carl.1	192.168.15.2/24
carl.2	192.168.24.1/24
doug.0	192.168.22.2/24
doug.1	192.168.24.2/24
don.0	192.168.21.2/24
don.1	192.168.23/24

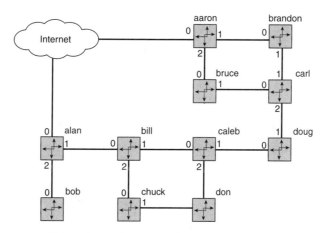

Figure 5.1   The routers of a small internetwork.

Each router in Table 5.1 has a different view of the network. alan and aaron both have a direct connection to the Internet and can act as default gateways for the networks behind them. doug and don are at the back of the network, and both have a variety of paths to get to the front. Let's start by looking at alan, bill, caleb, and doug's view of the world, as well as the routing information they will pass along.

alan has a default entry of 0.0.0.0/0 through interface 0. It will be configured not to pass any routing information out that interface, to avoid broadcasting internal (RFC 1918) addresses. It also has one-hop routes to the 192.168.4.0/24, 192.168.5.0/24, and 192.168.6.0/24 networks. It will broadcast all three of these routes on its eth1 and eth2 interfaces. (alan will eventually find out about other networks, but that comes along in a bit.)

bill is configured to use 192.168.5.1 as its default gateway. It also has one-hop routes to the 192.168.5.0/24, 192.168.12.1.0/24, and 192.168.13.0/24 networks, and it will broadcast these on all three of its interfaces. After alan has made a RIP broadcast, bill also knows about two-hop routes to the 192.168.4.0/24, 192.168.5.0/24, and 192.168.6.0/24 networks.[2] Because bill already has a one-hop route for the 192.168.5.0/24 network, it ignores this entry. The others are added to its routing table. On its next broadcast, bill sends information about all the one- and two-hop entries in its routing table. (Now alan knows about the 192.168.13.0/24 network as well.)

Routing Loops and Split Horizon

This is where we hit our first major problem with RIP. What would happen if alan.3 failed? bill would send a RIP broadcast showing a two-hop entry for the 192.168.6.0/24 network. Normally, alan would ignore these because they have a higher hop count than alan's own entries, but without the eth3 interface, bill's routes become the best available—except that they involve a jump right back to alan.

RIP doesn't carry enough information to stop these kinds of routing loops. Instead, it relies on a method called *split horizon*. No RIP participant will rebroadcast a route out the interface that it received it on.

If bill follows this rule, alan never receives the bogus routes to bob, and the routing loop is avoided.

To continue our example, caleb has one-hop routes to the 192.168.12.0/24, 192.168.22.0/24, and 192.168.23.0/24 networks. When it receives bill's broadcast, caleb learns about two-hop routes to the 192.168.13.0/24 and 192.168.5.0/24 networks, and about three–hop routes to the 192.168.4.0/24 and 192.168.6.0/24 networks. It will broadcast its own routing table, and bill and alan will learn about the 192.168.22.0/24 and 192.168.23.0/24 networks (with two and three hops, respectively).

doug begins with one-hop routes to the 192.168.22.0/24 and 192.168.24.0/24 networks. After receiving updates from caleb, doug also will have two-hop routes to the 192.168.23.0/24 and 192.168.12.0/24 networks, three-hop routes to the 192.168.13.0/24 and 192.168.5.0/24 networks, and four-hop routes to the 192.168.4.0/24 and 192.168.6.0/24 networks.

In the preceding descriptions, we've looked at the flow of RIP data in only one direction. In reality, it flows in both directions. After the network has been up for a while, routes will have propagated throughout the network. At that point, alan will have a routing table like the one shown in Table 5.2.

Table 5.2 **alan's Routing Table**

Network	Next Hop	Hop Count
192.168.4.0/24	192.168.4.1	1
192.168.5.0/24	192.168.5.1	1
192.168.6.0/24	192.168.6.1	1
192.168.12.0/24	192.168.6.2	2
192.168.13.0/24	192.168.5.2	2
192.168.21.0/24	192.168.5.2	3
192.168.22.0/24	192.168.5.2	3
192.168.23.0/24	192.168.5.2	3
192.168.24.0/24	192.168.5.2	4
192.168.14.0/24	192.168.5.2	5
192.168.15.0/24	192.168.5.2	5
192.168.3.0/24	192.168.5.2	6
192.168.2.0/24	192.168.5.2	6
192.168.1.0/24	192.168.5.2	7

RIP-2 Protocol Trace

Figure 5.2 shows a RIP-2 request. The packet is addressed to the IP broadcast address. Both the source port and the destination port are set to 520. Within the RIP datagram, the Command field is set to 1 (Request). The RIP Version field is set to 2.

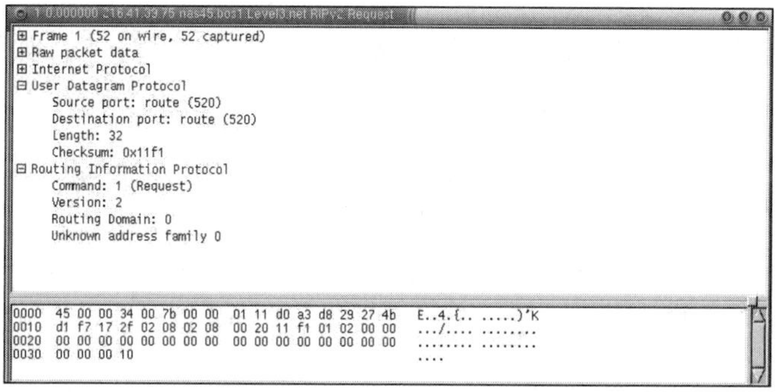

Figure 5.2   A RIP route advertisement.

TFTP

The *Trivial File Transfer Protocol* (TFTP) is a *User Datagram Protocol* (UDP) based protocol for exchanging files between systems. It was designed to be fast and easy to implement on a host with limited resources. TFTP is defined in RFC 1350.

Protocol Review

TFTP is implemented with five kinds of packets:

- Read requests
- Write requests
- File data
- Acknowledgments
- Error handling

Each of these packet types (except read and write requests) has a slightly different packet structure. We'll take a look at each of them in turn.

Read and write request packets have five fields. The first field is 2 bytes long and is the Op Code field; read requests are 0x0001, and write requests are 0x0002. The next field is of variable length and is the filename to be read. This is followed by a 1-byte separator, which is always 0x00. The fourth field is the Data Mode field and can be one of three values:

- Netascii

- Binary

- The recipient's email address (for write requests only)

The fourth field is of variable length. The fifth field is 1 byte long and is an *End Of File* (EOF) marker; this is always 0x00.

Data packets have only three fields. The first field is the Op Code field and is 2 bytes long; it is always 0x0003. The second field is the Block Number field and is 2 bytes long. The remainder of the packet (with a maximum length of 512 bytes) is the data. When TFTP transfers data, it uses a simple mechanism to track where it is in the data to be transferred. The data is divided into 512-byte blocks, and each is sent and acknowledged individually.[3] The last packet of a transfer is a data packet with a data field of less than 512 bytes. If the data is evenly divided into 512-byte blocks, an empty packet will be sent as the last packet (with 0 bytes being less than 512).

Each block of data is answered by an acknowledgment packet. The acknowledgment packet is 4 bytes long and has two fields. The first field is the 2-byte Op Code field (0x0004). The second field is the 2-byte block number of the block being acknowledged.

Because nothing is perfect, TFTP has a simple error-handling system built around an error-handling packet. These packets have four fields and are of variable length. The first field is the Op Code field; it is 2 bytes long and is always 0x0005. The second field is 2 bytes long and carries the error code. The third field is the error text, of variable length. The valid error codes and their corresponding error texts are shown in Table 5.3.

Table 5.3   **TFTP Error Codes**

Error Code	Error Text
0x0000	Undefined Error
0x0001	File Not Found
0x0002	Access Violation
0x0003	Disk Space Exceeded
0x0004	Illegal Operation
0x0005	Unknown Transfer ID
0x0006	File Exists
0x0007	No Such User

An error-handling packet ends with a 1-byte EOF field that is set to 0x00.

TFTP Protocol Trace

Figure 5.3 shows a TFTP read request; the Op Code field is 0x0001. The next field is the name of the file to be read, testout. This is followed by an EOF marker, 0x00. The fourth field is the data mode, netascii. The final field is another EOF marker, 0x00.

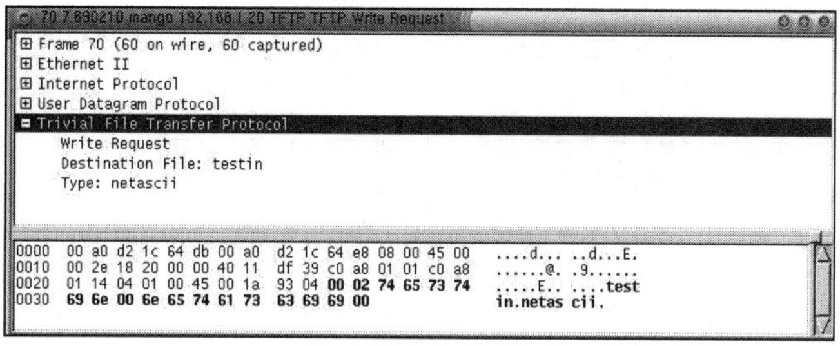

Figure 5.3   A TFTP read request.

Figure 5.4 shows a TFTP write request; the Op Code field is 0x0002. The name of the file to be written is testin, which is followed by 0x00 (the EOF marker). The data mode is netascii and is also followed with the 0x00 EOF marker.

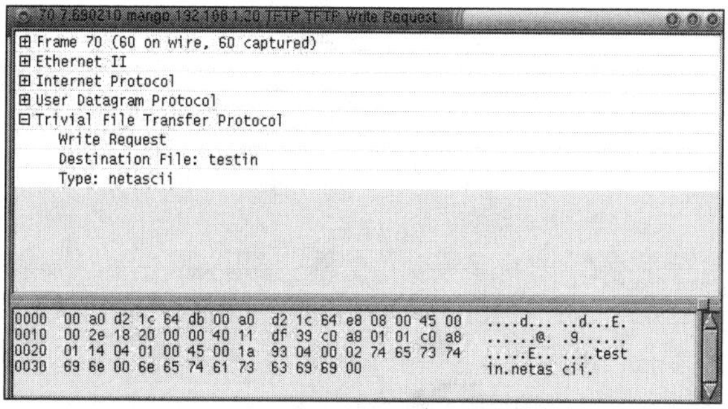

Figure 5.4   A TFTP write request packet.

A TFTP data packet is shown in Figure 5.5. The Op Code field is 0x0003; the block number is 0x0001. The rest of the packet is a large Data field. It is 512 bytes long, so we know that there are more packets to come.

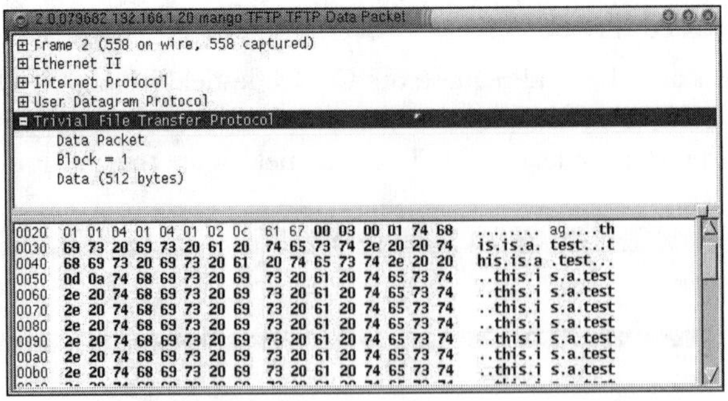

Figure 5.5 A TFTP data packet.

Figure 5.6 shows a TFTP acknowledgment packet. Its Op Code field is 0x0004, and its block number is 0x0001. The rest of the packet is padded out to meet the minimum data size for an Ethernet II packet.

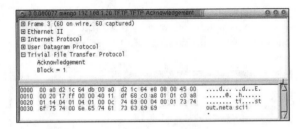

Figure 5.6 A TFTP acknowledgment packet.

The last TFTP packet type, a TFTP error packet, is shown in Figure 5.7. The Op Code field is 0x0005. The error code is 0x0001, and the error text is "File not found."

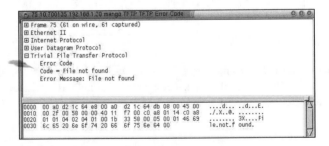

Figure 5.7 A TFTP error packet.

Setting Up a Server for TFTP

Setting up a Linux box to serve TFTP is a pretty simple task. TFTP is a notorious security hole, but it can also be an important part of your network. Diskless systems and a variety of other hardware often use TFTP to retrieve configuration files from a specified server.

Two major security problems exist with TFTP: First, it allows anonymous read and write access to a well-known port. Second, it is a UDP-based application, so it is harder to handle with a firewall (short of just blocking it altogether).

Like most protocols, if you don't need TFTP, don't run it. If you do need a TFTP server, run it on just one box and do your best to keep it as secure as possible. The following paragraphs explain how to do it.

Starting up the TFTP server is as simple as modifying your /etc/inetd.conf file and sending inetd the HUP signal.[4] The section you'll want to change looks like the one shown in Example 5.1 (at least on a Red Hat 6.2-based system).

Example 5.1   **An inetd.conf Without TFTP Enabled**

```
# TFTP service is provided primarily for booting.  Most sites
# run this only on machines acting as "boot servers." Do not uncomment
# this unless you *need* it.
#
#tftp   dgram   udp     wait    root    /usr/sbin/tcpd   in.tftpd
#bootps dgram   udp     wait    root    /usr/sbin/tcpd   bootpd
#
```

You need to change it to look like the one shown in Example 5.2.

Example 5.2   **An inetd.conf With TFTP Enabled**

```
# TFTP service is provided primarily for booting.  Most sites
# run this only on machines acting as "boot servers." Do not uncomment
# this unless you *need* it.
#
#tftp   dgram   udp     wait    root    /usr/sbin/tcpd   in.tftpd
#bootps dgram   udp     wait    root    /usr/sbin/tcpd   bootpd
#
```

After you've made this change, you can kill the inetd server. The process is shown in Example 5.3.

Example 5.3   **HUPing inetd**

```
[root@cherry /root]# ps -aux | grep inetd
root       482  0.0  0.0  1148    0 ?       SW   Aug08   0:00 [inetd]
root      2791  0.0  0.8  1360  508 pts/1   R    04:31   0:00 grep inetd
[root@cherry /root]# ps -ef | grep inetd
root       482     1  0 Aug08 ?      00:00:00 [inetd]
[root@cherry /root]# kill -1 482
[root@cherry /root]# ps -aux | grep inetd
root       482  0.0  0.3  1148  240 ?       S    Aug08   0:00 inetd
root      2795  0.0  0.8  1364  524 pts/1   S    04:32   0:00 grep inetd
[root@cherry /root]#
```

After you accomplish this, you've got a running TFTP server. The big question now is, "What will it do?" By default, `tftpd` serves files out of the /tftpboot directory. You might want to change this to something in its own file system to help mitigate file system stuffing attacks.[5] You can adjust the directory that `tftpd` serves files out of by adjusting your /etc/inetd.conf file, like so:

```
tftp    dgram   udp     wait    root    /usr/sbin/tcpd  in.tftpd /mnt/tftpserve
```

After making this file and HUPing `inetd`, `tftpd` will provide services from the /mnt/tftpserve file system.

You will need to put any files that you want to serve into this directory. The directory and any files that you want to serve will need to be world-readable (mode 666 for files and 777 for directories) because `tftpd` doesn't use any authentication for file transfers. `tftpd` will allow only write access to files that exist and that are world-writable (mode 555).

Using TFTP

The TFTP protocol client is implemented as the executable /usr/bin/tftp. This command is not installed on all Linux distributions.

Command-Line Options

/usr/bin/tftp allows only one command-line option: the remote host name or IP address. The command is used as shown in Example 5.4.

Example 5.4   **Starting TFTP**

```
[pate@cherry pate] tftp crashtestdummy
tftp?
```

The command in Example 5.4 starts a TFTP session to the host crashtestdummy. The remote host portion of the command is optional and can just as easily be done as shown in Example 5.5.

Example 5.5   **Another Way to Start TFTP**

```
[pate@router pate]$ tftp
tftp?
[pate@router pate]$
```

Interactive Commands

TFTP allows for a number of interactive commands. The most important are these:

- `connect`
- `get`
- `mode`
- `put`
- `status`
- `trace`
- `verbose`
- `?`

We'll cover each of these in this section. I'll start with `trace` and `status` because they will shed a great deal of light on later discussions.

The `status` command shows you the current status of the TFTP session. This is shown in Example 5.6.

Example 5.6   **The TFTP *status* Command**

```
tftp? status
Not connected.
Mode: netascii Verbose: off Tracing: off
Rexmt-interval: 5 seconds, Max-timeout: 25 seconds
tftp?
```

The `trace` command sends a report to the terminal for each TFTP packet. It is shown in Example 5.7.

Example 5.7   **The TFTP *trace* Command**

```
tftp? trace
tftp*rang; get testin
tftp> Packet tracing on.
tftp> sent RRQ ?file=testin, mode=netascii?
sent RRQ ?file=testin, mode=netascii?
sent RRQ ?file=testin, mode=netascii?
sent RRQ ?file=testin, mode=netascii?
sent RRQ ?file=testin, mode=netascii?
Transfer timed out.
```

If you do not specify a remote host, the `connect` command enables you to specify one. You can use `connect` with a new host even if you are already connected to one. This command is used as shown in Example 5.8.

Example 5.8   **The TFTP** *connect* **Command**

```
tftp? 192.168.1.20
tftp? status
Connected to 192.168.1.20.
Mode: netascii Verbose: off Tracing: off
Rexmt-interval: 5 seconds, Max-timeout: 25 seconds
tftp?
```

To retrieve a file, you use the get command. You can specify filenames in several ways:

- get filename

- get remotefile localfile

- get file1 file2 file3 ... fileN

- get

The second and third options can cause some confusion: If you list only two filenames, you read from the first and write to a local file named the second. If you list more than two filenames, each of the files will be read from the server and written into files of the same name on the client. If you use the fourth form, you are prompted for the file(s) that you want to download; the format is the same as the first three forms of get. You also can specify a host name with the get command; the format is get host:file. Example 5.9 shows several methods of getting files with this command.

Example 5.9   **The TFTP** *get* **Command**

```
tftp? trace
tftp? get testout
sent RRQ ?file=testout, mode=netascii?
received DATA ?block=1, 17 bytes?
Received 17 bytes in 0.1 seconds
tftp? get
(files) testin testout
sent RRQ ?file=testin, mode=netascii?
received DATA ?block=1, 448 bytes?
Received 448 bytes in 0.1 seconds
tftp? get
(files) testin testout foo
sent RRQ ?file=testin, mode=netascii?
received DATA ?block=1, 448 bytes?
Received 448 bytes in 0.0 seconds
sent RRQ ?file=testout, mode=netascii?
received DATA ?block=1, 17 bytes?
Received 17 bytes in 0.0 seconds
sent RRQ ?file=foo, mode=netascii?
received ERROR ?code=1, msg=File not found?
Error code 1: File not found
tftp?
```

The `mode` command is used to set the data mode for all following transfers. It can be used repeatedly to change back and forth from netascii to binary as needed. `mode` expects a single argument describing the data mode that you want to use. If you do not give a data mode, TFTP responds with the current data mode. The `mode` command is shown in Example 5.10.

Example 5.10   **The TFTP *mode* Command**

```
tftp? mode
Using netascii mode to transfer files.
tftp? mode binary
tftp? mode
Using octet mode to transfer files.
tftp? mode netascii
tftp?
```

You can write a file to the remote host with the `put` command. Its syntax is like that of `get`, explained previously.

For a quick review of these commands (and the other commands not covered here), you can use the ? command. It returns a list of commands with brief descriptions, as shown in Example 5.11.

Example 5.11   **The TFTP *?* Command**

```
tftp? ?
Commands may be abbreviated.  Commands are:

connect         connect to remote tftp
mode            set file transfer mode
put             send file
get             receive file
quit            exit tftp
verbose         toggle verbose mode
trace           toggle packet tracing
status          show current status
binary          set mode to octet
ascii           set mode to netascii
rexmt           set per-packet retransmission timeout
timeout         set total retransmission timeout
?               print help information
tftp?
```

HTTP

The *Hypertext Transfer Protocol* (HTTP), described in RFC 1945 and RFC 2616, provides an application-layer protocol for the distribution of data across a network. It allows several means of requesting and submitting data. HTTP provides a method for typing the data being transmitted.

Unlike the previous two protocols discussed, HTTP is implemented over the TCP transmission-layer protocol. The TCP protocol provides session information that allows HTTP to avoid doing some of the work that a UDP-based protocol would need to.

HTTP is similar in some ways to the TFTP protocol: Both are designed to pass data between two network-connected hosts. HTTP does not need to worry about dividing the data into explicitly sized blocks and signaling an End of Data condition. It does, however, have to carry the burden of TCP session setup and teardown.

The simplest description of HTTP is that it follows a four-step process:[6]

1. The client and server establish a TCP session. The server usually resides at TCP port 80.

2. The client sends an HTTP request. Often this is a `GET` request and looks like this: `GET /file.html HTTP/1.0`.

3. The server responds by sending the requested data to the client.

4. The hosts close their TCP session.

After the session is set up, the client send a (potentially) multiline HTTP request to the server. The parts of the request are shown in Example 5.12.

Example 5.12   **The HTTP Request Format**

```
method absolute-path (HTTP/1.0|HTTP/1.1)
(optional directives)
```

The method referred to in Example 5.12 can be one of several types; these are explained in Table 5.4.

Table 5.4   **Selected HTTP Methods**

Method	Description
DELETE	The DELETE method requests that the server delete the information referenced.
GET	The GET method retrieves the information that it references. GET requests can be conditional.
HEAD	The HEAD method is similar to the GET method, except that the response includes only its header, not the information referenced.
POST	The POST method indicates that data is being transferred to the server to be used with the information referenced.
PUT	The PUT method requests that the server store the information accompanying it in the location given.

The HTTP response is similar to the HTTP request. The format of the response is shown in Example 5.13.

Example 5.13 **An HTTP Response**

```
[HTTP/1.0 | HTTP/1.1] status-code description
(additional information lines)
[data]
```

The status code mentioned in Example 5.13 can have many possible values. All of them fit into a broad classification, shown in Table 5.5, and some of the more important status codes are shown in Table 5.6.

Table 5.5 **HTTP Status Code Base Values**

Value	Description
1yx	Informational
2yz	Success
3yz	Redirection
4yz	Client Error
5yz	Server Error

Table 5.6 **Selected HTTP Status Codes**

Code	Description
100	Continue
200	OK
204	No Content
206	Partial Content
301	Moved Permanently
304	Not Modified
400	Bad Request
401	Unauthorized
403	Forbidden
404	Not Found
405	Method Not Allowed
408	Request Timeout
500	Internal Server Error
501	Not Implemented
505	HTTP Version Not Supported

HTTP over SSL (HTTPS) is a secure extension to HTTP. It passes HTTP traffic though the *Secure Socket Layer* (SSL) to encrypt the traffic and to provide some authentication of the end systems. HTTPS uses port 443 instead of the typical port 80 of HTTP.

The *Common Gateway Interface* (CGI) is a widely used interface to provide dynamic content to Web sites. CGI programs can be written in any language available but are frequently written in Perl and C. Parameters to CGI programs can be sent to the host as part of the URL with a GET, or in a more hidden manner with a POST. A sample CGI program is shown in Example 5.14. This sample outputs a page of HTML containing a list of all parameters sent to it. (It isn't secure at all, but it is useful for testing links to CGI programs to ensure that the correct parameters and values are being passed.)

Example 5.14   **An Example CGI Program in Perl**

```
#!/usr/bin/perl

use CGI qw(:standard);

# print a http header, the html <head> section, a level 1 headline, and
# a horizontal rule
print header,
      start_html('A Simple Example'),
      h1('A Simple Example'),
      hr;

# get a list of all parameters
@param = param();

# for each parameter, print its value
foreach $key (@param) {
      $param = param($key);
      print p,"$key is $param\n";
}
```

HTTP Protocol Trace

In this section, we look at HTTP three different ways. First, we'll see a session trace of a Web page being downloaded. Second, we'll look at an ASCII representation of the download of one file from that page. Our last look at HTTP is a packet decode of an HTTP GET request.

The session trace in Figure 5.8 begins with a DNS lookup of the Web server in packets 1 and 2. Packets 3, 5, and 6 are the packets making up the three-step handshake. Packets 7–15 contain the first GET request and the accompanying response. Packets 17–19 then represent the three-step handshake for the next request. You can see the beginning of a second GET request and the accompanying response, but the remainder of the session is truncated.

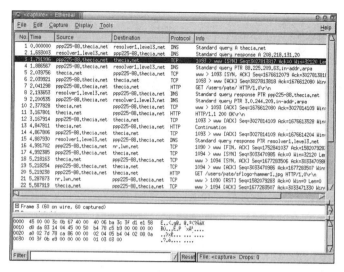

Figure 5.8   Downloading a Web page.

Figure 5.9 shows an ASCII representation of the first GET request and its response from Figure 5.8. The first block represents the GET request and the directives passed to the server by the client. The second block of data represents the response header from the server. The final block (which has been truncated) shows the actual data transferred between the two hosts.

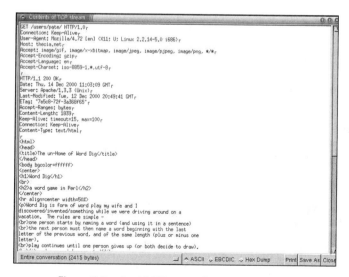

Figure 5.9   An ASCII trace of an HTTP session.

Figure 5.10 shows the HTTP message containing the first GET request from Figure 5.8. This is an HTTP 1.0 request; it requests English content and attempts to establish an ongoing connection.

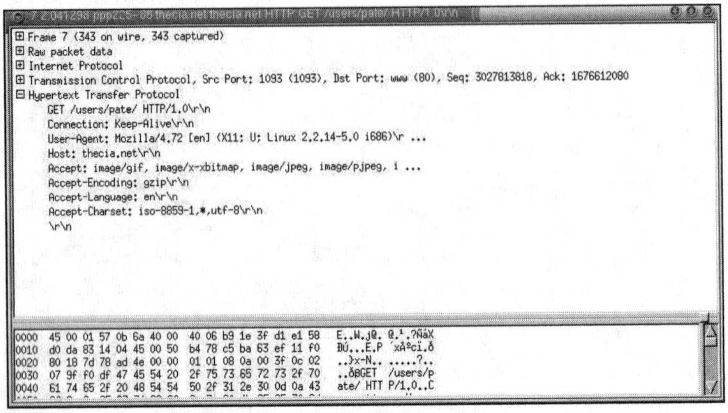

Figure 5.10   A GET request.

Using HTTP from the Command Line

One of the rarely used methods of interacting with (or testing) an HTTP server is a command-line connection. Connecting to the server in this manner offers you a great degree of control over the session. It also gives you immediate feedback on the data being returned. An example of testing a connection is shown in Example 5.14.

Example 5.14   **Using HTTP at the Command Line**

```
[pate@cherry figures]$ telnet thecia.net 80
Trying 208.218.131.20...
Connected to thecia.net.
Escape character is '^]'.
GET /users/pate/ HTTP/1.1
HOST: thecia.net
Connection: Keep-Alive

HTTP/1.1 200 OK
Date: Thu, 14 Dec 2000 11:39:54 GMT
Server: Apache/1.3.3 (Unix)
Last-Modified: Tue, 12 Dec 2000 20:49:41 GMT
ETag: "7e5c8-72f-3a368f65"
Accept-Ranges: bytes
Content-Length: 1839
Keep-Alive: timeout=15, max=100
Connection: Keep-Alive
Content-Type: text/html
```

```
<html>
<head>
<title>The un-Home of Word Dig</title>
</head>
<body bgcolor=ffffff>
<center>
<h1>Word Dig</h1>
<br>
<h2>a word game in Perl</h2>
</center>
<hr align=center width=50%>
[remainder of output truncated]
```

In Example 5.14 you can see three distinct blocks: the user-generated HTTP request, the server-generated HTTP response, and the HTML data being transferred from the server. In the HTTP request, we used the HOST parameter (which is required for HTTP/1.1) and the Connection parameter.

The HTTP response contains a number of interesting parameters. The Last-Modified parameter can be used by HTTP proxy servers that cache content. The server then knows when to replace their local content with a fresh download from the HTTP server. The Content-Length parameter lets the client process know how much data to expect (this is used to update the status bar in most Web browsers). The Keep-Alive parameter has two important values: The timeout value is the number of seconds that the session will be open for follow-on transmissions, and the max value is the total number of file transfers that can be passed in this session.

Endnotes

1. For more information on routing, see the section "Routing" in Chapter 3, "Network-Layer Protocols."

2. These are all two-hop routes because bill has added one to the hop count for each route, indicating that it must pass through alan.

3. This can lead to an unfortunate complication. The sender keeps a timer on the data that it sends. If the receiver hasn't acknowledged a block of data before the timer expires, the sender will send another copy. If the receiver was merely late, it will have sent an acknowledgment for the block and then will send another acknowledgment when it receives the second copy. As this continues to happen, it creates a snowball effect congesting the network. This is often called the Sorcerer's Apprentice bug, named after the scene in Fantasia in which Mickey Mouse conjures up an army of mops to clean the sorcerer's tower—the mops rapidly get out of hand, just like the runaway TFTP process that's suffering from this bug.

4. HUP (or Hang UP) is sent with the command `kill -1 [pid]`.

5. It is possible to write incredibly large files to a system using TFTP, eventually filling the filesystem and (if it's the root filesystem) shutting down the system.

6. In practice, there are many variations on these four steps. The most common is the use of additional steps to multiplex file requests into a single TCP session.

II

Using the Protocols Effectively

6

A Problem-Solving Pattern

THIS CHAPTER IS DEVOTED TO BUILDING a problem-solving pattern for you. It will be of benefit only with a solid grasp of the fundamentals of networking presented in the previous chapters. Whatever other tools you use in troubleshooting network issues, it will be your knowledge and ability to use the tools that will enable you to solve the problem. *You* are the most important tool.

Now that you know how TCP/IP is supposed to work, you will be able to quickly identify things that aren't running properly. Coupled with a plan, or pattern, for troubleshooting, your knowledge will steer you through the often murky waters of network problems.

Troubleshooting Pattern Is Helpful Whether or Not You're Familiar with the Technology

At one point, I was doing some volunteer work cataloging documents. The local network was acting up, so I decided to take a look at it. It was a Novell-based network (a technology that I was—and still am—not very familiar with), but I was able to follow the troubleshooting pattern presented in this chapter to narrow the problem to a misbehaving file server.

A pattern is just that: It is not a firm set of rules; it's a set of guidelines. If you follow a troubleshooting method consistently, it will help you to find solutions more easily. You will be able to zero in on the root cause of the issue and quickly resolve it. One nice thing about this pattern is that it is neither Linux- nor TCP/IP-specific. You can apply it to a variety of problems. (I make no promises about in-law problems, though.)

To try to set this pattern into context, each step of the pattern is described in its own section. Each section contains a short example at the beginning, as well as part of a continuing example that runs through each section. A true story showing both the problem with not using a pattern like this one and the benefit of using one comes at the end of the chapter. Later, in Chapter 8, "In The Moment—Case Studies," I'll point out the pattern in each case study. Nine steps are involved in the pattern, as shown in Figure 6.1.

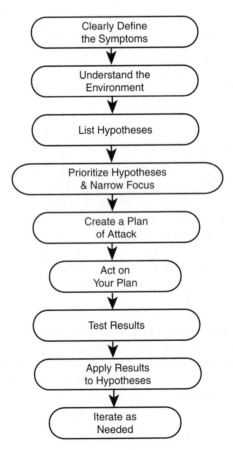

Figure 6.1   A nine-step problem-solving pattern.

Step 1: Clearly Describe the Symptoms

There's no good way to attack a problem until you know what the problem really is. Far too often, system and network administrators hear a rather poor (if not outright misleading) description of the problem. It's then your job to dig in and find out what's really going on.

Ask the Right Questions

Once, when I was working in a network management center, I received a call from a user claiming that he had a "network problem." When I asked what was wrong, he responded that his PC could not see the network. "Okay, what error messages are you getting?" I asked. He responded that when he booted his computer, it displayed the error message "Non-system Disk in Drive A:." Obviously, this was not a networking issue.

I could have jumped into diagnostic testing of the network segment that he was on or tried pinging his PC. By asking questions first, so that I could clearly describe the symptoms, I was able to save myself a lot of time and trouble. I was also able to get the caller back to work much more quickly.

As you can probably guess, you'll need some interviewing skills to get a clear description of the symptoms from a user. People don't want to hide the truth from you, but they often have predetermined the problem, coloring their perception of the issues involved.

It's a good idea to take notes as you're talking with someone, periodically summarizing the problem description as you go. This can help you spot follow-up questions to ask the user. It can also help jog a user's memory for other tidbits.

Never hesitate to call or email the user back with further questions to clarify the situation. It is certainly better to get all the answers you need up-front, but the reality is that you might not know all the questions that you need to ask until you've gotten your hands dirty working on the problem. If you need more detail, go get it.

Holding your interview at the customer's location also gives you a chance to say, "Show me." This enables you to see what the user is doing and perhaps to identify some more key points about the problem. Sometimes it will also reveal the problem as one of those transient things that just won't show up when you're there to see it.

If you run into a problem that you can't reproduce, you have yet another problem on your hands—what to do about it. The best thing is often to set up a monitoring plan with the user. Get all the details that you can, and tell the user to call you back when the problem recurs. Leave the user with a list of questions to try to answer when calling you back. On your end, you should maintain a log so that you can track details about the problem.

There is no good rule to determine when a problem is clearly stated. This is fairly objective. If you think it's clear enough, it probably is. If you're not sure, try to describe the problem to someone else. (It really doesn't matter whether that person understands networking. In fact you could try explaining it to a house plant; it's the process of talking through the problem while describing the symptoms that helps clarify things for you.)

As you're talking with users about the problem, see if there are other hosts with the same symptoms. If users haven't seen this problem, ask them to try to reproduce it. If there isn't anyone else available, try to reproduce it yourself. Knowing whether this problem affects a single host, a local group of hosts, or all the hosts on a network will help you when you hit Step 2.

Some key questions that you should know the answers to are listed here:

- What applications or protocols are affected?
- What hosts are involved?
- What is common between affected hosts?
- When did the problem start?
- Is this a constant problem?
- If the problem is not constant, does it occur at a regular time or interval?

To further illustrate, let's look at three pairs of problem descriptions. The first description in each pair is an inadequate description; the second provides enough information to start solving the problem.

- **Inadequate**—"Whenever I make a connection to the Internet, things seem really slow."
- **Better**—"When I try connecting to external Web sites in the morning, my connection seems slow. I've tried at other times, and it doesn't seem so bad. If I try connecting to our internal Web server, everything seems fine, even in the morning."
- **Inadequate**—"I can't use email."
- **Better**—"I'm receiving email from our mail host, but when I try to send something, it normally fails. Mail addressed to people inside the company works, but not mail addressed to external addresses."
- **Inadequate**—"The network is really slow."
- **Better**—"My NFS-mounted partitions really seem bogged down, especially right at the beginning of the day. ssh, `ping`, and Web connections all seem to run at the normal speed, though."

It isn't easy to turn an inadequate description of a problem into something that you can work from. As you read each pair of descriptions, did you think about which questions you could ask to clarify the situation? Which questions would you need to ask a user to help that person describe the problem?

Example 6.1: An ssh Example Using Step 1

As a running example in this chapter, let's take a look at one problem specifically. You're a network administrator for a small business, Frobnitzim R Us (FRU). A user calls you and complains, "I can't use ssh."

If you were confronted with the first description, you might ask the user, "Have you ever been able to connect to that host? Does anyone else have the same problem? Is it just that host, or are other hosts affected?" The answers to these questions would help lead you to a better description, such as this:

"Well, yesterday, I could ssh to our Web server and to external hosts. Today I can't get to our Web server. I can still connect to external hosts, though. I asked some other people, and they have the same problem."

Step 2: Understand the Environment

When you have a clear description of the symptoms, you must be able to understand the environment that the problem occurs in to effectively troubleshoot it. Gaining this understanding is really a twofold job: It requires both identifying the pieces involved in the problem and understanding how those pieces should act when they are not experiencing the problem.

A Problem-Solving Experience

Many years ago, I was trying to solve a sendmail problem on a host I was responsible for. At that time, sendmail had two configuration files, the sendmail.cf file (the obvious one) and the sendmail.fc file (the less obvious one). The sendmail.fc file was actually the "frozen" version of the sendmail.cf file. At that point in my career, I wasn't aware of the distinction.

I had made a needed change to the sendmail.cf, but I never "froze" it. When the anticipated behavioral change didn't occur, I started troubleshooting. It took far longer than I want to admit to figure out what was going on.

The first task typically means creating a subset of your network map, showing the portions of the network that are involved in the problem. Sometimes this new map will be a logical map, and sometimes you will want to draw it out.

The second task, understanding how things should be behaving, is made much easier if you look at a snapshot of how your network acted before the problem occurred. These snapshots are called *baselines* and are covered in more detail in the next chapter. In the absence of a baseline, you will need to create a model of the proper behavior of the network from your understanding of its layout, components, and configuration.

Example 6.2: An ssh Example Using Step 2

Figure 6.2 contains the network map used to troubleshoot the ssh problem given as an example in Step 1. This map shows the following components:

- Hosts on an internal network, connected via a switch
- Hosts on the other internal network, connected via a switch
- A router connecting the two internal networks
- A packet-filtering router connecting the internal, external, and protected networks
- Hosts on the protected network, interconnected via a switch
- The Internet
- A sample host on the Internet

After you've looked over your map of FRU's network, you'll need to isolate those systems involved in the problem.

The systems involved in the ssh problem are highlighted in gray in Figure 6.3. Notice that the internal router and the second internal switch are not highlighted, nor are the Internet and connected hosts.

We built the map in Figure 6.3 by comparing the hosts and networks with the problem description. Because all the internal hosts were affected, we know that the internal router is not at fault (not all the internal systems use the router to reach the Web server). Likewise, the second internal switch can be excluded. The problem does not affect traffic bound for arbitrary hosts on the Internet, so both the token Internet connect host and the Internet itself can be excluded.

By the time we reach the second task of this step, we know that only the following hosts are involved:

- Internal hosts, which should be capable of using ssh to connect to the Web server
- The first internal switch, which shouldn't be doing any packet filtering and should have a fairly light traffic load
- The packet filtering router, which should allow ssh connections from any internal host to any external host or any protected host
- The protected LAN, which shouldn't be doing any packet filtering and should have a very light load
- The company Web server, which should allow ssh connections from any internal hosts

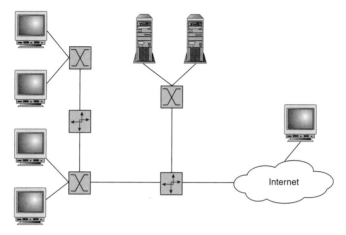

Figure 6.2 First network map.

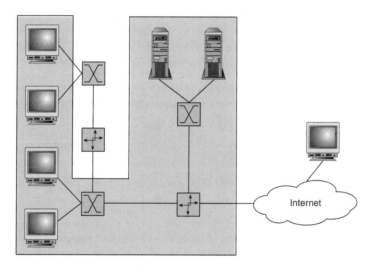

Figure 6.3 Map of affected portions.

Step 3: List Hypotheses

Having made a list of the affected systems (in Step 2), we can begin to list potential causes of the problem. It's safe to brainstorm at this stage because we will be narrowing our search later. In fact, it is better to be overly creative here and end up with extra hypotheses than to miss the actual cause and chase blind leads.

Be Thorough When Listing Hypotheses

Some time ago, I was called in to help troubleshoot a networking problem at a library. The library was on a college campus and was already part of a working LAN. When the Library Application Server was brought up, it could not talk to the other hosts on the LAN.

My initial thought was that it was probably one of three things:

- A bad 10BASE-2 connection

- A bad NIC

- A bad transceiver[1]

I first asked about lights on the back of the host. Sure enough, all lights were accounted for. I asked the same question about the transceiver and got the same answer. If I logged into the server and ran `net-stat`, I could see Ethernet packets coming in. The machine just didn't seem to make sense of them.

I asked the network technician from the school to check the same thing on the local router. Sure enough, there were packets arriving from the library's server. They just weren't being handled.

Obviously I'd missed something in my list. If the packets were moving around, the physical connection was fine. That ruled out media, transceiver, and NIC. I was stumped—until the network technician mentioned something that turned on a light for me.

He said that the only time he'd seen something like this was when the new Novell server had had problems on another LAN at the school. Back then, Novell ran on 802.3 networks, not Ethernet II.

The library's server was running AIX, which allowed you to define an interface as either 802.3 or Ethernet II. Sure enough, it had been configured to run in 802.3 mode. A quick configuration change later, and the server could see the rest of the network.

I had allowed myself to stop listing hypotheses after I had covered the first possibility, a physical problem. If I had spent a little more time working on a good list of possible causes, I might have saved myself (and everyone else) quite a bit of frustration.

Just like the maps of the problem environment, your list of hypotheses doesn't need to be anything formal. A mental list is normally fine; something scrawled on a piece of scratch paper is even better. Sometimes, though, you'll want a formal document; big network issues affecting lots of people just cry out for formal documents (well, at least the managers involved cry a lot).

Example 6.3: An ssh Example Using Step 3

Some of the possible causes of our ssh problem are listed here (in no particular order):

- It could be an ssh configuration problem.
- It could be an sshd configuration problem.
- It could be a switch configuration problem on the internal network switch.
- It could be a switch configuration problem on the protected network switch.
- It could be a problem with the filtering rules on the packet-filtering router.

Step 4: Prioritize Hypotheses and Narrow Focus

This is the step where we stop making work for ourselves and start making our jobs easier. Although we've just made a list of things that *could* be the problem, we don't want to research every item on the list if we don't have to. Instead, we can prioritize the potential causes and chase down the most likely ones first. Eventually, we'll either solve the problem or run out of possible causes (in which case we need to go back to Step 3).

Prioritizing Potential Problems

While I was trying to track down the source of dropped connections at a remote site, I was able to come up with the following list of possible problems:

- There could be a problem on the server that all the terminals were connecting to, which has shown up only on the affected terminals so far.

- All the affected terminal servers could be misconfigured, although the unaffected terminal servers were properly configured.

- There could be a wiring problem that affected only some of the terminals in the system.

- There could be a common environmental problem among the affected terminals.

We were able to push the first possibility to the bottom of the list because it was rather unlikely. The last possibility also seemed to be too contrived to be the problem. This left the two possibilities in the middle of our list as equally likely in our eyes. We decided to start looking at the third option because it was the easiest to check.

As you're prioritizing your list, pay particular attention to recent changes. These are often the source of your problems. Changes meant to improve the environment often have unintended consequences.

Example 6.4: An ssh Example Using Step 4

To continue the ssh example, I've prioritized the list of possible causes:

1. Last night's changes on the packet filter

2. A configuration problem on the Web server

3. A configuration problem on the highlighted internal switch

4. A configuration problem on the protected network switch

5. A problem on the internal PCs

We know that the problem started today, so it's most likely part of the changes from last night. The next most likely assumption is that it was a change on the Web server itself because that host is the only one in common with all the failing ssh connections. One of the two highlighted switches is also possible, but because they aren't supposed to be doing any packet filtering, we'll count them toward the bottom of the priority pile. Finally, it could be a new problem on all the internal PCs, although this is a pretty big stretch.

Step 5: Create a Plan of Attack

Now that you've identified the most likely causes of the problem, it's time to disprove each of the possible causes in turn. As each of the potential causes is eliminated, you narrow your search further. Eventually you will reach a problem that you can't disprove, and your most recent attempt will have corrected the problem.

Narrowing Down Potential Causes of Problems with Testing

Recently, I was working with another system administrator on a *remote console server* (RCS), a system that provided console access to several hosts at a remote location. For some reason, the console software wasn't operating correctly. We decided that the possible causes of software problems were these (from most likely to least likely):

- The physical connections between the RCS box and the other hosts could have been mangled as the boxes were physically installed.

- The TTY devices could have been installed incorrectly.

- The software could have been installed incorrectly.

- The software could have been misconfigured.

We decided to first test the physical connection. The best way to do this was to use a different software package (one that would use the same hardware) to make a serial connection to a remote host. If that worked, we would know that the physical connections were not the problem and would be able to focus on other things. (This test actually would help eliminate our second cause for suspicion because the TTY device would have to be correctly installed for our test to succeed.)

One thing you don't want to do is make changes in many areas at once. Making one change at a time, working on only one component per change, ensures that you'll be able to identify the modifications that actually fixed the problem.

You don't need a hard and fast plan for the follow-up steps to take if a test doesn't solve or identify the problem. However, you should at least think about where you're going to go next. Your prioritized list will be of great help as you make plans for the future. Don't be too surprised if your plans take a slight detour, though; crystal balls are notoriously vague.

A final step in preparing your plan is to review it with those holding a stake in solving the problem. This probably includes management, the customer suffering the problem, and anyone working with you in troubleshooting.

Example 6.5: An ssh Example Using Step 5

When creating a plan for our ssh example, we'll want to focus on the changes made to the packet filter last night. A simple first plan would be to back out the changes made last night. If this restores ssh connectivity, you'll have to rewrite and reinstall the changes to restore the new functionality without blocking ssh. If that doesn't work, it will be time to look at any packet-filtering rules that you find on the switches.

Step 6: Act on Your Plan

With a plan in place—and reviewed by those with a stake in solving the problem—you're prepared to act.

Troubleshooting Difficulties

While involved in a long troubleshooting sequence on a server, our group brought in the hardware vendor, the software vendor, and our own experts. The problem seemed to indicate a hardware problem, but there were some anomalies. We decided to run a prolonged stress test on the hardware with a clean OS install (on separate disks installed for just the test).

We started the exerciser and left it to run through the middle of the night. About two hours later, the system died with the same symptoms we had been seeing. Unfortunately, the night operator (who hadn't been well briefed in our plan) caught the failure and restarted the test suite. He did this without taking any notes about what had happened or informing any of the experts involved in the test.

The next day, when we found out what had happened, we were in a quandary. The system had failed, which seemed to indicate a hardware problem, but there were no details recorded that could have identified which component had failed.

While you're acting on the plan, take good notes and make sure that you keep copies of configuration files that you're changing. Nothing is worse than finishing off a series of tests, finding that they didn't solve the problem, and then discovering that you introduced a new problem and can't easily back out your changes. It can also be disheartening to have insufficient or misleading information to report at the conclusion of your test.

Example 6.6: An ssh Example Using Step 6

In our ssh example, we'll grab a copy of the most recent packet-filtering rules from the router. Just to be picky, we'll also grab them from the CVS repository where they're stored. Comparing the two copies (with the `diff` command), we find that they're the same. Reading the file however, we find a problem. The rule that's supposed to stop all ssh traffic is applied to the internal interface, not the external interface. Ouch! This means that anyone on the Internet can start an ssh session with our host, but no one inside can do so.

We modify the rules so that the ssh block is applied on the external interface, not the internal interface. Then we check the file into CVS, load it onto the router, and reload the packet-filtering process so that it sees the new rule set.

Step 7: Test Results

You'll never know whether your test has done anything without checking to see if the problem still exists. You'll also never know whether you've introduced new problems with your changes if you don't test. Testing gives you confidence that all is as it should be.

Testing Functionality

I once was asked to add some functionality to a log rotation package that we used in our shop. After I added the code to perform the new function, I tested it to ensure that things worked. A simple test showed that the new function worked as desired. I then ran a more complete test and found that I had broken another bit of functionality. Had I not run the full test suite, I would have released a broken tool onto our servers. (The good news is, it was a simple mistake to fix, and the fix pointed out a way to make the code smaller and easier to maintain.)

I recommend that you make it a practice to keep a suite of tests that exercise the main functionality of your network. Each time you run into a problem, add a test or two to check for it as well. Given a suite like this and a system to run all the tests, you can feel confident that your network is solid at the end of the day.

Example 6.7: An ssh Example Using Step 7

When we reload the packet filter in our ssh example, we can immediately check to see if we can use ssh to connect to our Web server. After verifying that it works, we can test to make sure that external connections to the Web server don't work (don't forget to add this to the test suite). Finally, we can verify that other major bits still work, all according to our existing test suite. For the sake of our example, we'll say that external hosts are still capable of making ssh connections to the Web server.

Step 8: Apply Results of Testing to Hypotheses

This is the pay-off step. If your testing has isolated and solved the problem, you're almost done. All that remains is to make the changes introduced in your test a permanent part of the network. If you haven't solved the problem yet, this is where you sit down with your results and your list of hypotheses to see what you've learned.

> **Applying Results**
>
> When I was first doing system administration work, I created a set of scripts to automate the creation of index files. When I ran the scripts from the command line, they worked perfectly. When I ran them from `cron`, they failed miserably.
>
> My first thought was that the `cron` user didn't have permission to run all the commands called by the script. I decided to test this by making every call explicitly and then logging them to a file.
>
> It turned out that permissions weren't a problem. Carefully examining the log file helped me find the problem, though. The file indicated that I was relying on environment variables that existed in my interactive session, but not in the environment that the `cron` job ran in.
>
> I was able to add the needed variables into the script, and all was well.

If the most recent test solved your problem, this step is unnecessary. You've found the problem and (hopefully) corrected it. If your efforts haven't solved the problem (or if you've created a new one), you need to look at how the data from this test affects your prioritized list of possible causes. Does your prioritization need to change? Are more possibilities pointed out by this test? If the test didn't identify and solve your problem, did it eliminate this possible cause? If not, what further tests are needed to make sure that this possible cause isn't the root of your problem?

Example 6.8: An ssh Example Using Step 8

Because we fixed only half of the problem in the previous steps, we need to check our data and see where we should look for our next step. The results of our test show that internal hosts can again connect to the Web server, but external hosts are no longer blocked. The rest of our test suite shows that other services are handled as expected.

Step 9: Iterate as Needed

Most often, you won't need to go all the way back to Step 1 or 2. Instead, you'll be able to go back to Step 4 to reprioritize and refocus. You might find that the things you learned in your most recent test point you in a slightly different direction. You might also find another possible cause of the problem; in this case, you can jump back to Step 3 and add it to your list.

Iterating

While I was writing this section, a Web hosting server that I help run died. After resuscitating it, I found that email wasn't working properly. My list of hypotheses was as follows:

- The MTA daemon hadn't been started.
- The MTA configuration was botched.

I logged in and checked. Sure enough, the MTA hadn't started. I started it up by hand and tested it; the local deliveries worked fine, but the remote deliveries didn't. Next I checked the configuration files, and everything looked fine. I also checked /var/log/messages, but I didn't see any sign of the MTA whining as it started.

Without a solution, I had to jump back to Step 3. What else could be wrong? I decided to try connecting directly to port 25 from a remote host to see what kind of errors I saw. I was a little surprised to find that the connection was refused, and then I remembered that our mailer sits behind a TCP wrapper daemon. (Sometimes you need a little reminder to put something on your list of possible causes.)

Going back to the server, I checked to see if the wrapper was running. It wasn't. After a quick restart of the daemon, all was well again. With everything running correctly, I went back and added the MTA and system startup scripts to ensure this would not happen again.

If you've completely run out of possible causes or found additional information, you might even want to go all the way back to Step 1 and restate the problem just to make sure that you've not missed the mark completely.

Example 6.9: An ssh Example Using Step 9

The ssh connection is supposed to be blocked at the router, so that's the most likely place to check for problems. Changes made on the fly (like the ones we made earlier) are notorious for having minor glitches that cause major headaches. Going back to the configuration, we might find that our shuffling of the file resulted in a bad mask being applied to the external hosts, allowing most of the Internet into our host. Again, it's a quick fix.

This time, when we run our test suite, everything runs as expected. It took us two trips through the pattern, but we got the problem licked.

Two Stories of Problem Solving

True to Life

The following two sections might read like something that really happened. That's not suprising—it did. I've changed the names to protect the innocent (and the guilty).

Well, this is really one story in two parts. The first section details the misguided attempts of someone to fix a problem he had come across. He doesn't use our nine-step pattern. The second section follows the actions of two system admins who came in behind the first attempt and had to clean things up. They did follow the pattern, and their results were much better.

Catching a Greased Pig

At one company I know of, a central mail server was located off-site. It not only received all the inbound mail and served it up via POP3, but it also relayed all the outgoing mail.

At one point, a user doing some systems administration work (we'll call him Rob) added a new machine to the network in one of the company's two offices. After assigning the remote machine as the SMTP gateway in pine for the new machine, he had someone send mail to the new user and verified that he could check his mail via the POP3 server. All worked as expected. Next he tried to send external mail. This time, it failed.

Thinking that he might have misconfigured his mail client, Rob tried reinstalling it. After configuring the SMTP gateway in pine to point to the central mail server, Rob tried sending mail to an external address again. It failed again. Next Rob tried setting up another mailer on the same host. He configured it to use the mail server as its SMTP gateway and tried to send external mail. Once more, it failed.

Rob decided that maybe he hadn't installed Linux correctly, so he installed Windows 98 on the machine to test things. After setting Outlook to use the mail server, he tried it again. Still no luck. At this point, Rob decided that it must be a server problem. He tried restarting the mail server and resending his test message, to no avail. Finally, he did an init 0^2 to shut off the box. After the other system administrators rebuilt things, they took a look around the system to see what was going on.

By the Book

The other two people doing system administration, Sara and Bill, asked Rob what had happened and eventually got this problem description from him: "I can't send mail to external addresses through our mail gateway, but I can receive mail from it."

Sara and Bill decided that they didn't quite have enough answers to really describe the problem. They wanted to know if Rob could send mail to internal addresses through the mail gateway and what kind of error messages he got. Giving him careful instructions, they sent him off to do the research for them.

After about 30 minutes, they got the answers that they needed. Yes, email could be sent to internal addresses. When messages failed, they generated an error message about relaying being denied.

Sara and Bill went to their white board and put together a map of the systems involved in the problem (as shown in Figure 6.4).

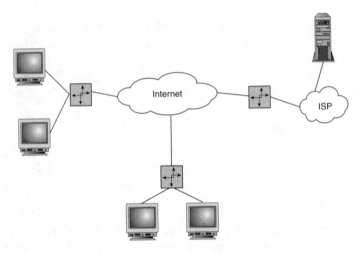

Figure 6.4   Email problem map.

They decided that the following items could be involved:

- The SMTP gateway
- The co-location network and routers
- The routers at the two office locations
- The client machines, including Rob's new machine, which could be the source of the problem

Sara and Bill decided that the problem was most likely on the server because there had been multiple MUAs and even two OSes involved on the client side. So that's where they started their list of possible causes:

- Misconfigured MTA
- Server IP problem
- Subnet mask problem on server
- Packet-filtering rules on the routers for the two office sites
- Subnet mask problem on the client

After a bit of thought, they where able to eliminate IP and subnet problems because the client and server could certainly pass IP traffic (including errors from the MTA).

They decided that their first test would be to verify that other hosts could still send external mail through the server. If not, it was a global problem on the MTA. If the other hosts could send mail, it might be related to the specific host in question.

To conduct the test, they sent mail from a box in the office where they worked, and they logged into a machine at the other office (where Rob worked) and sent mail from that host as well. Then they waited for delivery of the messages.

After a short wait, they checked the Hotmail account to which they had sent the email. Both boxes delivered their mail to the external address used in testing.

Applying the results of this test to their hypothesis meant that Sara and Bill could eliminate some of the possible causes from their list. They now knew that the only client box affected was the new one that Rob had installed. They redrew their map as shown in Figure 6.5.

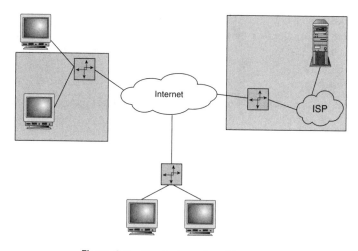

Figure 6.5   Revised email problem map.

The router and hosts from their office were crossed off the list of involved systems. Sara and Bill also dropped the remaining hosts at the other office from their list. They didn't see anything to add to their list of possible causes, and they couldn't drop the MTA as the culprit yet.

They decided that they needed to see what caused the MTA to generate relaying errors, so they hit the books (or in this case, the Web site). It turned out that their MTA relied on an external program called tcpserver to block relaying, and this program used a configuration file called /etc/tcp.smtp to control access. The next test would be to check /etc/tcp.smtp and change it, if needed.

Looking at the file revealed that the office where Bill and Sara were located was IP masqueraded, and the single IP address for the site was in the configuration file. The other office was using individual IP addresses, and not all of them were listed in the configuration file. Sara added the rest of the IP address from the other office to the file and restarted the tcpserver process. While she was doing that, Bill called Rob and asked him to try sending mail from the new box again.

This time the mail was sent to the external address. A couple follow-up tests showed that the other internal hosts were still capable of sending mail as well. With the problem solved and no new problems evident from their testing, Sara and Bill were able to go back to what they had been doing before this fiasco had interrupted them.

Endnotes

1. At that time, nearly all NICs had only a multipin AUI connection. If you wanted to connect to a network, you used a transceiver with an appropriate hardware connector to make the connection. This device was a small box that connected to the NIC and provided a single kind of Ethernet connection for the host.

2. `init 0` is like shuting down power to the box. Things just stop. It's bad.

7

Before Things Break—Building a Baseline

SOMETIMES WHEN YOU TALK TO A SEASONED SYSTEM or network administrator, he'll tell you that he knows that something is wrong when things don't feel right. This isn't an admission of paranormal powers; it's just a shorthand method for explaining that these experts know how their system or network is supposed to behave and that it isn't acting like that now. These administrators have created a baseline for their environment. Not all of them have done it formally, but the ones who have will have gained significant added benefits.

In this chapter, we'll cover what a baseline can do for you, what it really is, how to create one, how to keep it up-to-date, and how your baseline affects your network monitoring plan (and vice versa).

Why Baselines Matter

Baselines give you two primary benefits. First, they let you know how your network behaves under normal conditions—this lets you see where something is going wrong while you're troubleshooting a problem. Second, they let you see how your network's behavior is changing over time—this will help you maintain a healthy network through careful expansion. Both of these provide you with some real value.

A Baseline, Your Troubleshooting Friend

While you're troubleshooting, you'll use your baseline in two ways. The most obvious use is that you'll be able to tell when things are behaving outside the norm for your network. It is less obvious, but just as important, that you can use the baseline as part of your diagnostic tool kit. When taken together, these two benefits make your troubleshooting life much easier.

When you're aware of your network's normal behavior, changes become obvious. If Wednesday afternoons feature low bandwidth utilization but a high load on one of your servers, you won't be concerned if that server is slow to respond while the others are okay. All of the servers being slow to respond would send up a warning flag right away, though. This awareness cannot replace monitoring your network, but it does serve as a good adjunct to it.

When in the midst of troubleshooting, having your baseline information accessible can make a world of difference. For example, if you know that hosts cherry and berry aren't typically big users of bandwidth, but they seem to be the culprits in your current network overload, you've got a head start on identifying the problem. If you further know that one or both of them were just upgraded, you have an even better map. (Of course, it could always be the users flexing their Quake muscles...)

Having baseline information about your network will help you spot problems earlier and solve them faster. It may take a bit of work to get it started, but the effort expended now will pay off in weekend and evenings free later!

Watching Your Network for Fun and Prophet

Beyond helping you with your troubleshooting, a network baseline will help you avoid problems that you would otherwise walk into. Watching your network's behavior change will help you see where you need to make changes. Is traffic building up on a LAN segment? Maybe you'll need to add another switch. Do you have a server acting as a bottleneck? It's probably time to upgrade.

As your base of users grows and their needs change, your network will need to change as well. When you watch your network and can foresee needed changes in topology or equipment, you'll save yourself time and money. This is one of the best reasons to not only develop a baseline, but also to actively monitor against it and keep it up-to-date.

What Is a Baseline?

Several things make up a baseline, but at its heart, a baseline is merely a snapshot of your network the way it normally acts. The least effective form of a baseline is the "sixth sense" that you develop when you've been around something for a while. It seems to work because you notice aberrations subconsciously because you're used to the way things ought to be. Better baselines will be less informal and may include the following components:

- Network traces
- Summarized network utilization data
- Logs of work done on the network
- Maps of the network
- Records of equipment on the network and related configuration data

Each of these will be discussed in this section.

Network Traces

In Chapter 10, "Monitoring Tools," we discuss the ethereal network analyzer. This tool's capability to save capture files (or traces) enables you to maintain a history of your network. If the only traces you have saved represent your troubleshooting efforts, you won't have a very good picture of your network.

You also need to be aware that a lot of things will influence the contents of the traces you collect. Weekend vs. weekday; Monday or Friday vs. the rest of the week; and time of day are all examples of the kinds of factors that will affect your data. Running ethereal (or some other analyzer) at least three times a day, every day, and saving the capture file will give you a much clearer idea of how things normally work.

Utilization Data

Several tools can give you a quick look at your network's behavior: netstat, traceroute, ping, and even the contents of your system logs are all good sources of information.

The netstat tool can show you several important bits of information. Running it with the -M, -i, and -a switches are especially helpful. I typically add the -n switch to netstat as well. This switch turns off name resolution, which is a real boon if DNS is broken or IP addresses don't resolve back to names properly. The -i switch gives you interface specific information:

```
[pate@cherry sgml]$ netstat -i
Kernel Interface table
Iface   MTU Met    RX-OK RX-ERR RX-DRP RX-OVR    TX-OK TX-ERR TX-DRP TX-OVR Flg
eth0   1500   0        0      0      0      0       39      0      0      0 BRU
lo     3924   0       36      0      0      0       36      0      0      0 LRU
[pate@cherry sgml]$
```

The -M switch gives information pertaining to masqueraded connections:

```
[pate@router pate]$ netstat -Mn
IP masquerading entries
prot   expire source           destination        ports
tcp  59:59.96 192.168.1.10     64.28.67.48        1028 -> 80 (61002)
tcp  58:43.75 192.168.1.10     206.66.240.72      622 -> 22 (61001)
udp  16:37.72 192.168.1.10     209.244.0.3        1025 -> 53 (61000)
[pate@router pate]$
```

The -a switch gives connection-oriented output (this output has been abbreviated):

```
[pate@cherry pate]$ netstat -an
Active Internet connections (servers and established)
Proto Recv-Q Send-Q Local Address      Foreign Address      State
tcp        0      0 0.0.0.0:6000        0.0.0.0:*            LISTEN
tcp        0      0 0.0.0.0:3306        0.0.0.0:*            LISTEN
tcp        0      0 0.0.0.0:80          0.0.0.0:*            LISTEN
udp        0      0 0.0.0.0:111         0.0.0.0:*
raw        0      0 0.0.0.0:1           0.0.0.0:*            7
raw        0      0 0.0.0.0:6           0.0.0.0:*            7
Active UNIX domain sockets (servers and established)
Proto RefCnt Flags     Type     State       I-Node Path
unix  1      [ ]       STREAM   CONNECTED   1332   /tmp/.X11-unix/X0
unix  1      [ ]       STREAM   CONNECTED   1330   /tmp/.X11-unix/X0
unix  0      [ ]       DGRAM                440
[pate@cherry pate]$
```

The traceroute tool is especially important for servers that handle connections from disparate parts of the Internet. Setting up several traceroutes to different remote hosts can give you an indication of remote users connection speeds to your server.

The ping tool can help you watch the performance of a local or remote network in much the same way that traceroute does. It does not give as much detail, but it requires less overhead.

When users connect to services on your hosts, they leave a trail through your log files. If you use a central logging host and a log reader to grab important entries, you can build a history of how often services are used and when they are most heavily utilized.

Work/Problem Logs

You will likely find yourself touching a lot of the equipment on your network, so it is important that you keep good records of what you do. Even seemingly blind trails in troubleshooting may lead you to discover information about your network. In addition, you will find that your documentation will be an invaluable aid the next time you need to troubleshoot a similar problem.

Some people like to carry around a paper notebook to keep their records in; others prefer to keep things online. Both camps have good points, many related to information access. If you keep everything in a notebook but don't have it handy, it does you no good. Similarly, if everything is online and the network is down, you're in bad shape.

My preference is to keep things online, but in a cvs repository. Then you can keep it on a central server or two while also keeping a copy on your laptop, PC, or palmtop. If you like, you can even grab printouts. A nice benefit to this is that several people can make updates to documentation and then commit their changes back to the cvs repository when they've finished.

I won't get into the Web vs. flatfile vs. database vs. XML vs. whatever conflict. They all have benefits. Choose the right option for your organization, and stick to it. The important bit is that you have the data, right?

Network Maps

A roundly ignored set of baseline information is the network map. If you have more than two systems in your network and don't have a map, set down this book for 20 minutes and sketch something out. It doesn't have to be pretty, just reasonably accurate. Are you back? Good. Now that you have a map showing what is where, we can get back to work.

Most people want to deal with two kinds of maps. The first is a topological/physical map, which shows what equipment is where and how it is connected. The second is a logical map. This shows what services are provided and what user communities are supported by which servers. If you can combine these two maps, so much the better; color coding, numeric coding, and outlined boxes are all mechanisms that can help with this. A sample map is shown in Figure 7.1.

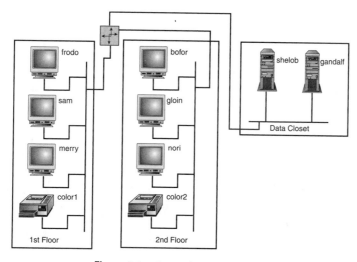

Figure 7.1   A sample network map.

Like the information discussed in the preceding "Work/Problem Logs" section, I recommend that you keep your maps online and in a couple of places. (cvs can be a good
solution here as well.) Nicely done maps also look good on your wall, not to mention
that this is a convenient place to find them when a problem breaks out and you need
to start troubleshooting.

Equipment Records

You should also have accurate records of the hardware and software in your network.
At a minimum, you should have a hardware listing of each box on the network, a list
of system and application levels (showing currently installed versions and patches), and
configurations of the same. If you keep this in cvs, you'll also have a nice mechanism
for looking at your history.[1]

If you decide to keep these records, it is vital that they be kept up-to-date. Every
time you make a change, you should edit the appropriate file and commit it to cvs.
If you fall behind, you'll miss something, and then you'll really be stuck.

How to Create a Baseline

Okay, I've talked a lot about what you should have, and I've created a daunting list of
stuff that you ought to do. How are you going to get it done? Never fear, most of this
can be done in small chunks. In addition, you'll find that much of the work can be
scripted and then run from cron.

In this section, I'll cover the following:

- Deciding what to do first
- Following naming convention
- Keeping logs and records
- Making maps
- Using cron to do your dirty work for you

What Do I Do Now?

To me, your baseline is pretty useless without a map and inventory. With this in mind,
I recommend that you do these second—yes, second. The first thing you'll want to
do is to decide how and where you're going to keep all your data, and then set it up.
(While you're at it, you might as well start your own logbook. You'll be touching a lot
of things while you make your map and inventory, so you'll get a chance to start
making entries.)

When you've got a repository for all your data set up (you did use cvs, right?), and when your maps and inventory are in it, you're ready to start on the next step. This is a good time to lay out a plan for what you want to watch and how often you want to check it. Some things should run constantly—log file watchers are a great example. Others, such as ethereal, traceroute, and netstat, will need to be run periodically.

Which of these you implement first depends a lot on your situation. Do you have any outstanding problems? If so, start building your baseline around your troubleshooting. Are you especially interested in watching certain areas? Start watching them. I think that it works well to start with something you're familiar with. You'll gain confidence in your plan and in your scripts with each success.

Another idea that bears mention is testing your baselining tools on small parts of your network. When you've got things working on a subsection, it is much simpler to extend them across your entire network.

Good Naming Conventions—Keeping It All Straight

Assuming that you're not throwing all your baseline data into a database, you're going to want a way to keep track of it. Even if you track only a couple of things, you'll soon have a huge collection of files. Without a way to track it all, it will be a mess of epic proportions. Your naming convention will go a long way toward helping here.

A large-grained approach is to separate all your files into monthly directories. From there, you can either divide like files into subdirectories or divide your files into daily subdirectories. Regardless, you'll want to name each file clearly showing what it contains, the date and time it was created, and which host it was created on (for example, ethereal-20001025-0900-mango_eth0.cap for an ethereal capture created on eth0 of mango at 9 A.M. on October 25, 2000). If you use different switches on a command, you might include that in the filename (for example, netstat-an-20001025-0900-mango, netstat-in-20001025-0900-mango, and netstat-Mn-20001025-mango).

Follow Naming Conventions Closely

Whatever naming convention you decide on, follow it religiously! You will want to be able to access the files from scripts, and a common naming scheme will make this far easier. If you ever decide that you do need to change your naming convention, having a regular system to change from will also make your life more pleasant.

Getting a Record Started

Starting your host-by-host record may seem like the hardest task of those outlined, but it can actually be pretty simple. Before I dive into hands-on advice, I'd like to weigh in on flatfiles vs. a database for system records. I think it's important to keep a local copy of this record on each host. To me, the best way to do this is to update it on the local host and to commit your changes to cvs after each change. This way, even if the box is isolated from the rest of the network, you have an accurate copy to work from.

Deciding what and how much to keep may seem like a difficult task, but (with the help of your system tools) it's pretty easy.

I recommend that you keep a list of installed software; if you use rpm to manage your system, this is not difficult. You can use the following command:

```
[root@cherry cherryconf]# rpm -qa |sort >rpm-qa
[root@cherry cherryconf]#
```

This will create a list of all installed packages in the following format:

```
ElectricFence-2.1-3
GConf-0.5-0_helix_2
GConf-devel-0.5-0_helix_2
Gtk-Perl-0.7003-0_helix_2
ImageMagick-4.2.9-3
MAKEDEV-2.5.2-1
```

Because the records are sorted, they are suitable for comparison with tools such as comm.

Using rpm can cause a bit of additional work for you because not all packages come in rpm packages. If you choose to use rpomm to simplify your record keeping and maintenance, you'll want to learn how to build your own rpms. This is not a difficult task, but it will require a bit of ramping up. The basic procedure is to move a tarball of the application you are planning to build into the /usr/src/redhat/SOURCES directory (it should be named foo-version.tgz). Then create a spec file in /usr/src/redhat/SPECS. Here's a sample spec file:

```
Summary: net-fu - a network foomigator
Name: net-fu
Version: 0.1
Release: 1
Copyright: GPL
Group: Applications/Terminal
Source: http://netfu.org/source/net-fu-0.1.tgz
Distribution: RedHat
Vendor: N/A
Packager: Pat Eyler

%description

%prep

%setup -q

%build
configure —prefix=/usr/local
make
```

```
%install
make install

%files
/usr/local/man/man1/net-fu
/usr/local/bin/net-fu

%clean
cd ..
rm -rf net-fu-0.1

%changelog
* Thu Dec 7 2000 Pat Eyler
- packaged as an example of an rpm
```

The %files Section

You'll want to pay special attention to the %files section. It controls which files are installed and managed by rpm. If the file isn't listed there, it won't be installed even if your make install would normally install it.

You'll also want to track the interface configuration and any access control configuration you have. Some of this information can be extracted automatically from the system, such as using ifconfig -a to collect interface information. Other bits of it must be read from config files such as /etc/hosts.allow or /etc/hosts.deny.

In addition to configuration information, you'll want to keep track of hardware installed on you server. This is a little bit harder to do, but it is well worth the effort. In this case, keeping a system's record on that system in addition to a central location is a good idea, but you might want to think about keeping it in a format that is easy to parse so that you can quickly find all the systems with similar hardware if you find yourself in the middle of a component recall (or similar situation).

Map Making

Map making can be a bit of an art, but anyone can make a serviceable map. Linux and GNOME even provide some great tools to help. One of my favorites is dia, a GNOME diagramming tool written by Alexander Larsson, James Henstridge, and a host of contributors. dia will give you a canvas to work on and icons representing systems on your network.

A simple map might look like the one in Figure 7.2.

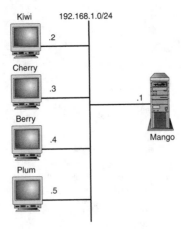

Figure 7.2 A simple network map.

A map that is this simple is going to rely on external documentation to keep track of many things, but it does show IP addresses and the mask for the network.

A more descriptive map is shown in Figure 7.3.

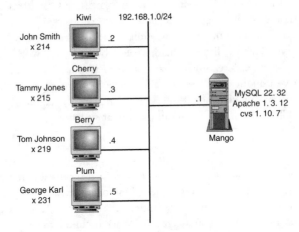

Figure 7.3 A more complete map.

This map includes contact information for workstations and information about which services are provided by a server. You could further improve the map with color coding to show additional information such as user department or project. Notes showing the physical location of each host or actual network connections to hubs or switches would also make your maps more useful.

Using cron

When you've started gathering this information, you'll want to automate it. Automating information gathering helps you in two ways: First, it enables you to collect the information at odd intervals (especially at times when you're not there). Second, it enables you to ensure that each item is gathered the same way every time.

For example, a convenient method of running ethereal every hour at 15 past the hour might be to run the following script from cron:

```
#!/bin/bash

export HOST=`hostname`
export DATE=`date +%y%m%d%I`

export FILE="${HOST}.${DATE}

tethereal -c 5000 -t r -w /var/log/ethereal/${FILE}

cd /var/log/ethereal

export CVS_RSH=ssh
cvs add ${FILE}
cvs commit -m "latest capture" ${FILE}
```

To run this script from cron, you will need to add a line like the following to the root crontab[2] (remember that only root can run ethereal/tethereal unless you allow other users to open an Ethernet interface in promiscuous mode):

```
15 * * * * /usr/local/bin/run_tethereal > /dev/null 2&>1
```

When you've put the whole thing into cron, including the cvs updates, you should write a script that ensures that all the changes were made by checking your cvs log files. There's nothing worse than having a nice data collection system and not noticing that some of the data isn't being collected. A cron-based script to do this is left as an exercise for the reader.

How to Keep Your Baseline Up-to-Date

There are two sides to keeping your records current. The first aspect is that you need to have an entry for every test each period; cron should take care of this for you. The second is that you need to add each new system into your baseline as it is added to your network. This one needs to be done by hand (well, sort of).

One way to help ensure that things get added is to make adding information as painless as possible. Again, we can turn to the system administrator's standby: scripting. If you write a script to add a new host and let that script take care of creating and adding the appropriate entries in the appropriate places, you'll find that your life seems a lot less complicated. You won't forget to do that one thing that always seems to be forgotten. You may even be able to hand the initial data entry off to the user of the equipment.

The adduser command is a good example of this. A better solution for host information might be to provide a script that the user can run when installing the system that puts the updates into a central repository. The needed additions and corrections to local configuration files can then be made by collecting data from this central repository.

If all my warnings in the last section weren't enough to convince you to use cvs and a naming standard, this is my last swing at it. Having these in place will make automatic maintenance and creation of the per-host files a lot simpler. Simpler means fewer mistakes and a greater chance that things will get done. It's a good idea. Do it.

Where Monitoring Fits into All of This

Okay, so where does monitoring fit into all of this? A lot of what I've talked about is monitoring, after all. Is this all you need to do? Not really.

Although the monitoring described previously helps you watch the general direction of your network and the ways it compares to the norm at any given time, it really represents only an occasional snapshot of the way things are. True monitoring is a near real-time view of reality. The two types of monitoring are complementary.

Monitoring should include frequent checks of systems and applications that you want to keep available to your users. You also want to ensure that you find out about failures through some alarm mechanism (pagers, email, or the like). Your monitoring plan will likely overlap your baseline by a bit. If this is the case, you should look into ways to combine the two functions.

The mon tool, which is discussed in Chapter 10, is a wonderful utility for watching your network. It enables you to send alarms to various users based on the results of your tests. Although mon is designed as a monitoring tool, extending it to write data into a record for your review is pretty trivial.

You might find that your baseline indicates that you need to adjust your alerting thresholds at times. This is really just another benefit of keeping a baseline. It helps keep your view of reality current. You might find that the reverse is true—something in your monitoring might suggest that you should add a test to your baseline. Again, this is just another benefit of really watching your network.

Endnotes

1. cvs is just good stuff. If you don't have it, you should go get it. And, no, I'm not a maintainer or a reseller, or otherwise involved with it.

2. To add a line to the crontab, use the crontab -e command.

8

In the Moment—Case Studies

For the purposes of our case studies, we'll create a small business to provide our examples. This should protect all the guilty parties who have had these problems.

The Network

Our office has two LANs (the server room LAN and the staff LAN), an Internet connection, and a remote server. mango is a combination file/print server and router for the staff and server room LANs. A map of the network is given in Figure 8.1.

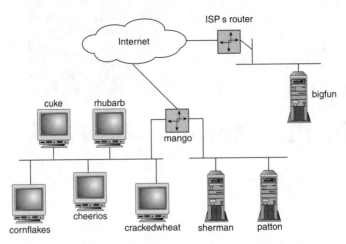

Figure 8.1   Network diagram of our example network.

The People

Eliza is the new network administrator, and Mike (a programmer) occasionally helps out. Tammy, Paul, and Tom are the users we'll deal with. These five people make up a small sample of the whole company. Eliza and Mike are on Linux platforms: rhubarb and cuke, respectively. Tammy, Paul, and Tom use Windows 98 platforms (named cornflakes, cheerios, and crackedwheat) for their day–to–day work.

The Case Studies

In this section, we'll present several problems, explicitly following the nine-step problem-solving pattern given in Chapter 6, "A Problem-Solving Pattern." Each problem will be introduced as it might occur in the real world, and then the path followed to the solution will be shown.

"The Network Is Always Slow in the Morning"

Eliza is pretty happy with herself as she settles into her new office Monday morning. She has just taken a job as the network administrator at a Web-based startup. About half of the staff has already been hired, and the network is already in place. That scares her a bit, but she took a look at it during her interview, and it didn't look too bad. She has already mapped out several fix-up projects. First on her docket, though, is to get a solid baseline.

"Why is this network always so slow in the mornings?" Tom's voice enters her office moments before he does. "Eliza, now that you're here, I hope you can get this mess cleared up for us. Every morning, it seems like our Internet connectivity just crawls until about 9:30. Then things pick up, and it is back to normal." He sits down across from her.

"I'll get right on it Tom," Eliza replies. Right now she could really use that baseline, but this gives her a good excuse to start working on it. It is already 9:15, so she doesn't have much time to see things this morning, but she can take a first look. Throughout the rest of the day she'll be able to watch the network under normal circumstances.

Step 1: Clearly Describe the Symptoms

Tom has provided Eliza with a pretty good description: Internet connectivity is slow every morning until about 9:30. Further probing on Eliza's part reveals that the slowness affects all services from all internal hosts.

Step 2: Understand the Environment

This is where Eliza runs into her first real problem. Because this is her first day on the job, she doesn't know the environment well enough to make any real judgments about the way things are supposed to be. She does have the tools to start looking at it, though, so she knows that she can start with those. She also has a map of the network that she can look at to determine which hosts might be involved.

While watching the network traffic, Eliza makes a discovery immediately. Most of the traffic is being passed between bigfun and patton. At 9:30, the traffic between these hosts dropped to almost nothing. Without a baseline to work from, this is probably the best information Eliza is going to get.

Step 3: List Your Hypotheses

From her initial investigation, Eliza thinks that the problem is probably one of four things:

- One or more applications running on bigfun and/or patton
- A hardware problem on one of the boxes
- A misconfiguration of either mango or the ISP's router
- A misconfiguration of the packet filter on mango

Step 4: Prioritize Your Hypotheses and Narrow Your Focus

Because the problem occurred only during a specific time window, Eliza feels pretty certain that it is an application problem. If it were a router issue, the problem would most likely be exhibited throughout the day. A hardware problem also would be unlikely to occur only within a specific time window.

Step 5: Create a Plan of Attack

If the problem was being caused by one or more applications, Eliza might have to dig a little bit to find the root cause. She can look at a couple things to start. Because the problem seems to have been occurring even before people arrived, it is likely to be a scheduled job. With this in mind, crontabs would be a good place to start. If that weren't fruitful, she could follow up with Tom.

Step 6: Act on Your Plan

Eliza logs in on patton to see what is going on there. Looking at the root crontab, she sees only one job, web-lint, set to go off in the morning. Logging in to bigfun, she checks the crontab there as well. There are two morning processes, full-dump and search-prep.

Looking at the cronjob on patton, Eliza identifies it as a link-checker. The cronjobs on bigfun prove to be an rsync-based backup of bigfun to patton (full-dump) and a Web site indexing job (search-prep). The link checker would be hard to optimize (you really do need to check every link), but perhaps it could be rescheduled. The backup might be something that could be optimized, but it could also be rescheduled. The indexing job didn't create any traffic, so she can ignore that one for now. She certainly will need to flag it for study later. A serious hit against the CPU or memory could really cause problems for anything else running on bigfun (such as the Web server).

Step 7: Test the Results of Your Actions

Eliza asks around to find out if there are any known conflicts with rescheduling the two jobs. Tom just wants to make sure that both jobs run after 9 p.m. so that any new content pushes can be finished before they start. He also wants the link checker to run before 10 a.m. so that the designers can fix anything on the Web site before the noon rush.

Because she has a big window to work with, Eliza decides to move the backup to 9:30 p.m. and the link checker to 1 a.m. She also wraps both cronjobs with a call to syslog to timestamp them. This allows her to check /var/log/messages to verify that things aren't taking too long. Finally, she sets up a cronjob on patton to watch the traffic with netstat, and a second one on mango to start up Ethereal for her.

The next morning, Eliza discovers that the slowness problem has evaporated: The two cronjobs that she'd rescheduled have run in reasonable time. She also has built herself a reputation as a miracle worker.

Step 8: Apply the Results

Because she already has changed the crontab, Eliza's fix is in place. She decides to canvas the other folks in the office over the next couple of weeks, just to ensure that things continue to look good. In addition, she notes all the changes in her notebook.

Step 9: Iterate as Needed

Because she found the solution to her problem, Eliza doesn't need to iterate over the problem-solving pattern.

Related Problems

Traffic problems can be hard to solve—they require digging into the traffic to see what is really going on. In this case, we had a couple high-bandwidth applications running at the same time. Other possibilities could have included these:

- A server being bogged down with people logging into it

- A poorly tuned application, creating far more traffic than it ought to

- A hardware problem causing many rebroadcasts

- A configuration problem on a router or bridge

"Our Web Site Loads Too Slowly"

Monday afternoon, Mike and Eliza go out to grab some lunch. While they are walking back to a table, Mike tells Eliza about the problem he is experiencing with the Web site: "I'm not sure what the problem is, but our users are complaining that the site takes forever to load. But I've checked it a few times, and it always seems alright to me."

Step 1: Clearly Describe the Symptoms

"Well, that's not a lot to go on, Mike. Why don't we sit down and sketch things out in a bit more detail." Eliza has her notebook and also has a couple ideas about where to look for problems. She wants to get a clear description of the symptoms before she starts chasing the wrong problem. As they sit down at the table, Eliza asks, "Do the users talk about any specific times? What about sections of the Web site or particular pages?"

"No, they don't say much at all," Mike answers. "I check it every day, though, just before lunch, and things always seem quick to me." They decide to follow up with some of the users to see if there is a pattern to the problem.

Step 2: Understand the Environment

Eliza also realizes that Mike is testing only from his machine at work, which means that there is only one hop between him and bigfun. She recommends that he test the Web page from somewhere else on the net. "Maybe you have a friend on the another coast who could look at things for us," she suggests. "Then, after we have that information, we'll know enough about the problem to try to solve it."

The next morning, Mike has some answers for Eliza. It seems that there are always some problems with response time, but they are worst in the afternoon. Mike's friend also reports that things were pretty bad—slow connects, dropped connects, and pages that seem stalled because of large, included images.

Step 3: List Your Hypotheses

Eliza digests the information that she and Mike gathered. Soon she is able to come up with a list of the possible problems:

- Too little bandwidth
- Underpowered servers
- Too few server resources (especially memory)

Step 4: Prioritize Your Hypotheses and Narrow Your Focus

After talking through their list for a bit, Eliza summarizes her thoughts for Mike: "I'd guess that we do have a bandwidth issue because things always seem to be slow, but there may be some other issues dogging us as well."

Mike cuts in, "But how can it be a bandwidth problem? I tested it from here, and it's not on our LAN."

"Well, that's more than a lot of Web guys do," admits Eliza. "But you've got to remember that we're only one hop away from bigfun—and it's a dedicated pipe. Everyone else has to share the upstream links, which can become congested rather easily. Maybe we're getting restricted service from the ISP. I'll check on it."

Step 5: Create a Plan of Attack

Eliza lays out a plan of action for the two of them: "While I'm talking to the ISP, you should probably look at the content we're serving up. Is there any way to cut down the size and number of files and still present a good face to our users?"

Step 6: Act on Your Plan

The two of them work on their separate tasks that day and meet back Wednesday morning to review their progress. "Well, I found a lot of big images," says Mike, "and I've convinced the design guys to cut back a bit. I think we've shaved about 50% off the size of our most heavily used pages."

Eliza explains that she hasn't found any restrictions placed on their bandwidth. The ISP did confirm that it sends a lot of bits during the afternoon, though. Eliza also was able to look over the Web server logs and found that their traffic has a sustained peak from about 12:30 until 15:30, matching the time frame of the worst slowdowns.

Step 7: Test the Results of Your Actions

"Well, I think we've got some leads to go on," says Eliza. "Let's see how the changes we made affect things today. If we've still got problems, we may have to start tweaking the hardware."

That afternoon they have Mike's friend check the Web site. They also send email to the users whom they have been working with. When all the results were in, they find that they've made some significant improvements.

Step 8: Apply the Results

Although things look good for the moment, Eliza and Mike know that they need to get some solid standards in place for Web developers going forward. In fact, they might even want to make a case for getting their server located at a facility with better upstream bandwidth.

Step 9: Iterate as Needed

Now that they have a pretty good handle on the problem, they don't really need to iterate through the pattern. Eliza would like to look at several areas to see if she can improve performance a bit more. The pattern provides a nice framework for this kind of project. She can put her thoughts into her logbook and work on things as time permits.

Related Information

Web servers are tricky things to tune well. In large measure this is because there are so many options. Other tuning areas to keep in mind are these:

- Dynamic content takes more resources to serve up. If you're going to build pages dynamically, make sure that you're optimizing things.

- If you're serving a lot of content from an underpowered server, you'll run into problems. Make sure that you have a fast enough CPU and enough RAM to carry the load.

- You might find that you just can't provide fast service to everyone from a single site. Consider using multiple servers at different locations, or look into a content distribution service such as Akamai.

"I Can't Connect to Any Remote Hosts"

"Hey, Eliza, I'm having some trouble here. I've got to push the new puzzle up to staging from my new workstation, but I can't get scp going." Eliza frowns as she reads Mike's email. She knows that when a user cannot connect to any remote hosts, the most common cause is a bad gateway. Either the local definition of the gateway may be bad, or the gateway may not be functioning properly. A quick ssh to bigfun proves that the gateway is working properly, so she logs in to cuke to try to get a better picture of what is going on.

Step 1: Clearly Describe the Symptoms

It doesn't take Eliza too long to get a clear picture of the problem. She finds that only cuke was affected by the problem. In fact, it is incapable of making connections to any hosts off its local network.

Step 2: Understand the Environment

Eliza has been on the job long enough to know the lay of the network by this point. In any case, not getting a connection off your local network gives a pretty good description of the environment.

Step 3: List Your Hypotheses

After looking at the situation, Eliza comes up with the following possibilities:

- cuke could have a bad network mask.
- mango could have a mask that excluded the new cuke's IP address.
- cuke could have a bad default gateway.
- cuke could have a hardware problem.

Step 4: Prioritize Your Hypotheses and Narrow Your Focus

Because cuke is a newly installed replacement for Mike's old machine, Eliza decides that the most likely causes of the problem are those on cuke. cuke is capable of talking to local machines (Mike had sent her an email), so she decides that hardware problems are pretty unlikely. She decides to start with the possibility that cuke has a bad gateway.

Step 5: Create a Plan of Attack

To test her hypothesis, Eliza needs to determine which host is configured as cuke's default gateway.

Step 6: Act on Your Plan

Checking the default gateway is a simple matter. Eliza executes the netstat command, as follows:

```
# netstat -rn
Kernel IP routing table
Destination     Gateway        Genmask          Flags   MSS Window   irtt Iface
127.0.0.0       0.0.0.0        255.0.0.0        U       3584 0          0 lo
192.168.2.0     192.168.2.10   255.255.255.0
0.0.0.0         192.168.1.1    255.255.255.0
```

Step 7: Test the Results of Your Actions

Her check of cuke's routing table indicates that cuke is, in fact, using the wrong gateway. To test this information, Eliza clears the incorrect default gateway and sets a new one with the following commands:

```
# route del -net default gw 192.168.1.1
# route add -net default gw 192.168.2.1
```

After that, she finds that she can ssh to bigfun and make other IP-based connections off the local network.

Step 8: Apply the Results

Now that she knows what the problem is and has fixed it, Eliza needs to set up cuke's configuration so that the next time it gets rebooted, it will retain the new configuration.

Step 9: Iterate as Needed

Eliza was able to solve the problem in her first step through the process, and she doesn't need to iterate back over it.

"I Can Connect to Only Some Remote Hosts"

Later that day, Mike sends Eliza another email: "Hey, thanks for fixing my box. Tammy just came by with the same problem, and I tried to do what you did, but it didn't work. Can you help her?"

Step 1: Clearly Describe the Symptoms

A problem description of "I'm seeing the same thing that Joe did yesterday" is normally not as good as it seems. End users often don't see the differences that can really affect the troubleshooting process. With this in mind, Eliza decides to talk to Tammy to see what's really going on. Tammy and Mike are both in Tammy's cube when she gets there, so Eliza can ask Mike about the troubleshooting that he has done so far.

This time, it turns out that Mike is right—it really is the same problem description. Tammy cannot make any connections from her host to any host off the local network.

Step 2: Understand the Environment

Because this occurred so recently after Mike's problem, Eliza has very little to do to understand the environment. In fact, the only major difference is that cornflakes (Tammy's host) is a Windows machine instead of a Linux machine, like cuke—not something that's likely to affect the diagnostics.

Step 3: List Your Hypotheses

Eliza can start with the same list of hypotheses she used in our last case study. She asks Mike, and he says that he already has chased down the default gateway and hardware problem options. Eliza is left with these options:

- cornflakes could have a bad network mask.
- mango could have a mask that excludes cornflakes' IP address.

Step 4: Prioritize Your Hypotheses and Narrow Your Focus

Just as with Mike's problem, it seems most likely that the problem is on the local host.

Step 5: Create a Plan of Attack

Eliza decides to start with cornflakes' subnet mask, an easy thing to check on a Windows machine.

Step 6: Act on Your Plan

Eliza opens the network Properties dialog box. Looking at the network mask, she sees that it is set to 255.255.0.0. "Here's the problem: You've got a Class B netmask, but you're in a Class C network. cornflakes doesn't think it needs to use a gateway to get to sherman, so it is trying to send the traffic locally," she says to Mike and Tammy.

Step 7: Test the Results of Your Actions

Eliza then sets the correct network mask, enabling her to ping sherman.

Step 8: Apply the Results

Because she had to reset the configuration for her test changes to take affect, Eliza already has applied the results in a lasting way. Given the two problems on two recently installed hosts, she decides to spend some time working with the PC technician straightening out the install procedure.

Step 9: Iterate as Needed

Again, Eliza doesn't need to iterate back through the process to find a solution. The iteration did occur, though; Mike has already stepped through the steps in trying to solve the problem by fixing the default gateway setting. Eliza actually entered this troubleshooting cycle on the second trip through the process.

Related Problems

Network mask-related problems can come into play in a number of ways:

- cornflakes' network mask could have excluded its default gateway.

- mango (cuke's gateway) could have had a network mask that excluded cuke.

- mango could have had IP forwarding turned off.

- mango could be down on one or both interfaces.

"My Connection Is Too Slow"

Eliza has been on the job for a couple of weeks, and things are starting to feel comfortable. She has sorted out most of the big problems, has done her initial baselining, and even has managed to get a project out of the way. She knows that something is bound to come up. As she is reviewing her "To Do" list, Paul walks in, sits down, and says, "I can't believe how slow our connection is!"

Step 1: Clearly Describe the Symptoms

Eliza knows that the connection to the net is pretty fast and that most of the nits have been worked out of their internal network. Paul's comment is so vague that she doesn't even know how to start defining the symptoms of his problem. She asks, "What do you mean, Paul?"

"Well, I installed the ssh client on my PC at home, like you asked me to," he answers. "Now every time I connect to our boxes, it just takes forever." In answer to further questions, it comes out that his connection seems to freeze for about a minute upon login and then proceeds at normal speed.

Step 2: Understand the Environment

When other people's computers are brought into the picture, your troubleshooting task becomes much more difficult. In this case, Eliza is able to find out that Paul has a static IP address and that he is running Windows with the recommended ssh client.

Eliza doesn't think that it sounds like a network problem, so she thinks that she'd better look into a session to see if she can dig up any more information. If that doesn't pan out, she can start looking at the configuration of Paul's home PC.

That evening, Eliza logs in from home and sets up an Ethereal session to watch Paul log in to the server. She sees that the session is set up immediately, and then there is a pause while the server sends out DNS requests. After the DNS requests times out, the session picks up again, and Paul seems to get logged in correctly. Eliza does an nslookup of Paul's IP and finds that it didn't resolve back to a host name, indicating a problem with the ISP's DNS configuration.

Step 3: List Your Hypotheses

In this case, Eliza's quest for more information seems to turn up the probable cause of the problem: Paul's static IP address is not resolvable, which causes a delay in logging him in to the server.

Step 4: Prioritize Your Hypotheses and Narrow Your Focus

With just one hypothesis to go on, Eliza is about as narrowly focused as she can get.

Step 5: Create a Plan of Attack

Eliza decides that the only way she can solve this is to create an entry for Paul's host in her /etc/hosts file. When this is completed, she can have Paul try again.

Step 6: Act on Your Plan

Popping open her favorite editor, Eliza makes the new entry in /etc/hosts.

Step 7: Test the Results of Your Actions

Now that the IP address can be mapped back to a host name, Eliza calls Paul and asks him to try to ssh in again. This time, his session starts without any delay.

Step 8: Apply the Results

Unless Eliza can convince Paul's ISP to fix its broken DNS, she has done about as much as she can to fix the problem going forward.

Step 9: Iterate as Needed

Because the problem was solved, there is no need for Eliza to iterate through the process.

Related Problems

Incorrect or missing DNS information can cause a number of problems:

- Application permissions can be broken.

- Licensing schemes for commercial software can become confused.

- Poorly configured access control can be thwarted or inadvertently triggered.

Tools for Your Toolkit

9

Troubleshooting Tools

THE PING, TRACEROUTE, ARP, AND NGREP TOOLS will help you as you're troubleshooting problems in your network or over the Internet. The first three are part of a stock Linux system, but the fourth will need to be downloaded and installed on your system before you can use it.

ping

ping is a diagnostic tool for verifying connectivity between two hosts on a network. It sends ICMP Echo Request packets to a remote IP address and watches for ICMP responses. The author of the initial version of the ping program used today was Mike Muss. Many other people have tweaked, rewritten, and variously abused ping since then.

The name *ping* itself is somewhat colorful. Some people claim that it is an acronym standing for the Packet INternet Groper, but this is not the case. ping was named after the sound of a sonar tracking system. There is even a story claiming that a system administrator wrote a script that repeatedly pinged a host on the network and made an audible "pinging" alert for each success. The system administrator was then able to methodically go through his network checking BNC connectors until he found the dodgy connector that had been plaguing his network. When the noises stopped, he'd found his culprit.

ping used to be a very good indicator of a machine's capability to receive and send IP packets in general. If you could ping a host, you could also make an FTP or HTTP connection. With the wider advent of packet filtering for security, this is becoming less true. Many firewalls explicitly disallow ICMP packets[1] on two grounds:

1. People don't need to know what your internal network looks like.

2. Any protocol, even ICMP, can be used to launch an attack.

Deciding whether to let ICMP through your firewall is a tough call to make. There are certainly good uses for ICMP, but there are also attacks based on ICMP (such as the "ping of death," which uses oversized ping packets to overload the IP stack of the target, often with spectacular results). If you choose to allow ICMP into your network, make sure you've thought about the repercussions.

Additional flavors of the `ping` command have been written for other purposes; among the most common is the `fping` command. The `fping` command was written to ping a range of addresses, and it is commonly used in network scanners and monitors such as satan, saint, and mon (which are covered in Chapter 10, "Monitoring Tools"). Another variant is the Net::ping module, which provides a perl implementation of ping functionality that can easily be used from within a script without calling an external program. You might use it in a script like that shown in Example 9.1.

Example 9.1 **Using Net::ping**

```
#!/usr/bin/perl -w

use strict;
use Net::ping;

my $host = $ARGV[0];

my $p = Net::ping->new("icmp");

if ($p->ping($host)) {
    print "$host is alive.\n";
} else {
    print "$host is not reachable.\n";
}
```

hping is another variant of the standard ping. It is actually a superset of ping, enabling you to ping hosts using non-ICMP protocols, elicit ICMP responses from UDP probes, and even craft your own packets to test for specific behavior.

ping at Work

ping is most often used without additional arguments and shut off with a Ctrl+C. The results are shown in Example 9.2.

Example 9.2 **The Results of a ping**

```
[pate@cherry pate]$ ping mango
PING mango (192.168.1.1) from 192.168.1.10 : 56(84) bytes of data.
64 bytes from mango (192.168.1.1): icmp_seq=0 ttl=255 time=0.5 ms
64 bytes from mango (192.168.1.1): icmp_seq=1 ttl=255 time=0.3 ms
64 bytes from mango (192.168.1.1): icmp_seq=2 ttl=255 time=0.3 ms
64 bytes from mango (192.168.1.1): icmp_seq=3 ttl=255 time=0.3 ms
64 bytes from mango (192.168.1.1): icmp_seq=4 ttl=255 time=0.3 ms
64 bytes from mango (192.168.1.1): icmp_seq=5 ttl=255 time=0.3 ms

— · mango ping statistics — ·
6 packets transmitted, 6 packets received, 0% packet loss
round-trip min/avg/max = 0.3/0.3/0.5 ms
[pate@cherry pate]$
```

This output can broken into three sections. The first section, the single line starting with PING, shows an overview of the command. The second section, the lines beginning with 64 bytes, shows a running tally of the responses received. The third section, everything after the line — · mango ping statistics — ·, shows a summary of the results. In this case, the results are good; none of the packets were dropped, and they were all passed fairly quickly.

This example also shows another important point: You should not rely on a single echo request to diagnose your network. A series of 5 or 10 is much better. You can attribute as much as 40% packet loss to congestion on a network; even a single packet dropped can be attributed to a busy host on the other end.

Several useful options exist for the ping command. These are summarized in Table 9.1.

Table 9.1 **ping Options**

Switch	Description
-c count	Stops sending and receiving packets after count packets
-d	Sets the SO_DEBUG on the socket used
-f	Sends the packets as fast as possible (flood)
-i wait	Sets an interval of wait seconds between packets
-I device	Sets the output interface
-l preload	Sends preload packets as fast as possible, and then drops back to normal mode
-n	Doesn't look up hostnames; just gives IP addresses (numeric)
-p pattern	Specifies up to 16 bytes of "pad data" to be sent with the packet
-q	Outputs only summary lines (quiet)

continues

Table 9.1 **Continued**

Switch	Description
-r	Doesn't use routing tables to send the packet; just drops it out the local interface
-R	Sets the Record Route option
-s packetsize	Sets the number of data bytes sent to packetsize
-T tsonly	Sends a ping with the timestamp option
-T tsandaddr	Collects timestamps and addresses
-T tsprespec [host1 [host2 [host3 [host4]]]]	Collects timestamps and addresses from prespecified hops

These options can be combined to make ping even more helpful. For example, the ping mango command used in the previous section is likely to take several seconds to run and report back. Using the -f switch will reduce the time spent waiting for the command. Combining this with the -c 10 and the -q switches will give you quick results and easier output to read, as shown in Example 9.3.

Example 9.3 **A More Readable ping**

```
        [root@cherry /root]# ping -c 10 -fq mango
PING mango (192.168.1.1) from 192.168.1.10 : 56(84) bytes of data.

— · mango ping statistics — ·
10 packets transmitted, 10 packets received, 0% packet loss
round-trip min/avg/max = 0.2/0.2/0.9 ms
[root@cherry /root]#
```

Dangerous Switches

The -f and -l switches can be used only by root because they can cause serious network degradation if they are misused.

It might be of some benefit to test larger packets; using ping -c10 -s 1024 -qf will send larger packets for you. This can be especially useful when you suspect problems with fragmented packets.

To see the route that your packets are traversing, you can use ping -c10 -R. This command produces the output shown in Example 9.4.

Example 9.4 **ping with Record Route**

```
      PING tbr.nailed.org (206.66.240.72) from 192.168.1.10 : 56(124) bytes of
➥data.
64 bytes from bigfun.whirlycott.com (206.66.240.72): icmp_seq=0 ttl=239 time=217.2
➥ms
RR:    192.168.1.10
       216.41.39.90
       serial0.mmgw32.bos1.Level3.net (209.244.39.25)
       208.218.130.22
```

```
166.90.184.2
so-6-0-0.mp2.NewYork1.level3.net (209.247.10.45)
137.39.52.10
180.ATM7-0.BR2.NYC9.ALTER.NET (152.63.22.229)
lo0.XR2.NYC9.ALTER.NET (137.39.4.175)


64 bytes from bigfun.whirlycott.com (206.66.240.72): icmp_seq=1 ttl=239
➥time=1940.8 ms  (same route)
64 bytes from bigfun.whirlycott.com (206.66.240.72): icmp_seq=2 ttl=239
➥time=250.6 ms   (same route)
64 bytes from bigfun.whirlycott.com (206.66.240.72): icmp_seq=3 ttl=239
➥time=230.3 ms   (same route)
64 bytes from bigfun.whirlycott.com (206.66.240.72): icmp_seq=4 ttl=239
➥time=289.8 ms   (same route)
64 bytes from bigfun.whirlycott.com (206.66.240.72): icmp_seq=5 ttl=239
➥time=1261.4 ms  (same route)
64 bytes from bigfun.whirlycott.com (206.66.240.72): icmp_seq=6 ttl=239
➥time=469.4 ms   (same route)
64 bytes from bigfun.whirlycott.com (206.66.240.72): icmp_seq=7 ttl=239
➥time=1272.3 ms  (same route)
64 bytes from bigfun.whirlycott.com (206.66.240.72): icmp_seq=8 ttl=239
➥time=353.1 ms   (same route)
64 bytes from bigfun.whirlycott.com (206.66.240.72): icmp_seq=9 ttl=239
➥time=1281.1 ms  (same route)

—· tbr.nailed.org ping statistics —·
10 packets transmitted, 10 packets received, 0% packet loss
round-trip min/avg/max = 217.2/756.6/1940.8 ms
```

Record Route Option

The Record Route option specified by the -R switch is not honored by all routers and hosts. Furthermore, because it contains only a limited space to hold router addresses, traceroute may be a better tool for identifying the path packets follow through a network.

traceroute

The traceroute tool provides a UDP-based system for tracing the flow of traffic through a network. traceroute uses the TTL field of the IP header to force each hop along the path to return an ICMP Time Exceeded message. The destination host is recognized because it returns an ICMP Destination Unreachable message.

The first set of packets is sent with a TTL of 1, which times out at the first router. The second set of packet has a TTL of 2 and times out at the second router. This pattern is followed until the destination host is reached.

traceroute at Work

As each packet is sent, the results are displayed. The results of a traceroute session are shown in Example 9.5.

Example 9.5   **traceroute Results**

```
[pate@router pate]$ traceroute
                bigfun.whirlycott.com

Password:
traceroute to bigfun.whirlycott.com (206.66.240.72), 30 hops max, 38 byte packets
 1  mmgw32.bos1.Level3.net (63.212.201.240)  113.711 ms  118.560 ms  109.549 ms
 2  mmcu32.bos1.Level3.net (209.244.39.26)  109.146 ms  109.135 ms  109.534 ms
 3  gis-gate.gis.net (209.113.128.1)  109.215 ms  109.112 ms  109.429 ms
 4  serial2-0-1.hsa1.bos1.Level3.net (166.90.184.1)  109.280 ms  109.070 ms
➥109.377 ms
 5  lo0.mp2.NewYork1.level3.net (209.247.8.252)  119.213 ms  118.905 ms  109.563
➥ms
 6  209.247.10.46 (209.247.10.46)  119.125 ms  118.996 ms  119.365 ms
 7  ATM1-0.BR2.NYC9.ALTER.NET (137.39.52.9)  119.551 ms  119.005 ms  119.413 ms
 8  518.at-5-0-0.XR2.NYC9.ALTER.NET (152.63.22.230)  119.254 ms  108.976 ms
➥119.354 ms
 9  180.ATM6-0.XR2.BOS1.ALTER.NET (152.63.16.217)  119.323 ms  119.070 ms  119.328
➥ms
10  190.ATM9-0-0.GW1.BOS1.ALTER.NET (146.188.176.237)  129.204 ms  118.981 ms
➥119.454 ms
11  mdc-gw.customer.ALTER.NET (157.130.1.178)  149.267 ms  129.104 ms  129.498 ms
12  bigfun.whirlycott.com (206.66.240.72)  139.251 ms  129.062 ms  139.349 ms

[pate@router pate]$
```

The first line of output gives a summary of the data to be sent. The following lines show which hop of the path, the hostname and/or IP address of the router for that hop, and the round-trip time for that packet. In this example everything looks pretty good—there are no big jumps in the round-trip time, no packets were dropped, and even the final round-trip time looks pretty small.

The results in Example 9.6 aren't quite so healthy, although they still aren't too bad. There are several spikes in the round-trip time and even a dropped packet at the destination host (the * marker).

Example 9.6   **A Less Healthy Route**

```
[root@cherry /root]# traceroute www.vii.com
traceroute to lonepeak.vii.com (206.71.77.2), 30 hops max, 38 byte packets
 1  mango (192.168.1.1)  0.504 ms  0.312 ms  0.290 ms
 2  mmgw32.bos1.Level3.net (63.212.201.240)  120.978 ms  108.857 ms  109.181 ms
 3  mmcu32.bos1.Level3.net (209.244.39.26)  105.202 ms  112.733 ms  115.206 ms
 4  gis-gate.gis.net (209.113.128.1)  105.302 ms  108.981 ms  1029.911 ms
 5  serial2-0-1.hsa1.bos1.Level3.net (166.90.184.1)  114.344 ms  108.968 ms
➥118.993 ms
```

```
    6  lo0.mp1.Chicago1.level3.net (209.247.8.243)  141.197 ms  139.011 ms  139.223
➥ms
    7  209.247.10.166 (209.247.10.166)  141.246 ms  149.155 ms  139.272 ms
    8  aads01.chcg.eli.net (206.220.243.97)  214.926 ms  217.502 ms  199.391 ms
    9  srp2-0.cr01.chcg.eli.net (208.186.20.81)  214.816 ms  208.874 ms  159.308 ms10
➥p10-0.cr02.slkc.eli.net (207.173.115.53)  214.941 ms  1079.453 ms  214.005 ms
   11  gw-VII3-DOM.slkc.eli.net (209.210.44.154)  214.463 ms  208.883 ms  281.402 ms
   12  gw-VII3-DOM.slkc.eli.net (209.210.44.154)  158.323 ms  208.855 ms  229.192 ms
   13  lonepeak.vii.com (206.71.77.2)  1092.011 ms  218.827 ms  *
[root@cherry /root]#
```

Just as many packet filters are configured to block ping, many are configured to stop traceroute from working as well. Although this limits the usefulness of traceroute for end-to-end troubleshooting, traceroute can still provide useful information about the path followed between the endpoints of the connections.

arp

If you have a host that isn't communicating with the other hosts on its network (for example, you can't ping it, nor can the host ping other boxes), looking in the arp cache is a quick check to see if the host is talking to the network or if there is already another host on the network with the same IP address.

An Overview of arp

The arp command takes a variety of options. The most important of these are summarized in Table 9.2.

Table 9.2 **arp Options**

Short Style Option	Long Style Option	Purpose
-a	(No long option)	Displays all hosts in the BSD style
-s	—set	Sets a new arp entry
-d	—delete	Deletes an arp entry
-n	—numeric	Displays contents without resolving names
-v	—version	Is verbose

Many of these options can be combined to provide better results. The -n option is of particular note here. If an IP address is not resolvable to a hostname, arp will hang for a long time waiting to resolve it. I almost always turn resolving off for networking commands.

arp at Work

In introducing arp as a troubleshooting tool, I mentioned using it to check for more than one host with the same IP address. Next is an example of using arp and ifconfig to find such a problem.

If I had problems communicating between crashtestdummy (at 192.168.1.20) and cherry (at 192.168.1.10), but could communicate between mango (192.168.1.1) and both of the others, I might start by checking the arp cache results on cherry and mango, and looking at the output from ifconfig on crashtestdummy. cherry's arp cache is shown in Example 9.7.

Example 9.7   **cherry's arp Cache**

```
[root@cherry /root]# arp -n
Address              HWtype  HWaddress          Flags Mask     Iface
mango                ether   00:A0:D2:1C:64:E8  C              eth0
192.168.1.20         ether   00:A0:D2:1C:64:F0  CM             eth0
[root@cherry /root]#
```

The arp cache for mango is shown in Example 9.8.

Example 9.8   **mango's arp Cache**

```
[root@mango /root]# arp -n
Address              HWtype  HWaddress          Flags Mask     Iface
cherry               ether   00:E0:98:7C:95:21  C              eth0
192.168.1.20         ether   00:A0:D2:1C:64:DB  C              eth0
[root@mango /root]#
```

The results of an ifconfig on crachtestdummy are shown in Example 9.9.

Example 9.9   **ifconfig on crashtestdummy**

```
[root@ctd /root]# ifconfig -a
eth0      Link encap:Ethernet  HWaddr 00:A0:D2:1C:64:DB
          inet addr:192.168.1.20  Bcast:192.168.1.255  Mask:255.255.255.0
          UP BROADCAST RUNNING MULTICAST  MTU:1500  Metric:1
          RX packets:1293 errors:0 dropped:0 overruns:0 frame:0
          TX packets:488 errors:0 dropped:0 overruns:0 carrier:0
          collisions:0 txqueuelen:100
          Interrupt:10 Base address:0xfc00
[root@ctd /root]#
```

If you look at the MAC address of crashtestdummy, you find that it's `00:A0:D2:1C:64:DB`, the same value as in mango's arp cache. A different value is lurking in cherry's arp cache, though, indicating our problem.

In this case, though, there is a bit more information to grab that will help us solve our problem: the `M` flag in 192.168.1.20's arp cache entry on cherry. This flag indicates a permanent entry, probably entered by hand. If you delete it, things should go back to normal, as shown in Example 9.10.

Example 9.10 **A Healthy Response**

```
[root@cherry /root]# arp -d 192.168.1.20
[root@cherry /root]# ping 192.168.1.20
PING 192.168.1.20 (192.168.1.20) from 192.168.1.10 : 56(84) bytes of data.
64 bytes from 192.168.1.20: icmp_seq=0 ttl=255 time=0.8 ms
64 bytes from 192.168.1.20: icmp_seq=1 ttl=255 time=0.3 ms

—· 192.168.1.20 ping statistics —·
2 packets transmitted, 2 packets received, 0% packet loss
round-trip min/avg/max = 0.3/0.5/0.8 ms
[root@cherry /root]# arp -n
Address           HWtype  HWaddress          Flags Mask        Iface
cherry            ether   00:E0:98:7C:95:21  C                 eth0
192.168.1.20      ether   00:A0:D2:1C:64:DB  C                 eth0
[root@cherry /root]#
```

ngrep

The ngrep is used for watching network traffic. It is based with the libpcap library, which provides packet-capturing functionality. ngrep allows regular expression style filters to be used to select traffic to be displayed.

ngrep is the first utility discussed that doesn't ship on most Linux systems. We'll talk about how to get and install it, how to start it up and use it, and more advanced use.

Getting and Installing ngrep

Source code for ngrep is available from http://ngrep.datasurge.net/, as are some binary packages. I'll only review installing the source code because the binary packages are fairly straightforward.

On a Red Hat 6.2 system, you'll need to install libpcap before you can install ngrep. This package is available from http://www.tcpdump.org/release. As of this writing, the most recent version is libpcap-0.5.2.tar.gz. After download, I put things like this into /usr/local/src; you should do something like Example 9.11.

Example 9.11 **Building libpcap**

```
$ tar xvzf libpcap-0.5.2.tar.gz
$ cd libpcap_0_5rel2
$ ./configure
$ make
$ su
Password: ********
# make install-incl
# make install-man
# exit
```

Your next step is to build ngrep itself. ngrep source code can be downloaded from `http://www.packetfactory.net/Projects/ngrep`. After downloading it, follow the steps in Example 9.12.

Example 9.12 **Building ngrep**

```
$ tar xzvf ngrep-1.38.tar.gz
$ cd ngrep
$ ./configure
$ make
$ su
Password: ********
# make install
# exit
```

Congratulations! At this point, you should have a working copy of ngrep installed on your system.

Using ngrep

To start using ngrep, you'll need to decide what pattern you want to search for. These can be either libpcap-style descriptions of network traffic or GNU grep-style regular expressions describing the contents of traffic. In the following example, you'll grab any packet containing the pattern ssword and display it in the alternative format (which I think is a lot more readable). The results are shown in Example 9.13.

Example 9.13 **Looking for Something with ngrep**

```
[root@cherry /root]# ngrep -x ssword
interface: eth0 (192.168.1.0/255.255.255.0)
match: ssword
##############################
T 192.168.1.20:23 -> 192.168.1.10:1056 [AP]
  50 61 73 73 77 6f 72 64    3a 20                    Password:
########################exit
59 received, 0 dropped
[root@cherry /root]#
```

Each hash mark in this example represents a packet not containing the pattern you're searching for; any packets containing the pattern are displayed.

In this example, you followed the basic syntax of ngrep: ngrep <options> [pattern]. You used only the -x option, which sets the alternative display format.

Doing More with ngrep

A number of additional twists are available for the way that you can use ngrep. Chief among them is the capability to include libpcap-style packet filtering. libpcap provides a fairly simple language for filtering traffic.

Filters are written by combining *primitives* with conjunctions (*and* and *or*). Primitives can be preceded with the term *not*.

Primitives are normally formed with an ID (which can be numeric or a symbolic name preceded by one or more qualifiers). There are three kinds of qualifiers: type, direction, and protocol.

- Type qualifiers describe what the ID refers to. Allowed options are host, net, and port. If not type is given, the primitive defaults to host. Examples of type primitives are host crashtestdummy, net 192.168.2, or port 80.

- Directional qualifiers indicate which direction traffic is flowing in. Allowable qualifiers are src and dst. Examples of direction primitives are src cherry, dst mango, and src or dst port http. This last example shows two qualifiers being used with a single ID.

- Protocol qualifiers limit the captured packets to those of a single protocol. In the absence of a protocol qualifier, all IP packets are captured (subject to other filtering rules). Protocols that can be filtered are TCP, UDP, and ICMP. You might use a protocol qualifier such as icmp or tcp dst port telnet.

Primitives can be negated and combined to develop more complex filters. If you want to see all traffic to rose except Telnet and FTP data, you could use the filter host dst rose and not port telnet and not port ftp-data.

Some command-line switches are worth noting as well. Table 9.3 shows the command-line switches likely to be of the most use. As usual, check the main page for more detail.

Table 9.3 **Command-Line Switches for ngrep**

Switch	Description
-e	Shows empty packets
-n [num]	Matches num packets and then exits
-i [expression]	Searches for the regular expression without regard to case
-v [expression]	Searches for packets not containing the regular expression
-t	Prints a YYYY/MM/DD HH:MM:SS.UUUUUU timestamp on each matched packet
-T	Displays a +S.UUUUUU timestamp on each matched packet
-x	Shows the packets in the alternate hex and ASCII style
-I [filename]	Reads from a pcap-style dump named filename instead of live traffic
-O filename	Writes output to a pcap-style file named filename
-D	Mimics real time by printing matched packets at their recorded timestamp

Wrapping Up ngrep

Using ngrep can help you quickly match and display packets during your troubleshooting. If you've got an application level problem, ngrep can help you isolate the problem.

For example, if I was trying to make a connection from cherry (192.168.1.10) to cuke (192.168.2.10) and the connection was failing, I might troubleshoot the problem like this:

Describe the symptoms—Cherry cannot make a connection to hosts on remote network, but it can connect to hosts on other networks. Other hosts on cherry's network can connect to hosts on the remote network.

Understand the environment—The hosts involved are cherry, rhubarb (the gateway to the remote network), and cuke.

List hypotheses—My problems might be a misconfiguration of cherry or of an intervening router.

Prioritize hypothesis and narrow focus—Because cuke seems to be the only host affected, start looking there. If you can't solve the problem on cuke, move to rhubarb.

Create a plan of attack—I can try to ping cuke from cherry while using ngrep to see what traffic I am sending, like this: ngrep host cherry.

Act on the plan—As you start pinging cuke, you can see the results of the ngrep session in Example 9.14.

Example 9.14   **Results of an ngrep Session**

```
[root@cherry /root]# ngrep -e -x host 192.168.1.10
interface: eth0 (192.168.1.0/255.255.255.0)
filter: ip and ( host 192.168.1.10 )
#
I 192.168.1.10 -> 192.168.2.10 8:0
    eb 07 00 00 31 86 a7 39    5e cd 0e 00 08 09 0a 0b    ....1..9^.......
    0c 0d 0e 0f 10 11 12 13    14 15 16 17 18 19 1a 1b    ................
    1c 1d 1e 1f 20 21 22 23    24 25 26 27 28 29 2a 2b    .... !"#$%&'()*+
    2c 2d 2e 2f 30 31 32 33    34 35 36 37                ,-./01234567
#
I 192.168.1.1 -> 192.168.1.10 5:1
    c0 a8 01 0b 45 00 00 54    25 f2 00 00 40 01 d0 52    ....E..T%...@..R
    c0 a8 01 0a c0 a8 02 0a    08 00 dc 67 eb 07 00 00    ...........g....
    31 86 a7 39 5e cd 0e 00    08 09 0a 0b 0c 0d 0e 0f    1..9^...........
    10 11 12 13 14 15 16 17    18 19 1a 1b 1c 1d 1e 1f    ................
    20 21 22 23 24 25 26 27    28 29 2a 2b 2c 2d 2e 2f     !"#$%&'()*+,-./
    30 31 32 33 34 35 36 37    b4 04 01 00 06 00 00 00    01234567........
    00 10 00 00 01 00 00 00    e8 40 00 00                .........@..
exit
2 received, 0 dropped
[root@cherry /root]#
```

This shows two packets. The first is an ICMP packet of Type 8 and Code 0, a ping request. It is destined for cuke. The second is an ICMP packet of Type 5 and Code 1 and ICMP Redirect. This is coming from mango, the gateway to the rest of the world.

Test the results—You shouldn't expect to see mango involved at all. If you look at the ICMP Redirects being sent (using the -v switch), you can see that you're being redirected to the 192.168.1.11 address, not rhubarb.

Apply results of the test to the hypothesis—If you're not sending your traffic to the right gateway, it will never get to the right place. You should be able to solve this by adding a route to the 192.168.2.0/24 network on cherry (a quick check of working hosts shows that this is the way they're configured). You'll probably want to fix the bad route on mango as well.

Iterate as needed—When you've made the change and tested it, you know that it works and don't need to go any further.

Endnotes

1. Not all ICMP packets are blocked by packet filters. Normally just the Echo Request and Response packets are blocked. Some administrators choose to block redirects, router advertisements, router solicitations, and other ICMP packets that should never come from an external host.

10

Monitoring Tools

E*THEREAL* AND *MON* ARE TWO GREAT TOOLS for monitoring your networks. Ethereal is the source of all the network traces and packet decodes in Part I, "The Protocols." It also provides some of the functions that you'll want to use when baselining your network, as described in Chapter 7, "Before Things Break—Building a Baseline." mon also provides functionality to help bolster your baselining.

Although neither of these tools is part of the Red Hat Linux distribution, they should both be installed on your Linux system as quickly as possible.

Ethereal

Ethereal is a very functional protocol analyzer.[1] It has both a GUI (Ethereal) and a command-line interface (Tethereal). Both provide very easy means of finding and watching network traffic.

Example 10.1 **Using Tetheral**

```
[root@cherry /root]# tethereal
Kernel filter, protocol ALL, raw packet socket
Capturing on eth0
00:e0:98:7c:95:21 -> ff:ff:ff:ff:ff:ff ARP Who has 192.168.1.100?  Tell
192.168.1.10
00:e0:98:7c:95:21 -> ff:ff:ff:ff:ff:ff ARP Who has 192.168.1.100?  Tell
192.168.1.10
00:e0:98:7c:95:21 -> ff:ff:ff:ff:ff:ff ARP Who has 192.168.1.100?  Tell
192.168.1.10

[root@cherry /root]#
```

Example 10.1 shows cherry ARPing for a nonexistent host. Figure 10.1 shows Ethereal having captured some Ethernet traffic.

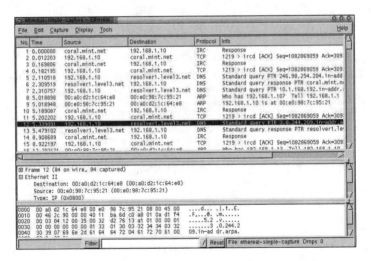

Figure 10.1 Ethereal screen shot.

Ethereal can give you a great deal of insight into the way things are really working on your network, but only in conjunction with a good understanding of the protocols themselves. In this section we'll look at the following topics:

- Getting and installing Ethereal
- Using Ethereal to capture packets
- Using Ethereal to view packets
- Filtering packets during both capture and display to make network diagnostics a bit simpler
- Dealing with bugs in Ethereal

Getting and Installing Ethereal

Ethereal is available for a wide range of platforms, including Linux, Windows, and several UNIX platforms. Although Ethereal has a command-line interface, it requires that GTK+ be installed on the system on which it is being built. Ethereal also relies on libpcap. I'll build it from source on Linux in this section. However, when you install it, it is important to ensure that you have Ethereal and the two software packages that it relies on. It should also be mentioned that although there are binary distributions of Ethereal available for many platforms, they are not always the most recent. You might want to take the extra time to build your own.

Downloading Binary Packages

Certainly the easiest way to install Ethereal is with the package-management system of your Linux distribution. The most recent binary packages for Ethereal are available at `http://ethereal.zing.org/download.html`. In addition to the Ethereal packages themselves, you'll also need to get packages for libpcap and perhaps for ucd-snmp (this will depend on what is installed on your system). After you've located the requisite packages, you're ready to go.

Downloading and Building Source

Building Ethereal is a bit more involved, but not too much. The following build instructions are based on a stock GNOME Workstation install of a Red Hat 6.2 box.

Don't forget that you'll need to install libpcap before you can build Ethereal. You can do this either with RPMs or by building it from source. Building from source isn't too hard, but you'll need to deal with a couple gotchas when building libpcap on Red Hat 6.2. First you'll need to make the /usr/local/include and /usr/local/include/net directories. You also must remember to do a `make install-incl` as well as the `make install`. The proper installation of libpcap is shown in Example 10.2.

Example 10.2 **Installing Libpcap**

```
[root@phred src] tar xzvf libpcap-0.5.2.tar.gz
[root@phred src] cd libpcap-0.5
[root@phred libpcap-0.5] ./configure
[root@phred libpcap-0.5] make
[root@phred libpcap-0.5] make install
[root@phred libpcap-0.5] mkdir -p /usr/local/lib/net
[root@phred libpcap-0.5] make install-incl
```

After libpcap is built, you've got smooth sailing in front of you. Ethereal is a three-step build. Building Ethereal is shown in Example 10.3.

Example 10.3 **Building Ethereal**

```
[root@phred src] tar xzvf ethereal-0.8.14.tar.gz
[root@phred src] cd ethereal-0.8.14
[root@phred ethereal-0.8.14] ./configure
[root@phred ethereal-0.8.14] make
[root@phred ethereal-0.8.14] make install
```

Using Ethereal to Capture Packets

Because the primary use of a protocol analyzer is to capture packets, that's just what we'll do. I'll start off with a simple example, move to some startup options for Ethereal and Tethereal, and wrap up with a more advanced example.

A Simple Example

Using Ethereal can be quite simple; typing **Ethereal** at the command line (as someone with permission to set the NIC into promiscuous mode) will start the GUI. When the GUI has started, you can select Capture, Start, which brings up the Capture Preferences window. This should have valid defaults set, but I like to click the Update List of Packets in Real Time and Automatic Scrolling in Live Capture buttons. Now press the Start button and watch your capture run.

While the capture is running, it displays the total number of packets captured in the Ethereal: Capture/Playback window. It also updates the main Ethereal window with each new packet that it grabs. After you've captured what you needed, you can stop the capture by hitting the Stop button in the Ethereal: Capture/Playback window. While the capture is running, you should see something similar to the display shown in Figure 10.2.

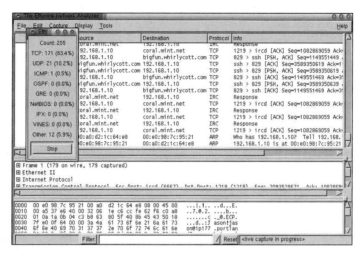

Figure 10.2   Ethereal capturing packets.

Starting Ethereal

A number of command-line options exist to help make starting Ethereal more pleasant. Table 10.1 shows some of the more likely candidates.

Table 10.1   **Command Line Options for Ethereal**

Option	Meaning
-i <interface>	This option sets the interface from which Ethereal will capture.
-k	This option causes Ethereal to begin capturing packets immediately upon startup. It must be used with the xs-i option.
-S	This option causes Ethereal to display packets as they are captured.
-c <count>	This option causes Ethereal to capture only *count* packets before stopping. It is useful only with the -k option.
-D	This option causes Ethereal to treat the TOS field of IP as the original TOS, not like Differentiated Services.
-f <capture filter>	This option enables you to set a libpcap-style capture filter. libpcap filter syntax is covered in the "ngrep" section of Chapter 9, "Troubleshooting Tools."
-n	This option disables name resolution; all packets will be displayed with numeric IP addresses, TCP ports, and UDP ports.

continues

Table 10.1 **Continued**

Option	Meaning
-r <infile>	This option causes Ethereal to read packets from a saved file instead of an interface. Using previous captures is covered in the upcoming section "Viewing Saved Captures."
-R <Read Filter>	This option enables you to set a read filter. Read filters are discussed in the upcoming section "Filtering Packets to Be Displayed."
-t <Time Stamp Format>	This option changes the format of the packet timestamps. The three possible formats are as follows: r—Relative to the first packet (the default) a—Actual date and time of the packet d—Relative to the previous packet
-w <savefile>	This option sets the name of the file to which the capture will be saved. Working with saved captures is covered in the upcoming section "Viewing Saved Captures."

A useful startup command for Ethereal might look like this:

```
[root@cherry /root]# ethereal -i eth0 -c 100 -D -t a -k -S &
```

This starts Ethereal, begins capturing from eth0 immediately, displays packets as they're captured using the original IPv4 TOS meaning for the TOS field, displays actual times for each packet, and stops capturing after 100 packets have been captured.

Starting Tethereal

Tethereal can be run in instances in which you have no good way to display the GUI for Ethereal or you don't need its extra weight to accomplish the task at hand (for example, you're just doing a file capture). Tethereal can be run like the session shown in Example 10.4.

Example 10.4 **Starting Tethereal**

```
[root@cherry /root]# tethereal
Kernel filter, protocol ALL, raw packet socket
Capturing on eth0
skull.eventloop.com -> 192.168.1.10 IRC Response
192.168.1.10 -> resolver1.level3.net DNS Standard query PTR 225.211.98.209.in-
addr.arpa
192.168.1.10 -> skull.eventloop.com TCP 1096 > ircd [ACK] Seq=984303403
↪Ack=994498041 Win=31856 Len=0
resolver1.level3.net -> 192.168.1.10 DNS Standard query response PTR
↪skull.eventloop.com
192.168.1.10 -> resolver1.level3.net DNS Standard query PTR 10.1.168.192.in-
↪addr.arpa
resolver1.level3.net -> 192.168.1.10 DNS Standard query response, Name error
192.168.1.10 -> resolver1.level3.net DNS Standard query PTR 3.0.244.209.in-
↪addr.arpa
```

```
resolver1.level3.net -> 192.168.1.10 DNS Standard query response PTR
➥resolver1.level3.net
```

```
[root@cherry /root]#
```

Like Ethereal, however, Tethereal is often better used with the command-line options
listed in Table 10.1. Some of the options either make no sense in the context of the
Tethereal interface (for instance, -t because there is no time display in Tethereal[2]) or
are not allowed (for instance, -S). A good example of a more useful Tethereal command might be this:

```
[root@cherry /root]# tethereal -i eth0 -c 10 -n -w quickcapture
```

This command captures the next 10 packets received on eth0 in the file quickcapture
without doing a name resolution.

Viewing Packets with Ethereal

The main window for Ethereal is divided into three sections, called *panes*. The top
pane is the packet list pane, which shows a summary of each packet captured. The
middle pane is the tree view pane, which shows a more detailed view of any packet
selected in the packet list pane. The bottom pane is the data view pane, which shows a
hex breakout and ASCII representation of any packet selected in the packet list pane.
There are also menu options of interest when viewing packets; we'll look at these in
more detail in the following sections.

A Simple Session Revisited

The simple Ethereal session described previously results in the final capture shown in
Figure 10.3.

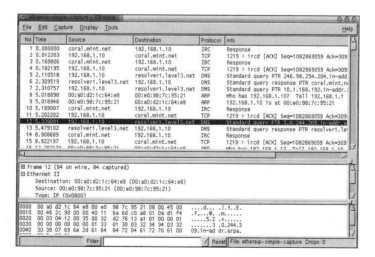

Figure 10.3 A simple Ethereal capture.

After the data is captured, you can look at it several ways, with a variety of tools.[3]

One way to look at the data is to review the Ethereal summary data, as shown in Figure 10.4.

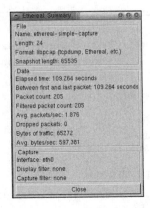

Figure 10.4 Ethereal summary data.

This summary shows the following:

- Information about the file (which we'll ignore)
- Information about the data (which we'll cover shortly)
- Information about the capture (which we'll cover right after the information about the data)

You can bring up the summary window by selecting Tools, Summary.

The information about the data provides some good information about the traffic in the capture. It tells us how long it took for the traffic to be sent, how many packets were sent, how much data was sent, how much data per packet (average), and how much data per second (average). This information can be made much more useful when combined with filters (see the upcoming section "Filtering Packets with Ethereal" for more information about writing filters). For example, if you want to determine the load that connecting to an IRC server will put on your network, you can capture a 15-minute IRC session while filtering for just IRC traffic. Then you can see the average amount of data that IRC transferred over those 15 minutes.[4] Bear in mind that you probably will want to check this at several points during the day, just to get a more realistic picture of the traffic load.

The capture information provides the context needed to make sense of the capture. It shows what interface the capture is from, what capture filter was used, and what display filter is in use. In the IRC example described in the previous paragraph, the data would be misleading if it also contained HTTP traffic. Looking at the capture information can help ensure that we're looking at just the data we want.

Another way of looking at the packets is to look at only those packets matching certain criteria. To be really effective at this, you'll need to write a display filter, but Ethereal provides a quick mechanism to create a simple filter for you. If you select a field in tree view pane, for example, selecting an Ethernet II Type field containing ARP, then clicking Display, Match Selected creates a display filter matching all packets with an Ethernet II type of ARP. This is shown in Figures 10.5 and 10.6.

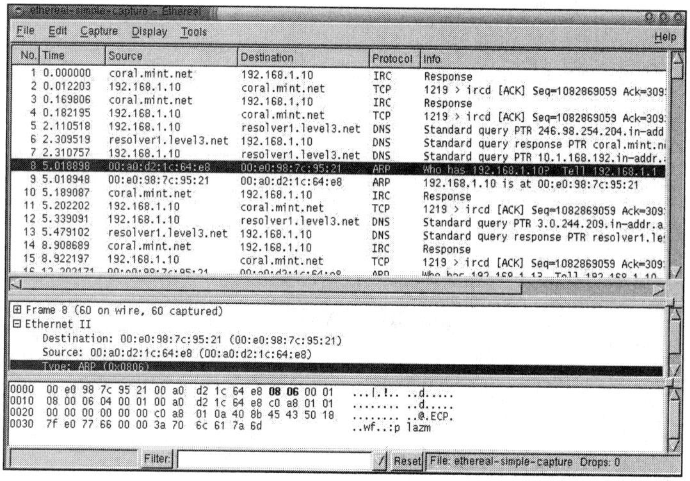

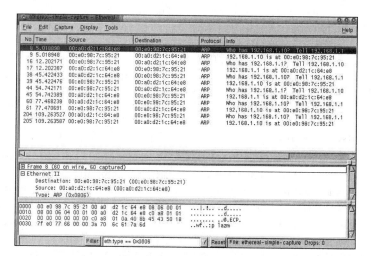

Figure 10.5 Selecting content to match.

Figure 10.6 Ethereal matching selected packets.

Because captured traffic is spread over several packets, it can be difficult to see just what traffic is being pushed around the network. Ethereal provides a way to do this, following a TCP stream. In Figure 10.7, you can see a TCP stream containing an HTTP session. You can follow a TCP session by selecting a TCP packet in the packet list pane and then clicking Tools, Follow TCP Stream.

```
Contents of TCP Stream
GET /daily HTTP/1.0
Connection: Keep-Alive
User-Agent: Mozilla/4.72 [en] (X11; U; Linux 2.2.14-5.0 i686)
Host: www.lwn.net
Accept: image/gif, image/x-xbitmap, image/jpeg, image/pjpeg, image/png, */*
Accept-Encoding: gzip
Accept-Language: en
Accept-Charset: iso-8859-1,*,utf-8

HTTP/1.1 301 Moved Permanently
Date: Tue, 29 Aug 2000 05:03:09 GMT
Server: Apache/1.3.3 (Unix) (Red Hat/Linux) mod_perl/1.15 PHP/3.0.5
Location: http://lwn.net/daily/
Connection: close
Content-Type: text/html

<!DOCTYPE HTML PUBLIC "-//IETF//DTD HTML 2.0//EN">
<HTML><HEAD>
<TITLE>301 Moved Permanently</TITLE>
</HEAD><BODY>
<H1>Moved Permanently</H1>
The document has moved <A HREF="http://lwn.net/daily/">here</A>. <P>
</BODY></HTML>
```

Figure 10.7   A TCP stream.

In this example, the first block of data is an HTTP request sent by the client. The second block of data is an HTTP error message returned by the server.

Saving a Capture File

Having captured a pile of network traffic, you'll probably want to look at it again later. Ethereal enables you to save your capture to a file. This can be done from the command line (the only way to do it with Tethereal), from the Capture Preferences screen, or after you've stopped a capture by selecting File, Save (which is also accessible from the keyboard shortcut Ctrl+S). This brings up the Save Capture File As window. This window enables you to save your capture in a number of formats; it also enables you to save only the currently displayed packets (using the Save Only Packets Currently Being Displayed button.)

Viewing Saved Captures

Sometimes you'll want to look at traffic that's no longer moving on the network (either for diagnostics or to review or learn more about a protocol). For these cases, Ethereal provides a convenient method for saving and viewing captured files. In fact, Ethereal even provides the capability to view captures saved from other applications.

To view a saved capture, select File, Open, which brings up the Open Capture File interface. This window presents a common file selection tool with which you should select the name of the capture file that you want to view. You can also select the file on startup, using `ethereal -r capturefile`.

Filtering Packets with Ethereal

Even a small network can have a lot of data running over it. Filters help you cut through the chaff to see just the data you are interested in. Two kinds of filters exist for Ethereal, capture filters and display filters. Capture filters are applied as the data is being read from the network. If traffic doesn't match the filter, it isn't read into Ethereal. Display filters are applied against traffic that Ethereal has already captured. Both styles of filters, with some pros and cons, are covered in the next two sections.

Filtering Packets to Be Captured

Capture filters are written in the libpcap syntax, which is covered in more detail in the section "ngrep" in Chapter 9. A quick overview is provided here as well. Capture filters are nice because they are very fast and because they operate on the raw traffic as it is being captured. This can be a huge benefit on a busy LAN; you'll get only the traffic you're interested in, not the other 8MB of traffic that you'd otherwise have to wade through. Capture filters are not a panacea, though; they may get you only 50% of the way to your goal. That's where display filters come in.

Libpcap-style filters use the `<not>` `[type]` `<direction>` `[id]` (such as host src 192.168.1.10). These filters can be combined with the conjunctions *and* and *or*. If you want to see all traffic between 192.168.1.1 and 192.168.1.10, you can use a filter such as `host 192.168.1.1` and `host 192.168.1.10`. To look at traffic going from 192.168.1.1 to host 192.168.1.10 and not the return traffic, you can do `host src 192.168.1.1` and `host dst 192.168.1.10`.

Filtering Packets to Be Displayed

The display filter syntax is much more expressive (and capable) than the capture filters described previously. Although capture filters are entered at the start of the capture (either on the command line or in the Capture Preferences window), display filters are entered after the capture is complete. With a capture buffer loaded, you can define a display filter in the filter section of the status bar at the bottom of the Main window. You can clear your active display filter by clicking the Reset button.

Display filters have an expressive syntax but can be quite basic. A simple filter to look at all the traffic from 192.168.1.1 to 192.168.1.10 would look like `ip.src == 192.168.1.1 && ip.dst == 192.168.1.10`.

A much cooler example would be to look at all traffic from 192.168.1.20 or 192.168.1.21 that has the TCP SYN bit set; this would be written as `(ip.src==192.168.1.21 or 192.168.1.20) and tcp.flags.syn`. If you want to extend the previous section to exclude HTTPS traffic, you could write `((ip.src==192.168.1.21 or 192.168.1.20) and tcp.flags.syn) ! tcp.port==443`.

Ethereal provides additional filter comparison operators as well. ==, !=, >, <, >=, and <= are all available in this C-style format or with English-style names. Beyond this, you can use a substring operator to match fields within a value. For example, you might want to match on the first three octets of an Ethernet source address; you could do that with `eth.src[0:3] == 00:a0:d2`.

Reporting Bugs

If you happen to find a bug in Ethereal, please report it. If you're a C hacker and think you know how to fix it, don't hesitate to send in a patch as well. (Your patch might not be used, but it will likely help the developers see where things are going wrong.) Bug reports can be directed to the ethereal-dev mailing list (you can subscribe through http://ethereal.zing.org/; click the Mailing Lists link on the left side). Your bug report should include the following three things (at a minimum):

- The version of Ethereal that you are using and the versions of software that it is linked against. This can be grabbed from ethereal -v, like so:

```
[pate@cherry sgml]$ ethereal -v
ethereal 0.8.7, with GTK+ 1.2.7, with libpcap 0.4, with libz 1.1.3, with UCD
➥SNMP 4.1.1
[pate@cherry sgml]$
```

- A traceback of Ethereal, if it crashed. To get a corefile, look for a corefile in your current working director, run file core against it to ensure that it is the Ethereal core file (you also might want to verify the date of the core file, just to be safe), and then run the following commands:

```
[pate@cherry pate]$ gdb /usr/bin/ethereal core >& backtrace.txt
backtrace
[pate@cherry pate]$
```

This will create a file called backtrace.txt, which you can mail in with your bug report.

- A description of what you were doing when Ethereal exhibited the bug. The more detail you can add here, the better.

Creating a good bug report is an art form, but it's something that should be taken seriously. The developers of Ethereal can't help fix problems if they don't know what is broken.

mon

mon is a resource-monitoring system designed to measure host or service availability. It was developed by Jim Trocki (trockij@transmeta.com) and is supported by an active community with a Web site at www.kernel.org/software/mon/ and a mailing list (information is available at the same location).

mon handles monitoring as two separate tasks: testing conditions and alerting on failures. Both functions are handled by external programs (usually scripts written in Perl). Many such scripts are distributed with mon.

mon itself is an engine that schedules tests based on your configuration and then passes the results of the test to appropriate alerting programs. This separation of functionality from mon enables you to make seamless changes to your monitoring system. All you need to do is add a new test or alert program and then modify your configuration. No changes to mon itself are needed (short of a `kill -HUP` to reread the config file).

In this section, we'll discuss getting and installing mon, configuring it, using it to monitor your network, and writing tests for it.

Getting and Installing mon

You can download mon from `ftp.kernel.org` at `/pub/software/admin/mon/` (the `kernel .org` maintainers ask that you use one of the `kernel.org` mirrors). Version 0.38.20 was current as of this writing. In addition to mon, you'll also need to grab several Perl modules: Time::Period, Time::HiRes, Convert::BER, and Mon::*. Some additional modules are required for the test and alert scripts (for instance, `telnet.monitor` requires Net::Telnet). The `fping.monitor` script relies on the fping package that is also available from the same place you got mon.

> **Download and Install First!**
> Please make sure that you download and install the required packages before starting in on mon. Installing Perl modules is a bit beyond the scope of this book, but building fping requires a bit of hackery that you'll need to know about. Line 222 of `fping.c` contains a redeclaration of `sys_errlist`, so you should comment out the entire line. Failure to do so will.cause the compilation to fail.

mon itself is a set of Perl scripts and configuration files, so you don't actually need to build it. Instead, you should configure it for local use (see the next section for details) and then test it. After it is configured properly, you can move it to its final location and set up a startup script in `/etc/rc.d/init.d`.

Configuring mon

You'll need to set up a mon.cf file representing your network. Example 10.5 contains a simple file representing a network with two monitored hosts. cherry is a Web server and a workstation. I usually check workstations every 15 minutes to make sure that I can Telnet into them; I check Web servers every 5 minutes to ensure that they're serving up pages.

Example 10.5   **A mon Configuration File**

```
#
# Example "mon.cf" configuration for "mon".
#


#
# global options
#  the eventual values for these options are commented out and values for
#  a test installation are currently in place
#

#cfbasedir   = /usr/local/lib/mon/etc
cfbasedir   = .
#alertdir    = /usr/local/lib/mon/alert.d
alertdir    = ./alert.d
#mondir      = /usr/local/lib/mon/mon.d
mondir      = ./mon.d
maxprocs    = 20
histlength = 100
randstart = 60s


#
# authentication types:
#   getpwnam      standard Unix passwd, NOT for shadow passwords
#   shadow        Unix shadow passwords (not implemented)
#   userfile      "mon" user file
#
authtype = userfile


#
# NB:  hostgroup and watch entries are terminated with a blank line (or
# end of file).  Don't forget the blank lines between them or you lose.
#


#
# group definitions (hostnames or IP addresses)
#
hostgroup workstations crash cherry

hostgroup wwwservers cherry

watch wwwservers
    service http
        interval 5m
        monitor http.monitor
        allow_empty_group
        period wd {Sun-Sat}
            alert mail.alert -S "web server has fallen down" pate
            upalert mail.alert -S "web server is back up" pate
            alertevery 45m
```

```
watch workstations
    service telnet
        interval 15m
        monitor telnet.monitor
        period wd {Sun-Sat}
            alert mail.alert pate
            alertevery 1h
```

After you've set your configuration file, you can start mon:

```
[root@cherry mon-0.38.20]# ./mon -f -c mon.cf -b `pwd`
```

And, after 2 or 3 minutes for the tests to start up, you can check the operating status of the hostgroups with the moncmd command:

```
[root@cherry mon-0.38.20]# ./clients/moncmd -s localhost list opstatus
group=workstations service=telnet opstatus=1 last_opstatus=7 exitval=0 timer=895
➥last_success=970580889 last_trap=0 last_check=970580887 ack=0 ackcomment=''
➥alerts_sent=0 depstatus=0 depend='' monitor='telnet.monitor' last_summary=''
➥last_detail='' interval=900
group=wwwservers service=http opstatus=1 last_opstatus=7 exitval=0 timer=289
➥last_success=970580883 last_trap=0 last_check=970580881 ack=0 ackcomment=''
➥alerts_sent=0 depstatus=0 depend='' monitor='http.monitor' last_summary=''
➥last_detail='HOST localhost: ok\0aHTTP/1.1 200 OK\0d\0aDate: Tue, 03 Oct 2000
➥13:48:01 GMT\0d\0aServer: Apache/1.3.12 (Unix)\0d\0aConnection:
➥close\0d\0aContent-Type: text/html\0a\0a' interval=300
220 list opstatus completed
[root@cherry mon-0.38.20]#
```

In addition to the moncmd interface and the alerts, there are three distinct Web front ends for mon. mon.cgi (by Andrew Ryan) seems to be the most widely accepted; it was designed to provide all the functionality of the command-line tools through a Web interface. mon.cgi can be obtained from www.nam-shub.com/files/. In addition to mon.cgi, there are also minotaure (by Gilles Lamiral) and monshow (by Jim Trocki). minotaure, in particular, has very nice documentation.

Writing Tests for mon

I've written a sample mon test to check for finger daemons that aren't running. Although this probably isn't useful for real life, it should serve as a model for writing your own tests. Example 10.6 contains a listing of the program:

Example 10.6   **A mon Test**

```
#!/usr/bin/perl -w

use strict;

use Net::Telnet;

my (@failures, @l);
my $debug = 0;
```

continues

Example 10.6 **Continued**

```perl
foreach my $host (@ARGV) {
    my $t = new Net::Telnet( Timeout => 10,
                             Port => 79,
                             Errmode => "return");
    if ($t -> open("$host")) {
        $t->print("");
        my $lines = $t->getlines;
        unless ($lines) {
            push @failures, [$host, $t->errmsg];
        }

    } else {
        push @failures, [$host, $t->errmsg];
    }
}

exit 0 if (0 == @failures);

foreach my $failed_host (@failures) {
    push @l, $$failed_host[0];
}

print "@l\n";

foreach my $error (@failures) {
    print "$$error[0]: $$error[1]\n";
}

exit 1;
```

Let's walk through this script to understand what's going on in a test script.

The first thing you'll need to know is how mon expects to pass the monitor script a list of hosts to test. mon calls external tests like this:

```
foo.monitor host1 host2 ... hostN
```

In the example script, we're grabbing those host names with the loop:

```perl
foreach my $host (@ARGV) {
    #do stuff
}
```

That "do stuff" thing is the important bit; we'll get back to it in a minute. Before we do, we need to look at one more thing—how mon expects to be told of failures by the test. mon is actually looking for three things: an exit code (0 if there are no errors, or 1 otherwise), a list of failed hosts, and a list of error messages associated with the failed hosts. Returning an exit code is not a big deal; the more interesting thing is the creation of the two lists that mon wants. This is done in the last two foreach loops in our sample.

Back to the "do stuff" section—in this example, I wanted to send alerts for boxes that weren't responding to finger requests. To perform the test, I used the Net::Telnet Perl module to make a TCP connection to the finger server (at port 79). Then I sent an empty string and waited for a response. If I got something back, I treated it as a working server. If there was no connection, or if I got an error, I treated it as a failure and popped the host and error message onto an array for later handling. After I had worked through the whole list of hosts, I could move on to the error-handling part of the test (if there were any failures).

That's all there is to it; not much magic there. The hardest part is sitting down to figure out how to test the condition you're looking for.

Endnotes

1. Protocol analyzers (or sniffers) enable you to capture some or all of the traffic on a network and display it in some meaningful way (this last part is called a *decode*). Because they typically are quite expensive (into the tens of thousands of dollars), they are not often used except in large networking shops or by expensive consultants brought in to solve a thorny problem.

2. Well, this is not entirely true. Tethereal will not display timestamps when capturing data; it will display timestamps when displaying a previously captured file, though.

3. By the way, if you look closely at this screen, you'll notice that I cheated. I saved a copy of the file so that I could go back to it. This copy has been put up at www.networkinglinuxbook.com along with the other materials for the book.

4. This is a simple form of benchmarking.

11

Security Tools

THIS CHAPTER PRESENTS SIX TOOLS that should become part of your security toolkit. *nmap* is a port scanner that has become the de facto standard for system and network administrators. *Nessus* is a security scanner that has replaced the older *SATAN* as the tool of choice for catching known security problems. *iptables* is the interface to the next generation of Linux packet filtering and IP masquerading. *Xinetd* and *tcp wrappers* provide two methods of controlling access to a specific host. They can be used separately or in conjunction with one another. *OPIE* provides a password-obscuring mechanism to allow fairly secure logins without encrypting the session between two hosts.

nmap

nmap is a tool for scanning a machine (or machines) for security problems and is exercised from the network. nmap is often run from the command line, but a GTK+-based front end (*nmapfe*) is also available. nmap is written and maintained by Fyodor <fyodor@insecure.org>. nmapfe was originally written by Zach Smith <key@aye.net> and is now maintained by Fyodor.

nmap and related tools are something of a mixed blessing, and thus have a murky reputation. While these tools are incredibly useful for a system or network administrator, they can also be used to the advantage of system crackers. Some people would prefer that tools like nmap weren't made publicly available. I tend to side with the other part of the community. If tools like this weren't available to the good guys, it would give the bad guys an incredible advantage because they certainly won't give up their tools.

nmap is an external security scanner, or a port scanner. It works by sending IP packets to the host(s) it is checking and by watching for what kind of response (if any) it receives.

nmap presents a summary of the responses it receives to provide a security overview of the target host(s). This overview can show

- A list of open ports
- Owners of remote processes on open ports
- RPC services matched against the port on which they are provided
- Information about TCP sequence numbers
- Remote operating systems

Getting and Installing nmap

Binaries and source of nmap are available from www.nmap.org. The binaries are as easy to install as you would expect. Building nmap and nmapfe is easy as well.

After putting the source tarball into /usr/local/source, you just follow the regular three step process:

```
[root@cherry nmap-2.53]# ./configure
[root@cherry nmap-2.53]# make
[root@cherry nmap-2.53]# make install
```

nmap at Work

After nmap has been built and installed, you're ready to run with it. nmap provides a number of different security-scanning options.

nmap on the Command Line

The simplest nmap scan is run as shown in Example 11.1.

Example 11.1 **Running an nmap Scan**

```
[root@cherry nmap-2.53]# nmap 192.168.1.20

Starting nmap V. 2.54BETA1 by fyodor@insecure.org
( www.insecure.org/nmap/ )
Interesting ports on (192.168.1.20):
(The 1519 ports scanned but not shown below are in state: closed)
Port State Service
25/tcp open smtp
111/tcp open sunrpc
113/tcp open auth
515/tcp open printer
939/tcp open unknown
1024/tcp open kdm

nmap run completed — 1 IP address (1 host up) scanned in 17 seconds
[root@cherry
nmap-2.53]#
```

Several different kinds of scans available through nmap are described in Table 11.1.

Table 11.1 **Scans Available Through nmap**

Scan Type	Switch	Description
TCP connect() scan	-sT	The most basic form of scanning. This opens a connection to every potentially interesting port on the target machine. Any user can use this kind of scan. It is easily detected, with many connection messages showing up in the logs of the target machine.
TCP SYN scan	-sS	The "half-open" scan. This scan sends a TCP SYN packet as though it is trying to open the connection. If it receives a SYN–ACK response, it sends an immediate RST to shut down the connection. Because this scan doesn't open the connection, it is less likely to be logged. Only users with root privilege can send TCP SYN scans.
Stealth FIN	-sF	This scan attempts to pass through packet filters by sending a TCP FIN packet.
Christmas Tree	-sX	This scan attempts to pass through packet filters by sending a packet with FIN, URG, and PUSH flags set.

continues

Table 11.1   **Continued**

Scan Type	Switch	Description
Null	-sN	This scan attempts to pass through packet filters by sending a packet without any flags turned on.
Ping	-sP	This limits the scan to only conducting a ping sweep to look for connected systems. It does not do port scans.
UDP scan	-sU	This sends 0 byte UDP packets to each port on the target machine(s).
ACK scan	-sA	This scan is used to help check packet filters. An ACK packet with random acknowledgment and sequence numbers is sent. If nothing is returned, the port is marked as filtered.
Window scan	-sW	This scan is similar to the ACK scan, but depends on anomalies in the TCP window size handling of some OSes.
RPC scan	-sR	This scan checks all open ports found by other scan types and sends RPC NULL commands to see if they are RPC ports. If they are RPC ports, this scan attempts to determine what program and version number they serve.
FTP bounce scan	-b <ftp relay host>	This scan relives a historical foible of FTP servers. Older FTP servers were able to serve bounced FTP sessions; that is, they connected to another host to deliver data to you. By providing a relay host in the format username:password@server:port, you can use this FTP bounce (mis)feature to scan ports that might otherwise be protected.

In addition to the types of scans that nmap can run, a number of options modify its behavior. These options include timing, target identification, output, and others. Some of the more useful options are shown in Table 11.2.

Table 11.2   **nmap Options**

Option	Explanation
-P0	Tells nmap not to ping hosts before scanning. (This is used to scan hosts that sit behind packet filters that don't allow ICMP traffic.)
-PT<PORT>	Uses TCP to look for hosts on the target network. ACK packets are sent, and nmap looks for RST packets to be returned. An optional PORT number can be given. It tells nmap which port to attempt its connections against.
–PS	Causes nmap to use SYN packets instead of ACK packets when checking for hosts on the target network (root users only).

Option	Explanation
-PI	Uses ICMP only when looking for hosts on the target network.
-PB	Uses both ICMP and TCP ACK to sweep the target network for hosts. This is the default behavior.
-O	Causes nmap to attempt remote host identification based on the way the target system handles TCP packets containing certain types of errors.
-I	Causes nmap to use an identd scan. This causes the owner of each server process to be shown as well.
-f	Causes nmap to fragment its scanning packets, making it more difficult to block the scan with packet filters.
-v	Puts nmap into verbose mode, causing it to display much more information about what it's doing.
-oN <logfile>	Writes output into a human readable logfile.
-oM <logfile>	Writes output into a machine-parsable logfile.
--resume <logfile&;	Resumes an incomplete scan from a logfile.
-iL <logfile>	Causes nmap to read input from a logfile instead of really scanning a host.
-g <portnumber>	Allows you to define the port nmap uses as its source port.
-p <port range>	Allows you to define the range of ports nmap will scan. If no range is given, nmap will scan all the ports listed in its own services file. A range of ports can be given in the following format: -p 20-30,79,6000-6010.

nmap allows you to list target IP addresses in one of four styles. For single hosts, you can write the IP address or hostname. For networks, you can write the number in slash notation using the CIDR-style network mask (for example, 192.168.1.0/24). The most flexible form of target listing allows you to wildcard portions of the address (or list them as ranges). This allows you to look at specific hosts within a group of networks (for instance, if you know that all your routers use the first IP address of their Class C address, you can scan your internal routers with a target such as 192.168.*.1). Finally, you are also able to provide a list of hosts (in any of the previous styles).

nmapfe

nmapfe makes it even easier. It provides a GTK+-based front end to nmap that you can use to select your targets, set your scanning options, and view the results of your scan. When initially launched, nmapfe looks like the screen shot in Figure 11.1.

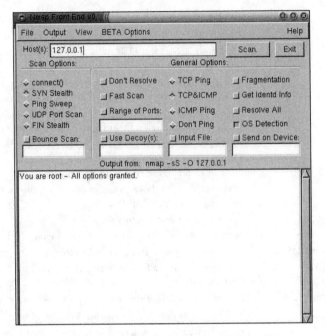

Figure 11.1   nmapfe upon launching.

A completed scan looks like the screen shot found in Figure 11.2.

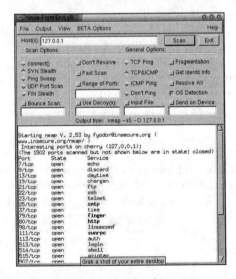

Figure 11.2   A completed nmap scan.

There are no nmap options that can be passed to nmapfe at this time. It accepts any X11 style options allowed by GTK+.

The buttons and menu items available in nmapfe correspond to some of the options available to nmap from the command line. Please see Table 11.2 for more details about these options.

Nessus

Nessus is a port-scanning vulnerability scanner. Nessus provides a scripting language to write additional tests. This section will give an overview of Nessus, discuss obtaining and installing it, and provide an introduction to its use.

Nessus was written by Renaud Deraison `<renaud@nessus.org>`, with a number of other contributors. It is available from `www.nessus.org`.

Nessus is a client-server pair of applications. *Nessusd* is the server. It runs as a daemon and is responsible for conducting all the tests. Nessus is a GTK+-based client application. It is responsible for providing the user with a convenient user interface.

Nessus begins scanning a host by conducting a port scan to see what avenues are available for attack. It relies on nmap for this functionality. When it has determined which ports it can look at, Nessus scans for known vulnerabilities. It uses plugins written in C or in the *Nessus Attack Scripting Language* (NASL) to carry out these tests. (Writing scripts in NASL is briefly covered later in this section.)

Getting and Installing Nessus

There are two major steps involved in getting Nessus to run on your system. First, you must obtain and build the software. After the software has been built, it needs to be installed and set up. This section covers both steps.

Getting and Building Nessus

Nessus is not hard to build, but there are four packages that you must download and build in the proper order:

- Nessus-libraries
- libnasl
- Nessus-core
- Nessus-plugins

Each of these packages follows the typical `configure`, `make`, `make install` pattern of building free software. Make sure you build and install the packages in the proper order and you will save yourself a good bit of grief.

Installing Nessus

Having completed the make install to install the programs and libraries, you can start Nessusd. The first time you start it, you need to go through an extended set up by starting with the nessus-adduser command, as shown in Example 11.2.

Example 11.2 **Adding a Nessus User**

```
[root@cherry /root]# nessus-adduser
Using /var/tmp as a temporary file holder

Add a new nessusd user
----------------------



Login : nessus
Authentication method (cipher/plaintext) [cipher] :

Source restriction
------------------

You can, if you will, configure this account so that it can only
be used from a given host or subnet. For instance, you may want
nessus to be able to connect to this nessusd server only from
his work machine.

Please enter the host (or subnet) nessus is allowed to connect from.
A blank entry will allow him to connect from anywhere

The entry format must be an IP address followed by an optional netmask.
Hostnames are *not* accepted

Examples of valid entries :
    192.168.1.5
    192.168.1.0/24
    192.168.1.0/255.255.255.0

Invalid entry :
    prof.fr.nessus.org

Source host or network [anywhere] :

One time password : foobarbaz
User rules
----------
nessusd has a rules system which allows you to restrict the hosts
that nessus has the right to test. For instance, you may want
him to be able to scan his own host only.
```

```
Please see the nessus-adduser(8) man page for the rules syntax

Enter the rules for this user, and hit ctrl-D once you are done :
(the user can have an empty rules set)

Login             : nessus
Auth. method      : cipher, can connect from anywhere
One time password : foobarbaz
Rules             :


Is that ok ? (y/n) [y]
user added.
[root@cherry /root]#
```

This example shows a very vanilla install. Any user can connect to the Nessus account using 'foobarbaz' as a password. After connected, you can use Nessus to scan any host. With a Nessus user added, you can start the Nessus daemon like this:

```
[root@cherry /root]# nessusd &
```

Nessus at Work

Nessus, like any other security tool, cannot be run just once to make your network secure. Ideally, you should run Nessus on a regular basis (perhaps weekly or biweekly), and again after any change has been made to your network.

Running Nessus from inside your network is important to help ensure the internal security of your hosts. It should also be run from an external host in order to get a real world picture of how things look from a cracker's perspective.

In this section, we'll look at just the internal scan of a single host in our internal network. Coverage includes running Nessus, saving and reading reports, and extending Nessus by writing tests in NASL.

Running Nessus

The first time Nessus is run, you need to configure your user. Nessus brings up a splash screen showing that it is building a key pair for your client, then a window where you can enter your pass phrase. If you are running Nessus for the second or later time, it just asks for your pass phrase.

After entering your pass phrase, Nessus brings up a login window for connecting to Nessusd (see Figure 11.3).

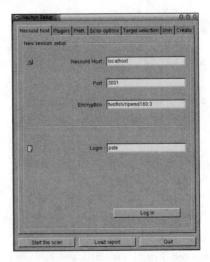

Figure 11.3   The Nessus login window.

This is also the main window for Nessus. The tabs that run across the top of the window provide access to additional functionality.

After you've logged in to Nessusd, you're automatically moved into the Plugins tab. Click the Enable All button to do a full scan or select and deselect scans manually by using the buttons on the left side of the window. Clicking the name of the scan family in the upper pane of the Plugins tab will bring up a list of individual scans in the lower pane (see Figure 11.4).

Figure 11.4   Nessus Plugins tab.

Having selected the scans you want to run, you can select your target. Move to the Target selection tab and enter your requested target (this could be a single host or a list of hosts). I've selected just a single host at 192.168.1.20 (see Figure 11.5).

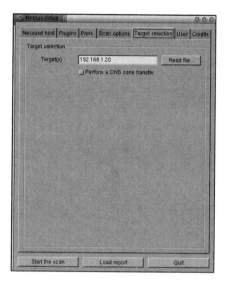

Figure 11.5   Nessus Target tab.

Now you can run the scan. Just click the Start the Scan button at the button of the window. The scan will take a while to run, so this might be a good time to go off and catch up on your email. You can watch the progress of your scan by watching the portscanning/attack status window (see Figure 11.6).

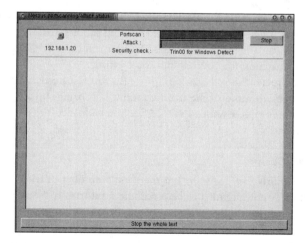

Figure 11.6   The Nessus portscanning/attack status window.

When Nessus has completed its scan, it brings up a report window. Clicking the host name or IP address brings up a cascading list of potential vulnerabilities on that host. In Figure 11.7, I've expanded a listed vulnerability to show the kind of detail Nessus is able to display.

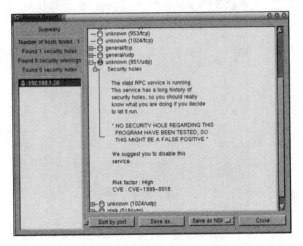

Figure 11.7   A Nessus report.

Saving and Reading Reports

Typically, you should save reports of scans so that you can keep a trail of what potential vulnerabilites show up in your network and when they do.

You can save a report by clicking the Save As button. Make sure that you use a consistent naming scheme and that you can readily interpret the names. Something like <hostname>-<date>.nsr is probably good. Depending on the number of hosts in your network, you might find that you need to keep subdirectories for LANs, for kinds of machines, and/or for time periods that you run the scans. In general, find the right level of organization for yourself and stick with it.

Going back to review an old scan report is easy. You just need to click the Load Report button at the bottom of the main window. This brings up a selection box for you to select the report you want to view. After you've loaded the report, it comes up in a report window.

Writing NASL Scripts

NASL scripts are fairly easy to write, but there are a number of tricks to getting them right. This section is not intended to be a complete tutorial. It should be enough for you to get your feet wet though. Please read the NASL guide and main page that come with the libnasl source for more details.

NASL is a C-like language, without a lot of the overhead. Variables need not be declared, nor are they typed (that you need to care about at least). If you need to use a variable, just do it:

```
myhostname = "cherry";
```

If you want to use a number, you can enter it in binary, decimal, or hex. NASL will take care of the conversion for you. If you're using a string, be aware that NASL will not interpolate special characters unless you tell it to:

```
a = "foo\nbar\nbaz";        # this equals "foo\nbar\nbaz"
a = string("foo\nbar\nbaz"); # this equals "foo
                            #             bar
                            #             baz"
```

As you can guess from the previous example, each line of comments is preceded with the # symbol. There are no multiline comments in NASL. You can define your own functions in NASL like this:

```
function sqr(n)
{
  return(n*n);
}

display("5 squared is ", sqr(5), "\n";
```

NASL provides the standard C operators *, /, %, +, -, |, and & (although it doesn't yet provide precedence for them). NASL also provides two additional operators. The 'x' operator repeats a function *n* times; for example, this will execute the display function 5 times:

```
display("a line of text\n") x 5;
```

The '><' operator functions like the grep command. It returns true if a string on the left of the operator appears in the string on the right.

```
a = "foo";
b = "Don't be a fool";
if (a >< b) {
  display(a, " is contained in ", b, "\n");
}
```

As an example, check the greeting message sent by the mailer daemon. All the internal hosts should be running qmail, so if someone is running Sendmail you want to know about it. The NASL script is shown in Example 11.3.

Example 11.3 **A NASL Script**

```
1.   if(description)
2.   {
3.    script_name(english:"sendmail message check");
4.    script_description(english:"This script looks for sendmail");
5.    script_summary(english:"connects on remote port 25");
6.    script_category(ACT_GATHER_INFO);
7.   script_family(english:"Administration toolbox");
8.   script_copyright(english:"Copyright Pat Eyler, licensed under GPL");
9.   script_dependencies("find_services.nes");
10.  exit(0);
11.  }
12.
13.  # get the smtp port from the knowledge base
14.  port = get_kb_item("Services/smtp");
15.
16.  # if we couldn't find the smtp port in the knowledge base, set it
17.  # to the standard
18.  if(!port) port = 25;
19.
20.  # warn is FALSE unless Sendmail is running
21.  warn = 0;
22.
23.  # check the knowledge base to see if the port is running
24.  if(get_port_state(port))
25.  {
26.
27.   # open a connection to the smtp port
28.   soc = open_sock_tcp(port);
29.   if(soc)
30.   {
31.
32.    # grab the first 200 bytes of data from our connection
33.    data = recv(socket:soc, length:200);
34.
35.    # look for "Sendmail" in the data, and set warn to TRUE
36.    # if it is
37.    if("Sendmail" >< data) warn = 1;
38.
39.   }
40.
41.   # clean up our connection
42.   close(soc);
43.  }
44.
45.  # do this only if we found Sendmail
46.  if(warn)
47.  {
```

```
48.    report = "Host is running Sendmail, not qmail.";
49.    security_warning(port:25, data:report);
50.    }
51.
52.    #
53.    # Check for Sendmail running instead of qmail
54.    #
55.
56.    # start by building a description of this script
```

While the example script above is heavily commented, it might be worth pointing some things out. In line 24, we used `get_port_state`. This function returns a Boolean FALSE value if the port is known to be closed. If the port is known to be open or has not been tested, the function returns a Boolean TRUE value. We also used conditional logic (the `if` statements) to control the flow of the script. NASL also provides looping logic with both `for` and `while` statements. Also note how values were assigned to variables being passed to functions in lines 33 and 49. The basic form is

```
function(variable:value);
```

Because Nessus runs your script for each host (assuming that you've selected it), and has a number of other scripts to run as well, it is important that you make your scripts as efficient as possible. NASL makes some provisions for doing this by allowing scripts to share information through a knowledge base. There are two examples of this in the script shown in Example 11.3.

iptables

The iptables tool is the next generation of TCP/IP filtering and monitoring for the Linux environment. The tool is an interface to the netfilter module of the Linux kernel. Netfilter provides *Network Address Translation* (NAT) and a security mechanism for your network.

iptables was written by Rusty Russell, who is also the author of the ipchains tool. The work was sponsored by Watchguard (`www.watchguard.com`), and the community is supported by Penguin Computing (`antarctica.penguincomputing.com/~netfilter/`), the Samba Team and SGI (`www.samba.org/netfilter/`), and Jim Pick (`netfilter.kernelnotes.org`). The Samba Team also maintains a mailing list (see `lists.samba.org` for more details).

An Overview of iptables and Netfilter

Netfilter is a kernel module for the 2.4 kernel series, and it is responsible for packet filtering. It looks at the headers of each packet moving through the gateway and makes a decision about what to do with them. Packets might be accepted (passed along to the routing process or the receiving protocol stack), dropped (not forwarded), or they might have some more complicated action taken. People choose to filter their traffic for many reasons. The most common reasons include segregating network traffic, securing an internal network, providing NAT for internal hosts, and controlling internal users' access to external services.

Netfilter starts with three sets of rules: INPUT, OUTPUT, and FORWARD. These rule sets are called *chains* (short for firewall chains). Traffic moves through these chains as shown in Figure 11.8.

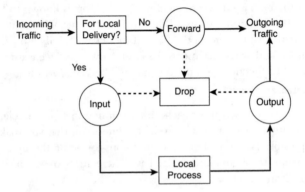

Figure 11.8   IP traffic moving through the firewall chains.

Each chain represents a list of rules that are consulted sequentially for each packet. As traffic moves through a rule chain, it is examined to determine what to do with it. If it is accepted, it passes to the next point in the diagram. If it is dropped, the packet stops there. If a rule doesn't specify what to do with a packet, the packet is examined by the next rule.

Setting Up iptables

The first step in setting up iptables is to build the appropriate kernel modules. These can either be built as separate modules or included in the kernel. To build them into the kernel, answer 'Y' to the question CONFIG_NETFILTER during kernel configuration on any kernel of 2.3.15 or better. You might find that there are additional kernel modules you want to build and install (such as ip_conntrack_ftp).

With the necessary kernel modules available, you can build and install the userspace tools. You can download iptables from `netfilter.kernelnotes.org` or either of the other sites mentioned previously. After downloaded, iptables follows the normal `configure`, `make`, `make install` pattern.

You can use the set of rules shown in Example 11.4 to test[1] your newly installed iptables and netfilter.

Example 11.4   **A Test Script for iptables**

```
# create a new table
iptables -N GATE

# set up rules for it
iptables -A GATE -m state —state ESTABLISHED, RELATED -j ACCEPT
iptables -A GATE -i eth0 -s 192.168.1.20 -j LOG —log-prefix \
  "connection from test bad machine, dropping:"
iptables -A GATE -s 192.168.1.20 -j DROP
iptables -A GATE -s 192.168.1.21 -j LOG —log-prefix \
  "connection from test good machine, accepting:"
iptables -A GATE -J LOG —log-prefix "Accepting packet:"
iptables -A GATE -j DROP

# apply it to the INPUT and FORWARD chains.
iptables -A INPUT -j GATE
```

After you've installed these rules, you can test them by trying to connect from 192.168.1.20 and 192.168.1.21. The first connection should fail (with a log entry), and the second should succeed (also with a log entry). If this happens, everything is fine and you can flush the rules:

```
iptables -F GATE
iptables -X GATE
iptables -F INPUT
```

Now that the tools have been built, installed, and verified you can configure them for use at your site.

iptables at Work

Before you start writing iptables rules, it is important to sit down and think about three things: What policy are you trying to implement, how can you keep the rules and chains manageable, and how can you keep the rules as efficient as possible without making them unmanageable. If the rules you write don't implement the policy you're trying to enforce, they might as well not be there. If you (and your coworkers) can't read and maintain the rules, someone is going to break them. If they don't work efficiently, they will throttle your network.

As important as efficiency is, we tend to overlook a major component of it—human time. If your rules are hard to read and understand, they will take a great deal of human time to maintain. In addition, as they get hairy, your chances of making a mistake increase dramatically. I don't like working late into the weekend trying to figure out why a needlessly complex set of rules isn't working the way I want it to, and I'm sure you don't either.

Remember that each rule a packet must traverse takes time. When you have lots of packets going through your packet filter, the little chunks of time add up. Keeping this in mind, you should make sure that (as much as possible) the rules that will be used most often should be the first rules in the chain. In addition, the more bytes you check in the packet headers the more work you're going to do. This means that again, you want to ensure that each rule checks as few bytes as possible—without compromising your security.

In order to actually work with your chains, you'll need to use the switches in Table 11.3.

Table 11.3 **iptables Chain Operations**

Switch	Function
-N	Creates a new rule chain.
-L	Lists the rules in a chain.
-P	Changes the policy for a built-in chain.
-Z	Zeroes the byte and packet counters in a chain.
-F	Flushes all the rules from a chain.
-X	Deletes an empty chain (except the built-in chains).

In addition to operations on chains, you also need to perform operations on individual rules within a chain. Table 11.4 shows some of the major operations on rules within a chain and the switches needed to invoke them. (Notice that these rules actually operate on the chain itself, modifying the content of the chain on a rule-by-rule basis.)

Table 11.4 **iptables Rule Operations**

Switch	Function
-A	Adds this rule to the end of a chain.
-I	Inserts this rule at the specified point in the chain.
-R	Replaces a rule at the specified point in the chain.
-D	Deletes a rule; can be specified by number or by matching content.

Using the rule and chains options from Table 11.4, you can start to modify the built-in chains or add your own. The additional information you'll need is in the following sections. Let's start by dissecting one of the rules from our GATE chain used in the preceding tests.

```
iptables -A GATE -s 192.168.1.20 -j DROP
```

The `-A GATE` statement means that this is a new rule being added to the end of the GATE chain. The `-s 192.168.1.20` statement applies this rule to any packet with a source address of 192.168.1.20. The `-j DROP` tells netfilter to drop this packet without further processing. Each rule that you build will follow this basic pattern.

Filtering by Address

In our example rule, we defined a source address with the `-s` option. This option can also be used to define a range of addresses using a network mask:

`-s 192.168.1.0/24`

or a hostname:

`-s crashtestdummy`

In addition to source addresses, we can also filter by destination address with the `-d` switch. (−source, −src, −destination, and −dst are all legal forms of this switch as well.)

Filtering by Interface

Instead of filtering by address, you can also define filters by the interface. `-i` and −in- interface define inbound interfaces, while `-o` and −out-interface define outbound interfaces.

The INBOUND chain only matches inbound interfaces and the OUTBOUND chain only matches outbound interfaces. The FORWARD chain can match either. If you define a non-existent interface, it will not match any packets until (or unless) that interface is brought up. There is also a special interface matching wildcard— the + indicates any interface matching the string preceding it:

`-o eth+`

That matches any packet destined to be sent out any Ethernet interface.

Filtering by Protocol

Protocols can be matched as well by using the `-p` switch. You can identify protocols either by the (IP) protocol number or (for the TCP, UDP, and ICMP) by its name. To specify all ICMP traffic, you could use

`-p ICMP`

Inverting a Selection

Sometimes it is easier to say "anything that isn't foo" than it is to specify all the individual things you want to talk about. iptables allows for this with an inversion prefix. To invert a selection, you use !. Selecting anything that doesn't come from the 192.168.1.0/24 network would look like this:

```
-s ! 192.168.1.0/24
```

Creating Your Own Selection Criteria

iptables is designed to be extensible, so you can define your own criteria. Definitions can be based upon existing TCP, UDP, ICMP, State, or other extensions.

TCP extensions include examination of TCP Flags and TCP Source and Destination Ports. To look for the SYN and ACK flags being set without any other flags being turned on, you could do this:

```
-p tcp —tcp-flags ALL SYN,ACK
```

To look for connections to X servers, you could do this:

```
-p tcp —destination-port 6000-6010
```

A —source-port extension is also provided. Both of these extensions allow four kinds of port listings: a single port, a range of ports (as above), all ports at or above a listed port (1024-), or all ports at or below a listed port (-1024).

UDP extensions are similar, but include only the —destination-port and —source-port options from the TCP extensions.

ICMP extensions provide searching of the ICMP Type and Code with the —icmp-type switch. ICMP Type name, the numeric value of the Type, or the Type and Code separated by a "/" are all allowed. To search for an ICMP Redirect for Host, you could do this:

```
-p icmp —icmp-type 5/1
```

Inspection of a connection's state can determine whether a packet is requesting a new connection, related to an existing connection (such as an ICMP error message), part of an existing connection, or indeterminate. To search for packets that are requesting new connections, you could do this:

```
-m state —state NEW
```

Defining and Using Chains

In our testing example, we created a new chain called GATE and applied it to both the INPUT and FORWARD chains. The flow of traffic through the INPUT chain looks something like Figure 11.9 after we've added these rules.

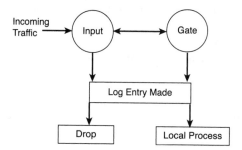

Figure 11.9 Flow of traffic through a netfilter chain.

We created the chain and set it into motion with the following steps:

1. Create the chain.
2. Add rules to it.
3. Apply the chain.

Creating the chain was done with the following command:

```
iptables -N GATE
```

The name is not required to be all uppercase, but cannot be the name of an existing rule chain.

Rules were added sequentially in our example, but we could have inserted them in any order using the -I switch instead. We could have also deleted or replaced existing rules had we so desired.

After the rules were written, we applied the rule with the following command:

```
iptables -A INPUT -j GATE
```

This command adds a rule to the INPUT chain that causes traffic to jump to the GATE chain for further processing. If you don't do this, no traffic will ever be checked by your rule chain!

Special Handling

At times you will want to log traffic that moves through your packet filter. This logging can take up a great deal of disk space, so it is normally done only on a reduced basis. Three switches are of special importance when logging. We used one of these options in the logging rules in our example.

```
iptables -A GATE -J LOG —log-prefix "Accepting packet:"
```

After declaring that packets matching this rule were to be logged, we gave the —log-prefix switch to prepend some text onto our log entries. The other switch used when logging is —log-level, which takes a syslog-style logging level as an argument, and directs the logging to that logging level. Because logging can take up so much disk space, it is most often used with the -m limit option as well. This command will limit the number of matches to a default of three matches per hour, with a burst of 5 matches.

When a packet is dropped, it is dropped silently. If you want to send an ICMP Port Unreachable message, you can specify that the packet be rejected with this:

```
-J REJECT
```

If you want to use multiple chains in conjunction with each other, you don't want to end a chain by dropping all remaining packets. Instead, you can pass control of the packet back to the parent chain with this:

```
-J RETURN
```

If this rule is hit and the chain is built-in, the default policy is executed. If the rule is hit in a user-defined chain, the packet begins to traverse the parent chain again at the point it jumped out to the current chain.

Xinetd

Xinetd is designed to be a secure replacement for the inetd program. It provides a more secure method for providing access to Internet services through a master daemon along with a number of other useful facilities. Xinetd was originally written by Panagiotis Tsirigotis (panos@cs.colorado.edu). Currently, it is maintained by Rob Braun (bbraun@synack.net). It is supported by a web page at www.xinetd.org and a mailing list hosted at synak.net.

Xinetd, like inetd, runs as a "super-server," or a switchboard. It listens on a number of ports and starts daemons as appropriate for incoming requests. Xinetd goes beyond the functionality of inetd in many ways. It takes advantage of its role as a switchboard operator to do a variety of things before it ever hands control off to the application daemon. Some of this functionality is used to create a more secure environment; other bits just make life better (or easier) for you, the administrator.

One of the most common tasks Xinetd performs is access control. Connections to a host can be allowed or disallowed based on the domain, name, or address of the remote host, and/or the time of access. If desired, Xinetd can be compiled with libwrap support to use the hosts.allow and hosts.deny files. Xinetd even allows you to bind specific services to specific IP addresses.

Xinetd is also used to prevent *denial of services* (DoS) attacks. Because it is looking at all the connections into a host instead of just one connection, Xinetd can limit the number of connections to given services. You can also set connection limits based on distinct client hosts.

One of the real strengths of Xinetd is its extensive logging capability. You can configure logging for each service individually. If you want to avoid syslog, you can write logs to log files directly. You can log information about failed connection attempts. You can even use Xinetd to log the connect and disconnect times of each connection.

Xinetd allows you to redirect TCP connections to a different host. These connections continue to run through the original host, so you could use this functionality to provide services from a privately addressed machine to the Internet.

Getting and Installing xinetd

Xinetd is now part of a stock Red Hat 7 system, but getting and building it is pretty straightforward as well. The sources are available from www.xinetd.org. There are currently two flavors: the stable release and the development release. Make sure that you grab the stable release.

Building Xinetd follows the normal `configure, make, make install` procedure. On a Red Hat 6.2 system it built and installed without any errors. If you do run into problems, please try the mailing list (see the section "What If I Have Problems" for information about subscribing).

The extra functionality provided by Xinetd means that it needs more information in its configuration file than inetd does. The two file formats are not interchangeable. A tool is provided to convert your existing `/etc/inetd.conf`, though, so things are relatively painless. To perform the conversion, do the following:

```
[root@cherry sbin]$ ./xconv.pl < inetd.conf > /etc/xinetd.conf
```

The resulting file is probably not exactly what you want, but it should work. The next section deals with making Xinetd do what you want it to.

Xinetd at Work

We'll take a small inetd.conf file and run it through xconv.pl to come up with a basic xinetd.conf. From there, we'll make incremental changes to our xinetd.conf to get it into shape for our own network.

A Basic Configuration

We'll start with a very short inetd.conf file, as shown in Example 11.5.

Example 11.5   **A Basic inetd.conf**

```
echo          stream  tcp    nowait  root    internal
echo    dgram   udp    wait    root    internal
ftp     stream  tcp    nowait  root    /usr/sbin/in.ftpd        in.ftpd -l -a
telnet  stream  tcp    nowait  root    /usr/sbin/in.telnet     in.telnetd
imap    stream  tcp    nowait  root    /usr/sbin/imapd imapd
finger  stream  tcp    nowait  nobody  /usr/local/sbin/my_safe.fingerd in.fingerd
```

This config file only runs four external services on an internal service to the TCP protocol. After running xconv.pl on it, we get the xinetd.conf file shown in Example 11.6.

Example 11.6 **The Converted xinetd.conf**

```
# The file is merely a translation of your inetd.conf file into
# the equivalent in xinetd.conf syntax.  xinetd has many
# features that may not be taken advantage of with this translation.

# The defaults section sets some information for all services
defaults
{
        #The maximum number of requests a particular service may handle
        # at once.
        instances    = 25

        # The type of logging.  This logs to a file that is specified.
        # Another option is: SYSLOG syslog_facility [syslog_level]
        log_type     = FILE /var/log/servicelog

        # What to log when the connection succeeds.
        # PID logs the pid of the server processing the request.
        # HOST logs the remote host's ip address.
        # USERID logs the remote user (using RFC 1413)
        # EXIT logs the exit status of the server.
        # DURATION logs the duration of the session.
        log_on_success = HOST PID

        # What to log when the connection fails.  Same options as above
        log_on_failure = HOST RECORD

        # The maximum number of connections a specific IP address can
        # have to a specific service.
        per_source   = 5
}

service echo
{
        flags       = REUSE NAMEINARGS
        socket_type = stream
        protocol    = tcp
        wait        = no
        user        = root
        type        = INTERNAL
        id          = echo-stream
```

```
}

service ftp
{
        flags       = REUSE NAMEINARGS
        socket_type = stream
        protocol    = tcp
        wait        = no
        user        = root
        server      = /usr/sbin/in.ftpd
        server_args = in.ftpd -l -a
}

service telnet
{
        flags       = REUSE NAMEINARGS
        socket_type = stream
        protocol    = tcp
        wait        = no
        user        = root
        server      = /usr/sbin/in.telnetd
        server_args = in.telnetd
}

service imap
{
        flags       = REUSE NAMEINARGS
        socket_type = stream
        protocol    = tcp
        wait        = no
        user        = root
        server      = /usr/sbin/imapd
        server_args = imapd
}

service finger
{
        flags       = REUSE NAMEINARGS
        socket_type = stream
        protocol    = tcp
        wait        = no
        user        = nobody
        server      = /usr/local/sbin/my_safe.fingerd
        server_args = my_safe.fingerd
}
```

This config file really doesn't do everything we want it to, so we'll make some changes to it. First, we only want 1 ftp connection at a time. Second, we're only going to allow telnet sessions from internal hosts (they'll have 192.168.1.0/24 addresses). We'll log all finger connections and connect them to /usr/local/my_safe.fingerd. Because we're not running imap on this host, we'll redirect all imap sessions to our imap server at 192.168.1.10.

Throttling ftp connections is fairly straightforward. We'll modify the ftp section to look like that shown in Example 11.7.

Example 11.7 **Defining ftp**

```
service ftp
{
        flags        = REUSE NAMEINARGS
socket_type = stream
        protocol     = tcp
        wait         = no
        user         = root
        server       = /usr/sbin/in.ftpd
        server_args  = in.ftpd -l -a
        instances    = 1
}
```

Controlling access is also straightforward. We'll modify the telnet session to match Example 11.8.

Example 11.8 **Defining Access Control for telnet**

```
service telnet
{
        flags        = REUSE NAMEINARGS
        socket_type = stream
        protocol     = tcp
        wait         = no
        user         = root
        server       = /usr/sbin/in.telnetd
        server_args  = in.telnetd
        only_from    = 192.168.1.0/24
}
```

What if we wanted to disallow connection from hosts within our local subnet during non-work hours? The following line could be added at the end of the section (after the only_from line):

```
access_time = 08:00-18:00
```

Similarly, you could disallow certain connections all the time by adding the rule:

```
# this guy is trouble
    no_access  = 192.168.1.20
```

We're logging information by default, but we're going to try and capture extra information about finger users. Example 11.9 shows how to do this.

Example 11.9   **Capturing _finger_ Data**

```
service finger
{
        flags       = REUSE NAMEINARGS
        socket_type = stream
        protocol    = tcp
        wait        = no
        user        = nobody
        server      = /usr/local/sbin/my_safe.fingerd
        server_args = my_safe.fingerd
        log_on_success = PID HOST USERID
}
```

Finally, to redirect imap users to the right place, we'll make the changes shown in Example 11.10.

Example 11.10   **Redirect imap Users**

```
service imap
{
        flags       = REUSE NAMEINARGS
        socket_type = stream
        protocol    = tcp
        wait        = no
        user        = root
        redirect    = 192.168.1.10 143
}
```

What If I Have Problems?

If you run into problems in installing, setting up, or using Xinetd, you should subscribe to the mailing list and ask for help.[2] You can subscribe by sending mail to majordomo@synack.net with a body of "subscribe xinetd".

> **If You Subscribe**
>
> When there, please try to make a good bug report. Be specific, include all the pertinent information, and be polite! Remember that the folks who will be answering your questions are just folks volunteering their time. They will get annoyed, and might ignore you entirely if you can't be bothered to write a decent note describing your problem, what you've done, and indicating that you've at least tried to read the docs.

tcp wrappers

tcp wrappers are a security tool for protecting access to internet services spawned by inetd or a similar daemon. By invoking tcpd instead of the standard daemon for the service, access control can be implemented on a host-by-host and service-by-service basis. tcp wrappers can be used in conjunction with Xinetd (see the previous section for more information on Xinetd) to provide an even greater level of security.

tcp wrappers are installed by default on most modern Linux distributions. They are not configured to provide any real protection though. In the remainder of this section, we'll look at using tcp rappers to make your system (or systems) more secure. To do this, we'll need to review how inetd works and then revise that system by introducing tcpd.

Instead of running a separate daemon for each service provided by a host, Unix and Linux run a "switchboard daemon" called *inetd*.[3] This daemon listens to many ports, and when it receives a request on a given port, it spawns the appropriate daemon to service that request. The list of ports it listens to, and the daemons associated with that port, are given in /etc/inetd.conf and use the following syntax (both the syntax and an example are given):

```
# <service_name> <sock_type> <proto> <flags> <user> <server_path> <args>
echo    stream  tcp    nowait  root    internal
```

In this example, the echo service (a built-in service of the TCP and UDP protocol stacks) is defined for TCP. inetd will look up the port number for echo in the /etc/services file:

```
echo            7/tcp
```

Then, whenever a TCP connection request is received on TCP port 7, inetd will hand the request to the echo server built into the TCP protocol stack. This same model is followed for every service listed in /etc/inetd.conf.

tcp wrappers are used by replacing the `<server_path>` portion of the /etc/inetd.conf entry with /usr/sbin/tcpd. The telnet service would be run through tcp wrappers like this:

```
telnet     stream  tcp    nowait  root    /usr/sbin/tcpd  in.telnetd
```

tcp wrappers will then check the IP address of the connecting client against its list of allowed and denied host rules. The allowed host rules are checked first, then the denied hosts. The checks stop at the first matching rule. If all the rules are processed without the connection being explicitly allowed or denied, the connection will be allowed.

As you can probably guess from the name, tcp wrappers are only suitable for protecting TCP-based services.[4] Because UDP does not create sessions, tcp wrappers are not used to control the start up of individual daemons. If you want to control access to UDP services, you should refer to the section "iptables" for more detail on how to set up a true packet filter.

tcp wrappers at Work

To put tcp wrappers to work, we'll take a look at where we might use it, create a policy for a host, and convert /etc/inetd.conf to implement that policy with tcp wrappers.

tcp wrappers is a good solution for providing security for a group of hosts behind a more involved firewall, or for a single host that is connected to the Internet intermittently. In the latter case, some thought should be given to using packet filtering tools as well as (or instead of) tcp wrappers. If you are using tcp wrappers to protect more than one host, remember that you will have to configure and maintain it on each host.

For our example, we'll look at a single host that is already behind a firewall. It is part of the IS LAN (192.168.1.0/24) and should provide only talk and echo services to any host internally (192.168.1.0/21) through inetd. Any host on the IS LAN or on the Data Center LAN (192.168.1.1/24) should also be able to use the finger service. Connectivity and file transfer are provided via SSH and HTTP, which are not run through inetd.

We'll start with a stripped down inetd.conf, which we can then modify to use tcp wrappers. This is shown in Example 11.11.

Example 11.11 **An *inetd.conf* Without tcp wrappers**

```
#
# inetd.conf  — this is a minimal inetd.conf for an IS machine.
#
echo    stream  tcp    nowait  root     internal
echo    dgram   udp    wait    root     internal
talk    dgram   udp    wait    nobody.tty      /usr/sbin/in.talkd      in.talkd
ntalk   dgram   udp    wait    nobody.tty      /usr/sbin/in.ntalkd     in.ntalkd
finger  stream  tcp    nowait  nobody /usr/sbin/in.fingerd      in.fingerd
```

The `echo` servers will not need to be changed because they are internal to the protocol stack. The `talk` and `ntalk` servers cannot be protected by tcp wrappers because they are UDP services. Fortunately, these services are going to be universally provided to internal hosts, so we will rely on our firewall to keep outside connections from getting in. `finger` is to be limited to only those users in the 192.168.1.0/23 address range.[5] This service is TCP-based, so we can use tcp wrappers to control access to it.

Our first step will be to modify `inetd.conf` to look like the one shown in Example 11.12.

Example 11.12 **Using tcp wrappers in** *inetd.conf*

```
#
echo    stream  tcp   nowait   root      internal
echo    dgram   udp   wait     root      internal
talk    dgram   udp   wait     nobody.tty       /usr/sbin/in.talkd     in.talkd
ntalk   dgram   udp   wait     nobody.tty       /usr/sbin/in.ntalkd    in.ntalkd
finger  stream  tcp   nowait   nobody /usr/sbin/tcpd  in.fingerd
```

This by itself will not control access. Our next step is to create entries in the /etc/hosts.allow and /etc/hosts.deny files to enforce the access controls we want. Our `hosts.allow` should look like this:

```
finger : 192.168.0.0/255.255.254.0
```

And our `hosts.deny` should look like this:

```
finger : ALL
```

After these files are in place, we can restart inetd, and we'll have implemented our policy on one host. We'll still need to go to each host on the IS LAN and make the same set of changes.

OPIE

One-time Passwords In Everything (OPIE) provides a more secure login environment without requiring encrypted traffic to be sent between hosts. It is based on the s/key system designed at Bell Labs, and was written at the Naval Research Labs.

Getting and Installing OPIE

OPIE can be had from `http://www.inner.net`. The most recent version as of this writing was 2.32. After downloading, building OPIE is a three-step process. If I've downloaded OPIE into /usr/local/src, I'd do the following:

```
# ./configure
# make
# make install
```

At this point, the real work begins: You need to get any users who will be using the
OPIE server to run `opiepassword` to generate an initial pass-phrase. It is important
that this is only done on a secure terminal.

Configuring OPIE

The server side of OPIE is taken care of when you do the `make install` step of the
installation. Each user must be separately added to the OPIE database. This is done
with the `opiepasswd` command, as shown in Example 11.13.

Example 11.13 **Using** *opiepasswd*

```
[pate@cherry sgml]$ opiepasswd -n 497 -c
Updating pate:
Reminder  -  Only  use  this method from the console;
NEVER from remote. If you
are using telnet, xterm, or a dial-in, type ^C now or
exit with no password.
Then run opiepasswd without the -c parameter.
Using MD5 to compute responses.
Enter old secret pass phrase:
Enter new secret pass phrase:
Again new secret pass phrase:

ID pate OPIE key is 497 cr1997
PHI CLAY MOOD VOID ELI BIRD
[pate@cherry sgml]$
```

OPIE at Work

After you've got OPIE installed and configured, the fun begins. When you telnet in to
the opiefied box, you'll go through the process shown in Example 11.14.

Example 11.14 **Connecting to a Remote Host with OPIE**

```
[pate@cherry sgml]$ telnet 192.168.1.20
Trying 192.168.1.20...
Connected to 192.168.1.20.
Escape character is '^]'.
Red Hat Linux release 6.2 (Zoot)
Kernel 2.2.14-5.0 on an i586
patelogin:
login: pate
otp-md5 497 cr1997 ext
```

continues

Example 11.14   **Continued**

```
Response: phi clay mood void eli bird
Last login: Fri Sep  1 05:27:20 from crashtestdummy

[pate@crashtestdummy pate]$
```

The actual response is generated from the otp-md5[6] program is given in Example 11.15.

Example 11.15   **Using otp5 on Your Local Host**

```
[pate@cherry pate]$ otp5 497 cr1997
Using the MD5 algorithm to compute response.
Reminder:  Don't use opiekey from telnet or dial-in sessions
Enter secret pass phrase:
PHI CLAY MOOD VOID ELI BIRD
[pate@cherry pate]$
```

The reminder shown in this output is important. OPIE does not do any encryption of your traffic, so if you were to use opiekey (under any of its names) you would be divulging your pass phrase to anyone capable of seeing the packets you're sending. In fact, if I tried to run this same command from my telnet session into crashtestdummy, it would fail with an error reminding that I was not on a secure terminal.

Endnotes

1. This set of rules is not something you'd want to use in real life, it is meant only to help exercise your installation of the tools.

2. Okay, you should go subscribe to the mailing list anyway. Go, do it now. I'll wait right here.

3. There are several replacements for inetd, including Xinetd, which is discussed in the section "Xinetd" in this chapter.

4. This is not entirely true; tcp wrappers can be used to control initial access to UDP-based services. Most of the services require that the daemon be left running for a short period of time after the most recent connection. This means that only the connections which require a daemon to be started will be logged and subjected to testing.

5. This is not a subnet mask. I'm using the CIDR-style notation to indicate the range of addresses used by the IS and Data Center LANs.

6. otp-md5 is actually another name for opiekey. Using it this way indicates that you are using md5-style encryption to generate the response from the pass phrase.

RFC-1122

Network Working Group—Internet Engineering Task Force
Request for Comments: 1122 R. Braden, Editor
October 1989

Requirements for Internet Hosts— Communication Layers

Status of This Memo

This RFC is an official specification for the Internet community. It incorporates by reference, amends, corrects, and supplements the primary protocol standards documents relating to hosts. Distribution of this document is unlimited.

Summary

This is one RFC of a pair that defines and discusses the requirements for Internet host software. This RFC covers the communications protocol layers: link layer, IP layer, and transport layer; its companion RFC-1123 covers the application and support protocols.

Table of Contents

1. INTRODUCTION

This document is one of a pair that defines and discusses the requirements for host system implementations of the Internet protocol suite. This RFC covers the communication protocol layers: link layer, IP layer, and transport layer. Its companion RFC, "Requirements for Internet Hosts—Application and Support" [INTRO:1], covers the application layer protocols. This document should also be read in conjunction with "Requirements for Internet Gateways" [INTRO:2].

These documents are intended to provide guidance for vendors, implementors, and users of Internet communication software. They represent the consensus of a large body of technical experience and wisdom, contributed by the members of the Internet research and vendor communities.

This RFC enumerates standard protocols that a host connected to the Internet must use, and it incorporates by reference the RFCs and other documents describing the current specifications for these protocols. It corrects errors in the referenced documents and adds additional discussion and guidance for an implementor.

For each protocol, this document also contains an explicit set of requirements, recommendations, and options. The reader must understand that the list of requirements in this document is incomplete by itself; the complete set of requirements for an Internet host is primarily defined in the standard protocol specification documents, with the corrections, amendments, and supplements contained in this RFC.

A good-faith implementation of the protocols that was produced after careful reading of the RFCs and with some interaction with the Internet technical community, and that followed good communications software engineering practices, should differ from the requirements of this document in only minor ways. Thus, in many cases, the "requirements" in this RFC are already stated or implied in the standard protocol documents, so that their inclusion here is, in a sense, redundant. However, they were included because some past implementation has made the wrong choice, causing problems of interoperability, performance, and/or robustness.

This document includes discussion and explanation of many of the requirements and recommendations. A simple list of requirements would be dangerous, because:

- Some required features are more important than others, and some features are optional.

- There may be valid reasons why particular vendor products that are designed for restricted contexts might choose to use different specifications.

However, the specifications of this document must be followed to meet the general goal of arbitrary host interoperation across the diversity and complexity of the Internet system. Although most current implementations fail to meet these requirements in various ways, some minor and some major, this specification is the ideal towards which we need to move.

These requirements are based on the current level of Internet architecture. This document will be updated as required to provide additional clarifications or to include additional information in those areas in which specifications are still evolving.

This introductory section begins with a brief overview of the Internet architecture as it relates to hosts, and then gives some general advice to host software vendors. Finally, there is some guidance on reading the rest of the document and some terminology.

1.1 The Internet Architecture

General background and discussion on the Internet architecture and supporting protocol suite can be found in the DDN Protocol Handbook [INTRO:3]; for background see for example [INTRO:9], [INTRO:10], and [INTRO:11]. Reference [INTRO:5] describes the procedure for obtaining Internet protocol documents, while [INTRO:6] contains a list of the numbers assigned within Internet protocols.

1.1.1 Internet Hosts

A host computer, or simply "host," is the ultimate consumer of communication services. A host generally executes application programs on behalf of user(s), employing network and/or Internet communication services in support of this function.

An Internet host corresponds to the concept of an "End-System" used in the OSI protocol suite [INTRO:13].

An Internet communication system consists of interconnected packet networks supporting communication among host computers using the Internet protocols. The networks are interconnected using packet-switching computers called "gateways" or "IP routers" by the Internet community, and "Intermediate Systems" by the OSI world [INTRO:13]. The RFC "Requirements for Internet Gateways" [INTRO:2] contains the official specifications for Internet gateways. That RFC together with the present document and its companion [INTRO:1] define the rules for the current realization of the Internet architecture.

Internet hosts span a wide range of size, speed, and function. They range in size from small microprocessors through workstations to mainframes and supercomputers. In function, they range from single-purpose hosts (such as terminal servers) to full-service hosts that support a variety of online network services, typically including remote login, file transfer, and electronic mail.

A host is generally said to be multihomed if it has more than one interface to the same or to different networks. See Section 1.3.3 on "Terminology."

1.1.2 Architectural Assumptions

The current Internet architecture is based on a set of assumptions about the communication system. The assumptions most relevant to hosts are as follows:

- The Internet is a network of networks—Each host is directly connected to some particular network(s); its connection to the Internet is only conceptual. Two hosts on the same network communicate with each other using the same set of protocols that they would use to communicate with hosts on distant networks.

- Gateways don't keep connection state information—To improve robustness of the communication system, gateways are designed to be stateless, forwarding each IP datagram independently of other datagrams. As a result, redundant paths can be exploited to provide robust service in spite of failures of intervening gateways and networks. All state information required for end-to-end flow control and reliability is implemented in the hosts, in the transport layer or in application programs. All connection control information is thus co-located with the end points of the communication, so it will be lost only if an end point fails.

- Routing complexity should be in the gateways—Routing is a complex and difficult problem, and ought to be performed by the gateways, not the hosts. An important objective is to insulate host software from changes caused by the inevitable evolution of the Internet routing architecture.

- The system must tolerate wide network variation—A basic objective of the Internet design is to tolerate a wide range of network characteristics—e.g., bandwidth, delay, packet loss, packet reordering, and maximum packet size. Another objective is robustness against failure of individual networks, gateways, and hosts, using whatever bandwidth is still available. Finally, the goal is full "open system interconnection": an Internet host must be able to interoperate robustly and effectively with any other Internet host, across diverse Internet paths. Sometimes host implementors have designed for less ambitious goals. For example, the LAN environment is typically much more benign than the Internet as a whole; LANs have low packet loss and delay and do not reorder packets. Some vendors have fielded host implementations that are adequate for a simple LAN environment, but work badly for general interoperation. The vendor justifies such a product as being economical within the restricted LAN market. However, isolated LANs seldom stay isolated for long; they are soon gatewayed to each other, to organization-wide internets, and eventually to the global Internet system. In the end, neither the customer nor the vendor is served by incomplete or substandard Internet host software. The requirements spelled out in this document are designed for a full-function Internet host, capable of full interoperation over an arbitrary Internet path.

1.1.3 Internet Protocol Suite

To communicate using the Internet system, a host must implement the layered set of protocols comprising the Internet protocol suite. A host typically must implement at least one protocol from each layer.

The protocol layers used in the Internet architecture are as follows [INTRO:4]:

- Application Layer—The application layer is the top layer of the Internet protocol suite. The Internet suite does not further subdivide the application layer, although some of the Internet application layer protocols do contain some internal sub-layering. The application layer of the Internet suite essentially combines the functions of the top two layers—Presentation and Application—of the OSI reference model. We distinguish two categories of application layer protocols: user protocols that provide service directly to users, and support protocols that provide common system functions. Requirements for user and support protocols will be found in the companion RFC [INTRO:1].

  The most common Internet user protocols are:

  - Telnet (remote login)
  - FTP (file transfer)
  - SMTP(electronic mail delivery)

  There are a number of other standardized user protocols [INTRO:4] and many private user protocols. Support protocols, used for host name mapping, booting, and management, include SNMP, BOOTP, RARP, and the Domain Name System (DNS) protocols.

- Transport Layer—The transport layer provides end-to-end communication services for applications. There are two primary transport layer protocols at present:

  - Transmission Control Protocol (TCP)
  - User Datagram Protocol (UDP)

  TCP is a reliable connection-oriented transport service that provides end-to-end reliability, resequencing, and flow control. UDP is a connectionless ("datagram") transport service. Other transport protocols have been developed by the research community, and the set of official Internet transport protocols may be expanded in the future. Transport layer protocols are discussed in Chapter 4.

- Internet Layer—All Internet transport protocols use the Internet Protocol (IP) to carry data from source host to destination host. IP is a connectionless or data-gram internetwork service, providing no end-to-end delivery guarantees. Thus, IP datagrams may arrive at the destination host damaged, duplicated, out of order, or not at all. The layers above IP are responsible for reliable delivery service when it is required. The IP protocol includes provision for addressing, type-of-service specification, fragmentation and reassembly, and security information. The datagram or connectionless nature of the IP protocol is a fundamental and characteristic feature of the Internet architecture. Internet IP was the model for the OSI Connectionless Network Protocol [INTRO:12]. ICMP is a control protocol that is considered to be an integral part of IP, although it is architecturally layered upon IP, i.e., it uses IP to carry its data end-to-end just as a transport protocol like TCP or UDP does. ICMP provides error reporting, congestion reporting, and first-hop gateway redirection. IGMP is an Internet layer protocol used for establishing dynamic host groups for IP multicasting. The Internet layer protocols IP, ICMP, and IGMP are discussed in Section 3.

- Link Layer—To communicate on its directly connected network, a host must implement the communication protocol used to interface to that network. We call this a link layer or media-access layer protocol. There is a wide variety of link layer protocols, corresponding to the many different types of networks. See Section 2.

1.1.4 Embedded Gateway Code

Some Internet host software includes embedded gateway functionality, so that these hosts can forward packets as a gateway would, while still performing the application layer functions of a host.

Such dual-purpose systems must follow the Gateway Requirements RFC [INTRO:2] with respect to their gateway functions, and must follow the present document with respect to their host functions. In all overlapping cases, the two specifications should be in agreement.

There are varying opinions in the Internet community about embedded gateway functionality. The main arguments are as follows:

- Pro: in a local network environment where networking is informal, or in isolated internets, it may be convenient and economical to use existing host systems as gateways. There is also an architectural argument for embedded gateway functionality: multihoming is much more common than originally foreseen, and multihoming forces a host to make routing decisions as if it were a gateway. If the multihomed host contains an embedded gateway, it will have full routing knowledge and as a result will be able to make more optimal routing decisions.

- Con: Gateway algorithms and protocols are still changing, and they will continue to change as the Internet system grows larger. Attempting to include a general gateway function within the host IP layer will force host system maintainers to track these (more frequent) changes. Also, a larger pool of gateway implementations will make coordinating the changes more difficult. Finally, the complexity of a gateway IP layer is somewhat greater than that of a host, making the implementation and operation tasks more complex. In addition, the style of operation of some hosts is not appropriate for providing stable and robust gateway service.

There is considerable merit in both of these viewpoints. One conclusion can be drawn: a host administrator must have conscious control over whether or not a given host acts as a gateway. See Section 3.1 for the detailed requirements.

1.2 General Considerations

There are two important lessons that vendors of Internet host software have learned and which a new vendor should consider seriously.

1.2.1 Continuing Internet Evolution

The enormous growth of the Internet has revealed problems of management and scaling in a large datagram-based packet communication system. These problems are being addressed, and as a result there will be continuing evolution of the specifications described in this document. These changes will be carefully planned and controlled, because there is extensive participation in this planning by the vendors and by the organizations responsible for operations of the networks.

Development, evolution, and revision are characteristic of computer network protocols today, and this situation will persist for some years. A vendor who develops computer communication software for the Internet protocol suite (or any other protocol suite!) and then fails to maintain and update that software for changing specifications is going to leave a trail of unhappy customers. The Internet is a large communication network, and the users are in constant contact through it. Experience has shown that knowledge of deficiencies in vendor software propagates quickly through the Internet technical community.

1.2.2 Robustness Principle

At every layer of the protocols, there is a general rule whose application can lead to enormous benefits in robustness and interoperability [IP:1]:

"Be liberal in what you accept, and conservative in what you send"

Software should be written to deal with every conceivable error, no matter how unlikely; sooner or later a packet will come in with that particular combination of errors and attributes, and unless the software is prepared, chaos can ensue. In general, it is best to assume that the network is filled with malevolent entities that will send in packets designed to have the worst possible effect. This assumption will lead to suitable protective design, although the most serious problems in the Internet have been caused by unenvisaged mechanisms triggered by low-probability events; mere human malice would never have taken so devious a course!

Adaptability to change must be designed into all levels of Internet host software. As a simple example, consider a protocol specification that contains an enumeration of values for a particular header field—e.g., a type field, a port number, or an error code; this enumeration must be assumed to be incomplete. Thus, if a protocol specification defines four possible error codes, the software must not break when a fifth code shows up. An undefined code might be logged (see below), but it must not cause a failure.

The second part of the principle is almost as important: software on other hosts may contain deficiencies that make it unwise to exploit legal but obscure protocol features. It is unwise to stray far from the obvious and simple, lest untoward effects result elsewhere. A corollary of this is "watch out for misbehaving hosts"; host software should be prepared, not just to survive other misbehaving hosts, but also to cooperate to limit the amount of disruption such hosts can cause to the shared communication facility.

1.2.3 Error Logging

The Internet includes a great variety of host and gateway systems, each implementing many protocols and protocol layers, and some of these contain bugs and misfeatures in their Internet protocol software. As a result of complexity, diversity, and distribution of function, the diagnosis of Internet problems is often very difficult. Problem diagnosis will be aided if host implementations include a carefully designed facility for logging erroneous or "strange" protocol events. It is important to include as much diagnostic information as possible when an error is logged. In particular, it is often useful to record the header(s) of a packet that caused an error. However, care must be taken to ensure that error logging does not consume prohibitive amounts of resources or otherwise interfere with the operation of the host.

There is a tendency for abnormal but harmless protocol events to overflow error logging files; this can be avoided by using a "circular" log, or by enabling logging only while diagnosing a known failure. It may be useful to filter and count duplicate successive messages. One strategy that seems to work well is: (1) always count abnormalities and make such counts accessible through the management protocol (see [INTRO:1]); and (2) allow the logging of a great variety of events to be selectively enabled. For example, it might useful to be able to "log everything" or to "log everything for host X."

Note that different management may have differing policies about the amount of error logging that they want normally enabled in a host. Some will say, "if it doesn't hurt me, I don't want to know about it," while others will want to take a more watchful and aggressive attitude about detecting and removing protocol abnormalities.

1.2.4 Configuration

It would be ideal if a host implementation of the Internet protocol suite could be entirely self-configuring. This would allow the whole suite to be implemented in ROM or cast into silicon, it would simplify diskless workstations, and it would be an immense boon to harried LAN administrators as well as system vendors. We have not reached this ideal; in fact, we are not even close.

At many points in this document, you will find a requirement that a parameter be a configurable option. There are several different reasons behind such requirements. In a few cases, there is current uncertainty or disagreement about the best value, and it may be necessary to update the recommended value in the future. In other cases, the value really depends on external factors—e.g., the size of the host and the distribution of its communication load, or the speeds and topology of nearby networks—and self-tuning algorithms are unavailable and may be insufficient. In some cases, configurability is needed because of administrative requirements.

Finally, some configuration options are required to communicate with obsolete or incorrect implementations of the protocols, distributed without sources, that unfortunately persist in many parts of the Internet. To make correct systems coexist with these faulty systems, administrators often have to "misconfigure" the correct systems. This problem will correct itself gradually as the faulty systems are retired, but it cannot be ignored by vendors.

When we say that a parameter must be configurable, we do not intend to require that its value be explicitly read from a configuration file at every boot time. We recommend that implementors set up a default for each parameter, so a configuration file is only necessary to override those defaults that are inappropriate in a particular installation. Thus, the configurability requirement is an assurance that it will be POSSIBLE to override the default when necessary, even in a binary-only or ROM-based product.

This document requires a particular value for such defaults in some cases. The choice of default is a sensitive issue when the configuration item controls the accommodation to existing faulty systems. If the Internet is to converge successfully to complete interoperability, the default values built into implementations must implement the official protocol, not "misconfigurations" to accommodate faulty implementations.

Although marketing considerations have led some vendors to choose misconfiguration defaults, we urge vendors to choose defaults that will conform to the standard.

Finally, we note that a vendor needs to provide adequate documentation on all configuration parameters, their limits and effects.

1.3 Reading this Document

1.3.1 Organization

Protocol layering, which is generally used as an organizing principle in implementing network software, has also been used to organize this document. In describing the rules, we assume that an implementation does strictly mirror the layering of the protocols. Thus, the following three major sections specify the requirements for the link layer, the internet layer, and the transport layer, respectively. A companion RFC [INTRO:1] covers application level software. This layerist organization was chosen for simplicity and clarity.

However, strict layering is an imperfect model, both for the protocol suite and for recommended implementation approaches. Protocols in different layers interact in complex and sometimes subtle ways, and particular functions often involve multiple layers. There are many design choices in an implementation, many of which involve creative "breaking" of strict layering. Every implementor is urged to read references [INTRO:7] and [INTRO:8].

This document describes the conceptual service interface between layers using a functional ("procedure call") notation, like that used in the TCP specification [TCP:1]. A host implementation must support the logical information flow implied by these calls, but need not literally implement the calls themselves. For example, many implementations reflect the coupling between the transport layer and the IP layer by giving them shared access to common data structures. These data structures, rather than explicit procedure calls, are then the agency for passing much of the information that is required.

In general, each major section of this document is organized into the following subsections:

1. Introduction

2. Protocol Walk-Through—Considers the protocol specification documents section-by-section, correcting errors, stating requirements that may be ambiguous or ill-defined, and providing further clarification or explanation.

3. Specific Issues—discusses protocol design and implementation issues that were not included in the walk-through.

4. Interfaces—Discusses the service interface to the next higher layer.

5. Summary—Contains a summary of the requirements of the section.

Under many of the individual topics in this document, there is parenthetical material labeled "DISCUSSION" or "IMPLEMENTATION." This material is intended to give clarification and explanation of the preceding requirement's text. It also includes some suggestions on possible future directions or developments. The implementation material contains suggested approaches that an implementor may want to consider.

The summary sections are intended to be guides and indexes to the text, but are necessarily cryptic and incomplete. The summaries should never be used or referenced separately from the complete RFC.

1.3.2 Requirements

In this document, the words that are used to define the significance of each particular requirement are capitalized. These words are:

- "MUST"—This word or the adjective "REQUIRED" means that the item is an absolute requirement of the specification.

- "SHOULD"—This word or the adjective "RECOMMENDED" means that there may exist valid reasons in particular circumstances to ignore this item, but the full implications should be understood and the case carefully weighed before choosing a different course.

- "MAY"—This word or the adjective "OPTIONAL" means that this item is truly optional. One vendor may choose to include the item because a particular marketplace requires it or because it enhances the product, for example; another vendor may omit the same item. An implementation is not compliant if it fails to satisfy one or more of the MUST requirements for the protocols it implements. An implementation that satisfies all the MUST and all the SHOULD requirements for its protocols is said to be "unconditionally compliant"; one that satisfies all the MUST requirements but not all the SHOULD requirements for its protocols is said to be "conditionally compliant."

1.3.3 Terminology

This document uses the following technical terms:

- Segment—A segment is the unit of end-to-end transmission in the TCP protocol. A segment consists of a TCP header followed by application data. A segment is transmitted by encapsulation inside an IP datagram.

- Message—In this description of the lower-layer protocols, a message is the unit of transmission in a transport layer protocol. In particular, a TCP segment is a message. A message consists of a transport protocol header followed by application protocol data. To be transmitted end-to-end through the Internet, a message must be encapsulated inside a datagram.

- IP Datagram—An IP datagram is the unit of end-to-end transmission in the IP protocol. An IP datagram consists of an IP header followed by transport layer data, i.e., of an IP header followed by a message. In the description of the internet layer (Section 3), the unqualified term "datagram" should be understood to refer to an IP datagram.

- Packet—A packet is the unit of data passed across the interface between the internet layer and the link layer. It includes an IP header and data. A packet may be a complete IP datagram or a fragment of an IP datagram.

- Frame—A frame is the unit of transmission in a link layer protocol, and consists of a link-layer header followed by a packet.

- Connected Network—A network to which a host is interfaced is often known as the "local network" or the "subnetwork" relative to that host. However, these terms can cause confusion, and therefore we use the term "connected network" in this document.

- Multihomed—A host is said to be multihomed if it has multiple IP addresses. For a discussion of multihoming, see Section 3.3.4.

- Physical network interface—This is a physical interface to a connected network and has a (possibly unique) link-layer address. Multiple physical network interfaces on a single host may share the same link-layer address, but the address must be unique for different hosts on the same physical network.

- Logical [network] interface—We define a logical [network] interface to be a logical path, distinguished by a unique IP address, to a connected network. See Section 3.3.4.

- Specific-destination address—This is the effective destination address of a datagram, even if it is broadcast or multicast; see Section 3.2.1.3.

- Path—At a given moment, all the IP datagrams from a particular source host to a particular destination host will typically traverse the same sequence of gateways. We use the term "path" for this sequence. Note that a path is unidirectional; it is not unusual to have different paths in the two directions between a given host pair.

- MTU—The maximum transmission unit, i.e., the size of the largest packet that can be transmitted.

The terms frame, packet, datagram, message, and segment are illustrated by the following schematic diagrams:

A. Transmission on connected network:

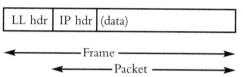

B. Before IP fragmentation or after IP reassembly:

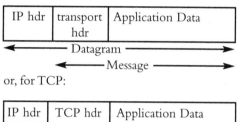

or, for TCP:

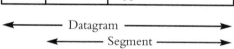

1.4 Acknowledgments

This document incorporates contributions and comments from a large group of Internet protocol experts, including representatives of university and research labs, vendors, and government agencies. It was assembled primarily by the Host Requirements Working Group of the Internet Engineering Task Force (IETF).

The Editor would especially like to acknowledge the tireless dedication of the following people, who attended many long meetings and generated 3 million bytes of electronic mail over the past 18 months in pursuit of this document: Philip Almquist, Dave Borman (Cray Research), Noel Chiappa, Dave Crocker (DEC), Steve Deering (Stanford), Mike Karels (Berkeley), Phil Karn (Bellcore), John Lekashman (NASA), Charles Lynn (BBN), Keith McCloghrie (TWG), Paul Mockapetris (ISI), Thomas Narten (Purdue), Craig Partridge (BBN), Drew Perkins (CMU), and James Van Bokkelen (FTP Software).

In addition, the following people made major contributions to the effort: Bill Barns (Mitre), Steve Bellovin (AT&T), Mike Brescia (BBN), Ed Cain (DCA), Annette DeSchon (ISI), Martin Gross (DCA), Phill Gross (NRI), Charles Hedrick (Rutgers), Van Jacobson (LBL), John Klensin (MIT), Mark Lottor (SRI), Milo Medin (NASA), Bill Melohn (Sun Microsystems), Greg Minshall (Kinetics), Jeff Mogul (DEC),

John Mullen (CMC), Jon Postel (ISI), John Romkey (Epilogue Technology), and Mike StJohns (DCA). The following also made significant contributions to particular areas: Eric Allman (Berkeley), Rob Austein (MIT), Art Berggreen (ACC), Keith Bostic (Berkeley), Vint Cerf (NRI), Wayne Hathaway (NASA), Matt Korn (IBM), Erik Naggum (Naggum Software, Norway), Robert Ullmann (Prime Computer), David Waitzman (BBN), Frank Wancho (USA), Arun Welch (Ohio State), Bill Westfield (Cisco), and Rayan Zachariassen (Toronto).

We are grateful to all, including any contributors who may have been inadvertently omitted from this list.

2. LINK LAYER

2.1 INTRODUCTION

All Internet systems, both hosts and gateways, have the same requirements for link layer protocols. These requirements are given in Chapter 3 of "Requirements for Internet Gateways" [INTRO:2], augmented with the material in this section.

2.2 PROTOCOL WALK-THROUGH

None.

2.3 SPECIFIC ISSUES

2.3.1 Trailer Protocol Negotiation

The trailer protocol [LINK:1] for link-layer encapsulation MAY be used, but only when it has been verified that both systems (host or gateway) involved in the link-layer communication implement trailers. If the system does not dynamically negotiate use of the trailer protocol on a per-destination basis, the default configuration MUST disable the protocol.

DISCUSSION:

The trailer protocol is a link-layer encapsulation technique that rearranges the data contents of packets sent on the physical network. In some cases, trailers improve the throughput of higher layer protocols by reducing the amount of data copying within the operating system. Higher layer protocols are unaware of trailer use, but both the sending and receiving host MUST understand the protocol if it is used.

Improper use of trailers can result in very confusing symptoms. Only packets with specific size attributes are encapsulated using trailers, and typically only a small fraction of the packets being exchanged have these attributes. Thus, if a system using trailers exchanges packets with a system that does not, some packets disappear into a black hole while others are delivered successfully.

IMPLEMENTATION:

On an Ethernet, packets encapsulated with trailers use a distinct Ethernet type [LINK:1], and trailer negotiation is performed at the time that ARP is used to discover the link-layer address of a destination system.

Specifically, the ARP exchange is completed in the usual manner using the normal IP protocol type, but a host that wants to speak trailers will send an additional "trailer ARP reply" packet, i.e., an ARP reply that specifies the trailer encapsulation protocol type but otherwise has the format of a normal ARP reply. If a host configured to use trailers receives a trailer ARP reply message from a remote machine, it can add that machine to the list of machines that understand trailers, e.g., by marking the corresponding entry in the ARP cache.

Hosts wishing to receive trailer encapsulations send trailer ARP replies whenever they complete exchanges of normal ARP messages for IP. Thus, a host that received an ARP request for its IP protocol address would send a trailer ARP reply in addition to the normal IP ARP reply; a host that sent the IP ARP request would send a trailer ARP reply when it received the corresponding IP ARP reply.

In this way, either the requesting or responding host in an IP ARP exchange may request that it receive trailer encapsulations.

This scheme, using extra trailer ARP reply packets rather than sending an ARP request for the trailer protocol type, was designed to avoid a continuous exchange of ARP packets with a misbehaving host that, contrary to any specification or common sense, responded to an ARP reply for trailers with another ARP reply for IP. This problem is avoided by sending a trailer ARP reply in response to an IP ARP reply only when the IP ARP reply answers an outstanding request; this is true when the hardware address for the host is still unknown when the IP ARP reply is received. A trailer ARP reply may always be sent along with an IP ARP reply responding to an IP ARP request.

2.3.2 Address Resolution Protocol—ARP

2.3.2.1 ARP Cache Validation

An implementation of the Address Resolution Protocol (ARP) [LINK:2] MUST provide a mechanism to flush out-of-date cache entries. If this mechanism involves a timeout, it SHOULD be possible to configure the timeout value.

A mechanism to prevent ARP flooding (repeatedly sending an ARP Request for the same IP address, at a high rate) MUST be included. The recommended maximum rate is 1 per second per destination.

DISCUSSION:

The ARP specification [LINK:2] suggests but does not require a timeout mechanism to invalidate cache entries when hosts change their Ethernet addresses. The prevalence of proxy ARP (see Section 2.4 of [INTRO:2]) has significantly increased the likelihood that cache entries in hosts will become invalid, and therefore some ARP-cache invalidation mechanism is now required for hosts. Even in the absence of proxy ARP, a long-period cache timeout is useful in order to automatically correct any bad ARP data that might have been cached.

IMPLEMENTATION:

Four mechanisms have been used, sometimes in combination, to flush out-of-date cache entries.

1. Timeout—Periodically time out cache entries, even if they are in use. Note that this timeout should be restarted when the cache entry is "refreshed" (by observing the source fields, regardless of target address, of an ARP broadcast from the system in question). For proxy ARP situations, the timeout needs to be on the order of a minute.

2. Unicast Poll—Actively poll the remote host by periodically sending a point-to-point ARP Request to it, and delete the entry if no ARP Reply is received from N successive polls. Again, the timeout should be on the order of a minute, and typically N is 2.

3. Link-Layer Advice—If the link-layer driver detects a delivery problem, flush the corresponding ARP cache entry.

4. Higher-layer Advice—Provide a call from the Internet layer to the link layer to indicate a delivery problem. The effect of this call would be to invalidate the corresponding cache entry. This call would be analogous to the "ADVISE_DELIVPROB()" call from the transport layer to the Internet layer (see Section 3.4), and in fact the ADVISE_DELIVPROB routine might in turn call the link-layer advice routine to invalidate the ARP cache entry.

Approaches (1) and (2) involve ARP cache timeouts on the order of a minute or less. In the absence of proxy ARP, a timeout this short could create noticeable overhead traffic on a very large Ethernet. Therefore, it may be necessary to configure a host to lengthen the ARP cache timeout.

2.3.2.2 ARP Packet Queue

The link layer SHOULD save (rather than discard) at least one (the latest) packet of each set of packets destined to the same unresolved IP address, and transmit the saved packet when the address has been resolved.

DISCUSSION:

Failure to follow this recommendation causes the first packet of every exchange to be lost. Although higher-layer protocols can generally cope with packet loss by retransmission, packet loss does impact performance. For example, loss of a TCP open request causes the initial round-trip time estimate to be inflated. UDP-based applications such as the Domain Name System are more seriously affected.

2.3.3 Ethernet and IEEE 802 Encapsulation

The IP encapsulation for Ethernets is described in RFC-894 [LINK:3], while RFC-1042 [LINK:4] describes the IP encapsulation for IEEE 802 networks. RFC-1042 elaborates and replaces the discussion in Section 3.4 of [INTRO:2].

Every Internet host connected to a 10Mbps Ethernet cable:

- MUST be able to send and receive packets using RFC-894 encapsulation

- SHOULD be able to receive RFC-1042 packets, intermixed with RFC-894 packets

- MAY be able to send packets using RFC-1042 encapsulation.

An Internet host that implements sending both the RFC-894 and the RFC-1042 encapsulations MUST provide a configuration switch to select which is sent, and this switch MUST default to RFC-894.

Note that the standard IP encapsulation in RFC-1042 does not use the protocol id value (K1=6) that IEEE reserved for IP; instead, it uses a value (K1=170) that implies an extension (the "SNAP") which can be used to hold the Ether-Type field.

An Internet system MUST NOT send 802 packets using K1=6. Address translation from Internet addresses to link-layer addresses on Ethernet and IEEE 802 networks MUST be managed by the Address Resolution Protocol (ARP).

The MTU for an Ethernet is 1500 and for 802.3 is 1492.

DISCUSSION:

The IEEE 802.3 specification provides for operation over a 10Mbps Ethernet cable, in which case Ethernet and IEEE 802.3 frames can be physically intermixed. A receiver can distinguish Ethernet and 802.3 frames by the value of the 802.3 Length field; this two-octet field coincides in the header with the Ether-Type field of an Ethernet frame. In particular, the 802.3 Length field must be less than or equal to 1500, while all valid Ether-Type values are greater than 1500.

Another compatibility problem arises with link-layer broadcasts. A broadcast sent with one framing will not be seen by hosts that can receive only the other framing. The provisions of this section were designed to provide direct interoperation between 894-capable and 1042-capable systems on the same cable, to the maximum extent possible. It is intended to support the present situation where 894-only systems predominate, while providing an easy transition to a possible future in which 1042-capable systems become common.

Note that 894-only systems cannot interoperate directly with 1042-only systems. If the two system types are set up as two different logical networks on the same cable, they can communicate only through an IP gateway.

Furthermore, it is not useful or even possible for a dual-format host to discover automatically which format to send, because of the problem of link-layer broadcasts.

2.4 LINK/INTERNET LAYER INTERFACE

The packet receive interface between the IP layer and the link layer MUST include a flag to indicate whether the incoming packet was addressed to a link-layer broadcast address.

DISCUSSION

Although the IP layer does not generally know link layer addresses (since every different network medium typically has a different address format), the broadcast address on a broadcast-capable medium is an important special case. See Section 3.2.2, especially the DISCUSSION concerning broadcast storms.

The packet send interface between the IP and link layers MUST include the 5-bit TOS field (see Section 3.2.1.6).

The link layer MUST NOT report a Destination Unreachable error to IP solely because there is no ARP cache entry for a destination.

Feature	Section	Must	Should	May	Should Not	Must Not	Footnote
Trailer encapsulation	2.3.1			x			
Send Trailers by default without negotiation	2.3.1					x	
ARP	2.3.2						
Flush out-of-date ARP cache entries	2.3.2.1	x					
Prevent ARP floods	2.3.2.1	x					
Cache timeout configurable	2.3.2.1		x				
Save at least one (latest) unresolved pkt	2.3.2.2		x				
Ethernet and IEEE 802 Encapsulation	2.3.3						
Host able to:	2.3.3						
Send & receive RFC-894 encapsulation	2.3.3	x					
Receive RFC-1042 encapsulation	2.3.3		x				

Feature	Section	Must	Should	May	Should Not	Must Not	Footnote
Send RFC-1042 encapsulation	2.3.3			x			
Then config. sw. to select, RFC-894 dflt	2.3.3	x					
Send K1=6 encapsulation	2.3.3					x	
Use ARP on Ethernet and IEEE 802 nets	2.3.3	x					
Link layer report b'casts to IP layer	2.4	x					
IP layer pass TOS to link layer	2.4	x					
No ARP cache entry treated as Dest. Unreach.	2.4					x	

3. INTERNET LAYER PROTOCOLS

3.1 INTRODUCTION

The Robustness Principle: "Be liberal in what you accept, and conservative in what you send" is particularly important in the Internet layer, where one misbehaving host can deny Internet service to many other hosts.

The protocol standards used in the Internet layer are:

- RFC-791 [IP:1] defines the IP protocol and gives an introduction to the architecture of the Internet.

- RFC-792 [IP:2] defines ICMP, which provides routing, diagnostic and error functionality for IP. Although ICMP messages are encapsulated within IP datagrams, ICMP processing is considered to be (and is typically implemented as) part of the IP layer. See Section 3.2.2.

- RFC-950 [IP:3] defines the mandatory subnet extension to the addressing architecture.

- RFC-1112 [IP:4] defines the Internet Group Management Protocol IGMP, as part of a recommended extension to hosts and to the host-gateway interface to support Internet-wide multicasting at the IP level. See Section 3.2.3.

The target of an IP multicast may be an arbitrary group of Internet hosts. IP multicasting is designed as a natural extension of the link-layer multicasting facilities of some networks, and it provides a standard means for local access to such link-layer multicasting facilities. Other important references are listed in Section 5 of this document.

The Internet layer of host software MUST implement both IP and ICMP. See Section 3.3.7 for the requirements on support of IGMP.

The host IP layer has two basic functions:

1. Choose the "next hop" gateway or host for outgoing IP datagrams

2. Reassemble incoming IP datagrams

The IP layer may also

3. Implement intentional fragmentation of outgoing datagrams

Finally, the IP layer must

4. Provide diagnostic and error functionality

We expect that IP layer functions may increase somewhat in the future, as further Internet control and management facilities are developed.

For normal datagrams, the processing is straightforward. For incoming datagrams, the IP layer:

1. Verifies that the datagram is correctly formatted

2. Verifies that it is destined to the local host

3. Processes options

4. Reassembles the datagram if necessary

5. Passes the encapsulated message to the appropriate transport-layer protocol module

For outgoing datagrams, the IP layer:

1. Sets any fields not set by the transport layer

2. Selects the correct first hop on the connected network (a process called "routing")

3. Fragments the datagram if necessary and if intentional fragmentation is implemented (see Section 3.3.3)

4. Passes the packet(s) to the appropriate link-layer driver

A host is said to be multihomed if it has multiple IP addresses.

Multihoming introduces considerable confusion and complexity into the protocol suite, and it is an area in which the Internet architecture falls seriously short of solving all problems. There are two distinct problem areas in multihoming:

1. Local multihoming—the host itself is multihomed

2. Remote multihoming—the local host needs to communicate with a remote multihomed host.

At present, remote multihoming MUST be handled at the application layer, as discussed in the companion RFC [INTRO:1]. A host MAY support local multihoming, which is discussed in this document, and in particular in Section 3.3.4.

Any host that forwards datagrams generated by another host is acting as a gateway and MUST also meet the specifications laid out in the gateway requirements RFC [INTRO:2]. An Internet host that includes embedded gateway code MUST have a configuration switch to disable the gateway function, and this switch MUST default to the non-gateway mode. In this mode, a datagram arriving through one interface will not be forwarded to another host or gateway (unless it is source-routed), regardless of whether the host is single-homed or multihomed. The host software MUST NOT automatically move into gateway mode if the host has more than one interface, as the operator of the machine may neither want to provide that service nor be competent to do so.

In the following, the action specified in certain cases is to "silently discard" a received datagram. This means that the datagram will be discarded without further processing and that the host will not send any ICMP error message (see Section 3.2.2) as a result. However, for diagnosis of problems a host SHOULD provide the capability of logging the error (see Section 1.2.3), including the contents of the silently-discarded datagram, and SHOULD record the event in a statistics counter.

DISCUSSION:

Silent discard of erroneous datagrams is generally intended to prevent "broadcast storms."

3.2 PROTOCOL WALK-THROUGH

3.2.1 Internet Protocol—IP

3.2.1.1 Version Number: RFC-791 Section 3.1

A datagram whose version number is not 4 MUST be silently discarded.

3.2.1.2 Checksum: RFC-791 Section 3.1

A host MUST verify the IP header checksum on every received datagram and silently discard every datagram that has a bad checksum.

3.2.1.3 Addressing: RFC-791 Section 3.2

There are now five classes of IP addresses: Class A through Class E. Class D addresses are used for IP multicasting [IP:4], while Class E addresses are reserved for experimental use. A multicast (Class D) address is a 28-bit logical address that stands for a group of hosts, and may be either permanent or transient. Permanent multicast addresses are allocated by the Internet Assigned Number Authority [INTRO:6], while transient addresses may be allocated dynamically to transient groups. Group membership is determined dynamically using IGMP [IP:4].

We now summarize the important special cases for Class A, B, and C IP addresses, using the following notation for an IP address:

{ <Network-number>, <Host-number> }

or { <Network-number>, <Subnet-number>, <Host-number> } and the notation "-1" for a field that contains all 1 bits. This notation is not intended to imply that the 1-bits in an address mask need be contiguous.

(a){ 0, 0 } This host on this network. MUST NOT be sent, except as a source address as part of an initialization procedure by which the host learns its own IP address. See also Section 3.3.6 for a non-standard use of {0,0}.

(b){ 0, <Host-number> } Specified host on this network. It MUST NOT be sent, except as a source address as part of an initialization procedure by which the host learns its full IP address.

(c) { -1, -1 } Limited broadcast. It MUST NOT be used as a source address. A datagram with this destination address will be received by every host on the connected physical network but will not be forwarded outside that network.

(d){ <Network-number>, -1 } Directed broadcast to the specified network. It MUST NOT be used as a source address.

(e){ <Network-number>, <Subnet-number>, -1 } Directed broadcast to the specified subnet. It MUST NOT be used as a source address.

(f){ <Network-number>, -1, -1 } Directed broadcast to all subnets of the specified subnetted network. It MUST NOT be used as a source address.

(g){ 127, <any> }

Internal host loopback address. Addresses of this form MUST NOT appear outside a host. The <Network-number> is administratively assigned so that its value will be unique in the entire world. IP addresses are not permitted to have the value 0 or -1 for any of the <Host-number>, <Network-number>, or <Subnet-number> fields (except in the special cases listed above). This implies that each of these fields will be at least two bits long. For further discussion of broadcast addresses, see Section 3.3.6. A host MUST support the subnet extensions to IP [IP:3]. As a result, there will be an address mask of the form:

{-1, -1, 0} associated with each of the host's local IP addresses; see Sections 3.2.2.9 and 3.3.1.1.

When a host sends any datagram, the IP source address MUST be one of its own IP addresses (but not a broadcast or multicast address).

A host MUST silently discard an incoming datagram that is not destined for the host. An incoming datagram is destined for the host if the datagram's destination address field is:

1. (One of) the host's IP address(es)

2. An IP broadcast address valid for the connected network

3. The address for a multicast group of which the host is a member on the incoming physical interface

For most purposes, a datagram addressed to a broadcast or multicast destination is processed as if it had been addressed to one of the host's IP addresses; we use the term "specific-destination address" for the equivalent local IP address of the host. The specific-destination address is defined to be the destination address in the IP header unless the header contains a broadcast or multicast address, in which case the specific-destination is an IP address assigned to the physical interface on which the datagram arrived.

A host MUST silently discard an incoming datagram containing an IP source address that is invalid by the rules of this section. This validation could be done in either the IP layer or by each protocol in the transport layer.

DISCUSSION:

A mis-addressed datagram might be caused by a link-layer broadcast of a unicast datagram or by a gateway or host that is confused or mis-configured. An architectural goal for Internet hosts was to allow IP addresses to be featureless 32-bit numbers, avoiding algorithms that required a knowledge of the IP address format. Otherwise, any future change in the format or interpretation of IP addresses will require host software changes. However, validation of broadcast and multicast addresses violates this goal; a few other violations are described elsewhere in this document. Implementers should be aware that applications depending upon the all-subnets directed broadcast address (f) may be unusable on some networks. All-subnets broadcast is not widely implemented in vendor gateways at present, and even when it is implemented, a particular network administration may disable it in the gateway configuration.

3.2.1.4 Fragmentation and Reassembly: RFC-791 Section 3.2

The Internet model requires that every host support reassembly. See Sections 3.3.2 and 3.3.3 for the requirements on fragmentation and reassembly.

3.2.1.5 Identification: RFC-791 Section 3.2

When sending an identical copy of an earlier datagram, a host MAY optionally retain the same Identification field in the copy.

DISCUSSION:

Some Internet protocol experts have maintained that when a host sends an identical copy of an earlier datagram, the new copy should contain the same Identification value as the original. There are two suggested advantages: (1) if the datagrams are fragmented and some of the fragments are lost, the receiver may be able to reconstruct a complete datagram from fragments of the original and the copies; (2) a congested gateway might use the IP Identification field (and Fragment Offset) to discard duplicate datagrams from the queue.

However, the observed patterns of datagram loss in the Internet do not favor the probability of retransmitted fragments filling reassembly gaps, while other mechanisms (e.g., TCP repacketizing upon retransmission) tend to prevent retransmission of an identical datagram [IP:9]. Therefore, we believe that retransmitting the same

Identification field is not useful. Also, a connectionless transport protocol like UDP would require the cooperation of the application programs to retain the same Identification value in identical datagrams.

3.2.1.6 Type-of-Service: RFC-791 Section 3.2

The "Type-of-Service" byte in the IP header is divided into two sections: he Precedence field (high-order 3 bits), and a field that is customarily called "Type-of-Service" or "TOS" (low-order 5 bits). In this document, all references to "TOS" or the "TOS field" refer to the low-order 5 bits only.

The Precedence field is intended for Department of Defense applications of the Internet protocols. The use of non-zero values in this field is outside the scope of this document and the IP standard specification. Vendors should consult the Defense Communication Agency (DCA) for guidance on the IP Precedence field and its implications for other protocol layers. However, vendors should note that the use of precedence will most likely require that its value be passed between protocol layers in just the same way as the TOS field is passed.

The IP layer MUST provide a means for the transport layer to set the TOS field of every datagram that is sent; the default is all zero bits. The IP layer SHOULD pass received TOS values up to the transport layer. The particular link-layer mappings of TOS contained in RFC-795 SHOULD NOT be implemented.

DISCUSSION:

While the TOS field has been little used in the past, it is expected to play an increasing role in the near future. The TOS field is expected to be used to control two aspects of gateway operations: routing and queuing algorithms. See Section 2 of [INTRO:1] for the requirements on application programs to specify TOS values. The TOS field may also be mapped into link-layer service selectors. This has been applied to provide effective sharing of serial lines by different classes of TCP traffic, for example. However, the mappings suggested in RFC-795 for networks that were included in the Internet as of 1981 are now obsolete.

3.2.1.7 Time-to-Live: RFC-791 Section 3.2

A host MUST NOT send a datagram with a Time-to-Live (TTL) value of zero. A host MUST NOT discard a datagram just because it was received with TTL less than 2. The IP layer MUST provide a means for the transport layer to set the TTL field of every datagram that is sent. When a fixed TTL value is used, it MUST be configurable. The current suggested value will be published in the "Assigned Numbers" RFC.

DISCUSSION:

The TTL field has two functions: limit the lifetime of TCP segments (see RFC-793 [TCP:1], p. 28), and terminate Internet routing loops. Although TTL is a time in seconds, it also has some attributes of a hop-count, since each gateway is required to reduce the TTL field by at least one. The intent is that TTL expiration will cause a datagram to be discarded by a gateway but not by the destination host; however, hosts that act as gateways by forwarding datagrams must follow the gateway rules for TTL. A higher-layer protocol may want to set the TTL in order to implement an "expanding scope" search for some Internet resource. his is used by some diagnostic tools, and is expected to be useful for locating the "nearest" server of a given class using IP multicasting, for example. A particular transport protocol may also want to specify its own TTL bound on maximum datagram lifetime.

A fixed value must be at least big enough for the Internet "diameter," i.e., the longest possible path. A reasonable value is about twice the diameter, to allow for continued Internet growth.

3.2.1.8 Options: RFC-791 Section 3.2

There MUST be a means for the transport layer to specify IP options to be included in transmitted IP datagrams (see Section 3.4).

All IP options (except NOP or END-OF-LIST) received in datagrams MUST be passed to the transport layer (or to ICMP processing when the datagram is an ICMP message). The IP and transport layer MUST each interpret those IP options that they understand and silently ignore the others. Later sections of this document discuss specific IP option support required by each of ICMP, TCP, and UDP.

DISCUSSION:

Passing all received IP options to the transport layer is a deliberate "violation of strict layering" that is designed to ease the introduction of new transport-relevant IP options in the future. Each layer must pick out any options that are relevant to its own processing and ignore the rest. For this purpose, every IP option except NOP and END-OF-LIST will include a specification of its own length. This document does not define the order in which a receiver must process multiple options in the same IP header. Hosts sending multiple options must be aware that this introduces an ambiguity in the meaning of certain options when combined with a source-route option.

IMPLEMENTATION:

The IP layer must not crash as the result of an option length that is outside the possible range. For example, erroneous option lengths have been observed to put some IP implementations into infinite loops.

Here are the requirements for specific IP options:

(a)Security Option—Some environments require the Security option in every datagram; such a requirement is outside the scope of this document and the IP standard specification. Note, however, that the security options described in RFC-791 and RFC-1038 are obsolete. For DoD applications, vendors should consult [IP:8] for guidance.

(b)Stream Identifier Option—This option is obsolete; it SHOULD NOT be sent, and it MUST be silently ignored if received.

(c)Source Route Options—A host MUST support originating a source route and MUST be able to act as the final destination of a source route.

If host receives a datagram containing a completed source route (i.e., the pointer points beyond the last field), the datagram has reached its final destination; the option as received (the recorded route) MUST be passed up to the transport layer (or to ICMP message processing). This recorded route will be reversed and used to form a return source route for reply datagrams (see discussion of IP Options in Section 4). When a return source route is built, it MUST be correctly formed even if the recorded route included the source host (see case (B) in the discussion below). An IP header containing more than one Source Route option MUST NOT be sent; the effect on routing of multiple Source Route options is implementation-specific. Section 3.3.5 presents the rules for a host acting as an intermediate hop in a source route, i.e., forwarding a source-routed datagram.

DISCUSSION:

If a source-routed datagram is fragmented, each fragment will contain a copy of the source route. Since the processing of IP options (including a source route) must precede reassembly, the original datagram will not be reassembled until the final destination is reached. Suppose a source routed datagram is to be routed from host S to host D via gateways G1, G2, ... Gn.

There was an ambiguity in the specification over whether the source route option in a datagram sent out by S should be (A) or (B):

(A): {>>G2, G3, ... Gn, D} <—— CORRECT

(B): {S, >>G2, G3, ... Gn, D} <—— WRONG

(where >> represents the pointer). If (A) is sent, the datagram received at D will contain the option: {G1, G2, ... Gn >>}, with S and D as the IP source and destination addresses. If (B) were sent, the datagram received at D would again contain S and D as the same IP source and destination addresses, but the option would be: {S, G1, ...Gn >>}; i.e., the originating host would be the first hop in the route.

(d) Record Route Option—Implementation of originating and processing the Record Route option is OPTIONAL.

(e) Timestamp Option—Implementation of originating and processing the Timestamp option is OPTIONAL. If it is implemented, the following rules apply:

- The originating host MUST record a timestamp in a Timestamp option whose Internet address fields are not pre-specified or whose first pre-specified address is the host's interface address.

- The destination host MUST (if possible) add the current timestamp to a Timestamp option before passing the option to the transport layer or to ICMP for processing.

- A timestamp value MUST follow the rules given in Section 3.2.2.8 for the ICMP Timestamp message.

3.2.2 Internet Control Message Protocol—ICMP

ICMP messages are grouped into two classes:

- ICMP error messages:

Destination Unreachable(see Section 3.2.2.1)

Redirect(see Section 3.2.2.2)

Source Quench (see Section 3.2.2.3)

Time Exceeded (see Section 3.2.2.4)

Parameter Problem(see Section 3.2.2.5)

- ICMP query messages:

Echo(see Section 3.2.2.6)

Information (see Section 3.2.2.7)

Timestamp (see Section 3.2.2.8)

Address Mask (see Section 3.2.2.9)

If an ICMP message of unknown type is received, it MUST be silently discarded. Every ICMP error message includes the Internet header and at least the first 8 data octets of the datagram that triggered the error; more than 8 octets MAY be sent; this header and data MUST be unchanged from the received datagram.

In those cases where the Internet layer is required to pass an ICMP error message to the transport layer, the IP protocol number MUST be extracted from the original header and used to select the appropriate transport protocol entity to handle the error. An ICMP error message SHOULD be sent with normal (i.e., zero) TOS bits. An ICMP error message MUST NOT be sent as the result of receiving:

- An ICMP error message
- A datagram destined to an IP broadcast or IP multicast address
- A datagram sent as a link-layer broadcast
- A non-initial fragment
- A datagram whose source address does not define a single host—e.g., a zero address, a loopback address, a broadcast address, a multicast address, or a Class E address

NOTE: THESE RESTRICTIONS TAKE PRECEDENCE OVER ANY REQUIREMENT ELSEWHERE IN THIS DOCUMENT FOR SENDING ICMP ERROR MESSAGES.

DISCUSSION:

These rules will prevent the "broadcast storms" that have resulted from hosts returning ICMP error messages in response to broadcast datagrams. For example, a broadcast

UDP segment to a non-existent port could trigger a flood of ICMP Destination
Unreachable datagrams from all machines that do not have a client for that destination
port. On a large Ethernet, the resulting collisions can render the network useless for a
second or more. Every datagram that is broadcast on the connected network should
have a valid IP broadcast address as its IP destination (see Section 3.3.6). However, some
hosts violate this rule. To be certain to detect broadcast datagrams, therefore, hosts are
required to check for a link-layer broadcast as well as an IP-layer broadcast address.
IMPLEMENTATION:
This requires that the link layer inform the IP layer when a link-layer broadcast datagram
has been received; see Section 2.4.

3.2.2.1 Destination Unreachable: RFC-792

The following additional codes are hereby defined:
6 = destination network unknown
7 = destination host unknown
8 = source host isolated
9 = communication with destination network administratively prohibited
10 = communication with destination host administratively prohibited
11 = network unreachable for type of service
12 = host unreachable for type of service
A host SHOULD generate Destination Unreachable messages with code:
2 (Protocol Unreachable), when the designated transport protocol is not supported; or
3 (Port Unreachable), when the designated transport protocol (e.g., UDP) is unable to
demultiplex the datagram but has no protocol mechanism to inform the sender.
A Destination Unreachable message that is received MUST be reported to the transport
layer. The transport layer SHOULD use the information appropriately; for example,
see Sections 4.1.3.3, 4.2.3.9, and 4.2.4 below. A transport protocol that has its own
mechanism for notifying the sender that a port is unreachable (e.g., TCP, which sends
RST segments) MUST nevertheless accept an ICMP Port Unreachable for the same
purpose. A Destination Unreachable message that is received with code 0 (Net), 1 (Host),
or 5 (Bad Source Route) may result from a outing transient and MUST therefore be
interpreted as only a hint, not proof, that the specified destination is unreachable [IP:11].
For example, it MUST NOT be used as proof of a dead gateway (see Section 3.3.1).

3.2.2.2 Redirect: RFC-792

A host SHOULD NOT send an ICMP Redirect message; redirects are to be sent
only by gateways. A host receiving a Redirect message MUST update its routing
information accordingly. Every host MUST be prepared to accept both Host and
Network Redirects and to process them as described in Section 3.3.1.2 below.
A Redirect message SHOULD be silently discarded if the new gateway address it
specifies is not on the same connected (sub-) net through which the Redirect arrived
[INTRO:2, Appendix A], or if the source of the Redirect is not the current first-hop
gateway for the specified destination (see Section 3.3.1).

3.2.2.3 Source Quench: RFC-792

A host MAY send a Source Quench message if it is approaching, or has reached, the point at which it is forced to discard incoming datagrams due to a shortage of reassembly buffers or other resources. See Section 2.2.3 of [INTRO:2] for suggestions on when to send Source Quench.

If a Source Quench message is received, the IP layer MUST report it to the transport layer (or ICMP processing). In general, the transport or application layer SHOULD implement a mechanism to respond to Source Quench for any protocol that can send a sequence of datagrams to the same destination and which can reasonably be expected to maintain enough state information to make this feasible. See Section 4 for the handling of Source Quench by TCP and UDP.

DISCUSSION:

A Source Quench may be generated by the target host or by some gateway in the path of a datagram. The host receiving a Source Quench should throttle itself back for a period of time, then gradually increase the transmission rate again. The mechanism to respond to Source Quench may be in the transport layer (for connection-oriented protocols like TCP) or in the application layer (for protocols that are built on top of UDP).

A mechanism has been proposed [IP:14] to make the IP layer respond directly to Source Quench by controlling the rate at which datagrams are sent, however, this proposal is currently experimental and not currently recommended.

3.2.2.4 Time Exceeded: RFC-792

An incoming Time Exceeded message MUST be passed to the transport layer.

DISCUSSION:

A gateway will send a Time Exceeded Code 0 (In Transit) message when it discards a datagram due to an expired TTL field. This indicates either a gateway routing loop or too small an initial TTL value. A host may receive a Time Exceeded Code 1 (Reassembly Timeout) message from a destination host that has timed out and discarded an incomplete datagram; see Section 3.3.2 below. In the future, receipt of this message might be part of some "MTU discovery" procedure, to discover the maximum datagram size that can be sent on the path without fragmentation.

3.2.2.5 Parameter Problem: RFC-792

A host SHOULD generate Parameter Problem messages. An incoming Parameter Problem message MUST be passed to the transport layer, and it MAY be reported to the user.

DISCUSSION:

The ICMP Parameter Problem message is sent to the source host for any problem not specifically covered by another ICMP message. Receipt of a Parameter Problem message generally indicates some local or remote implementation error.

A new variant on the Parameter Problem message is hereby defined:
Code 1 = required option is missing.
DISCUSSION:
This variant is currently in use in the military community for a missing security option.

3.2.2.6 Echo Request/Reply: RFC-792

Every host MUST implement an ICMP Echo server function that receives Echo Requests and sends corresponding Echo Replies. A host SHOULD also implement an application-layer interface for sending an Echo Request and receiving an Echo Reply, for diagnostic purposes. An ICMP Echo Request destined to an IP broadcast or IP multicast address MAY be silently discarded.
DISCUSSION:
This neutral provision results from a passionate debate between those who feel that ICMP Echo to a broadcast address provides a valuable diagnostic capability and those who feel that misuse of this feature can too easily create packet storms.
The IP source address in an ICMP Echo Reply MUST be the same as the specific-destination address (defined in Section 3.2.1.3) of the corresponding ICMP Echo Request message. Data received in an ICMP Echo Request MUST be entirely included in the resulting Echo Reply. However, if sending the Echo Reply requires intentional fragmentation that is not implemented, the datagram MUST be truncated to maximum transmission size (see Section 3.3.3) and sent. Echo Reply messages MUST be passed to the ICMP user interface, unless the corresponding Echo Request originated in the IP layer.
If a Record Route and/or Time Stamp option is received in an ICMP Echo Request, this option (these options) SHOULD be updated to include the current host and included in the IP header of the Echo Reply message, without "truncation." Thus, the recorded route will be for the entire round trip. If a Source Route option is received in an ICMP Echo Request, the return route MUST be reversed and used as a Source Route option for the Echo Reply message.

3.2.2.7 Information Request/Reply: RFC-792

A host SHOULD NOT implement these messages.
DISCUSSION:
The Information Request/Reply pair was intended to support self-configuring systems such as diskless workstations, to allow them to discover their IP network numbers at boot time. However, the RARP and BOOTP protocols provide better mechanisms for a host to discover its own IP address.

3.2.2.8 Timestamp and Timestamp Reply: RFC-792

A host MAY implement Timestamp and Timestamp Reply. If they are implemented, the following rules MUST be followed.

- The ICMP Timestamp server function returns a Timestamp Reply to every Timestamp message that is received. If this function is implemented, it SHOULD be designed for minimum variability in delay (e.g., implemented in the kernel to avoid delay in scheduling a user process).

The following cases for Timestamp are to be handled according to the corresponding rules for ICMP Echo:

- An ICMP Timestamp Request message to an IP broadcast or IP multicast address MAY be silently discarded.
- The IP source address in an ICMP Timestamp Reply MUST be the same as the specific-destination address of the corresponding Timestamp Request message.
- If a Source Route option is received in an ICMP Echo Request, the return route MUST be reversed and used as a Source Route option for the Timestamp Reply message.
- If a Record Route and/or Timestamp option is received in a Timestamp Request, this (these) option(s) SHOULD be updated to include the current host and included in the IP header of the Timestamp Reply message.
- Incoming Timestamp Reply messages MUST be passed up to the ICMP user interface.

The preferred form for a timestamp value (the "standard value") is in units of milliseconds since midnight Universal Time. However, it may be difficult to provide this value with millisecond resolution. For example, many systems use clocks that update only at line frequency, 50 or 60 times per second. Therefore, some latitude is allowed in a "standard value":

(a) A "standard value" MUST be updated at least 15 times per second (i.e., at most the six low-order bits of the value may be undefined).

(b) The accuracy of a "standard value" MUST approximate that of operator-set CPU clocks, i.e., correct within a few minutes.

3.2.2.9 Address Mask Request/Reply: RFC-950

A host MUST support the first, and MAY implement all three, of the following methods for determining the address mask(s) corresponding to its IP address(es):

1. Static configuration information
2. Obtaining the address mask(s) dynamically as a side-effect of the system initialization process (see [INTRO:1])
3. Sending ICMP Address Mask Request(s) and receiving ICMP Address Mask Reply(s).

The choice of method to be used in a particular host MUST be configurable. When method (3), the use of Address Mask messages, is enabled, then:

(a) When it initializes, the host MUST broadcast an Address Mask Request message on the connected network corresponding to the IP address. It MUST retransmit this message a small number of times if it does not receive an immediate Address Mask Reply.

(b) Until it has received an Address Mask Reply, the host SHOULD assume a mask appropriate for the address class of the IP address, i.e., assume that the connected network is not subnetted.

(c) The first Address Mask Reply message received MUST be used to set the address mask corresponding to the particular local IP address. This is true even if the first Address Mask Reply message is "unsolicited," in which case it will have been broadcast and may arrive after the host has ceased to retransmit Address Mask Requests. When the mask has been set by an Address Mask Reply, later Address Mask Reply messages MUST be (silently) ignored.

Conversely, if Address Mask messages are disabled, no ICMP Address Mask Requests will be sent, and any ICMP Address Mask Replies received for that local IP address MUST be (silently) ignored. A host SHOULD make some reasonableness check on any address mask it installs; see IMPLEMENTATION section on the next page.

A system MUST NOT send an Address Mask Reply unless it is an authoritative agent for address masks. An authoritative agent may be a host or a gateway, but it MUST be explicitly configured as a address mask agent. Receiving an address mask via an Address Mask Reply does not give the receiver authority and MUST NOT be used as the basis for issuing Address Mask Replies.

With a statically configured address mask, there SHOULD be an additional configuration flag that determines whether the host is to act as an authoritative agent for this mask, i.e., whether it will answer Address Mask Request messages using this mask.

If it is configured as an agent, the host MUST broadcast an Address Mask Reply for the mask on the appropriate interface when it initializes. See "System Initialization" in [INTRO:1] for more information about the use of Address Mask Request/Reply messages.

DISCUSSION

Hosts that casually send Address Mask Replies with invalid address masks have often been a serious nuisance. To prevent this, Address Mask Replies ought to be sent only by authoritative agents that have been selected by explicit administrative action. When an authoritative agent receives an Address Mask Request message, it will send a unicast Address Mask Reply to the source IP address. If the network part of this address is zero (see (a) and (b) in 3.2.1.3), the Reply will be broadcast.

Getting no reply to its Address Mask Request messages, a host will assume there is no agent and use an unsubnetted mask, but the agent may be only temporarily unreachable.

An agent will broadcast an unsolicited Address Mask Reply whenever it initializes in order to update the masks of all hosts that have initialized in the meantime.
IMPLEMENTATION:
The following reasonableness check on an address mask is suggested: the mask is not all 1 bits, and it is either zero or else the 8 highest-order bits are on.

3.2.3 Internet Group Management Protocol IGMP

IGMP [IP:4] is a protocol used between hosts and gateways on a single network to establish hosts' membership in particular multicast groups. The gateways use this information, in conjunction with a multicast routing protocol, to support IP multicasting across the Internet.

At this time, implementation of IGMP is OPTIONAL; see Section 3.3.7 for more information. Without IGMP, a host can still participate in multicasting local to its connected networks.

3.3 SPECIFIC ISSUES

3.3.1 Routing Outbound Datagrams

The IP layer chooses the correct next hop for each datagram it sends. If the destination is on a connected network, the datagram is sent directly to the destination host; otherwise, it has to be routed to a gateway on a connected network.

3.3.1.1 Local/Remote Decision

To decide if the destination is on a connected network, the following algorithm MUST be used [see IP:3]:

(a) The address mask (particular to a local IP address for a multihomed host) is a 32-bit mask that selects the network number and subnet number fields of the corresponding IP address.

(b) If the IP destination address bits extracted by the address mask match the IP source address bits extracted by the same mask, then the destination is on the corresponding connected network, and the datagram is to be transmitted directly to the destination host.

(c) If not, then the destination is accessible only through a gateway. Selection of a gateway is described in Section 3.3.1.2.

A special-case destination address is handled as follows:

- For a limited broadcast or a multicast address, simply pass the datagram to the link layer for the appropriate interface.

- For a (network or subnet) directed broadcast, the datagram can use the standard routing algorithms.

The host IP layer MUST operate correctly in a minimal network environment, and in particular, when there are no gateways. For example, if the IP layer of a host insists on finding at least one gateway to initialize, the host will be unable to operate on a single isolated broadcast net.

3.3.1.2 Gateway Selection

To efficiently route a series of datagrams to the same destination, the source host MUST keep a "route cache" of mappings to next-hop gateways. A host uses the following basic algorithm on this cache to route a datagram; this algorithm is designed to put the primary routing burden on the gateways [IP:11]:

(a)If the route cache contains no information for a particular destination, the host chooses a "default" gateway and sends the datagram to it. It also builds a corresponding Route Cache entry.

(b)If that gateway is not the best next hop to the destination, the gateway will forward the datagram to the best next-hop gateway and return an ICMP Redirect message to the source host.

(c)When it receives a Redirect, the host updates the next-hop gateway in the appropriate route cache entry, so later datagrams to the same destination will go directly to the best gateway.

Because the subnet mask appropriate to the destination address is generally not known, a Network Redirect message SHOULD be treated identically to a Host Redirect message; i.e., the cache entry for the destination host (only) would be updated (or created, if an entry for that host did not exist) for the new gateway.
DISCUSSION:
This recommendation is to protect against gateways that erroneously send Network Redirects for a subnetted network, in violation of the gateway requirements [INTRO:2].
When there is no route cache entry for the destination host address (and the destination is not on the connected network), the IP layer MUST pick a gateway from its list of "default" gateways. The IP layer MUST support multiple default gateways.
As an extra feature, a host IP layer MAY implement a table of "static routes." Each such static route MAY include a flag specifying whether it may be overridden by ICMP Redirects.
DISCUSSION:
A host generally needs to know at least one default gateway to get started. This information can be obtained from a configuration file or else from the host startup sequence, e.g., the BOOTP protocol (see [INTRO:1]).
It has been suggested that a host can augment its list of default gateways by recording any new gateways it learns about. For example, it can record every gateway to which it is ever redirected. Such a feature, while possibly useful in some circumstances, may cause problems in other cases (e.g., gateways are not all equal), and it is not recommended.

A static route is typically a particular preset mapping from destination host or network into a particular next-hop gateway; it might also depend on the Type-of-Service (see next section). Static routes would be set up by system administrators to override the normal automatic routing mechanism, to handle exceptional situations. However, any static routing information is a potential source of failure as configurations change or equipment fails.

3.3.1.3 Route Cache

Each route cache entry needs to include the following fields:

1. Local IP address (for a multihomed host)
2. Destination IP address
3. Type(s)-of-Service
4. Next-hop gateway IP address

Field (2) MAY be the full IP address of the destination host, or only the destination network number. Field (3), the TOS, SHOULD be included. See Section 3.3.4.2 for a discussion of the implications of multihoming for the lookup procedure in this cache.
DISCUSSION:
Including the Type-of-Service field in the route cache and considering it in the host route algorithm will provide the necessary mechanism for the future when Type-of-Service routing is commonly used in the Internet. See Section 3.2.1.6. Each route cache entry defines the endpoints of an Internet path. Although the connecting path may change dynamically in an arbitrary way, the transmission characteristics of the path tend to remain approximately constant over a time period longer than a single typical host-host transport connection. Therefore, a route cache entry is a natural place to cache data on the properties of the path. Examples of such properties might be the maximum unfragmented datagram size (see Section 3.3.3), or the average round-trip delay measured by a transport protocol. This data will generally be both gathered and used by a higher layer protocol, e.g., by TCP, or by an application using UDP. Experiments are currently in progress on caching path properties in this manner. There is no consensus on whether the route cache should be keyed on destination host addresses alone, or allow both host and network addresses. Those who favor the use of only host addresses argue that:

1. As required in Section 3.3.1.2, Redirect messages will generally result in entries keyed on destination host addresses; the simplest and most general scheme would be to use host addresses always.
2. The IP layer may not always know the address mask for a network address in a complex subnetted environment.
3. The use of only host addresses allows the destination address to be used as a pure 32-bit number, which may allow the Internet architecture to be more easily extended in the future without any change to the hosts.

The opposing view is that allowing a mixture of destination hosts and networks in the route cache:

1. Saves memory space.

2. Leads to a simpler data structure, easily combining the cache with the tables of default and static routes (see below).

3. Provides a more useful place to cache path properties, as discussed earlier.

IMPLEMENTATION:

The cache needs to be large enough to include entries for the maximum number of destination hosts that may be in use at one time. A route cache entry may also include control information used to choose an entry for replacement. This might take the form of a "recently used" bit, a use count, or a last-used timestamp, for example. It is recommended that it include the time of last modification of the entry, for diagnostic purposes. An implementation may wish to reduce the overhead of scanning the route cache for every datagram to be transmitted. This may be accomplished with a hash table to speed the lookup, or by giving a connection-oriented transport protocol a "hint" or temporary handle on the appropriate cache entry, to be passed to the IP layer with each subsequent datagram. Although we have described the route cache, the lists of default gateways, and a table of static routes as conceptually distinct, in practice they may be combined into a single "routing table" data structure.

3.3.1.4 Dead Gateway Detection

The IP layer MUST be able to detect the failure of a "next-hop" gateway that is listed in its route cache and to choose an alternate gateway (see Section 3.3.1.5). Dead gateway detection is covered in some detail in RFC-816 [IP:11]. Experience to date has not produced a complete algorithm which is totally satisfactory, though it has identified several forbidden paths and promising techniques.

- A particular gateway SHOULD NOT be used indefinitely in the absence of positive indications that it is functioning.

- Active probes such as "pinging" (i.e., using an ICMP Echo Request/Reply exchange) are expensive and scale poorly. In particular, hosts MUST NOT actively check the status of a first-hop gateway by simply pinging the gateway continuously.

- Even when it is the only effective way to verify a gateway's status, pinging MUST be used only when traffic is being sent to the gateway and when there is no other positive indication to suggest that the gateway is functioning.

- To avoid pinging, the layers above and/or below the Internet layer SHOULD be able to give "advice" on the status of route cache entries when either positive (gateway OK) or negative (gateway dead) information is available.

DISCUSSION:

If an implementation does not include an adequate mechanism for detecting a dead gateway and re-routing, a gateway failure may cause datagrams to apparently vanish into a "black hole." This failure can be extremely confusing for users and difficult for network personnel to debug.

The dead-gateway detection mechanism must not cause unacceptable load on the host, on connected networks, or on first-hop gateway(s). The exact constraints on the timeliness of dead gateway detection and on acceptable load may vary somewhat depending on the nature of the host's mission, but a host generally needs to detect a failed first-hop gateway quickly enough that transport-layer connections will not break before an alternate gateway can be selected. Passing advice from other layers of the protocol stack complicates the interfaces between the layers, but it is the preferred approach to dead gateway detection. Advice can come from almost any part of the IP/TCP INTERNET LAYER architecture, but it is expected to come primarily from the transport and link layers. Here are some possible sources for gateway advice:

- TCP or any connection-oriented transport protocol should be able to give negative advice, e.g., triggered by excessive retransmissions.

- TCP may give positive advice when (new) data is acknowledged. Even though the route may be asymmetric, an ACK for new data proves that the acknowledged data must have been transmitted successfully.

- An ICMP Redirect message from a particular gateway should be used as positive advice about that gateway.

- Link-layer information that reliably detects and reports host failures (e.g., ARPANET Destination Dead messages) should be used as negative advice.

- Failure to ARP or to re-validate ARP mappings may be used as negative advice for the corresponding IP address.

- Packets arriving from a particular link-layer address are evidence that the system at this address is alive. However, turning this information into advice about gateways requires mapping the link-layer address into an IP address, and then checking that IP address against the gateways pointed to by the route cache. This is probably prohibitively inefficient. Note that positive advice that is given for every datagram received may cause unacceptable overhead in the implementation.

While advice might be passed using required arguments in all interfaces to the IP layer, some transport and application layer protocols cannot deduce the correct advice. These interfaces must therefore allow a neutral value for advice, since either always-positive or always-negative advice leads to incorrect behavior. There is another technique for dead gateway detection that has been commonly used but is not recommended.

This technique depends upon the host passively receiving ("wiretapping") the Interior Gateway Protocol (IGP) datagrams that the gateways are broadcasting to each other. This approach has the drawback that a host needs to recognize all the interior gateway protocols that gateways may use (see [INTRO:2]). In addition, it only works on a broadcast network.

At present, pinging (i.e., using ICMP Echo messages) is the mechanism for gateway probing when absolutely required. A successful ping guarantees that the addressed interface and its associated machine are up, but it does not guarantee that the machine is a gateway as opposed to a host. The normal inference is that if a Redirect or other evidence indicates that a machine was a gateway, successful pings will indicate that the machine is still up and hence still a gateway. However, since a host silently discards packets that a gateway would forward or redirect, this assumption could sometimes fail. To avoid this problem, a new ICMP message under development will ask "are you a gateway?"

IMPLEMENTATION:

The following specific algorithm has been suggested:

- Associate a "reroute timer" with each gateway pointed to by the route cache. Initialize the timer to a value Tr, which must be small enough to allow detection of a dead gateway before transport connections time out.

- Positive advice would reset the reroute timer to Tr. Negative advice would reduce or zero the reroute timer.

- Whenever the IP layer used a particular gateway to route a datagram, it would check the corresponding reroute timer. If the timer had expired (reached zero), the IP layer would send a ping to the gateway, followed immediately by the datagram.

- The ping (ICMP Echo) would be sent again if necessary, up to N times. If no ping reply was received in N tries, the gateway would be assumed to have failed, and a new first-hop gateway would be chosen for all cache entries pointing to the failed gateway.

Note that the size of Tr is inversely related to the amount of advice available. Tr should be large enough to insure that

- Any pinging will be at a low level (e.g., <10%) of all packets sent to a gateway from the host

- Pinging is infrequent (e.g., every 3 minutes). Since the recommended algorithm is concerned with the gateways pointed to by route cache entries, rather than the cache entries themselves, a two level data structure (perhaps coordinated with ARP or similar caches) may be desirable for implementing a route cache.

3.3.1.5 New Gateway Selection

If the failed gateway is not the current default, the IP layer can immediately switch to a default gateway. If it is the current default that failed, the IP layer MUST select a different default gateway (assuming more than one default is known) for the failed route and for establishing new routes.

DISCUSSION:

When a gateway does fail, the other gateways on the connected network will learn of the failure through some inter-gateway routing protocol. However, this will not happen instantaneously, since gateway routing protocols typically have a settling time of 30-60 seconds. If the host switches to an alternative gateway before the gateways have agreed on the failure, the new target gateway will probably forward the datagram to the failed gateway and send a Redirect back to the host pointing to the failed gateway (!). The result is likely to be a rapid oscillation in the contents of the host's route cache during the gateway settling period. It has been proposed that the dead-gateway logic should include some hysteresis mechanism to prevent such oscillations. However, experience has not shown any harm from such oscillations, since service cannot be restored to the host until the gateways' routing information does settle down.

IMPLEMENTATION:

One implementation technique for choosing a new default gateway is to simply round-robin among the default gateways in the host's list. Another is to rank the gateways in priority order, and when the current default gateway is not the highest priority one, to "ping" the higher-priority gateways slowly to detect when they return to service. This pinging can be at a very low rate, e.g., 0.005 per second.

3.3.1.6 Initialization

The following information MUST be configurable:

1. IP address(es)

2. Address mask(s)

3. A list of default gateways, with a preference level

A manual method of entering this configuration data MUST be provided. In addition, a variety of methods can be used to determine this information dynamically; see the section on "Host Initialization" in [INTRO:1].

DISCUSSION:

Some host implementations use "wiretapping" of gateway protocols on a broadcast network to learn what gateways exist. A standard method for default gateway discovery is under development.

3.3.2 Reassembly

The IP layer MUST implement reassembly of IP datagrams. We designate the largest datagram size that can be reassembled by EMTU_R ("Effective MTU to receive"); this is sometimes called the "reassembly buffer size." EMTU_R MUST be greater than

or equal to 576, SHOULD be either configurable or indefinite, and SHOULD be greater than or equal to the MTU of the connected network(s).
DISCUSSION:
A fixed EMTU_R limit should not be built into the code because some application layer protocols require EMTU_R values larger than 576.
IMPLEMENTATION:
An implementation may use a contiguous reassembly buffer for each datagram, or it may use a more complex data structure that places no definite limit on the reassembled datagram size; in the latter case, EMTU_R is said to be "indefinite."
Logically, reassembly is performed by simply copying each fragment into the packet buffer at the proper offset. Note that fragments may overlap if successive retransmissions use different packetizing but the same reassembly Id. The tricky part of reassembly is the bookkeeping to determine when all bytes of the datagram have been reassembled. We recommend Clark's algorithm [IP:10] that requires no additional data space for the bookkeeping. However, note that, contrary to [IP:10], the first fragment header needs to be saved for inclusion in a possible ICMP Time Exceeded (Reassembly Timeout) message.
There MUST be a mechanism by which the transport layer can learn MMS_R, the maximum message size that can be received and reassembled in an IP datagram (see GET_MAXSIZES calls in Section 3.4). If EMTU_R is not indefinite, then the value of MMS_R is given by:
MMS_R = EMTU_R - 20
because 20 is the minimum size of an IP header. There MUST be a reassembly time-out. The reassembly timeout value SHOULD be a fixed value, not set from the remaining TTL.
It is recommended that the value lie between 60 seconds and 120 seconds. If this timeout expires, the partially-reassembled datagram MUST be discarded and an ICMP Time Exceeded message sent to the source host (if fragment zero has been received).
DISCUSSION:
The IP specification says that the reassembly timeout should be the remaining TTL from the IP header, but this does not work well because gateways generally treat TTL as a simple hop count rather than an elapsed time. If the reassembly timeout is too small, datagrams will be discarded unnecessarily, and communication may fail. The timeout needs to be at least as large as the typical maximum delay across the Internet. A realistic minimum reassembly timeout would be 60 seconds.
It has been suggested that a cache might be kept of round-trip times measured by transport protocols for various destinations, and that these values might be used to dynamically determine a reasonable reassembly timeout value. Further investigation of this approach is required.
If the reassembly timeout is set too high, buffer resources in the receiving host will be tied up too long, and the MSL (Maximum Segment Lifetime) [TCP:1] will be larger than necessary. The MSL controls the maximum rate at which fragmented datagrams

can be sent using distinct values of the 16-bit Ident field; a larger MSL lowers the maximum rate. The TCP specification [TCP:1] arbitrarily assumes a value of 2 minutes for MSL. This sets an upper limit on a reasonable reassembly timeout value.

3.3.3 Fragmentation

Optionally, the IP layer MAY implement a mechanism to fragment outgoing datagrams intentionally.

We designate by EMTU_S ("Effective MTU for sending") the maximum IP datagram size that may be sent, for a particular combination of IP source and destination addresses and perhaps TOS.

A host MUST implement a mechanism to allow the transport layer to learn MMS_S, the maximum transport-layer message size that may be sent for a given {source, destination, TOS} triplet (see GET_MAXSIZES call in Section 3.4). If no local fragmentation is performed, the value of MMS_S will be:

MMS_S = EMTU_S - <IP header size>

and EMTU_S must be less than or equal to the MTU of the network interface corresponding to the source address of the datagram. Note that <IP header size> in this equation will be 20, unless the IP reserves space to insert IP options for its own purposes in addition to any options inserted by the transport layer. A host that does not implement local fragmentation MUST ensure that the transport layer (for TCP) or the application layer (for UDP) obtains MMS_S from the IP layer and does not send a datagram exceeding MMS_S in size.

It is generally desirable to avoid local fragmentation and to choose EMTU_S low enough to avoid fragmentation in any gateway along the path. In the absence of actual knowledge of the minimum MTU along the path, the IP layer SHOULD use EMTU_S <= 576 whenever the destination address is not on a connected network, and otherwise use the connected network's MTU.

The MTU of each physical interface MUST be configurable. A host IP layer implementation MAY have a configuration flag "All-Subnets-MTU," indicating that the MTU of the connected network is to be used for destinations on different subnets within the same network, but not for other networks. Thus, this flag causes the network class mask, rather than the subnet address mask, to be used to choose an EMTU_S. For a multihomed host, an "All-Subnets-MTU" flag is needed for each network interface.

DISCUSSION:

Picking the correct datagram size to use when sending data is a complex topic [IP:9].

   (a) In general, no host is required to accept an IP datagram larger than 576 bytes (including header and data), so a host must not send a larger datagram without explicit knowledge or prior arrangement with the destination host. Thus, MMS_S is only an upper bound on the datagram size that a transport protocol may send; even when MMS_S exceeds 556, the transport layer must limit its messages to 556 bytes in the absence of other knowledge about the destination host.

(b)Some transport protocols (e.g.,TCP) provide a way to explicitly inform the sender about the largest datagram the other end can receive and reassemble [IP:7]. There is no corresponding mechanism in the IP layer. A transport protocol that assumes an EMTU_R larger than 576 (see Section 3.3.2), can send a datagram of this larger size to another host that implements the same protocol.

(c)Hosts should ideally limit their EMTU_S for a given destination to the minimum MTU of all the networks along the path, to avoid any fragmentation. IP fragmentation, while formally correct, can create a serious transport protocol performance problem, because loss of a single fragment means all the fragments in the segment must be retransmitted [IP:9].

Since nearly all networks in the Internet currently support an MTU of 576 or greater, we strongly recommend the use of 576 for datagrams sent to non-local networks. It has been suggested that a host could determine the MTU over a given path by sending a zero-offset datagram fragment and waiting for the receiver to time out the reassembly (which cannot complete!) and return an ICMP Time Exceeded message. This message would include the largest remaining fragment header in its body. More direct mechanisms are being experimented with, but have not yet been adopted (see e.g., RFC-1063).

3.3.4 Local Multihoming

3.3.4.1 Introduction

A multihomed host has multiple IP addresses, which we may think of as "logical interfaces." These logical interfaces may be associated with one or more physical interfaces, and these physical interfaces may be connected to the same or different networks. Here are some important cases of multihoming:

(a)Multiple Logical Networks—The Internet architects envisioned that each physical network would have a single unique IP network (or subnet) number. However, LAN administrators have sometimes found it useful to violate this assumption, operating a LAN with multiple logical networks per physical connected network. If a host connected to such a physical network is configured to handle traffic for each of N different logical networks, then the host will have N logical interfaces. These could share a single physical interface, or might use N physical interfaces to the same network.

(b)Multiple Logical Hosts—When a host has multiple IP addresses that all have the same <Network-number> part (and the same <Subnet-number> part, if any), the logical interfaces are known as "logical hosts." These logical interfaces might share a single physical interface or might use separate physical interfaces to the same physical network.

(c)Simple Multihoming—In this case, each logical interface is mapped into a separate physical interface and each physical interface is connected to a different physical network. The term "multihoming" was originally applied only to this case, but it is now applied more generally. A host with embedded gateway functionality will typically fall into the simple multihoming case. Note, however, that a host may be simply multihomed without containing an embedded gateway, i.e., without forwarding datagrams from one connected network to another.

This case presents the most difficult routing problems. The choice of interface (i.e., the choice of first-hop network) may significantly affect performance or even reachability of remote parts of the Internet.

Finally, we note another possibility that is NOT multihoming: one logical interface may be bound to multiple physical interfaces, in order to increase the reliability or throughput between directly connected machines by providing alternative physical paths between them. For instance, two systems might be connected by multiple point-to-point links. We call this "link-layer multiplexing." With link-layer multiplexing, the protocols above the link layer are unaware that multiple physical interfaces are present; the link-layer device driver is responsible for multiplexing and routing packets across the physical interfaces.

In the Internet protocol architecture, a transport protocol instance ("entity") has no address of its own, but instead uses a single Internet Protocol (IP) address. This has implications for the IP, transport, and application layers, and for the interfaces between them. In particular, the application software may have to be aware of the multiple IP addresses of a multihomed host; in other cases, the choice can be made within the network software.

3.3.4.2 Multihoming Requirements

The following general rules apply to the selection of an IP source address for sending a datagram from a multihomed host.

1. If the datagram is sent in response to a received datagram, the source address for the response SHOULD be the specific-destination address of the request. See Sections 4.1.3.5 and 4.2.3.7 and the "General Issues" section of [INTRO:1] for more specific requirements on higher layers. Otherwise, a source address must be selected.

2. An application MUST be able to explicitly specify the source address for initiating a connection or a request.

3. In the absence of such a specification, the networking software MUST choose a source address. Rules for this choice are described below.

There are two key requirement issues related to multihoming:

(A) A host MAY silently discard an incoming datagram whose destination address does not correspond to the physical interface through which it is received.

(B) A host MAY restrict itself to sending (non-source-routed) IP datagrams only through the physical interface that corresponds to the IP source address of the datagrams.

DISCUSSION:

Internet host implementors have used two different conceptual models for multihoming, briefly summarized in the following discussion. This document takes no stand on which model is preferred; each seems to have a place. This ambivalence is reflected in the issues (A) and (B) being optional.

- Strong ES Model—The Strong ES (End System, i.e., host) model emphasizes the host/gateway (ES/IS) distinction, and would therefore substitute MUST for MAY in issues (A) and (B) above. It tends to model a multihomed host as a set of logical hosts within the same physical host.

With respect to (A), proponents of the Strong ES model note that automatic Internet routing mechanisms could not route a datagram to a physical interface that did not correspond to the destination address. Under the Strong ES model, the route computation for an outgoing datagram is the mapping:

route(src IP addr, dest IP addr, TOS) -> gateway

Here the source address is included as a parameter in order to select a gateway that is directly reachable on the corresponding physical interface. Note that this model logically requires that in general there be at least one default gateway, and preferably multiple defaults, for each IP source address.

- Weak ES Model—This view de-emphasizes the ES/IS distinction, and would therefore substitute MUST NOT for MAY in issues (A) and (B). This model may be the more natural one for hosts that wiretap gateway routing protocols, and is necessary for hosts that have embedded gateway functionality.

The Weak ES Model may cause the Redirect mechanism to fail. If a datagram is sent out a physical interface that does not correspond to the destination address, the first-hop gateway will not realize when it needs to send a Redirect. On the other hand, if the host has embedded gateway functionality, then it has routing information without listening to Redirects.

In the Weak ES model, the route computation for an outgoing datagram is the mapping:

route(dest IP addr, TOS) -> gateway, interface

3.3.4.3 Choosing a Source Address

DISCUSSION:

When it sends an initial connection request (e.g., a TCP "SYN" segment) or a datagram service request (e.g., a UDP-based query), the transport layer on a multihomed host needs to know which source address to use. If the application does not specify it, the transport layer must ask the IP layer to perform the conceptual mapping:

GET_SRCADDR(remote IP addr, TOS) -> local IP address

Here TOS is the Type-of-Service value (see Section 3.2.1.6), and the result is the desired source address. The following rules are suggested for implementing this mapping:

(a) If the remote Internet address lies on one of the (sub-) nets to which the host is directly connected, a corresponding source address may be chosen, unless the corresponding interface is known to be down.

(b) The route cache may be consulted, to see if there is an active route to the specified destination network through any network interface; if so, a local IP address corresponding to that interface may be chosen.

(c) The table of static routes, if any (see Section 3.3.1.2) may be similarly consulted.

(d) The default gateways may be consulted. If these gateways are assigned to different interfaces, the interface corresponding to the gateway with the highest preference may be chosen. In the future, there may be a defined way for a multihomed host to ask the gateways on all connected networks for advice about the best network to use for a given destination.

IMPLEMENTATION:
It will be noted that this process is essentially the same as datagram routing (see Section 3.3.1), and therefore hosts may be able to combine the implementation of the two functions.

3.3.5 Source Route Forwarding

Subject to restrictions given below, a host MAY be able to act as an intermediate hop in a source route, forwarding a source-routed datagram to the next specified hop. However, in performing this gateway-like function, the host MUST obey all the relevant rules for a gateway forwarding source-routed datagrams [INTRO:2]. This includes the following specific provisions, which override the corresponding host provisions given earlier in this document:

(A) TTL (ref. Section 3.2.1.7)—The TTL field MUST be decremented and the datagram perhaps discarded as specified for a gateway in [INTRO:2].

(B) ICMP Destination Unreachable (ref. Section 3.2.2.1)—A host MUST be able to generate Destination Unreachable messages with the following codes:

4 (Fragmentation Required but DF Set) when a source-routed datagram cannot be fragmented to fit into the target network;

5 (Source Route Failed) when a source-routed datagram cannot be forwarded, e.g., because of a routing problem or because the next hop of a strict source route is not on a connected network.

(C) IP Source Address (ref. Section 3.2.1.3)—A source-routed datagram being forwarded MAY (and normally will) have a source address that is not one of the IP addresses of the forwarding host.

(D) Record Route Option (ref. Section 3.2.1.8d)—A host that is forwarding a source-routed datagram containing a Record Route option MUST update that option, if it has room.

(E) Timestamp Option (ref. Section 3.2.1.8e)—A host that is forwarding a source-routed datagram containing a Timestamp Option MUST add the current timestamp to that option, according to the rules for this option.

To define the rules restricting host forwarding of source-routed datagrams, we use the term "local source-routing" if the next hop will be through the same physical interface through which the datagram arrived; otherwise, it is "non-local source-routing."

- A host is permitted to perform local source-routing without restriction.
- A host that supports non-local source-routing MUST have a configurable switch to disable forwarding, and this switch MUST default to disabled.
- The host MUST satisfy all gateway requirements for configurable policy filters [INTRO:2] restricting non-local forwarding.

If a host receives a datagram with an incomplete source route but does not forward it for some reason, the host SHOULD return an ICMP Destination Unreachable (code 5, Source Route Failed) message, unless the datagram was itself an ICMP error message.

3.3.6 Broadcasts

Section 3.2.1.3 defined the four standard IP broadcast address forms:
Limited Broadcast: {-1, -1}
Directed Broadcast: {<Network-number>,-1}
Subnet Directed Broadcast: {<Network-number>,<Subnet-number>,-1}
All-Subnets Directed Broadcast: {<Network-number>,-1,-1} A host MUST recognize any of these forms in the destination address of an incoming datagram.
There is a class of hosts (4.2BSD Unix and its derivatives, but not 4.3BSD) that use non-standard broadcast address forms, substituting 0 for -1. All hosts SHOULD recognize and accept any of these non-standard broadcast addresses as the destination address of an incoming datagram.
A host MAY optionally have a configuration option to choose the 0 or the -1 form of broadcast address, for each physical interface, but this option SHOULD default to the standard (-1) form.
When a host sends a datagram to a link-layer broadcast address, the IP destination address MUST be a legal IP broadcast or IP multicast address.
A host SHOULD silently discard a datagram that is received via a link-layer broadcast (see Section 2.4) but does not specify an IP multicast or broadcast destination address.
Hosts SHOULD use the Limited Broadcast address to broadcast to a connected network.
DISCUSSION:
Using the Limited Broadcast address instead of a Directed Broadcast address may improve system robustness. Problems are often caused by machines that do not understand the plethora of broadcast addresses (see Section 3.2.1.3), or that may have different ideas about which broadcast addresses are in use. The prime example of the latter is machines that do not understand subnetting but are attached to a subnetted net. Sending a Subnet Broadcast for the connected network will confuse those machines, which will see it as a message to some other host. There has been discussion on whether a datagram addressed to the Limited Broadcast address ought to be sent from all the interfaces of a multihomed host. This specification takes no stand on the issue.

3.3.7 IP Multicasting

A host SHOULD support local IP multicasting on all connected networks for which a mapping from Class D IP addresses to link-layer addresses has been specified (see below). Support for local IP multicasting includes sending multicast datagrams, joining multicast groups and receiving multicast datagrams, and leaving multicast groups. This implies support for all of [IP:4] except the IGMP protocol itself, which is OPTIONAL.
DISCUSSION:
IGMP provides gateways that are capable of multicast routing with the information required to support IP multicasting across multiple networks. At this time, multicast-routing gateways are in the experimental stage and are not widely available. For hosts that are not connected to networks with multicast-routing gateways or that do not need to receive multicast datagrams originating on other networks, IGMP serves no purpose and is therefore optional for now. However, the rest of [IP:4] is currently recommended for the purpose of providing IP-layer access to local network multicast addressing, as a preferable alternative to local broadcast addressing. It is expected that IGMP will become recommended at some future date, when multicast-routing gateways have become more widely available. If IGMP is not implemented, a host SHOULD still join the "all-hosts" group (224.0.0.1) when the IP layer is initialized and remain a member for as long as the IP layer is active.
DISCUSSION:
Joining the "all-hosts" group will support strictly local uses of multicasting, e.g., a gateway discovery protocol, even if IGMP is not implemented.
The mapping of IP Class D addresses to local addresses is currently specified for the following types of networks:

- Ethernet/IEEE 802.3, as defined in [IP:4].

- Any network that supports broadcast but not multicast, addressing: all IP Class D addresses map to the local broadcast address.

- Any type of point-to-point link (e.g., SLIP or HDLC links): no mapping required. All IP multicast datagrams are sent as-is, inside the local framing. Mappings for other types of networks will be specified in the future.

A host SHOULD provide a way for higher-layer protocols or applications to determine which of the host's connected network(s) support IP multicast addressing.

3.3.8 Error Reporting

Wherever practical, hosts MUST return ICMP error datagrams on detection of an error, except in those cases where returning an ICMP error message is specifically prohibited.
DISCUSSION:
A common phenomenon in datagram networks is the "black hole disease": datagrams are sent out, but nothing comes back. Without any error datagrams, it is difficult for the user to figure out what the problem is.

3.4 INTERNET/TRANSPORT LAYER INTERFACE

The interface between the IP layer and the transport layer MUST provide full access to all the mechanisms of the IP layer, including options, Type-of-Service, and Time-to-Live. The transport layer MUST either have mechanisms to set these interface parameters, or provide a path to pass them through from an application, or both.

DISCUSSION:

Applications are urged to make use of these mechanisms where applicable, even when the mechanisms are not currently effective in the Internet (e.g., TOS). This will allow these mechanisms to be immediately useful when they do become effective, without a large amount of retrofitting of host software.

We now describe a conceptual interface between the transport layer and the IP layer, as a set of procedure calls. This is an extension of the information in Section 3.3 of RFC-791 [IP:1].

- Send Datagram—SEND(src, dst, prot, TOS, TTL, BufPTR, len, Id, DF, opt => result)

  where the parameters are defined in RFC-791. Passing an Id parameter is optional; see Section 3.2.1.5.

- Receive Datagram—RECV(BufPTR, prot => result, src, dst, SpecDest, TOS, len, opt)

All the parameters are defined in RFC-791, except for SpecDest = specific-destination address of datagram (defined in Section 3.2.1.3) The result parameter dst contains the datagram's destination address. Since this may be a broadcast or multicast address, the SpecDest parameter (not shown in RFC-791) MUST be passed. The parameter opt contains all the IP options received in the datagram; these MUST also be passed to the transport layer.

- Select Source Address—GET_SRCADDR(remote, TOS) -> local remote = remote IP address

  TOS = Type-of-Service

  local = local IP address

  See Section 3.3.4.3.

- Find Maximum Datagram Sizes—GET_MAXSIZES(local, remote, TOS) -> MMS_R, MMS_S

  MMS_R = maximum receive transport-message size.

  MMS_S = maximum send transport-message size.

  (local, remote, TOS defined above)

  See Sections 3.3.2 and 3.3.3.

- Advice on Delivery Success—ADVISE_DELIVPROB(sense, local, remote, TOS)

Here the parameter sense is a 1-bit flag indicating whether positive or negative advice is being given; see the discussion in Section 3.3.1.4. The other parameters were defined earlier.

- Send ICMP Message—SEND_ICMP(src, dst, TOS, TTL, BufPTR, len, Id, DF, opt) -> result (Parameters defined in RFC-791).

Passing an Id parameter is optional; see Section 3.2.1.5. The transport layer MUST be able to send certain ICMP messages: Port Unreachable or any of the query-type messages. This function could be considered to be a special case of the SEND() call, of course; we describe it separately for clarity.

- Receive ICMP Message—RECV_ICMP(BufPTR) -> result, src, dst, len, opt (Parameters defined in RFC-791).

The IP layer MUST pass certain ICMP messages up to the appropriate transport-layer routine. This function could be considered to be a special case of the RECV() call, of course; we describe it separately for clarity.

For an ICMP error message, the data that is passed up MUST include the original Internet header plus all the octets of the original message that are included in the ICMP message. This data will be used by the transport layer to locate the connection state information, if any.

In particular, the following ICMP messages are to be passed up:

- Destination Unreachable
- Source Quench
- Echo Reply (to ICMP user interface, unless the Echo Request originated in the IP layer)
- Timestamp Reply (to ICMP user interface)
- Time Exceeded

DISCUSSION:
In the future, there may be additions to this interface to pass path data (see Section 3.3.1.3) between the IP and transport layers.

3.5 INTERNET LAYER REQUIREMENTS SUMMARY

Feature	Section	Must	Should	May	Should Not	Must Not	Footnote
Implement IP and ICMP	3.1	x					
Handle remote multihoming in application layer	3.1	x					
Support local multihoming	3.1			x			

continues

3.5 INTERNET LAYER REQUIREMENTS SUMMARY (Continued)

Feature	Section	Must	Should	May	Should Not	Must Not	Footnote
Meet gateway specs if forward datagrams	3.1	x					
Configuration switch for embedded gateway	3.1	x					1
Config switch default to non-gateway	3.1	x					1
Auto-config based on number of interfaces	3.1					x	1
Able to log discarded datagrams	3.1		x				
Record in counter	3.1		x				
Silently discard Version != 4	3.2.1.1	x					
Verify IP checksum, silently discard bad dgram	3.2.1.2	x					
Addressing:							
Subnet addressing (RFC-950)	3.2.1.3	x					
Src address must be host's own IP address	3.2.1.3	x					
Silently discard datagram with bad dest addr	3.2.1.3	x					
Silently discard datagram with bad src addr	3.2.1.3	x					
Support reassembly	3.2.1.4	x					
Retain same Id field in identical datagram	3.2.1.5			x			
TOS:							
Allow transport layer to set TOS	3.2.1.6	x					
Pass received TOS up to transport layer	3.2.1.6		x				
Use RFC-795 link-layer mappings for TOS	3.2.1.6				x		
TTL:							
Send packet with TTL of 0	3.2.1.7				x		
Discard received packets with TTL < 2	3.2.1.7				x		

Feature	Section	Must	Should	May	Should Not	Must Not	Footnote
Allow transport layer to set TTL	3.2.1.7	x					
Fixed TTL is configurable	3.2.1.7	x					
IP Options:							
Allow transport layer to send IP options	3.2.1.8	x					
Pass all IP options rcvd to higher layer	3.2.1.8	x					
IP layer silently ignore unknown options	3.2.1.8	x					
Security option	3.2.1.8a			x			
Send Stream Identifier option	3.2.1.8b				x		
Silently ignore Stream Identifier option	3.2.1.8b	x					
Record Route option	3.2.1.8d			x			
Timestamp option	3.2.1.8e			x			
Source Route Option:							
Originate & terminate Source Route options	3.2.1.8c	x					
Datagram with completed SR passed up to TL	3.2.1.8c	x					
Build correct (non-redundant) return route	3.2.1.8c	x					
Send multiple SR options in one header	3.2.1.8c					x	
ICMP:							
Silently discard ICMP msg with unknown type	3.2.2	x					
Include more than 8 octets of orig datagram	3.2.2					x	

continues

3.5 INTERNET LAYER REQUIREMENTS SUMMARY (Continued)

Feature	Section	Must	Should	May	Should Not	Must Not	Footnote
Included octets same as received	3.2.2	x					
Demux ICMP Error to transport protocol	3.2.2	x					
Send ICMP error message with TOS=0	3.2.2		x				
Send ICMP error message for:							
– ICMP error msg	3.2.2					x	
– IP b'cast or IP m'cast	3.2.2					x	
– Link-layer b'cast	3.2.2					x	
– Non-initial fragment	3.2.2					x	
– Datagram with non-unique src address	3.2.2					x	
Return ICMP error msgs (when not prohibited)	3.3.8	x					
Dest Unreachable:							
Generate Dest Unreachable (code 2/3)	3.2.2.1		x				
Pass ICMP Dest Unreachable to higher layer	3.2.2.1	x					
Higher layer act on Dest Unreach	3.2.2.1		x				
Interpret Dest Unreach as only hint	3.2.2.1	x					
Redirect:							
Host send Redirect	3.2.2.2			x			
Update route cache when recv Redirect	3.2.2.2	x					
Handle both Host and Net Redirects	3.2.2.2	x					
Discard illegal Redirect	3.2.2.2		x				
Source Quench:							
Send Source Quench if buffering exceeded	3.2.2.3			x			

Feature	Section	Must	Should	May	Should Not	Must Not	Footnote
Pass Source Quench to higher layer	3.2.2.3	x					
Higher layer act on Source Quench	3.2.2.3		x				
Time Exceeded: pass to higher layer	3.2.2.4	x					
Parameter Problem:							
Send Parameter Problem messages	3.2.2.5		x				
Pass Parameter Problem to higher layer	3.2.2.5	x					
Report Parameter Problem to user	3.2.2.5			x			
ICMP Echo Request or Reply:							
Echo server and Echo client	3.2.2.6	x					
Echo client	3.2.2.6		x				
Discard Echo Request to broadcast address	3.2.2.6			x			
Discard Echo Request to multicast address	3.2.2.6			x			
Use specific-dest addr as Echo Reply src	3.2.2.6	x					
Send same data in Echo Reply	3.2.2.6	x					
Pass Echo Reply to higher layer	3.2.2.6	x					
Reflect Record Route, Time Stamp options	3.2.2.6		x				
Reverse and reflect Source Route option	3.2.2.6	x					
ICMP Information Request or Reply:	3.2.2.7				x		
ICMP Timestamp and Timestamp Reply:	3.2.2.8			x			
Minimize delay variability	3.2.2.8		x				1

continues

3.5 INTERNET LAYER REQUIREMENTS SUMMARY (Continued)

Feature	Section	Must	Should	May	Should Not	Must Not	Footnote
Silently discard b'cast Timestamp	3.2.2.8			x			1
Silently discard m'cast Timestamp	3.2.2.8			x			1
Use specific-dest addr as TS Reply src	3.2.2.8	x					1
Reflect Record Route, Time Stamp options	3.2.2.6		x				1
Reverse and reflect Source Route option	3.2.2.8	x					1
Pass Timestamp Reply to higher layer	3.2.2.8	x					1
Obey rules for "standard value"	3.2.2.8	x					1
ICMP Address Mask Request and Reply:							
Addr Mask source configurable	3.2.2.9	x					
Support static configuration of addr mask	3.2.2.9	x					
Get addr mask dynamically during booting	3.2.2.9		x				
Get addr via ICMP Addr Mask Request/Reply	3.2.2.9		x				
Retransmit Addr Mask Req if no Reply	3.2.2.9	x					3
Assume default mask if no Reply	3.2.2.9		x				3
Update address mask from first Reply only	3.2.2.9	x					3
Reasonableness check on Addr Mask	3.2.2.9		x				
Send unauthorized Addr Mask Reply msgs	3.2.2.9					x	
Explicitly configured to be agent	3.2.2.9	x					

Feature	Section	Must	Should	May	Should Not	Must Not	Footnote
Static config=> Addr-Mask-Authoritative flag	3.2.2.9		x				
Broadcast Addr Mask Reply when init.	3.2.2.9	x					3
ROUTING OUTBOUND DATAGRAMS:							
Use address mask in local/remote decision	3.3.1.1	x					
Operate with no gateways on conn network	3.3.1.1	x					
Maintain "route cache" of next-hop gateways	3.3.1.2	x					
Treat Host and Net Redirect the same	3.3.1.2		x				
no cache entry, use default gateway	3.3.1.2	x					
Support multiple default gateways	3.3.1.2	x					
Provide table of static routes	3.3.1.2			x			
Flag: route overridable by Redirects	3.3.1.2			x			
Key route cache on host, not net address	3.3.1.3			x			
Include TOS in route cache	3.3.1.3		x				
Able to detect failure of next-hop gateway	3.3.1.4	x					
Assume route is good forever	3.3.1.4				x		
Ping gateways continuously	3.3.1.4					x	
Ping only when traffic being sent	3.3.1.4	x					
Ping only when no positive indication	3.3.1.4	x					

continues

3.5 INTERNET LAYER REQUIREMENTS SUMMARY (Continued)

Feature	Section	Must	Should	May	Should Not	Must Not	Footnote
Higher and lower layers give advice	3.3.1.4		x				
Switch from failed default g'way to another	3.3.1.5	x					
Manual method of entering config info	3.3.1.6	x					
REASSEMBLY and FRAGMENTATION:							
Able to reassemble incoming datagrams	3.3.2	x					
At least 576 byte datagrams	3.3.2	x					
EMTU_R configurable or indefinite	3.3.2		x				
Transport layer able to learn MMS_R	3.3.2	x					
Send ICMP Time Exceeded on reassembly timeout	3.3.2	x					
Fixed reassembly timeout value	3.3.2		x				
Pass MMS_S to higher layers	3.3.3	x					
Local fragmentation of outgoing packets	3.3.3			x			
Else don't send bigger than MMS_S	3.3.3	x					
Send max 576 to off-net destination	3.3.3		x				
All-Subnets-MTU configuration flag	3.3.3			x			
MULTIHOMING:							
Reply with same addr as spec-dest addr	3.3.4.2		x				
Allow application to choose local IP addr	3.3.4.2	x					
Silently discard d'gram in "wrong" interface	3.3.4.2			x			

Feature	Section	Must	Should	May	Should Not	Must Not	Footnote
Only send d'gram through "right" interface	3.3.4.2			x			4
SOURCE-ROUTE FORWARDING:							
Forward datagram with Source Route option	3.3.5			x			1
Obey corresponding gateway rules	3.3.5	x					1
Update TTL by gateway rules	3.3.5	x					1
Able to generate ICMP err code 4, 5	3.3.5	x					1
IP src addr not local host	3.3.5			x			1
Update Timestamp, Record Route options	3.3.5	x					1
Configurable switch for non-local Sring	3.3.5	x					1
Defaults to OFF	3.3.5	x					1
Satisfy gwy access rules for non-local SRing	3.3.5	x					1
If not forward, send Dest Unreach (cd 5)	3.3.5		x				2
BROADCAST:							
Broadcast addr as IP source addr	3.2.1.3					x	
Receive 0 or –1 broadcast formats OK	3.3.6		x				
Config'ble option to send 0 or –1 b'cast	3.3.6			x			
Default to –1 broadcast	3.3.6		x				
Recognize all broadcast address formats	.3.6	x					
Use IP b'cast/ m'cast addr in link-layer b'cast	3.3.6	x					

continues

3.5 INTERNET LAYER REQUIREMENTS SUMMARY (Continued)

Feature	Section	Must	Should	May	Should Not	Must Not	Footnote
Silently discard link-layer-only b'cast dg's	3.3.6		x				
Use Limited Broadcast addr for connected net	3.3.6		x				
MULTICAST:							
Support local IP multicasting (RFC-1112)	3.3.7		x				
Support IGMP (RFC-1112)	3.3.7			x			
Join all-hosts group at startup	3.3.7		x				
Higher layers learn i'face m'cast capability	3.3.7		x				
INTERFACE:							
Allow transport layer to use all IP mechanisms	3.4	x					
Pass interface ident up to transport layer	3.4	x					
Pass all IP options up to transport layer	3.4	x					
Transport layer can send certain ICMP messages	3.4	x					
Pass spec'd ICMP messages up to transp. layer	3.4	x					
Include IP hdr+8 octets or more from orig.	3.4	x					
Able to leap tall buildings at a single bound	3.5		x				

Footnotes:
1 Only if feature is implemented.
2 This requirement is overruled if datagram is an ICMP error message.
3 Only if feature is implemented and is configured "on."
4 Unless has embedded gateway functionality or is source routed.

4. TRANSPORT PROTOCOLS

4.1 USER DATAGRAM PROTOCOL—UDP

4.1.1 INTRODUCTION

The User Datagram Protocol UDP [UDP:1] offers only a minimal transport service—non-guaranteed datagram delivery—and gives applications direct access to the datagram service of the IP layer. UDP is used by applications that do not require the level of service of TCP or that wish to use communications services (e.g., multicast or broadcast delivery) not available from TCP.

UDP is almost a null protocol; the only services it provides over IP are checksumming of data and multiplexing by port number. Therefore, an application program running over UDP must deal directly with end-to-end communication problems that a connection-oriented protocol would have handled—e.g., retransmission for reliable delivery, packetization and reassembly, flow control, congestion avoidance, etc., when these are required. The fairly complex coupling between IP and TCP will be mirrored in the coupling between UDP and many applications using UDP.

4.1.2 PROTOCOL WALK-THROUGH

There are no known errors in the specification of UDP.

4.1.3 SPECIFIC ISSUES

4.1.3.1 Ports

UDP well-known ports follow the same rules as TCP well-known ports; see Section 4.2.2.1 below. If a datagram arrives addressed to a UDP port for which there is no pending LISTEN call, UDP SHOULD send an ICMP Port Unreachable message.

4.1.3.2 IP Options

UDP MUST pass any IP option that it receives from the IP layer transparently to the application layer. An application MUST be able to specify IP options to be sent in its UDP datagrams, and UDP MUST pass these options to the IP layer.

DISCUSSION:

At present, the only options that need be passed through UDP are Source Route, Record Route, and Time Stamp. However, new options may be defined in the future, and UDP need not and should not make any assumptions about the format or content of options it passes to or from the application; an exception to this might be an IP-layer security option. An application based on UDP will need to obtain a source route from a request datagram and supply a reversed route for sending the corresponding reply.

4.1.3.3 ICMP Messages

UDP MUST pass to the application layer all ICMP error messages that it receives from the IP layer. Conceptually at least, this may be accomplished with an upcall to the ERROR_REPORT routine (see Section 4.2.4.1).

DISCUSSION:

Note that ICMP error messages resulting from sending a UDP datagram are received asynchronously. A UDP-based application that wants to receive ICMP error messages is responsible for maintaining the state necessary to demultiplex these messages when they arrive; for example, the application may keep a pending receive operation for this purpose. The application is also responsible to avoid confusion from a delayed ICMP error message resulting from an earlier use of the same port(s).

4.1.3.4 UDP Checksums

A host MUST implement the facility to generate and validate UDP checksums. An application MAY optionally be able to control whether a UDP checksum will be generated, but it MUST default to checksumming on.

If a UDP datagram is received with a checksum that is non-zero and invalid, UDP MUST silently discard the datagram. An application MAY optionally be able to control whether UDP datagrams without checksums should be discarded or passed to the application.

DISCUSSION:

Some applications that normally run only across local area networks have chosen to turn off UDP checksums for efficiency. As a result, numerous cases of undetected errors have been reported. The advisability of ever turning off UDP checksumming is very controversial.

IMPLEMENTATION:

There is a common implementation error in UDP checksums. Unlike the TCP checksum, the UDP checksum is optional; the value zero is transmitted in the checksum field of a UDP header to indicate the absence of a checksum. If the transmitter really calculates a UDP checksum of zero, it must transmit the checksum as all 1's (65535). No special action is required at the receiver, since zero and 65535 are equivalent in 1's complement arithmetic.

4.1.3.5 UDP Multihoming

When a UDP datagram is received, its specific-destination address MUST be passed up to the application layer. An application program MUST be able to specify the IP source address to be used for sending a UDP datagram or to leave it unspecified (in which case the networking software will choose an appropriate source address). There SHOULD be a way to communicate the chosen source address up to the application layer (e.g. so that the application can later receive a reply datagram only from the corresponding interface).

DISCUSSION:

A request/response application that uses UDP should use a source address for the response that is the same as the specific destination address of the request. See the "General Issues" section of [INTRO:1].

4.1.3.6 Invalid Addresses

A UDP datagram received with an invalid IP source address (e.g., a broadcast or multicast address) must be discarded by UDP or by the IP layer (see Section 3.2.1.3). When a host sends a UDP datagram, the source address MUST be (one of) the IP address(es) of the host.

4.1.4 UDP/APPLICATION LAYER INTERFACE

The application interface to UDP MUST provide the full services of the IP/transport interface described in Section 3.4 of this document. Thus, an application using UDP needs the functions of the GET_SRCADDR(), GET_MAXSIZES(), ADVISE_DELIVPROB(), and RECV_ICMP() calls described in Section 3.4. For example, GET_MAXSIZES() can be used to learn the effective maximum UDP maximum datagram size for a particular {interface,remote host,TOS} triplet.

An application-layer program MUST be able to set the TTL and TOS values as well as IP options for sending a UDP datagram, and these values must be passed transparently to the IP layer. UDP MAY pass the received TOS up to the application layer.

4.1.5 UDP REQUIREMENTS SUMMARY

Feature	Section	Must	Should	May	Should Not	Must Not	Footnote
UDP							
UDP send Port Unreachable	4.1.3.1		x				
IP Options in UDP							
– Pass rcv'd IP options to applic layer	4.1.3.2	x					
– Applic layer can specify IP options in Send	4.1.3.2	x					
– UDP passes IP options down to IP layer	4.1.3.2	x					
Pass ICMP msgs up to applic layer	4.1.3.3	x					
UDP checksums:							
– Able to generate/ check checksum	4.1.3.4	x					

continues

4.1.5 UDP REQUIREMENTS SUMMARY (Continued)

Feature	Section	Must	Should	May	Should Not	Must Not	Footnote
– Silently discard bad checksum	4.1.3.4	x					
– Sender Option to not generate checksum	4.1.3.4			x			
– Default is to checksum	4.1.3.4	x					
– Receiver Option to require checksum	4.1.3.4			x			
UDP Multihoming							
– Pass spec-dest addr to application	4.1.3.5	x					
– Applic layer can specify Local IP addr	4.1.3.5	x					
– Applic layer specify wild Local IP addr	4.1.3.5	x					
– Applic layer notified of Local IP addr used	4.1.3.5		x				
Bad IP src addr silently discarded by UDP/IP	4.1.3.6	x					
Only send valid IP source address	4.1.3.6	x					
UDP Application Interface Services							
Full IP interface of 3.4 for application	4.1.4	x					
– Able to spec TTL, TOS, IP opts when send dg	4.1.4	x					
– Pass received TOS up to applic layer	4.1.4			x			

4.2 TRANSMISSION CONTROL PROTOCOL—TCP

4.2.1 INTRODUCTION

The Transmission Control Protocol TCP [TCP:1] is the primary virtual-circuit transport protocol for the Internet suite. TCP provides reliable, in-sequence delivery of a full-duplex stream of octets (8-bit bytes). TCP is used by those applications needing reliable, connection-oriented transport service, e.g., mail (SMTP), file transfer (FTP), and virtual terminal service (Telnet); requirements for these application-layer protocols are described in [INTRO:1].

4.2.2 PROTOCOL WALK-THROUGH

4.2.2.1 Well-Known Ports: RFC-793 Section 2.7

DISCUSSION:

TCP reserves port numbers in the range 0-255 for "well-known" ports, used to access services that are standardized across the Internet. The remainder of the port space can be freely allocated to application processes. Current well-known port definitions are listed in the RFC entitled "Assigned Numbers" [INTRO:6]. A prerequisite for defining a new well-known port is an RFC documenting the proposed service in enough detail to allow new implementations. Some systems extend this notion by adding a third subdivision of the TCP port space: reserved ports, which are generally used for operating-system-specific services. For example, reserved ports might fall between 256 and some system-dependent upper limit. Some systems further choose to protect well-known and reserved ports by permitting only privileged users to open TCP connections with those port values. This is perfectly reasonable as long as the host does not assume that all hosts protect their low-numbered ports in this manner.

4.2.2.2 Use of Push: RFC-793 Section 2.8

When an application issues a series of SEND calls without setting the PUSH flag, the TCP MAY aggregate the data internally without sending it. Similarly, when a series of segments is received without the PSH bit, a TCP MAY queue the data internally without passing it to the receiving application.

The PSH bit is not a record marker and is independent of segment boundaries. The transmitter SHOULD collapse successive PSH bits when it packetizes data, to send the largest possible segment.

A TCP MAY implement PUSH flags on SEND calls. If PUSH flags are not implemented, then the sending TCP: (1) must not buffer data indefinitely, and (2) MUST set the PSH bit in the last buffered segment (i.e., when there is no more queued data to be sent).

The discussion in RFC-793 on pages 48, 50, and 74 erroneously implies that a received PSH flag must be passed to the application layer. Passing a received PSH flag to the application layer is now OPTIONAL.

An application program is logically required to set the PUSH flag in a SEND call whenever it needs to force delivery of the data to avoid a communication deadlock. However, a TCP SHOULD send a maximum-sized segment whenever possible, to improve performance (see Section 4.2.3.4).

DISCUSSION:

When the PUSH flag is not implemented on SEND calls, i.e., when the application/TCP interface uses a pure streaming model, responsibility for aggregating any tiny data fragments to form reasonable sized segments is partially borne by the application layer. Generally, an interactive application protocol must set the PUSH flag at least in the last SEND call in each command or response sequence. A bulk transfer protocol like FTP should set the PUSH flag on the last segment of a file or when necessary to prevent buffer deadlock. At the receiver, the PSH bit forces buffered data to be delivered to the application (even if less than a full buffer has been received). Conversely, the lack of a PSH bit can be used to avoid unnecessary wakeup calls to the application process; this can be an important performance optimization for large time-sharing hosts. Passing the PSH bit to the receiving application allows an analogous optimization within the application.

4.2.2.3 Window Size: RFC-793 Section 3.1

The window size MUST be treated as an unsigned number, or else large window sizes will appear like negative windows and TCP will not work. It is RECOMMENDED that implementations reserve 32-bit fields for the send and receive window sizes in the connection record and do all window computations with 32 bits.
DISCUSSION:
It is known that the window field in the TCP header is too small for high-speed, long-delay paths. Experimental TCP options have been defined to extend the window size; see for example [TCP:11]. In anticipation of the adoption of such an extension, TCP implementors should treat windows as 32 bits.

4.2.2.4 Urgent Pointer: RFC-793 Section 3.1

The second sentence is in error: the urgent pointer points to the sequence number of the LAST octet (not LAST+1) in a sequence of urgent data. The description on page 56 (last sentence) is correct.
A TCP MUST support a sequence of urgent data of any length. A TCP MUST inform the application layer asynchronously whenever it receives an Urgent pointer and there was previously no pending urgent data, or whenever the Urgent pointer advances in the data stream. There MUST be a way for the application to learn how much urgent data remains to be read from the connection, or at least to determine whether or not more urgent data remains to be read.
DISCUSSION:
Although the Urgent mechanism may be used for any application, it is normally used to send "interrupt"-type commands to a Telnet program (see "Using Telnet Synch Sequence" section in [INTRO:1]). The asynchronous or "out-of-band" notification will allow the application to go into "urgent mode," reading data from the TCP connection. This allows control commands to be sent to an application whose normal input buffers are full of unprocessed data.
IMPLEMENTATION:
The generic ERROR-REPORT() upcall described in Section 4.2.4.1 is a possible mechanism for informing the application of the arrival of urgent data.

4.2.2.5 TCP Options: RFC-793 Section 3.1

A TCP MUST be able to receive a TCP option in any segment. A TCP MUST ignore without error any TCP option it does not implement, assuming that the option has a length field (all TCP options defined in the future will have length fields). TCP MUST be prepared to handle an illegal option length (e.g., zero) without crashing; a suggested procedure is to reset the connection and log the reason.

4.2.2.6 Maximum Segment Size Option: RFC-793 Section 3.1

TCP MUST implement both sending and receiving the Maximum Segment Size option [TCP:4].

TCP SHOULD send an MSS (Maximum Segment Size) option in every SYN segment when its receive MSS differs from the default 536, and MAY send it always. If an MSS option is not received at connection setup, TCP MUST assume a default send MSS of 536 (576-40) [TCP:4].

The maximum size of a segment that TCP really sends, the "effective send MSS," MUST be the smaller of the send MSS (which reflects the available reassembly buffer size at the remote host) and the largest size permitted by the IP layer:

Eff.snd.MSS = min(SendMSS+20, MMS_S) - TCPhdrsize - IPoptionsize

where:

- SendMSS is the MSS value received from the remote host, or the default 536 if no MSS option is received.

- MMS_S is the maximum size for a transport-layer message that TCP may send.

- TCPhdrsize is the size of the TCP header; this is normally 20, but may be larger if TCP options are to be sent.

- IPoptionsize is the size of any IP options that TCP will pass to the IP layer with the current message. The MSS value to be sent in an MSS option must be less than or equal to:

  MMS_R - 20

  where MMS_R is the maximum size for a transport-layer message that can be received (and reassembled). TCP obtains MMS_R and MMS_S from the IP layer; see the generic call GET_MAXSIZES in Section 3.4.

DISCUSSION:

The choice of TCP segment size has a strong effect on performance. Larger segments increase throughput by amortizing header size and per-datagram processing overhead over more data bytes; however, if the packet is so large that it causes IP fragmentation, efficiency drops sharply if any fragments are lost [IP:9]. Some TCP implementations send an MSS option only if the destination host is on a non-connected network. However, in general the TCP layer may not have the appropriate information to make this decision, so it is preferable to leave to the IP layer the task of determining a suitable MTU for the Internet path. We therefore recommend that TCP always send the option (if not 536) and that the IP layer determine MMS_R as specified in 3.3.3 and 3.4. A proposed IP-layer mechanism to measure the MTU would then modify the IP layer without changing TCP.

4.2.2.7 TCP Checksum: RFC-793 Section 3.1

Unlike the UDP checksum (see Section 4.1.3.4), the TCP checksum is never optional. The sender MUST generate it and the receiver MUST check it.

4.2.2.8 TCP Connection State Diagram: RFC-793 Section 3.2

There are several problems with this diagram:

(a)The arrow from SYN-SENT to SYN-RCVD should be labeled with "snd SYN,ACK," to agree with the text on page 68 and with Figure 8.

(b)There could be an arrow from SYN-RCVD state to LISTEN state, conditioned on receiving a RST after a passive open (see text page 70).

(c)It is possible to go directly from FIN-WAIT-1 to the TIME-WAIT state (see page 75 of the spec).

4.2.2.9 Initial Sequence Number Selection: RFC-793 Section 3.3

A TCP MUST use the specified clock-driven selection of initial sequence numbers.

4.2.2.10 Simultaneous Open Attempts: RFC-793 Section 3.4

There is an error in Figure 8: the packet on line 7 should be identical to the packet on line 5. A TCP MUST support simultaneous open attempts.

DISCUSSION:

It sometimes surprises implementors that if two applications attempt to simultaneously connect to each other, only one connection is generated instead of two. This was an intentional design decision; don't try to "fix" it.

4.2.2.11 Recovery from Old Duplicate SYN: RFC-793 Section 3.4

Note that a TCP implementation MUST keep track of whether a connection has reached SYN_RCVD state as the result of a passive OPEN or an active OPEN.

4.2.2.12 RST Segment: RFC-793 Section 3.4

A TCP SHOULD allow a received RST segment to include data.

DISCUSSION

It has been suggested that a RST segment could contain ASCII text that encoded and explained the cause of the RST. No standard has yet been established for such data.

4.2.2.13 Closing a Connection: RFC-793 Section 3.5

A TCP connection may terminate in two ways: (1) the normal TCP close sequence using a FIN handshake, and (2) an "abort" in which one or more RST segments are sent and the connection state is immediately discarded. If a TCP connection is closed by the remote site, the local application MUST be informed whether it closed normally or was aborted.

The normal TCP close sequence delivers buffered data reliably in both directions. Since the two directions of a TCP connection are closed independently, it is possible for a connection to be "half closed," i.e., closed in only one direction, and a host is permitted to continue sending data in the open direction on a half-closed connection. A host MAY implement a "half-duplex" TCP close sequence, so that an application that has called CLOSE cannot continue to read data from the connection. If such a host issues a CLOSE call while received data is still pending in TCP, or if new data is received after CLOSE is called, its TCP SHOULD send a RST to show that data was lost.

When a connection is closed actively, it MUST linger in TIME-WAIT state for a time 2xMSL (Maximum Segment Lifetime). However, it MAY accept a new SYN from the remote TCP to reopen the connection directly from TIME-WAIT state, if it

1. Assigns its initial sequence number for the new connection to be larger than the largest sequence number it used on the previous connection incarnation

2. Returns to TIME-WAIT state if the SYN turns out to be an old duplicate

DISCUSSION:
TCP's full-duplex data-preserving close is a feature that is not included in the analogous ISO transport protocol TP4.

Some systems have not implemented half-closed connections, presumably because they do not fit into the I/O model of their particular operating system. On these systems, once an application has called CLOSE, it can no longer read input data from the connection; this is referred to as a "half-duplex" TCP close sequence. The graceful close algorithm of TCP requires that the connection state remain defined on (at least) one end of the connection, for a timeout period of 2xMSL, i.e., 4 minutes. During this period, the (remote socket, local socket) pair that defines the connection is busy and cannot be reused. To shorten the time that a given port pair is tied up, some TCPs allow a new SYN to be accepted in TIME-WAIT state.

4.2.2.14 Data Communication: RFC-793 Section 3.7

Since RFC-793 was written, there has been extensive work on TCP algorithms to achieve efficient data communication. Later sections of the present document describe required and recommended TCP algorithms to determine when to send data (Section 4.2.3.4), when to send an acknowledgment (Section 4.2.3.2), and when to update the window (Section 4.2.3.3).

DISCUSSION:
One important performance issue is "Silly Window Syndrome" or "SWS" [TCP:5], a stable pattern of small incremental window movements resulting in extremely poor TCP performance. Algorithms to avoid SWS are described below for both the sending side (Section 4.2.3.4) and the receiving side (Section 4.2.3.3).

In brief, SWS is caused by the receiver advancing the right window edge whenever it has any new buffer space available to receive data and by the sender using any incremental window, no matter how small, to send more data [TCP:5]. The result can be a stable pattern of sending tiny data segments, even though both sender and receiver have a large total buffer space for the connection. SWS can only occur during the transmission of a large amount of data; if the connection goes quiescent, the problem will disappear. It is caused by typical straightforward implementation of window management, but the sender and receiver algorithms given below will avoid it.

Another important TCP performance issue is that some applications, especially remote login to character-at-a-time hosts, tend to send streams of one-octet data segments. To avoid deadlocks, every TCP SEND call from such applications must be "pushed," either explicitly by the application or else implicitly by TCP. The result may be a stream of TCP segments that contain one data octet each, which makes very inefficient use of the Internet and contributes to Internet congestion.

The Nagle Algorithm described in Section 4.2.3.4 provides a simple and effective solution to this problem. It does have the effect of clumping characters over Telnet connections; this may initially surprise users accustomed to single-character echo, but user acceptance has not been a problem.

Note that the Nagle algorithm and the send SWS avoidance algorithm play complementary roles in improving performance. The Nagle algorithm discourages sending tiny segments when the data to be sent increases in small increments, while the SWS avoidance algorithm discourages small segments resulting from the right window edge advancing in small increments. A careless implementation can send two or more acknowledgment segments per data segment received. For example, suppose the receiver acknowledges every data segment immediately. When the application program subsequently consumes the data and increases the available receive buffer space again, the receiver may send a second acknowledgment segment to update the window at the sender. The extreme case occurs with single-character segments on TCP connections using the Telnet protocol for remote login service. Some implementations have been observed in which each incoming 1-character segment generates three return segments: (1) the acknowledgment, (2) a one byte increase in the window, and (3) the echoed character, respectively.

4.2.2.15 Retransmission Timeout: RFC-793 Section 3.7

The algorithm suggested in RFC-793 for calculating the retransmission timeout is now known to be inadequate; see Section 4.2.3.1.

Recent work by Jacobson [TCP:7] on Internet congestion and TCP retransmission stability has produced a transmission algorithm combining "slow start" with "congestion avoidance." A TCP MUST implement this algorithm. If a retransmitted packet is identical to the original packet (which implies not only that the data boundaries have not changed, but also that the window and acknowledgment fields of the header have not changed), then the same IP Identification field MAY be used (see Section 3.2.1.5).

IMPLEMENTATION:

Some TCP implementors have chosen to "packetize" the data stream, i.e., to pick segment boundaries when segments are originally sent and to queue these segments in a "retransmission queue" until they are acknowledged. Another design (which may be simpler) is to defer packetizing until each time data is transmitted or retransmitted, so there will be no segment retransmission queue.

In an implementation with a segment retransmission queue, TCP performance may be enhanced by repacketizing the segments awaiting acknowledgment when the first retransmission timeout occurs. That is, the outstanding segments that fitted would be combined into one maximum-sized segment, with a new IP Identification value. The TCP would then retain this combined segment in the retransmit queue until it was acknowledged. However, if the first two segments in the retransmission queue totaled more than one maximum-sized segment, the TCP would retransmit only the first segment using the original IP Identification field.

4.2.2.16 Managing the Window: RFC-793 Section 3.7

A TCP receiver SHOULD NOT shrink the window, i.e., move the right window edge to the left. However, a sending TCP MUST be robust against window shrinking, which may cause the "useable window" (see Section 4.2.3.4) to become negative. If this happens, the sender SHOULD NOT send new data, but SHOULD retransmit normally the old unacknowledged data between SND.UNA and SND.UNA+SND.WND. The sender MAY also retransmit old data beyond SND.UNA+SND.WND, but SHOULD NOT time out the connection if data beyond the right window edge is not acknowledged. If the window shrinks to zero, the TCP MUST probe it in the standard way (see next Section).

DISCUSSION:

Many TCP implementations become confused if the window shrinks from the right after data has been sent into a larger window. Note that TCP has a heuristic to select the latest window update despite possible datagram reordering; as a result, it may ignore a window update with a smaller window than previously offered if neither the sequence number nor the acknowledgment number is increased.

4.2.2.17 Probing Zero Windows: RFC-793 Section 3.7

Probing of zero (offered) windows MUST be supported. A TCP MAY keep its offered receive window closed indefinitely. As long as the receiving TCP continues to send acknowledgments in response to the probe segments, the sending TCP MUST allow the connection to stay open.

DISCUSSION:

It is extremely important to remember that ACK (acknowledgment) segments that contain no data are not reliably transmitted by TCP. If zero window probing is not supported, a connection may hang forever when an ACK segment that re-opens the window is lost. The delay in opening a zero window generally occurs when the receiving application stops taking data from its TCP. For example, consider a printer daemon application, stopped because the printer ran out of paper.

The transmitting host SHOULD send the first zero-window probe when a zero window has existed for the retransmission timeout period (see Section 4.2.2.15), and SHOULD increase exponentially the interval between successive probes.

DISCUSSION:

This procedure minimizes delay if the zero-window condition is due to a lost ACK segment containing a window-opening update. Exponential backoff is recommended, possibly with some maximum interval not specified here. This procedure is similar to that of the retransmission algorithm, and it may be possible to combine the two procedures in the implementation.

4.2.2.18 Passive OPEN Calls: RFC-793 Section 3.8

Every passive OPEN call either creates a new connection record in LISTEN state, or it returns an error; it MUST NOT affect any previously created connection record. A TCP that supports multiple concurrent users MUST provide an OPEN call that will functionally allow an application to LISTEN on a port while a connection block with the same local port is in SYN-SENT or SYN-RECEIVED state.

DISCUSSION:

Some applications (e.g., SMTP servers) may need to handle multiple connection attempts at about the same time. The probability of a connection attempt failing is reduced by giving the application some means of listening for a new connection at the same time that an earlier connection attempt is going through the three-way handshake.

IMPLEMENTATION:

Acceptable implementations of concurrent opens may permit multiple passive OPEN calls, or they may allow "cloning" of LISTEN-state connections from a single passive OPEN call.

4.2.2.19 Time to Live: RFC-793 Section 3.9

RFC-793 specified that TCP was to request the IP layer to send TCP segments with TTL = 60. This is obsolete; the TTL value used to send TCP segments MUST be configurable. See Section 3.2.1.7 for discussion.

4.2.2.20 Event Processing: RFC-793 Section 3.9

While it is not strictly required, a TCP SHOULD be capable of queuing out-of-order TCP segments. Change the "may" in the last sentence of the first paragraph on page 70 to "should."

DISCUSSION:

Some small-host implementations have omitted segment queuing because of limited buffer space. This omission may be expected to adversely affect TCP throughput, since loss of a single segment causes all later segments to appear to be "out of sequence."

(The smoothed variance is to be initialized to the value that will result in this RTO). The recommended upper and lower bounds on the RTO are known to be inadequate on large internets. The lower bound SHOULD be measured in fractions of a second (to accommodate high speed LANs) and the upper bound should be 2*MSL, i.e., 240 seconds.

DISCUSSION:

Experience has shown that these initialization values are reasonable, and that in any case the Karn and Jacobson algorithms make TCP behavior reasonably insensitive to the initial parameter choices.

4.2.3.2 When to Send an ACK Segment

A host that is receiving a stream of TCP data segments can increase efficiency in both the Internet and the hosts by sending fewer than one ACK (acknowledgment) segment per data segment received; this is known as a "delayed ACK" [TCP:5]. A TCP SHOULD implement a delayed ACK, but an ACK should not be excessively delayed; in particular, the delay MUST be less than 0.5 seconds, and in a stream of full-sized segments there SHOULD be an ACK for at least every second segment.

DISCUSSION:

A delayed ACK gives the application an opportunity to update the window and perhaps to send an immediate response. In particular, in the case of character-mode remote login, a delayed ACK can reduce the number of segments sent by the server by a factor of 3 (ACK, window update, and echo character all combined in one segment). In addition, on some large multi-user hosts, a delayed ACK can substantially reduce protocol processing overhead by reducing the total number of packets to be processed [TCP:5]. However, excessive delays on ACK's can disturb the round-trip timing and packet "clocking" algorithms [TCP:7].

4.2.3.3 When to Send a Window Update

A TCP MUST include a SWS avoidance algorithm in the receiver [TCP:5].

IMPLEMENTATION:

The receiver's SWS avoidance algorithm determines when the right window edge may be advanced; this is customarily known as "updating the window." This algorithm combines with the delayed ACK algorithm (see Section 4.2.3.2) to determine when an ACK segment containing the current window will really be sent to the receiver. We use the notation of RFC-793; see Figures 4 and 5 in that document.

The solution to receiver SWS is to avoid advancing the right window edge RCV.NXT+RCV.WND in small increments, even if data is received from the network in small segments.

Suppose the total receive buffer space is RCV.BUFF. At any given moment, RCV.USER octets of this total may be tied up with data that has been received and acknowledged but which the user process has not yet consumed. When the connection is quiescent, RCV.WND = RCV.BUFF and RCV.USER = 0.

Keeping the right window edge fixed as data arrives and is acknowledged requires that the receiver offer less than its full buffer space, i.e., the receiver must specify a RCV.WND that keeps RCV.NXT+RCV.WND constant as RCV.NXT increases. Thus, the total buffer space RCV.BUFF is generally divided into three parts:

```
|<———— RCV.BUFF ————————>|
1 23
——|————-|————————|———|———
RCV.NXT^
(Fixed)
```

1. RCV.USER = data received but not yet consumed;

2. RCV.WND = space advertised to sender;

3. Reduction = space available but not yet advertised.

The suggested SWS avoidance algorithm for the receiver is to keep RCV.NXT+RCV.WND fixed until the reduction satisfies:

RCV.BUFF - RCV.USER - RCV.WND >=

min(Fr $\star$ RCV.BUFF, Eff.snd.MSS)

where Fr is a fraction whose recommended value is 1/2, and Eff.snd.MSS is the effective send MSS for the connection (see Section 4.2.2.6). When the inequality is satisfied, RCV.WND is set to RCV.BUFF-RCV.USER. Note that the general effect of this algorithm is to advance RCV.WND in increments of Eff.snd.MSS (for realistic receive buffers: Eff.snd.MSS < RCV.BUFF/2). Note also that the receiver must use its own Eff.snd.MSS, assuming it is the same as the sender's.

4.2.3.4 When to Send Data

A TCP MUST include a SWS avoidance algorithm in the sender.

A TCP SHOULD implement the Nagle Algorithm [TCP:9] to coalesce short segments. However, there MUST be a way for an application to disable the Nagle algorithm on an individual connection. In all cases, sending data is also subject to the limitation imposed by the Slow Start algorithm (Section 4.2.2.15).

DISCUSSION:

The Nagle algorithm is generally as follows:

If there is unacknowledged data (i.e., SND.NXT > SND.UNA), then the sending TCP buffers all user data (regardless of the PSH bit), until the outstanding data has been acknowledged or until the TCP can send a full-sized segment (Eff.snd.MSS bytes; see Section 4.2.2.6).

Some applications (e.g., real-time display window updates) require that the Nagle algorithm be turned off, so small data segments can be streamed out at the maximum rate.

IMPLEMENTATION:

The sender's SWS avoidance algorithm is more difficult than the receiver's, because the sender does not know (directly) the receiver's total buffer space RCV.BUFF. An approach which has been found to work well is for the sender to calculate Max (SND.WND), the maximum send window it has seen so far on the connection, and to use this value as an estimate of RCV.BUFF. Unfortunately, this can only be an estimate; the receiver may at any time reduce the size of RCV.BUFF. To avoid a resulting dead-lock, it is necessary to have a timeout to force transmission of data, overriding the SWS avoidance algorithm. In practice, this timeout should seldom occur.

The "useable window" [TCP:5] is:

$$U = SND.UNA + SND.WND - SND.NXT$$

i.e., the offered window less the amount of data sent but not acknowledged. If D is the amount of data queued in the sending TCP but not yet sent, then the following set of rules is recommended.

Send data:

(1) if a maximum-sized segment can be sent, i.e, if:

$$min(D,U) >= Eff.snd.MSS;$$

(2) or if the data is pushed and all queued data can be sent now, i.e., if:

$$[SND.NXT = SND.UNA \text{ and}] \text{ PUSHED and } D <= U$$

(the bracketed condition is imposed by the Nagle algorithm);

(3) or if at least a fraction Fs of the maximum window can be sent, i.e., if:

$$[SND.NXT = SND.UNA \text{ and}]$$
$$min(D.U) >= Fs \star Max(SND.WND);$$

(4) or if data is PUSHed and the override timeout occurs.

Here Fs is a fraction whose recommended value is 1/2. The override timeout should be in the range 0.1–1.0 seconds. It may be convenient to combine this timer with the timer used to probe zero windows (Section 4.2.2.17). Finally, note that the SWS avoidance algorithm just specified is to be used instead of the sender-side algorithm contained in [TCP:5].

4.2.3.5 TCP Connection Failures

Excessive retransmission of the same segment by TCP indicates some failure of the remote host or the Internet path. This failure may be of short or long duration. The following procedure MUST be used to handle excessive retransmissions of data segments [IP:11]:

(a) There are two thresholds R1 and R2 measuring the amount of retransmission that has occurred for the same segment. R1 and R2 might be measured in time units or as a count of retransmissions.

(b) When the number of transmissions of the same segment reaches or exceeds threshold R1, pass negative advice (see Section 3.3.1.4) to the IP layer, to trigger dead-gateway diagnosis.

(c) When the number of transmissions of the same segment reaches a threshold R2 greater than R1, close the connection.

(d) An application MUST be able to set the value for R2 for a particular connection. For example, an interactive application might set R2 to "infinity," giving the user control over when to disconnect.

(e) TCP SHOULD inform the application of the delivery problem (unless such information has been disabled by the application; see Section 4.2.4.1), when R1 is reached and before R2. This will allow a remote login (User Telnet) application program to inform the user, for example.

The value of R1 SHOULD correspond to at least 3 retransmissions, at the current RTO. The value of R2 SHOULD correspond to at least 100 seconds.

An attempt to open a TCP connection could fail with excessive retransmissions of the SYN segment or by receipt of a RST segment or an ICMP Port Unreachable. SYN retransmissions MUST be handled in the general way just described for data retransmissions, including notification of the application layer.

However, the values of R1 and R2 may be different for SYN and data segments. In particular, R2 for a SYN segment MUST be set large enough to provide retransmission of the segment for at least 3 minutes. The application can close the connection (i.e., give up on the open attempt) sooner, of course.

DISCUSSION:

Some Internet paths have significant setup times, and the number of such paths is likely to increase in the future.

4.2.3.6 TCP Keep-Alives

Implementors MAY include "keep-alives" in their TCP implementations, although this practice is not universally accepted. If keep-alives are included, the application MUST be able to turn them on or off for each TCP connection, and they MUST default to off. Keep-alive packets MUST only be sent when no data or acknowledgement packets have been received for the connection within an interval. This interval MUST be configurable and MUST default to no less than two hours.

It is extremely important to remember that ACK segments that contain no data are not reliably transmitted by TCP. Consequently, if a keep-alive mechanism is implemented it MUST NOT interpret failure to respond to any specific probe as a dead connection.

An implementation SHOULD send a keep-alive segment with no data; however, it MAY be configurable to send a keep-alive segment containing one garbage octet, for compatibility with erroneous TCP implementations.

DISCUSSION:

A "keep-alive" mechanism periodically probes the other end of a connection when the connection is otherwise idle, even when there is no data to be sent. The TCP specification does not include a keep-alive mechanism because it could: (1) cause perfectly good connections to break during transient Internet failures; (2) consume unnecessary bandwidth ("if no one is using the connection, who cares if it is still good?"); and (3) cost money for an Internet path that charges for packets.

Some TCP implementations, however, have included a keep-alive mechanism. To confirm that an idle connection is still active, these implementations send a probe segment designed to elicit a response from the peer TCP. Such a segment generally contains SEG.SEQ = SND.NXT-1 and may or may not contain one garbage octet of data. Note that on a quiet connection SND.NXT = RCV.NXT, so that this SEG.SEQ will be outside the window. Therefore, the probe causes the receiver to return an acknowledgment segment, confirming that the connection is still live. If the peer has dropped the connection due to a network partition or a crash, it will respond with a RST instead of an acknowledgment segment.

Unfortunately, some misbehaved TCP implementations fail to respond to a segment with SEG.SEQ = SND.NXT-1 unless the segment contains data. Alternatively, an implementation could determine whether a peer responded correctly to keep-alive packets with no garbage data octet. A TCP keep-alive mechanism should only be invoked in server applications that might otherwise hang indefinitely and consume resources unnecessarily if a client crashes or aborts a connection during a network failure.

4.2.3.7 TCP Multihoming

If an application on a multihomed host does not specify the local IP address when actively opening a TCP connection, then the TCP MUST ask the IP layer to select a local IP address before sending the (first) SYN. See the function GET_SRCADDR() in Section 3.4.

At all other times, a previous segment has either been sent or received on this connection, and TCP MUST use the same local address is used that was used in those previous segments.

4.2.3.8 IP Options

When received options are passed up to TCP from the IP layer, TCP MUST ignore options that it does not understand.

A TCP MAY support the Time Stamp and Record Route options. An application MUST be able to specify a source route when it actively opens a TCP connection, and this MUST take precedence over a source route received in a datagram.

When a TCP connection is OPENed passively and a packet arrives with a completed IP Source Route option (containing a return route), TCP MUST save the return route and use it for all segments sent on this connection. If a different source route arrives in a later segment, the later definition SHOULD override the earlier one.

4.2.3.9 ICMP Messages

TCP MUST act on an ICMP error message passed up from the IP layer, directing it to the connection that created the error. The necessary demultiplexing information can be found in the IP header contained within the ICMP message.

■ Source Quench—TCP MUST react to a Source Quench by slowing transmission on the connection. The RECOMMENDED procedure is for a Source Quench to trigger a "slow start," as if a retransmission timeout had occurred.

■ Destination Unreachable—codes 0, 1, 5. Since these Unreachable messages indicate soft error conditions, TCP MUST NOT abort the connection, and it SHOULD make the information available to the application.

DISCUSSION:
TCP could report the soft error condition directly to the application layer with an upcall to the ERROR_REPORT routine, or it could merely note the message and report it to the application only when and if the TCP connection times out.

■ Destination Unreachable—codes 2-4. These are hard error conditions, so TCP SHOULD abort the connection.

■ Time Exceeded—codes 0, 1. This should be handled the same way as Destination Unreachable codes 0, 1, 5 (see above).

■ Parameter Problem—This should be handled the same way as Destination Unreachable codes 0, 1, 5 (see above).

4.2.3.10 Remote Address Validation

A TCP implementation MUST reject as an error a local OPEN call for an invalid remote IP address (e.g., a broadcast or multicast address).
An incoming SYN with an invalid source address must be ignored either by TCP or by the IP layer (see Section 3.2.1.3).
A TCP implementation MUST silently discard an incoming SYN segment that is addressed to a broadcast or multicast address.

4.2.3.11 TCP Traffic Patterns

IMPLEMENTATION:
The TCP protocol specification [TCP:1] gives the implementor much freedom in designing the algorithms that control the message flow over the connection—packetizing, managing the window, sending acknowledgments, etc. These design decisions are difficult because a TCP must adapt to a wide range of traffic patterns. Experience has shown that a TCP implementor needs to verify the design on two extreme traffic patterns:

■ Single-character Segments—Even if the sender is using the Nagle Algorithm, when a TCP connection carries remote login traffic across a low-delay LAN the receiver will generally get a stream of single-character segments. If remote terminal echo mode is in effect, the receiver's system will generally echo each character as it is received.

■ Bulk Transfer—When TCP is used for bulk transfer, the data stream should be made up (almost) entirely of segments of the size of the effective MSS. Although TCP uses a sequence number space with byte (octet) granularity, in bulk-transfer

Feature	Section	Must	Should	May	Should Not	Must Not	Footnote
Ask IP for src address for SYN if necc.	4.2.3.7	x					
Otherwise, use local addr of conn.	4.2.3.7	x					
OPEN to broadcast/ multicast IP Address	4.2.3.14					x	
Silently discard seg to bcast/mcast addr	4.2.3.14	x					
Closing Connections							
RST can contain data	4.2.2.12		x				
Inform application of aborted conn	4.2.2.13	x					
Half-duplex close connections	4.2.2.13			x			
Send RST to indicate data lost	4.2.2.13		x				
In TIME-WAIT state for 2xMSL seconds	4.2.2.13	x					
Accept SYN from TIME-WAIT state	4.2.2.13			x			
Retransmissions							
Jacobson Slow Start algorithm	4.2.2.15	x					
Jacobson Congestion-Avoidance algorithm	4.2.2.15	x					
Retransmit with same IP ident	4.2.2.15			x			
Karn's algorithm	4.2.3.1	x					
Jacobson's RTO estimation alg.	4.2.3.1	x					
Exponential backoff	4.2.3.1	x					
SYN RTO calc same as data	4.2.3.1		x				
Recommended initial values and bounds	4.2.3.1		x				
Generating ACK's:							
Queue out-of-order segments	4.2.2.20		x				
Process all Q'd before send ACK	4.2.2.20	x					

continues

4.2.5 TCP REQUIREMENT SUMMARY (Continued)

Feature	Section	Must	Should	May	Should Not	Must Not	Footnote
Send ACK for out-of-order segment	4.2.2.21			x			
Delayed ACK's	4.2.3.2		x				
Delay < 0.5 seconds	4.2.3.2	x					
Every 2nd full-sized segment ACK'd	4.2.3.2	x					
Receiver SWS-Avoidance Algorithm	4.2.3.3	x					
Sending data							
Configurable TTL	4.2.2.19	x					
Sender SWS-Avoidance Algorithm	4.2.3.4	x					
Nagle algorithm	4.2.3.4		x				
Application can disable Nagle algorithm	4.2.3.4	x					
Connection Failures:							
Negative advice to IP on R1 retxs	4.2.3.5	x					
Close connection on R2 retxs	4.2.3.5	x					
ALP can set R2	4.2.3.5	x					1
Inform ALP of R1<=retxs<R2	4.2.3.5		x				1
Recommended values for R1, R2	4.2.3.5		x				
Same mechanism for SYNs	4.2.3.5	x					
R2 at least 3 minutes for SYN	4.2.3.5	x					
Send Keep-alive Packets:	4.2.3.6			x			
- Application can request	4.2.3.6	x					
- Default is "off"	4.2.3.6	x					
- Only send if idle for interval	4.2.3.6	x					
- Interval configurable	4.2.3.6	x					
- Default at least 2 hrs.	4.2.3.6	x					
- Tolerant of lost ACK's	4.2.3.6	x					

Feature	Section	Must	Should	May	Should Not	Must Not	Footnote
IP Options							
Ignore options TCP doesn't understand	4.2.3.8	x					
Time Stamp support	4.2.3.8			x			
Record Route support	4.2.3.8			x			
Source Route:							
ALP can specify	4.2.3.8	x					1
Overrides src rt in datagram	4.2.3.8	x					
Build return route from src rt	4.2.3.8	x					
Later src route overrides	4.2.3.8		x				
Receiving ICMP Messages from IP	4.2.3.9	x					
Dest. Unreach (0,1,5) => inform ALP	4.2.3.9		x				
Dest. Unreach (0,1,5) => abort conn	4.2.3.9				x		
Dest. Unreach (2-4) => abort conn	4.2.3.9		x				
Source Quench => slow start	4.2.3.9		x				
Time Exceeded => tell ALP, don't abort	4.2.3.9		x				
Param Problem => tell ALP, don't abort	4.2.3.9		x				
Address Validation							
Reject OPEN call to invalid IP address	4.2.3.10	x					
Reject SYN from invalid IP address	4.2.3.10	x					
Silently discard SYN to bcast/mcast addr	4.2.3.10	x					
TCP/ALP Interface Services							
Error Report mechanism	4.2.4.1	x					
ALP can disable Error Report Routine	4.2.4.1		x				

continues

4.2.5 TCP REQUIREMENT SUMMARY (Continued)

Feature	Section	Must	Should	May	Should Not	Must Not	Footnote
ALP can specify TOS for sending	4.2.4.2	x					
Passed unchanged to IP	4.2.4.2		x				
ALP can change TOS during connection	4.2.4.2		x				
Pass received TOS up to ALP	4.2.4.2			x			
FLUSH call	4.2.4.3			x			
Optional local IP addr parm. in OPEN	4.2.4.4	x					

FOOTNOTES:
(1) "ALP" means Application-Layer program.

5. REFERENCES

INTRODUCTORY REFERENCES

[INTRO:1] "Requirements for Internet Hosts — Application and Support," IETF Host Requirements Working Group, R. Braden, Ed., RFC-1123, October 1989.

[INTRO:2] "Requirements for Internet Gateways," R. Braden and J. Postel, RFC-1009, June 1987.

[INTRO:3] "DDN Protocol Handbook," NIC-50004, NIC-50005, NIC-50006, (three volumes), SRI International, December 1985.

[INTRO:4] "Official Internet Protocols," J. Reynolds and J. Postel, RFC-1011, May 1987.

This document is republished periodically with new RFC numbers; the latest version must be used.

[INTRO:5] "Protocol Document Order Information," O. Jacobsen and J. Postel, RFC-980, March 1986.

[INTRO:6] "Assigned Numbers," J. Reynolds and J. Postel, RFC-1010, May 1987.

This document is republished periodically with new RFC numbers; the latest version must be used.

[INTRO:7] "Modularity and Efficiency in Protocol Implementations," D. Clark, RFC-817, July 1982.

[INTRO:8] "The Structuring of Systems Using Upcalls," D. Clark, 10th ACM SOSP, Orcas Island, Washington, December 1985.

Secondary References:

[INTRO:9] "A Protocol for Packet Network Intercommunication," V. Cerf and R. Kahn, IEEE Transactions on Communication, May 1974.

[INTRO:10] "The ARPA Internet Protocol," J. Postel, C. Sunshine, and D. Cohen, Computer Networks, Vol. 5, No. 4, July 1981.

[INTRO:11] "The DARPA Internet Protocol Suite," B. Leiner, J. Postel, R. Cole and D. Mills, Proceedings INFOCOM 85, IEEE, Washington DC, March 1985. Also in: IEEE Communications Magazine, March 1985. Also available as ISI-RS-85-153.

[INTRO:12] "Final Text of DIS8473, Protocol for Providing the Connectionless Mode Network Service," ANSI, published as RFC-994, March 1986.

[INTRO:13] "End System to Intermediate System Routing Exchange Protocol," ANSI X3S3.3, published as RFC-995, April 1986.

LINK LAYER REFERENCES

[LINK:1] "Trailer Encapsulations," S. Leffler and M. Karels, RFC-893, April 1984.

[LINK:2] "An Ethernet Address Resolution Protocol," D. Plummer, RFC-826, November 1982.

[LINK:3] "A Standard for the Transmission of IP Datagrams over Ethernet Networks," C. Hornig, RFC-894, April 1984.

[LINK:4] "A Standard for the Transmission of IP Datagrams over IEEE 802 "Networks," J. Postel and J. Reynolds, RFC-1042, February 1988. This RFC contains a great deal of information of importance to Internet implementers planning to use IEEE 802 networks.

IP LAYER REFERENCES

[IP:1] "Internet Protocol (IP)," J. Postel, RFC-791, September 1981.

[IP:2] "Internet Control Message Protocol (ICMP)," J. Postel, RFC-792, September 1981.

[IP:3] "Internet Standard Subnetting Procedure," J. Mogul and J. Postel, RFC-950, August 1985.

[IP:4] "Host Extensions for IP Multicasting," S. Deering, RFC-1112, August 1989.

[IP:5] "Military Standard Internet Protocol," MIL-STD-1777, Department of Defense, August 1983.

This specification, as amended by RFC-963, is intended to describe the Internet Protocol but has some serious omissions (e.g., the mandatory subnet extension [IP:3] and the optional multicasting extension [IP:4]). It is also out of date. If there is a conflict, RFC-791, RFC-792, and RFC-950 must be taken as authoritative, while the present document is authoritative over all.

[IP:6] "Some Problems with the Specification of the Military Standard Internet Protocol," D. Sidhu, RFC-963, November 1985.

[IP:7] "The TCP Maximum Segment Size and Related Topics," J. Postel, RFC-879, November 1983.

Discusses and clarifies the relationship between the TCP Maximum Segment Size option and the IP datagram size.

[IP:8] "Internet Protocol Security Options," B. Schofield, RFC-1108, October 1989.

[IP:9] "Fragmentation Considered Harmful," C. Kent and J. Mogul, ACM SIG-COMM-87, August 1987. Published as ACM Comp Comm Review, Vol. 17, no. 5. This useful paper discusses the problems created by Internet fragmentation and presents alternative solutions.

[IP:10] "IP Datagram Reassembly Algorithms," D. Clark, RFC-815, July 1982. This and the following paper should be read by every implementor.

[IP:11] "Fault Isolation and Recovery," D. Clark, RFC-816, July 1982.

SECONDARY IP REFERENCES:

[IP:12] "Broadcasting Internet Datagrams in the Presence of Subnets," J. Mogul, RFC-922, October 1984.

[IP:13] "Name, Addresses, Ports, and Routes," D. Clark, RFC-814, July 1982.

[IP:14] "Something a Host Could Do with Source Quench: The Source Quench Introduced Delay (SQUID)," W. Prue and J. Postel, RFC-1016, July 1987. This RFC first described directed broadcast addresses. However, the bulk of the RFC is concerned with gateways, not hosts.

UDP REFERENCE:

[UDP:1] "User Datagram Protocol," J. Postel, RFC-768, August 1980.

TCP REFERENCES:

[TCP:1] "Transmission Control Protocol," J. Postel, RFC-793, September 1981.

[TCP:2] "Transmission Control Protocol," MIL-STD-1778, US Department of Defense, August 1984. This specification as amended by RFC-964 is intended to describe the same protocol as RFC-793 [TCP:1]. If there is a conflict, RFC-793 takes precedence, and the present document is authoritative over both.

[TCP:3] "Some Problems with the Specification of the Military Standard Transmission Control Protocol," D. Sidhu and T. Blumer, RFC-964, November 1985.

[TCP:4] "The TCP Maximum Segment Size and Related Topics," J. Postel, RFC-879, November 1983.

[TCP:5] "Window and Acknowledgment Strategy in TCP," D. Clark, RFC-813, July 1982.

[TCP:6] "Round Trip Time Estimation," P. Karn & C. Partridge, ACM SIGCOMM-87, August 1987.

[TCP:7] "Congestion Avoidance and Control," V. Jacobson, ACM SIGCOMM-88, August 1988.

SECONDARY TCP REFERENCES:

[TCP:8] "Modularity and Efficiency in Protocol Implementation," D. Clark, RFC-817, July 1982.

[TCP:9] "Congestion Control in IP/TCP," J. Nagle, RFC-896, January 1984.

[TCP:10] "Computing the Internet Checksum," R. Braden, D. Borman, and C. Partridge, RFC-1071, September 1988.

[TCP:11] "TCP Extensions for Long-Delay Paths," V. Jacobson & R. Braden, RFC-1072, October 1988.

Security Considerations

There are many security issues in the communication layers of host software, but a full discussion is beyond the scope of this RFC.

The Internet architecture generally provides little protection against spoofing of IP source addresses, so any security mechanism that is based upon verifying the IP source address of a datagram should be treated with suspicion. However, in restricted environments some source-address checking may be possible. For example, there might be a secure LAN whose gateway to the rest of the Internet discarded any incoming datagram with a source address that spoofed the LAN address. In this case, a host on the LAN could use the source address to test for local vs. remote source. This problem is complicated by source routing, and some have suggested that source-routed datagram forwarding by hosts (see Section 3.3.5) should be outlawed for security reasons.

Security-related issues are mentioned in sections concerning the IP Security option (Section 3.2.1.8), the ICMP Parameter Problem message (Section 3.2.2.5), IP options in UDP datagrams (Section 4.1.3.2), and reserved TCP ports (Section 4.2.2.1).

Author's Address

Robert Braden

USC/Information Sciences Institute

4676 Admiralty Way

Marina del Rey, CA 90292-6695

Phone: (213) 822 1511

EMail: Braden@ISI.EDU

RFC-1123

Network Working Group—Internet Engineering Task Force
Request for Comments: 1123   R. Braden, Editor
October 1989

Requirements for Internet Hosts—Application and Support

Status of This Memo

This RFC is an official specification for the Internet community. It incorporates by reference, amends, corrects, and supplements the primary protocol standards documents relating to hosts. Distribution of this document is unlimited.

Summary

This RFC is one of a pair that defines and discusses the requirements for Internet host software. This RFC covers the application and support protocols; its companion RFC-1122 covers the communication protocol layers: link layer, IP layer, and transport layer.

Table of Contents

1. INTRODUCTION

This document is one of a pair that defines and discusses the requirements for host system implementations of the Internet protocol suite. This RFC covers the applications layer and support protocols. Its companion RFC, "Requirements for Internet Hosts—Communications Layers" [INTRO:1] covers the lower layer protocols: transport layer, IP layer, and link layer.

These documents are intended to provide guidance for vendors, implementors, and users of Internet communication software. They represent the consensus of a large body of technical experience and wisdom, contributed by members of the Internet research and vendor communities.

This RFC enumerates standard protocols that a host connected to the Internet must use, and it incorporates by reference the RFCs and other documents describing the current specifications for these protocols. It corrects errors in the referenced documents and adds additional discussion and guidance for an implementor.

For each protocol, this document also contains an explicit set of requirements, recommendations, and options. The reader must understand that the list of requirements in this document is incomplete by itself; the complete set of requirements for an Internet host is primarily defined in the standard protocol specification documents, with the corrections, amendments, and supplements contained in this RFC.

A good-faith implementation of the protocols that was produced after careful reading of the RFC's and with some interaction with the Internet technical community, and that followed good communications software engineering practices, should differ from the requirements of this document in only minor ways. Thus, in many cases, the "requirements" in this RFC are already stated or implied in the standard protocol documents, so that their inclusion here is, in a sense, redundant. However, they were included because some past implementation has made the wrong choice, causing problems of interoperability, performance, and/or robustness.

This document includes discussion and explanation of many of the requirements and recommendations. A simple list of requirements would be dangerous, because:

- Some required features are more important than others, and some features are optional.

- There may be valid reasons why particular vendor products that are designed for restricted contexts might choose to use different specifications.

However, the specifications of this document must be followed to meet the general goal of arbitrary host interoperation across the diversity and complexity of the Internet system. Although most current implementations fail to meet these requirements in various ways, some minor and some major, this specification is the ideal toward which we need to move.

These requirements are based on the current level of Internet architecture. This document will be updated as required to provide additional clarifications or to include additional information in those areas in which specifications are still evolving.

This introductory section begins with general advice to host software vendors, and then gives some guidance on reading the rest of the document. Section 2 contains general requirements that may be applicable to all application and support protocols. Sections 3, 4, and 5 contain the requirements on protocols for the three major applications: Telnet, file transfer, and electronic mail, respectively. Section 6 covers the support applications: the domain name system, system initialization, and management. Finally, all references are found in Section 7.

1.1 The Internet Architecture

For a brief introduction to the Internet architecture from a host viewpoint, see Section 1.1 of [INTRO:1]. That section also contains recommended references for general background on the Internet architecture.

1.2 General Considerations

There are two important lessons that vendors of Internet host software have learned and which a new vendor should consider seriously.

1.2.1 Continuing Internet Evolution

The enormous growth of the Internet has revealed problems of management and scaling in a large datagram-based packet communication system. These problems are being addressed, and as a result there will be continuing evolution of the specifications described in this document. These changes will be carefully planned and controlled, since there is extensive participation in this planning by the vendors and by the organizations responsible for operations of the networks.

Development, evolution, and revision are characteristic of computer network protocols today, and this situation will persist for some years. A vendor who develops computer communication software for the Internet protocol suite (or any other protocol suite!) and then fails to maintain and update that software for changing specifications is going to leave a trail of unhappy customers. The Internet is a large communication network, and the users are in constant contact through it. Experience has shown that knowledge of deficiencies in vendor software propagates quickly through the Internet technical community.

1.2.2 Robustness Principle

At every layer of the protocols, there is a general rule whose application can lead to enormous benefits in robustness and interoperability:

"Be liberal in what you accept, and conservative in what you send."

Software should be written to deal with every conceivable error, no matter how unlikely; sooner or later a packet will come in with that particular combination of errors and attributes, and unless the software is prepared, chaos can ensue. In general, it is best to assume that the network is filled with malevolent entities that will send in packets designed to have the worst possible effect. This assumption will lead to suitable protective design, although the most serious problems in the Internet have been caused by unenvisaged mechanisms triggered by low-probability events; mere human malice would never have taken so devious a course!

Adaptability to change must be designed into all levels of Internet host software. As a simple example, consider a protocol specification that contains an enumeration of values for a particular header field—e.g., a type field, a port number, or an error code; this enumeration must be assumed to be incomplete. Thus, if a protocol specification defines four possible error codes, the software must not break when a fifth code shows up. An undefined code might be logged (see below), but it must not cause a failure. The second part of the principle is almost as important: software on other hosts may contain deficiencies that make it unwise to exploit legal but obscure protocol features. It is unwise to stray far from the obvious and simple, lest untoward effects result elsewhere. A corollary of this is "watch out for misbehaving hosts"; host software should be prepared, not just to survive other misbehaving hosts, but also to cooperate to limit the amount of disruption such hosts can cause to the shared communication facility.

1.2.3 Error Logging

The Internet includes a great variety of host and gateway systems, each implementing many protocols and protocol layers, and some of these contain bugs and misfeatures in their Internet protocol software. As a result of complexity, diversity, and distribution of function, the diagnosis of user problems is often very difficult. Problem diagnosis will be aided if host implementations include a carefully designed facility for logging erroneous or "strange" protocol events. It is important to include as much diagnostic information as possible when an error is logged. In particular, it is often useful to record the header(s) of a packet that caused an error. However, care must be taken to ensure that error logging does not consume prohibitive amounts of resources or otherwise interfere with the operation of the host.

There is a tendency for abnormal but harmless protocol events to overflow error logging files; this can be avoided by using a "circular" log, or by enabling logging only while diagnosing a known failure. It may be useful to filter and count duplicate successive messages. One strategy that seems to work well is: (1) always count abnormalities and make such counts accessible through the management protocol (see Section 6.3); and (2) allow the logging of a great variety of events to be selectively enabled. For example, it might useful to be able to "log everything" or to "log everything for host X."

Note that different management may have differing policies about the amount of error logging that they want normally enabled in a host. Some will say, "if it doesn't hurt me, I don't want to know about it," while others will want to take a more watchful and aggressive attitude about detecting and removing protocol abnormalities.

1.2.4 Configuration

It would be ideal if a host implementation of the Internet protocol suite could be entirely self-configuring. This would allow the whole suite to be implemented in ROM or cast into silicon, it would simplify diskless workstations, and it would be an immense boon to harried LAN administrators as well as system vendors. We have not reached this ideal; in fact, we are not even close.

At many points in this document, you will find a requirement that a parameter be a configurable option. There are several different reasons behind such requirements. In a few cases, there is current uncertainty or disagreement about the best value, and it may be necessary to update the recommended value in the future. In other cases, the value really depends on external factors—e.g., the size of the host and the distribution of its communication load, or the speeds and topology of nearby networks—and self-tuning algorithms are unavailable and may be insufficient. In some cases, configurability is needed because of administrative requirements.

Finally, some configuration options are required to communicate with obsolete or incorrect implementations of the protocols, distributed without sources, that unfortunately persist in many parts of the Internet. To make correct systems coexist with these faulty systems, administrators often have to "misconfigure" the correct systems. This problem will correct itself gradually as the faulty systems are retired, but it cannot be ignored by vendors.

When we say that a parameter must be configurable, we do not intend to require that its value be explicitly read from a configuration file at every boot time. We recommend that implementors set up a default for each parameter, so a configuration file is only necessary to override those defaults that are inappropriate in a particular installation. Thus, the configurability requirement is an assurance that it will be POSSIBLE to override the default when necessary, even in a binary-only or ROM-based product.

This document requires a particular value for such defaults in some cases. The choice of default is a sensitive issue when the configuration item controls the accommodation to existing faulty systems. If the Internet is to converge successfully to complete interoperability, the default values built into implementations must implement the official protocol, not "misconfigurations" to accommodate faulty implementations.

Although marketing considerations have led some vendors to choose misconfiguration defaults, we urge vendors to choose defaults that will conform to the standard.

Finally, we note that a vendor needs to provide adequate documentation on all configuration parameters, their limits and effects.

1.3 Reading this Document

1.3.1 Organization

In general, each major section is organized into the following subsections:

1. Introduction

2. Protocol Walk-Through—Considers the protocol specification documents section-by-section, correcting errors, stating requirements that may be ambiguous or ill-defined, and providing further clarification or explanation.

3. Specific Issues—Discusses protocol design and implementation issues that were not included in the walk-through.

4. Interfaces—Discusses the service interface to the next higher layer.

5. Summary—Contains a summary of the requirements of the section.

Under many of the individual topics in this document, there is parenthetical material labeled "DISCUSSION" or "IMPLEMENTATION." This material is intended to give clarification and explanation of the preceding requirements text. It also includes some suggestions on possible future directions or developments. The implementation material contains suggested approaches that an implementor may want to consider. The summary sections are intended to be guides and indexes to the text, but are necessarily cryptic and incomplete. The summaries should never be used or referenced separately from the complete RFC.

1.3.2 Requirements

In this document, the words that are used to define the significance of each particular requirement are capitalized. These words are:

- "MUST"—This word or the adjective "REQUIRED" means that the item is an absolute requirement of the specification.

- "SHOULD"—This word or the adjective "RECOMMENDED" means that there may exist valid reasons in particular circumstances to ignore this item, but the full implications should be understood and the case carefully weighed before choosing a different course.

- "MAY"—This word or the adjective "OPTIONAL" means that this item is truly optional. One vendor may choose to include the item because a particular marketplace requires it or because it enhances the product, for example; another vendor may omit the same item.

An implementation is not compliant if it fails to satisfy one or more of the MUST requirements for the protocols it implements. An implementation that satisfies all the MUST and all the SHOULD requirements for its protocols is said to be "unconditionally compliant"; one that satisfies all the MUST requirements but not all the SHOULD requirements for its protocols is said to be "conditionally compliant."

1.3.3 Terminology

This document uses the following technical terms:

- Segment—A segment is the unit of end-to-end transmission in the TCP protocol. A segment consists of a TCP header followed by application data. A segment is transmitted by encapsulation in an IP datagram.

- Message—This term is used by some application layer protocols (particularly SMTP) for an application data unit.

- Datagram—A [UDP] datagram is the unit of end-to-end transmission in the UDP protocol.

- Multihomed—A host is said to be multihomed if it has multiple IP addresses to connected networks.

1.4 Acknowledgments

This document incorporates contributions and comments from a large group of Internet protocol experts, including representatives of university and research labs, vendors, and government agencies. It was assembled primarily by the Host Requirements Working Group of the Internet Engineering Task Force (IETF).

The Editor would especially like to acknowledge the tireless dedication of the following people, who attended many long meetings and generated 3 million bytes of electronic mail over the past 18 months in pursuit of this document: Philip Almquist, Dave Borman (Cray Research), Noel Chiappa, Dave Crocker (DEC), Steve Deering (Stanford), Mike Karels (Berkeley), Phil Karn (Bellcore), John Lekashman (NASA), Charles Lynn (BBN), Keith McCloghrie (TWG), Paul Mockapetris (ISI), Thomas Narten (Purdue), Craig Partridge (BBN), Drew Perkins (CMU), and James Van Bokkelen (FTP Software).

In addition, the following people made major contributions to the effort: Bill Barns (Mitre), Steve Bellovin (AT&T), Mike Brescia (BBN), Ed Cain (DCA), Annette DeSchon (ISI), Martin Gross (DCA), Phill Gross (NRI), Charles Hedrick (Rutgers), Van Jacobson (LBL), John Klensin (MIT), Mark Lottor (SRI), Milo Medin (NASA), Bill Melohn (Sun Microsystems), Greg Minshall (Kinetics), Jeff Mogul (DEC), John Mullen (CMC), Jon Postel (ISI), John Romkey (Epilogue Technology), and Mike StJohns (DCA). The following also made significant contributions to particular areas: Eric Allman (Berkeley), Rob Austein (MIT), Art Berggreen (ACC), Keith Bostic (Berkeley), Vint Cerf (NRI), Wayne Hathaway (NASA), Matt Korn (IBM), Erik Naggum (Naggum Software, Norway), Robert Ullmann (Prime Computer), David Waitzman (BBN), Frank Wancho (USA), Arun Welch (Ohio State), Bill Westfield (Cisco), and Rayan Zachariassen (Toronto).

We are grateful to all, including any contributors who may have been inadvertently omitted from this list.

2. GENERAL ISSUES

This section contains general requirements that may be applicable to all application-layer protocols.

2.1 Host Names and Numbers

The syntax of a legal Internet host name was specified in RFC-952 [DNS:4]. One aspect of host name syntax is hereby changed: the restriction on the first character is relaxed to allow either a letter or a digit. Host software MUST support this more liberal syntax.

Host software MUST handle host names of up to 63 characters and SHOULD handle host names of up to 255 characters.

Whenever a user inputs the identity of an Internet host, it SHOULD be possible to enter either (1) a host domain name or (2) an IP address in dotted-decimal ("#.#.#.#") form. The host SHOULD check the string syntactically for a dotted-decimal number before looking it up in the Domain Name System.

DISCUSSION:

This last requirement is not intended to specify the complete syntactic form for entering a dotted-decimal host number; that is considered to be a user-interface issue. For example, a dotted-decimal number must be enclosed within "[ ]" brackets for SMTP mail (see Section 5.2.17). This notation could be made universal within a host system, simplifying the syntactic checking for a dotted-decimal number.

If a dotted-decimal number can be entered without such identifying delimiters, then a full syntactic check must be made, because a segment of a host domain name is now allowed to begin with a digit and could legally be entirely numeric (see Section 6.1.2.4). However, a valid host name can never have the dotted-decimal form #.#.#.#, since at least the highest-level component label will be alphabetic.

2.2 Using Domain Name Service

Host domain names MUST be translated to IP addresses as described in Section 6.1. Applications using domain name services MUST be able to cope with soft error conditions. Applications MUST wait a reasonable interval between successive retries due to a soft error, and MUST allow for the possibility that network problems may deny service for hours or even days.

An application SHOULD NOT rely on the ability to locate a WKS record containing an accurate listing of all services at a particular host address, since the WKS RR type is not often used by Internet sites. To confirm that a service is present, simply attempt to use it.

2.3 Applications on Multihomed Hosts

When the remote host is multihomed, the name-to-address translation will return a list of alternative IP addresses. As specified in Section 6.1.3.4, this list should be in order of decreasing preference. Application protocol implementations SHOULD be prepared to try multiple addresses from the list until success is obtained. More specific requirements for SMTP are given in Section 5.3.4.

When the local host is multihomed, a UDP-based request/response application SHOULD send the response with an IP source address that is the same as the specific destination address of the UDP request datagram. The "specific destination address" is defined in the "IP Addressing" section of the companion RFC [INTRO:1]. Similarly, a server application that opens multiple TCP connections to the same client SHOULD use the same local IP address for all.

2.4 Type-of-Service

Applications MUST select appropriate TOS values when they invoke transport layer services, and these values MUST be configurable. Note that a TOS value contains 5 bits, of which only the most significant 3 bits are currently defined; the other two bits MUST be zero.

DISCUSSION:

As gateway algorithms are developed to implement Type-of-Service, the recommended values for various application protocols may change. In addition, it is likely that particular combinations of users and Internet paths will want non-standard TOS values. For these reasons, the TOS values must be configurable.

See the latest version of the "Assigned Numbers" RFC [INTRO:5] for the recommended TOS values for the major application protocols.

2.5 GENERAL APPLICATION REQUIREMENTS SUMMARY

Feature	Section	Must	Should	May	Should Not	Must Not	Footnote
User interfaces:							
Allow host name to begin with digit	2.1	x					
Host names of up to 635 characters	2.1	x					
Host names of up to 255 characters	2.1		x				
Support dotted-decimal host numbers	2.1		x				
Check syntactically for dotted-dec first	2.1		x				
Map domain names per Section 6.1	2.2	x					
Cope with soft DNS errors	2.2	x					
Reasonable interval between retries	2.2	x					
Allow for long outages	2.2	x					

continues

2.5 GENERAL APPLICATION REQUIREMENTS SUMMARY (Continued)

Feature	Section	Must	Should	May	Should Not	Must Not	Footnote
Expect WKS records to be available	2.2				x		
Try multiple addr's for remote multihomed host	2.3		x				
UDP reply src addr is specific dest of request	2.3		x				
Use same IP addr for related TCP connections	2.3		x				
Specify appropriate TOS values	2.4	x					
TOS values configurable	2.4	x					
Unused TOS bits zero	2.4	x					

3. REMOTE LOGIN—TELNET PROTOCOL

3.1 INTRODUCTION

Telnet is the standard Internet application protocol for remote login. It provides the encoding rules to link a user's keyboard/display on a client ("user") system with a command interpreter on a remote server system. A subset of the Telnet protocol is also incorporated within other application protocols, e.g., FTP and SMTP.

Telnet uses a single TCP connection, and its normal data stream ("Network Virtual Terminal" or "NVT" mode) is 7-bit ASCII with escape sequences to embed control functions. Telnet also allows the negotiation of many optional modes and functions. The primary Telnet specification is to be found in RFC-854 [TELNET:1], while the options are defined in many other RFCs; see Section 7 for references.

3.2 PROTOCOL WALK-THROUGH

3.2.1 Option Negotiation: RFC-854, pp. 2-3

Every Telnet implementation MUST include option negotiation and subnegotiation machinery [TELNET:2].

A host MUST carefully follow the rules of RFC-854 to avoid option-negotiation loops. A host MUST refuse (i.e, reply WONT/DONT to a DO/WILL) an unsupported option. Option negotiation SHOULD continue to function (even if all requests are refused) throughout the lifetime of a Telnet connection.

If all option negotiations fail, a Telnet implementation MUST default to, and support, an NVT.

DISCUSSION:

Even though more sophisticated "terminals" and supporting option negotiations are becoming the norm, all implementations must be prepared to support an NVT for any user-server communication.

3.2.2 Telnet Go-Ahead Function: RFC-854, p. 5, and RFC-858

On a host that never sends the Telnet command Go Ahead (GA), the Telnet Server MUST attempt to negotiate the Suppress Go Ahead option (i.e., send "WILL Suppress Go Ahead"). A User or Server Telnet MUST always accept negotiation of the Suppress Go Ahead option.

When it is driving a full-duplex terminal for which GA has no meaning, a User Telnet implementation MAY ignore GA commands.

DISCUSSION:

Half-duplex ("locked-keyboard") line-at-a-time terminals for which the Go-Ahead mechanism was designed have largely disappeared from the scene. It turned out to be difficult to implement sending the Go-Ahead signal in many operating systems, even some systems that support native half-duplex terminals. The difficulty is typically that the Telnet server code does not have access to information about whether the user process is blocked awaiting input from the Telnet connection, i.e., it cannot reliably determine when to send a GA command. Therefore, most Telnet Server hosts do not send GA commands.

The effect of the rules in this section is to allow either end of a Telnet connection to veto the use of GA commands. There is a class of half-duplex terminals that is still commercially important: "data entry terminals," which interact in a full-screen manner. However, supporting data entry terminals using the Telnet protocol does not require the Go Ahead signal; see Section 3.3.2.

3.2.3 Control Functions: RFC-854, pp. 7-8

The list of Telnet commands has been extended to include EOR (End-of-Record), with code 239 [TELNET:9].

Both User and Server Telnets MAY support the control functions EOR, EC, EL, and Break, and MUST support AO, AYT, DM, IP, NOP, SB, and SE.

A host MUST be able to receive and ignore any Telnet control functions that it does not support.

DISCUSSION:

Note that a Server Telnet is required to support the Telnet IP (Interrupt Process) function, even if the server host has an equivalent in-stream function (e.g., Control-C in many systems). The Telnet IP function may be stronger than an in-stream interrupt command, because of the out-of-band effect of TCP urgent data.

The EOR control function may be used to delimit the stream. An important application is data entry terminal support (see Section 3.3.2). There was concern that since EOR had not been defined in RFC-854, a host that was not prepared to correctly ignore unknown Telnet commands might crash if it received an EOR. To protect such hosts, the End-of-Record option [TELNET:9] was introduced; however, a properly implemented Telnet program will not require this protection.

3.2.4 Telnet "Synch" Signal: RFC-854, pp. 8-10

When it receives "urgent" TCP data, a User or Server Telnet MUST discard all data except Telnet commands until the DM (and end of urgent) is reached.

When it sends Telnet IP (Interrupt Process), a User Telnet SHOULD follow it by the Telnet "Synch" sequence, i.e., send as TCP urgent data the sequence "IAC IP IAC DM." The TCP urgent pointer points to the DM octet.

When it receives a Telnet IP command, a Server Telnet MAY send a Telnet "Synch" sequence back to the user, to flush the output stream. The choice ought to be consistent with the way the server operating system behaves when a local user interrupts a process.

When it receives a Telnet AO command, a Server Telnet MUST send a Telnet "Synch" sequence back to the user, to flush the output stream.

A User Telnet SHOULD have the capability of flushing output when it sends a Telnet IP; see also Section 3.4.5.

DISCUSSION:

There are three possible ways for a User Telnet to flush the stream of server output data:

1. Send AO after IP. This will cause the server host to send a "flush-buffered-output" signal to its operating system. However, the AO may not take effect locally, i.e., stop terminal output at the User Telnet end, until the Server Telnet has received and processed the AO and has sent back a "Synch."

2. Send DO TIMING-MARK [TELNET:7] after IP, and discard all output locally until a WILL/WONT TIMING-MARK is received from the Server Telnet. Since the DO TIMING-MARK will be processed after the IP at the server, the reply to it should be in the right place in the output data stream. However, the TIMING-MARK will not send a "flush buffered output" signal to the server operating system. Whether or not this is needed is dependent upon the server system.

3. Do both. The best method is not entirely clear, since it must accommodate a number of existing server hosts that do not follow the Telnet standards in various ways. The safest approach is probably to provide a user-controllable option to select (1), (2), or (3).

3.2.5 NVT Printer and Keyboard: RFC-854, p. 11

In NVT mode, a Telnet SHOULD NOT send characters with the high-order bit 1, and MUST NOT send it as a parity bit. Implementations that pass the high-order bit to applications SHOULD negotiate binary mode (see Section 3.2.6).

DISCUSSION:

Implementors should be aware that a strict reading of RFC-854 allows a client or server expecting NVT ASCII to ignore characters with the high-order bit set. In general, binary mode is expected to be used for transmission of an extended (beyond 7-bit) character set with Telnet.

However, there exist applications that really need an 8-bit NVT mode, which is currently not defined, and these existing applications do set the high-order bit during part or all of the life of a Telnet connection. Note that binary mode is not the same as 8-bit NVT mode, since binary mode turns off end-of-line processing. For this reason, the requirements on the high-order bit are stated as SHOULD, not MUST.

RFC-854 defines a minimal set of properties of a "network virtual terminal" or NVT; this is not meant to preclude additional features in a real terminal. A Telnet connection is fully transparent to all 7-bit ASCII characters, including arbitrary ASCII control characters.

For example, a terminal might support full-screen commands coded as ASCII escape sequences; a Telnet implementation would pass these sequences as uninterpreted data. Thus, an NVT should not be conceived as a terminal type of a highly-restricted device.

3.2.6 Telnet Command Structure: RFC-854, p. 13

Because options may appear at any point in the data stream, a Telnet escape character (known as IAC, with the value 255) to be sent as data MUST be doubled.

3.2.7 Telnet Binary Option: RFC-856

When the Binary option has been successfully negotiated, arbitrary 8-bit characters are allowed. However, the data stream MUST still be scanned for IAC characters, any embedded Telnet commands MUST be obeyed, and data bytes equal to IAC MUST be doubled. Other character processing (e.g., replacing CR by CR NUL or by CR LF) MUST NOT be done. In particular, there is no end-of-line convention (see Section 3.3.1) in binary mode.

DISCUSSION:

The Binary option is normally negotiated in both directions, to change the Telnet connection from NVT mode to "binary mode."

The sequence IAC EOR can be used to delimit blocks of data within a binary-mode Telnet stream.

3.2.8 Telnet Terminal-Type Option: RFC-1091

The Terminal-Type option MUST use the terminal type names officially defined in the Assigned Numbers RFC [INTRO:5], when they are available for the particular terminal. However, the receiver of a Terminal-Type option MUST accept any name.

DISCUSSION:

RFC-1091 [TELNET:10] updates an earlier version of the Terminal-Type option defined in RFC-930. The earlier version allowed a server host capable of supporting multiple terminal types to learn the type of a particular client's terminal, assuming that each physical terminal had an intrinsic type. However, today a "terminal" is often really a terminal emulator program running in a PC, perhaps capable of emulating a range of terminal types. Therefore, RFC-1091 extends the specification to allow a more general terminal-type negotiation between User and Server Telnets.

3.3 SPECIFIC ISSUES

3.3.1 Telnet End-of-Line Convention

The Telnet protocol defines the sequence CR LF to mean "end-of-line." For terminal input, this corresponds to a command-completion or "end-of-line" key being pressed on a user terminal; on an ASCII terminal, this is the CR key, but it may also be labelled "Return" or "Enter."

When a Server Telnet receives the Telnet end-of-line sequence CR LF as input from a remote terminal, the effect MUST be the same as if the user had pressed the "end-of-line" key on a local terminal. On server hosts that use ASCII, in particular, receipt of the Telnet sequence CR LF must cause the same effect as a local user pressing the CR key on a local terminal. Thus, CR LF and CR NUL MUST have the same effect on an ASCII server host when received as input over a Telnet connection.

A User Telnet MUST be able to send any of the forms: CR LF, CR NUL, and LF. A User Telnet on an ASCII host SHOULD have a user-controllable mode to send either CR LF or CR NUL when the user presses the "end-of-line" key, and CR LF SHOULD be the default.

The Telnet end-of-line sequence CR LF MUST be used to send Telnet data that is not terminal-to-computer (e.g., for Server Telnet sending output, or the Telnet protocol incorporated another application protocol).

DISCUSSION:

To allow interoperability between arbitrary Telnet clients and servers, the Telnet protocol defined a standard representation for a line terminator. Since the ASCII character set includes no explicit end-of-line character, systems have chosen various representations, e.g., CR, LF, and the sequence CR LF. The Telnet protocol chose the CR LF sequence as the standard for network transmission.

Unfortunately, the Telnet protocol specification in RFC-854 [TELNET:1] has turned out to be somewhat ambiguous on what character(s) should be sent from client to server for the "end-of-line" key. The result has been a massive and continuing inter-operability headache, made worse by various faulty implementations of both User and Server Telnets.

Although the Telnet protocol is based on a perfectly symmetric model, in a remote login session the role of the user at a terminal differs from the role of the server host. For example, RFC-854 defines the meaning of CR, LF, and CR LF as output from the server, but does not specify what the User Telnet should send when the user presses the "end-of-line" key on the terminal; this turns out to be the point at issue. When a user presses the "end-of-line" key, some User Telnet implementations send CR LF, while others send CR NUL (based on a different interpretation of the same sentence in RFC-854). These will be equivalent for a correctly-implemented ASCII server host, as discussed previously. For other servers, a mode in the User Telnet is needed.

The existence of User Telnets that send only CR NUL when CR is pressed creates a dilemma for non-ASCII hosts: they can either treat CR NUL as equivalent to CR LF in input, thus precluding the possibility of entering a "bare" CR, or else lose complete interworking.

Suppose a user on host A uses Telnet to log into a server host B, and then execute B's User Telnet program to log into server host C. It is desirable for the Server/User Telnet combination on B to be as transparent as possible, i.e., to appear as if A were connected directly to C. In particular, correct implementation will make B transparent to Telnet end-of-line sequences, except that CR LF may be translated to CR NUL or vice versa.

IMPLEMENTATION:

To understand Telnet end-of-line issues, one must have at least a general model of the relationship of Telnet to the local operating system. The Server Telnet process is typically coupled into the terminal driver software of the operating system as a pseudo-terminal. A Telnet end-of-line sequence received by the Server Telnet must have the same effect as pressing the end-of-line key on a real locally-connected terminal.

Operating systems that support interactive character-at-a-time applications (e.g., editors) typically have two internal modes for their terminal I/O: a formatted mode, in which local conventions for end-of-line and other formatting rules have been applied to the data stream, and a "raw" mode, in which the application has direct access to every character as it was entered. A Server Telnet must be implemented in such a way that these modes have the same effect for remote as for local terminals. For example, suppose a CR LF or CR NUL is received by the Server Telnet on an ASCII host. In raw mode, a CR character is passed to the application; in formatted mode, the local system's end-of-line convention is used.

3.3.2 Data Entry Terminals

DISCUSSION:

In addition to the line-oriented and character-oriented ASCII terminals for which Telnet was designed, there are several families of video display terminals that are some-times known as "data entry terminals" or DETs. The IBM 3270 family is a well-known example.

Two Internet protocols have been designed to support generic DETs: SUPDUP [TELNET:16, TELNET:17], and the DET option [TELNET:18, TELNET:19]. The DET option drives a data entry terminal over a Telnet connection using (sub-) negotiation. SUPDUP is a completely separate terminal protocol, which can be entered from Telnet by negotiation.

Although both SUPDUP and the DET option have been used successfully in particular environments, neither has gained general acceptance or wide implementation.

A different approach to DET interaction has been developed for supporting the IBM 3270 family through Telnet, although the same approach would be applicable to any DET. The idea is to enter a "native DET" mode, in which the native DET input/output stream is sent as binary data. The Telnet EOR command is used to delimit logical records (e.g., "screens") within this binary stream.

IMPLEMENTATION:

The rules for entering and leaving native DET mode are as follows:

- The Server uses the Terminal-Type option [TELNET:10] to learn that the client is a DET.

- It is conventional, but not required, that both ends negotiate the EOR option [TELNET:9].

- Both ends negotiate the Binary option [TELNET:3] to enter native DET mode.

- When either end negotiates out of binary mode, the other end does too, and the mode then reverts to normal NVT.

3.3.3 Option Requirements

Every Telnet implementation MUST support the Binary option [TELNET:3] and the Suppress Go Ahead option [TELNET:5], and SHOULD support the Echo [TELNET:4], Status [TELNET:6], End-of-Record [TELNET:9], and Extended Options List [TELNET:8] options.

A User or Server Telnet SHOULD support the Window Size Option [TELNET:12] if the local operating system provides the corresponding capability.

DISCUSSION:

Note that the End-of-Record option only signifies that a Telnet can receive a Telnet EOR without crashing; therefore, every Telnet ought to be willing to accept negotiation of the End-of-Record option. See also the discussion in Section 3.2.3.

3.3.4 Option Initiation

When the Telnet protocol is used in a client/server situation, the server SHOULD initiate negotiation of the terminal interaction mode it expects.

DISCUSSION:

The Telnet protocol was defined to be perfectly symmetrical, but its application is generally asymmetric. Remote login has been known to fail because NEITHER side initiated negotiation of the required non-default terminal modes. It is generally the server that determines the preferred mode, so the server needs to initiate the negotiation; since the negotiation is symmetric, the user can also initiate it.

A client (User Telnet) SHOULD provide a means for users to enable and disable the initiation of option negotiation.

DISCUSSION:

A user sometimes needs to connect to an application service (e.g., FTP or SMTP) that uses Telnet for its control stream but does not support Telnet options. User Telnet may be used for this purpose if initiation of option negotiation is disabled.

3.3.5 Telnet Linemode Option

DISCUSSION:

An important new Telnet option, LINEMODE [TELNET:12], has been proposed. The LINEMODE option provides a standard way for a User Telnet and a Server Telnet to agree that the client rather than the server will perform terminal character processing. When the client has prepared a complete line of text, it will send it to the server in (usually) one TCP packet. This option will greatly decrease the packet cost of Telnet sessions and will also give much better user response over congested or long-delay networks.

The LINEMODE option allows dynamic switching between local and remote character processing. For example, the Telnet connection will automatically negotiate into single-character mode while a full screen editor is running, and then return to linemode when the editor is finished.

We expect that when this RFC is released, hosts should implement the client side of this option, and may implement the server side of this option. To properly implement the server side, the server needs to be able to tell the local system not to do any input character processing, but to remember its current terminal state and notify the Server Telnet process whenever the state changes. This will allow password echoing and full screen editors to be handled properly, for example.

3.4 TELNET/USER INTERFACE

3.4.1 Character Set Transparency

User Telnet implementations SHOULD be able to send or receive any 7-bit ASCII character. Where possible, any special character interpretations by the user host's operating system SHOULD be bypassed so that these characters can conveniently be sent and received on the connection.

Some character value MUST be reserved as "escape to command mode"; conventionally, doubling this character allows it to be entered as data. The specific character used SHOULD be user selectable.

On binary-mode connections, a User Telnet program MAY provide an escape mechanism for entering arbitrary 8-bit values, if the host operating system doesn't allow them to be entered directly from the keyboard.

IMPLEMENTATION:

The transparency issues are less pressing on servers, but implementors should take care in dealing with issues like: masking off parity bits (sent by an older, non-conforming client) before they reach programs that expect only NVT ASCII, and properly handling programs that request 8-bit data streams.

3.4.2 Telnet Commands

A User Telnet program MUST provide a user the capability of entering any of the Telnet control functions IP, AO, or AYT, and SHOULD provide the capability of entering EC, EL, and Break.

3.4.3 TCP Connection Errors

A User Telnet program SHOULD report to the user any TCP errors that are reported by the transport layer (see "TCP/Application Layer Interface" section in [INTRO:1]).

3.4.4 Non-Default Telnet Contact Port

A User Telnet program SHOULD allow the user to optionally specify a non-standard contact port number at the Server Telnet host.

3.4.5 Flushing Output

A User Telnet program SHOULD provide the user the ability to specify whether or not output should be flushed when an IP is sent; see Section 3.2.4.

For any output flushing scheme that causes the User Telnet to flush output locally until a Telnet signal is received from the Server, there SHOULD be a way for the user to manually restore normal output, in case the Server fails to send the expected signal.

3.5 TELNET REQUIREMENTS SUMMARY

Feature	Section	Must	Should	May	Should Not	Must Not	Footnote
Option Negotiation	3.2.1	x					
Avoid negotiation loops	3.2.1	x					
Refuse unsupported options	3.2.1	x					
Negotiation OK anytime on connection	3.2.1			x			
Default to NVT	3.2.1	x					
Send official name in Term-Type option	3.2.8	x					
Accept any name in Term-Type option	3.2.8	x					
Implement Binary, Suppress-GA options	3.3.3	x					

Feature	Section	Must	Should	May	Should Not	Must Not	Footnote
Echo, Status, EOL, Ext-Opt-List options	3.3.3		x				
Implement Window-Size option if appropriate	3.3.3		x				
Server initiate mode negotiations	3.3.4		x				
User can enable/disable init negotiations	3.3.4		x				
Go-Aheads							
Non-GA server negotiate SUPPRESS-GA option	3.2.2	x					
User or Server accept SUPPRESS-GA option	3.2.2	x					
User Telnet ignore GA's	3.2.2			x			
Control Functions							
Support SE NOP DM IP AO AYT SB	3.2.3	x					
Support EOR EC EL Break	3.2.3			x			
Ignore unsupported control functions	3.2.3	x					
User, Server discard urgent data up to DM	3.2.4	x					
User Telnet send "Synch" after IP, AO, AYT	3.2.4		x				
Server Telnet reply Synch to IP	3.2.4			x			
Server Telnet reply Synch to AO	3.2.4	x					
User Telnet can flush output when send IP	3.2.4		x				
Encoding							
Send high-order bit in NVT mode	3.2.5				x		
Send high-order bit as parity bit	3.2.5					x	
Negot. BINARY if pass high-ord. bit to applic	3.2.5		x				
Always double IAC data byte	3.2.6	x					

continues

3.5 TELNET REQUIREMENTS SUMMARY (Continued)

Feature	Section	Must	Should	May	Should Not	Must Not	Footnote
Double IAC data byte in binary mode	3.2.7	x					
Obey Telnet cmds in binary mode	3.2.7	x					
End-of-line, CR NUL in binary mode	3.2.7					x	
End-of-Line							
EOL at Server same as local end-of-line	3.3.1	x					
ASCII Server accept CR LF or CR NUL for EOL	3.3.1	x					
User Telnet able to send CR LF, CR NUL, or LF	3.3.1	x					
ASCII user able to select CR LF/CR NUL	3.3.1		x				
User Telnet default mode is CR LF	3.3.1		x				
Non-interactive uses CR LF for EOL	3.3.1	x					
User Telnet interface							
Input & output all 7-bit characters	3.4.1		x				
Bypass local op sys interpretation	3.4.1		x				
Escape character	3.4.1	x					
User-settable escape character	3.4.1		x				
Escape to enter 8-bit values	3.4.1			x			
Can input IP, AO, AYT	3.4.2	x					
Can input EC, EL, Break	3.4.2		x				
Report TCP connection errors to user	3.4.3		x				
Optional non-default contact port	3.4.4		x				
Can spec: output flushed when IP sent	3.4.5		x				
Can manually restore output mode	3.4.5		x				

4. FILE TRANSFER

4.1 FILE TRANSFER PROTOCOL—FTP

4.1.1 INTRODUCTION

The File Transfer Protocol FTP is the primary Internet standard for file transfer. The current specification is contained in RFC-959 [FTP:1].

FTP uses separate simultaneous TCP connections for control and for data transfer. The FTP protocol includes many features, some of which are not commonly implemented. However, for every feature in FTP, there exists at least one implementation. The minimum implementation defined in RFC-959 was too small, so a somewhat larger minimum implementation is defined here.

Internet users have been unnecessarily burdened for years by deficient FTP implementations. Protocol implementors have suffered from the erroneous opinion that implementing FTP ought to be a small and trivial task. This is wrong, because FTP has a user interface, because it has to deal (correctly) with the whole variety of communication and operating system errors that may occur, and because it has to handle the great diversity of real file systems in the world.

4.1.2. PROTOCOL WALK-THROUGH

4.1.2.1 LOCAL Type: RFC-959 Section 3.1.1.4

An FTP program MUST support TYPE I ("IMAGE" or binary type) as well as TYPE L 8 ("LOCAL" type with logical byte size 8). A machine whose memory is organized into m-bit words, where m is not a multiple of 8, MAY also support TYPE L m.
DISCUSSION:
The command "TYPE L 8" is often required to transfer binary data between a machine whose memory is organized into (e.g.) 36-bit words and a machine with an 8-bit byte organization. For an 8-bit byte machine, TYPE L 8 is equivalent to IMAGE.

"TYPE L m" is sometimes specified to the FTP programs on two m-bit word machines to ensure the correct transfer of a native-mode binary file from one machine to the other. However, this command should have the same effect on these machines as "TYPE I."

4.1.2.2 Telnet Format Control: RFC-959 Section 3.1.1.5.2

A host that makes no distinction between TYPE N and TYPE T SHOULD implement TYPE T to be identical to TYPE N.
DISCUSSION:
This provision should ease interoperation with hosts that do make this distinction.

Many hosts represent text files internally as strings of ASCII characters, using the embedded ASCII format effector characters (LF, BS, FF, ...) to control the format when a file is printed. For such hosts, there is no distinction between "print" files and other files. However, systems that use record structured files typically need a special format for printable files (e.g., ASA carriage control). For the latter hosts, FTP allows a choice of TYPE N or TYPE T.

4.1.2.3 Page Structure: RFC-959 Section 3.1.2.3 and Appendix I

Implementation of page structure is NOT RECOMMENDED in general. However, if a host system does need to implement FTP for "random access" or "holey" files, it MUST use the defined page structure format rather than define a new private FTP format.

4.1.2.4 Data Structure Transformations: RFC-959 Section 3.1.2

An FTP transformation between record-structure and file-structure SHOULD be invertible, to the extent possible while making the result useful on the target host.

DISCUSSION:

RFC-959 required strict invertibility between record-structure and file-structure, but in practice, efficiency and convenience often preclude it. Therefore, the requirement is being relaxed. There are two different objectives for transferring a file: processing it on the target host, or just storage. For storage, strict invertibility is important. For processing, the file created on the target host needs to be in the format expected by application programs on that host.

As an example of the conflict, imagine a record-oriented operating system that requires some data files to have exactly 80 bytes in each record. While storing a file on such a host, an FTP Server must be able to pad each line or record to 80 bytes; a later retrieval of such a file cannot be strictly invertible.

4.1.2.5 Data Connection Management: RFC-959 Section 3.3

A User-FTP that uses STREAM mode SHOULD send a PORT command to assign a non-default data port before each transfer command is issued.

DISCUSSION:

This is required because of the long delay after a TCP connection is closed until its socket pair can be reused, to allow multiple transfers during a single FTP session. Sending a port command can be avoided if a transfer mode other than stream is used, by leaving the data transfer connection open between transfers.

4.1.2.6 PASV Command: RFC-959 Section 4.1.2

A server-FTP MUST implement the PASV command. If multiple third-party transfers are to be executed during the same session, a new PASV command MUST be issued before each transfer command, to obtain a unique port pair.

IMPLEMENTATION:
The format of the 227 reply to a PASV command is not well standardized. In particular, an FTP client cannot assume that the parentheses shown on page 40 of RFC-959 will be present (and in fact, Figure 3 on page 43 omits them). Therefore, a User-FTP program that interprets the PASV reply must scan the reply for the first digit of the host and port numbers.

Note that the host number h1,h2,h3,h4 is the IP address of the server host that is sending the reply, and that p1,p2 is a non-default data transfer port that PASV has assigned.

4.1.2.7 LIST and NLST Commands: RFC-959 Section 4.1.3

The data returned by an NLST command MUST contain only a simple list of legal pathnames, such that the server can use them directly as the arguments of subsequent data transfer commands for the individual files.

The data returned by a LIST or NLST command SHOULD use an implied TYPE AN, unless the current type is EBCDIC, in which case an implied TYPE EN SHOULD be used.

DISCUSSION:
Many FTP clients support macro-commands that will get or put files matching a wildcard specification, using NLST to obtain a list of pathnames. The expansion of "multiple-put" is local to the client, but "multiple-get" requires cooperation by the server.

The implied type for LIST and NLST is designed to provide compatibility with existing User-FTPs, and in particular with multiple-get commands.

4.1.2.8 SITE Command: RFC-959 Section 4.1.3

A Server-FTP SHOULD use the SITE command for non-standard features, rather than invent new private commands or unstandardized extensions to existing commands.

4.1.2.9 STOU Command: RFC-959 Section 4.1.3

The STOU command stores into a uniquely named file. When it receives an STOU command, a Server-FTP MUST return the actual file name in the "125 Transfer Starting" or the "150 Opening Data Connection" message that precedes the transfer (the 250 reply code mentioned in RFC-959 is incorrect). The exact format of these messages is hereby defined to be as follows:

    125 FILE: pppp

where pppp represents the unique pathname of the file that will be written.

4.1.2.10 Telnet End-of-line Code: RFC-959, Page 34

Implementors MUST NOT assume any correspondence between READ boundaries on the control connection and the Telnet EOL sequences (CR LF).

DISCUSSION:

Thus, a server-FTP (or User-FTP) must continue reading characters from the control connection until a complete Telnet EOL sequence is encountered, before processing the command (or response, respectively). Conversely, a single READ from the control connection may include more than one FTP command.

4.1.2.11 FTP Replies: RFC-959 Section 4.2, Page 35

A Server-FTP MUST send only correctly formatted replies on the control connection. Note that RFC-959 (unlike earlier versions of the FTP spec) contains no provision for a "spontaneous" reply message.

A Server-FTP SHOULD use the reply codes defined in RFC-959 whenever they apply. However, a server-FTP MAY use a different reply code when needed, as long as the general rules of Section 4.2 are followed. When the implementor has a choice between a 4xx and 5xx reply code, a Server-FTP SHOULD send a 4xx (temporary failure) code when there is any reasonable possibility that a failed FTP will succeed a few hours later.

A User-FTP SHOULD generally use only the highest-order digit of a 3-digit reply code for making a procedural decision, to prevent difficulties when a Server-FTP uses non-standard reply codes.

A User-FTP MUST be able to handle multi-line replies. If the implementation imposes a limit on the number of lines and if this limit is exceeded, the User-FTP MUST recover, e.g., by ignoring the excess lines until the end of the multi-line reply is reached.

A User-FTP SHOULD NOT interpret a 421 reply code ("Service not available, closing control connection") specially, but SHOULD detect closing of the control connection by the server.

DISCUSSION:

Server implementations that fail to strictly follow the reply rules often cause FTP user programs to hang. Note that RFC-959 resolved ambiguities in the reply rules found in earlier FTP specifications and must be followed.

It is important to choose FTP reply codes that properly distinguish between temporary and permanent failures, to allow the successful use of file transfer client daemons. These programs depend on the reply codes to decide whether or not to retry a failed transfer; using a permanent failure code (5xx) for a temporary error will cause these programs to give up unnecessarily.

When the meaning of a reply matches exactly the text shown in RFC-959, uniformity will be enhanced by using the RFC-959 text verbatim. However, a Server-FTP implementor is encouraged to choose reply text that conveys specific system-dependent information, when appropriate.

4.1.2.12 Connections: RFC-959 Section 5.2

The words "and the port used" in the second paragraph of this section of RFC-959 are erroneous (historical), and they should be ignored.

On a multihomed server host, the default data transfer (L-1) MUST be associated with the same local IP address as the corresponding control connection to port L.

A user-FTP MUST NOT send any Telnet controls other than SYNCH and IP on an FTP control connection. In particular, it MUST NOT attempt to negotiate Telnet options on the control connection. However, a server-FTP MUST be capable of accepting and refusing Telnet negotiations (i.e., sending DONT/WONT).

DISCUSSION:

Although the RFC says: "Server- and User- processes should follow the conventions for the Telnet protocol [on the control connection]," it is not the intent that Telnet option negotiation is to be employed.

4.1.2.13 Minimum Implementation; RFC-959 Section 5.1

The following commands and options MUST be supported by every server-FTP and user-FTP, except in cases where the underlying file system or operating system does not support a particular command.

Type: ASCII Non-print, IMAGE, LOCAL 8
Mode: Stream
Structure: File, Record★
Commands:

USER, PASS, ACCT, PORT, PASV, TYPE, MODE, STRU, RETR, STOR, APPE, RNFR, RNTO, DELE, CWD, CDUP, RMD, MKD, PWD, LIST, NLST, SYST, STAT, HELP, NOOP, QUIT.

★Record structure is REQUIRED only for hosts whose file systems support record structure.

DISCUSSION:

Vendors are encouraged to implement a larger subset of the protocol. For example, there are important robustness features in the protocol (e.g., Restart, ABOR, block mode) that would be an aid to some Internet users but are not widely implemented. A host that does not have record structures in its file system may still accept files with STRU R, recording the byte stream literally.

4.1.3 SPECIFIC ISSUES

4.1.3.1 Non-standard Command Verbs

FTP allows "experimental" commands, whose names begin with "X." If these commands are subsequently adopted as standards, there may still be existing implementations using the "X" form. At present, this is true for the directory commands:

RFC-959 "Experimental"

MKD	XMKD
RMD	XRMD

PWD	XPWD
CDUP	XCUP
CWD	XCWD

All FTP implementations SHOULD recognize both forms of these commands, by simply equating them with extra entries in the command lookup table.
IMPLEMENTATION:
A User-FTP can access a server that supports only the "X" forms by implementing a mode switch, or automatically using the following procedure: if the RFC-959 form of one of the above commands is rejected with a 500 or 502 response code, then try the experimental form; any other response would be passed to the user.

4.1.3.2 Idle Timeout

A Server-FTP process SHOULD have an idle timeout, which will terminate the process and close the control connection if the server is inactive (i.e., no command or data transfer in progress) for a long period of time. The idle timeout time SHOULD be configurable, and the default should be at least 5 minutes.
A client FTP process ("User-PI" in RFC-959) will need timeouts on responses only if it is invoked from a program.
DISCUSSION:
Without a timeout, a Server-FTP process may be left pending indefinitely if the corresponding client crashes without closing the control connection.

4.1.3.3 Concurrency of Data and Control

DISCUSSION:
The intent of the designers of FTP was that a user should be able to send a STAT command at any time while data transfer was in progress and that the server-FTP would reply immediately with status—e.g., the number of bytes transferred so far. Similarly, an ABOR command should be possible at any time during a data transfer. Unfortunately, some small-machine operating systems make such concurrent programming difficult, and some other implementers seek minimal solutions, so some FTP implementations do not allow concurrent use of the data and control connections. Even such a minimal server must be prepared to accept and defer a STAT or ABOR command that arrives during data transfer.

4.1.3.4 FTP Restart Mechanism

The description of the 110 reply on pp. 40-41 of RFC-959 is incorrect; the correct description is as follows. A restart reply message, sent over the control connection from the receiving FTP to the User-FTP, has the format:

```
110 MARK ssss = rrrr
```

Here:

- ssss is a text string that appeared in a Restart Marker in the data stream and encodes a position in the sender's file system
- rrrr encodes the corresponding position in the receiver's file system.

The encoding, which is specific to a particular file system and network implementation, is always generated and interpreted by the same system, either sender or receiver. When an FTP that implements restart receives a Restart Marker in the data stream, it SHOULD force the data to that point to be written to stable storage before encoding the corresponding position rrrr. An FTP sending Restart Markers MUST NOT assume that 110 replies will be returned synchronously with the data, i.e., it must not await a 110 reply before sending more data.

Two new reply codes are hereby defined for errors encountered in restarting a transfer:

- 554 Requested action not taken: invalid REST parameter—A 554 reply may result from a FTP service command that follows a REST command. The reply indicates that the existing file at the Server-FTP cannot be repositioned as specified in the REST.

- 555 Requested action not taken: type or stru mismatch. A 555 reply may result from an APPE command or from any FTP service command following a REST command. The reply indicates that there is some mismatch between the current transfer parameters (type and stru) and the attributes of the existing file.

DISCUSSION:

Note that the FTP Restart mechanism requires that Block or Compressed mode be used for data transfer, to allow the Restart Markers to be included within the data stream. The frequency of Restart Markers can be low. Restart Markers mark a place in the data stream, but the receiver may be performing some transformation on the data as it is stored into stable storage. In general, the receiver's encoding must include any state information necessary to restart this transformation at any point of the FTP data stream. For example, in TYPE A transfers, some receiver hosts transform CR LF sequences into a single LF character on disk. If a Restart Marker happens to fall between CR and LF, the receiver must encode in rrrr that the transfer must be restarted in a "CR has been seen and discarded" state.

Note that the Restart Marker is required to be encoded as a string of printable ASCII characters, regardless of the type of the data.

RFC-959 says that restart information is to be returned "to the user." This should not be taken literally. In general, the User-FTP should save the restart information (ssss,rrrr) in stable storage, e.g., append it to a restart control file. An empty restart control file should be created when the transfer first starts and deleted automatically when the transfer completes successfully. It is suggested that this file have a name derived in an easily-identifiable manner from the name of the file being transferred and the remote host name; this is analogous to the means used by many text editors for naming "backup" files.

There are three cases for FTP restart:

1. User-to-Server Transfer—The User-FTP puts Restart Markers <ssss> at convenient places in the data stream. When the Server-FTP receives a Marker, it writes all prior data to disk, encodes its file system position and transformation state as rrrr, and returns a "110 MARK ssss = rrrr" reply over the control connection. The User-FTP appends the pair (ssss,rrrr) to its restart control file. To restart the transfer, the User-FTP fetches the last (ssss,rrrr) pair from the restart control file, repositions its local file system and transformation state using ssss, and sends the command "REST rrrr" to the Server-FTP.

2. Server-to-User Transfer—The Server-FTP puts Restart Markers <ssss> at convenient places in the data stream. When the User-FTP receives a Marker, it writes all prior data to disk, encodes its file system position and transformation state as rrrr, and appends the pair (rrrr,ssss) to its restart control file. To restart the transfer, the User-FTP fetches the last (rrrr,ssss) pair from the restart control file, repositions its local file system and transformation state using rrrr, and sends the command "REST ssss" to the Server-FTP.

3. Server-to-Server ("Third-Party") Transfer—The sending Server-FTP puts Restart Markers <ssss> at convenient places in the data stream. When it receives a Marker, the receiving Server-FTP writes all prior data to disk, encodes its file system position and transformation state as rrrr, and sends a "110 MARK ssss = rrrr" reply over the control connection to the User. The User-FTP appends the pair (ssss,rrrr) to its restart control file. To restart the transfer, the User-FTP fetches the last (ssss,rrrr) pair from the restart control file, sends "REST ssss" to the sending Server-FTP, and sends "REST rrrr" to the receiving Server-FTP.

4.1.4 FTP/USER INTERFACE

This section discusses the user interface for a User-FTP program.

4.1.4.1 Pathname Specification

Because FTP is intended for use in a heterogeneous environment, User-FTP implementations MUST support remote pathnames as arbitrary character strings, so that their form and content are not limited by the conventions of the local operating system.
DISCUSSION:
In particular, remote pathnames can be of arbitrary length, and all the printing ASCII characters as well as space (0x20) must be allowed. RFC-959 allows a pathname to contain any 7-bit ASCII character except CR or LF.

4.1.4.2 "QUOTE" Command

A User-FTP program MUST implement a "QUOTE" command that will pass an arbitrary character string to the server and display all resulting response messages to the user.

To make the "QUOTE" command useful, a User-FTP SHOULD send transfer control commands to the server as the user enters them, rather than saving all the commands and sending them to the server only when a data transfer is started.
DISCUSSION:
The "QUOTE" command is essential to allow the user to access servers that require system-specific commands (e.g., SITE or ALLO), or to invoke new or optional features that are not implemented by the User-FTP. For example, "QUOTE" may be used to specify "TYPE A T" to send a print file to hosts that require the distinction, even if the User-FTP does not recognize that TYPE.

4.1.4.3 Displaying Replies to User

A User-FTP SHOULD display to the user the full text of all error reply messages it receives. It SHOULD have a "verbose" mode in which all commands it sends and the full text and reply codes it receives are displayed, for diagnosis of problems.

4.1.4.4 Maintaining Synchronization

The state machine in a User-FTP SHOULD be forgiving of missing and unexpected reply messages, in order to maintain command synchronization with the server.

4.1.5 FTP REQUIREMENTS SUMMARY

Feature	Section	Must	Should	May	Should Not	Must Not	Footnote
Implement TYPE T if same as TYPE N	4.1.2.2		x				
File/Record transform invertible if poss.	4.1.2.4		x				
User-FTP send PORT cmd for stream mode	4.1.2.5		x				
Server-FTP implement PASV	4.1.2.6	x					
PASV is per-transfer	4.1.2.6	x					
NLST reply usable in RETR cmds	4.1.2.7	x					
Implied type for LIST and NLST	4.1.2.7		x				
SITE cmd for non-standard features	4.1.2.8		x				
STOU cmd return pathname as specified	4.1.2.9	x					
Use TCP READ boundaries on control conn.	4.1.2.10					x	

continues

4.1.5 FTP REQUIREMENTS SUMMARY (Continued)

Feature	Section	Must	Should	May	Should Not	Must Not	Footnote
Server-FTP send only correct reply format	4.1.2.11	x					
Server-FTP use defined reply code if poss.	4.1.2.11		x				
New reply code following Section 4.2	4.1.2.11			x			
User-FTP use only high digit of reply	4.1.2.11		x				
User-FTP handle multi-line reply lines	4.1.2.11	x					
User-FTP handle 421 reply specially	4.1.2.11				x		
Default data port same IP addr as ctl conn	4.1.2.12	x					
User-FTP send Telnet cmds exc. SYNCH, IP	4.1.2.12					x	
User-FTP negotiate Telnet options	4.1.2.12					x	
Server-FTP handle Telnet options	4.1.2.12	x					
Handle "Experimental" directory cmds	4.1.3.1		x				
Idle timeout in server-FTP	4.1.3.2		x				
Configurable idle timeout	4.1.3.2		x				
Receiver checkpoint data at Restart Marker	4.1.3.4		x				
Sender assume 110 replies are synchronous	4.1.3.4				x		
Support TYPE:							
ASCII - Non-Print (AN)	4.1.2.13	x					
ASCII - Telnet (AT)— if same as AN	4.1.2.2		x				
ASCII - Carriage Control (AC)	959 3.1.1.5.2			x			
EBCDIC - (any form)	959 3.1.1.2			x			
IMAGE	4.1.2.1	x					
LOCAL 8	4.1.2.1	x					
LOCAL m	4.1.2.1			x			2

Feature	Section	Must	Should	May	Should Not	Must Not	Footnote
Support MODE:							
Stream	4.1.2.13	x					
Block	959 3.4.2			x			
Support STRUCTURE:							
File	4.1.2.13	x					
Record	4.1.2.13	x					3
Page	4.1.2.3			x			
Support commands:							
USER	4.1.2.13	x					
PASS	4.1.2.13	x					
ACCT	4.1.2.13	x					
CWD	4.1.2.13	x					
CDUP	4.1.2.13	x					
SMNT	959 5.3.1			x			
REIN	959 5.3.1			x			
QUIT	4.1.2.13	x					
PORT	4.1.2.13	x					
PASV	4.1.2.6	x					
TYPE	4.1.2.13	x					1
STRU	4.1.2.13	x					1
MODE	4.1.2.13	x					1
RETR	4.1.2.13	x					
STOR	4.1.2.13	x					
STOU	959 5.3.1			x			
APPE	4.1.2.13	x					
ALLO	959 5.3.1			x			
REST	959 5.3.1			x			
RNFR	4.1.2.13	x					
RNTO	4.1.2.13	x					
ABOR	959 5.3.1			x			
DELE	4.1.2.13	x					
RMD	4.1.2.13	x					
MKD	4.1.2.13	x					
PWD	4.1.2.13	x					
LIST	4.1.2.13	x					

continues

4.1.5 FTP REQUIREMENTS SUMMARY (Continued)

Feature	Section	Must	Should	May	Should Not	Must Not	Footnote
NLST	4.1.2.13	x					
SITE	4.1.2.8			x			
STAT	4.1.2.13	x					
SYST	4.1.2.13	x					
HELP	4.1.2.13	x					
NOOP	4.1.2.13	x					
User Interface:							
Arbitrary pathnames	4.1.4.1	x					
Implement "QUOTE" command	4.1.4.2	x					
Transfer control commands immediately	4.1.4.2		x				
Display error messages to user	4.1.4.3		x				
Verbose mode	4.1.4.3		x				
Maintain synchronization with server	4.1.4.4		x				

Footnotes:

(1) For the values shown earlier.

(2) Here m is number of bits in a memory word.

(3) Required for host with record-structured file system, optional otherwise.

4.2 TRIVIAL FILE TRANSFER PROTOCOL—TFTP

4.2.1 INTRODUCTION

The Trivial File Transfer Protocol TFTP is defined in RFC-783 [TFTP:1]. TFTP provides its own reliable delivery with UDP as its transport protocol, using a simple stop-and-wait acknowledgment system. Because TFTP has an effective window of only one 512 octet segment, it can provide good performance only over paths that have a small delay*bandwidth product. The TFTP file interface is very simple, providing no access control or security.

TFTP's most important application is bootstrapping a host over a local network, since it is simple and small enough to be easily implemented in EPROM [BOOT:1, BOOT:2]. Vendors are urged to support TFTP for booting.

4.2.2 PROTOCOL WALK-THROUGH

The TFTP specification [TFTP:1] is written in an open style, and does not fully specify many parts of the protocol.

4.2.2.1 Transfer Modes: RFC-783, Page 3

The transfer mode "mail" SHOULD NOT be supported.

4.2.2.2 UDP Header: RFC-783, Page 17

The Length field of a UDP header is incorrectly defined; it includes the UDP header length (8).

4.2.3 SPECIFIC ISSUES

4.2.3.1 Sorcerer's Apprentice Syndrome

There is a serious bug, known as the "Sorcerer's Apprentice Syndrome," in the protocol specification. While it does not cause incorrect operation of the transfer (the file will always be transferred correctly if the transfer completes), this bug may cause excessive retransmission, which may cause the transfer to time out.

Implementations MUST contain the fix for this problem: the sender (i.e., the side originating the DATA packets) must never resend the current DATA packet on receipt of a duplicate ACK.

DISCUSSION:

The bug is caused by the protocol rule that either side, on receiving an old duplicate datagram, may resend the current datagram. If a packet is delayed in the network but later successfully delivered after either side has timed out and retransmitted a packet, a duplicate copy of the response may be generated. If the other side responds to this duplicate with a duplicate of its own, then every datagram will be sent in duplicate for the remainder of the transfer (unless a datagram is lost, breaking the repetition). Worse yet, since the delay is often caused by congestion, this duplicate transmission usually causes more congestion, leading to more delayed packets, etc.

The following example may help to clarify this problem.

TFTP A	TFTP B
(1)Receive ACK X-1 Send DATA X	
	(2)Receive DATA X Send ACK X
(ACK X is delayed in network, and A times out):	
(3)Retransmit DATA X	
	(4)Receive DATA X again Send ACK X again
(5)Receive (delayed) ACK X Send DATA X+1	
	(6)Receive DATA X+1 Send ACK X+1
(7)Receive ACK X again Send DATA X+1 again	

continues

TFTP A	**TFTP B**
	(8)Receive DATA X+1 again
	Send ACK X+1 again
(9)Receive ACK X+1	
Send DATA X+2	
	(10)Receive DATA X+2
	Send ACK X+3
(11)Receive ACK X+1 again	
Send DATA X+2 again	
	(12)Receive DATA X+2 again
	Send ACK X+3 again

Notice that after the delayed ACK arrives, the protocol settles down to duplicate all further packets (sequences 5-8 and 9-12). The problem is caused not by either side timing out, but by both sides retransmitting the current packet when they receive a duplicate.

The fix is to break the retransmission loop, as indicated above. This is analogous to the behavior of TCP. It is then possible to remove the retransmission timer on the receiver, since the resent ACK will never cause any action; this is a useful simplification where TFTP is used in a bootstrap program. It is OK to allow the timer to remain, and it may be helpful if the retransmitted ACK replaces one that was genuinely lost in the network. The sender still requires a retransmit timer, of course.

4.2.3.2 Timeout Algorithms

A TFTP implementation MUST use an adaptive timeout.
IMPLEMENTATION:
TCP retransmission algorithms provide a useful base to work from. At least an exponential backoff of retransmission timeout is necessary.

4.2.3.3 Extensions

A variety of non-standard extensions have been made to TFTP, including additional transfer modes and a secure operation mode (with passwords). None of these have been standardized.

4.2.3.4 Access Control

A server TFTP implementation SHOULD include some configurable access control over what pathnames are allowed in TFTP operations.

4.2.3.5 Broadcast Request

A TFTP request directed to a broadcast address SHOULD be silently ignored.
DISCUSSION:
Due to the weak access control capability of TFTP, directed broadcasts of TFTP requests to random networks could create a significant security hole.

DISCUSSION:

For example, suppose a host that does not implement the relay function receives a message with the SMTP command: "RCPT TO:<@ALPHA,@BETA:joe@GAMMA>," where ALPHA, BETA, and GAMMA represent domain names. Rather than immediately refusing the message with a 550 error reply as suggested on page 20 of RFC-821, the host should try to forward the message to GAMMA directly, using: "RCPT TO:<joe@GAMMA>."

Because this host does not support relaying, it is not required to update the reverse path.

Some have suggested that source routing may be needed occasionally for manually routing mail around failures; however, the reality and importance of this need is controversial. The use of explicit SMTP mail relaying for this purpose is discouraged, and in fact it may not be successful, as many host systems do not support it. Some have used the "%-hack" (see Section 5.2.16) for this purpose.

5.2.7 RCPT Command: RFC-821 Section 4.1.1

A host that supports a receiver-SMTP MUST support the reserved mailbox "Postmaster."

The receiver-SMTP MAY verify RCPT parameters as they arrive; however, RCPT responses MUST NOT be delayed beyond a reasonable time (see Section 5.3.2). Therefore, a "250 OK" response to a RCPT does not necessarily imply that the delivery address(es) are valid. Errors found after message acceptance will be reported by mailing a notification message to an appropriate address (see Section 5.3.3).

DISCUSSION:

The set of conditions under which a RCPT parameter can be validated immediately is an engineering design choice. Reporting destination mailbox errors to the Sender-SMTP before mail is transferred is generally desirable to save time and network bandwidth, but this advantage is lost if RCPT verification is lengthy.

For example, the receiver can verify immediately any simple local reference, such as a single locally-registered mailbox. On the other hand, the "reasonable time" limitation generally implies deferring verification of a mailing list until after the message has been transferred and accepted, since verifying a large mailing list can take a very long time. An implementation might or might not choose to defer validation of addresses that are non-local and therefore require a DNS lookup. If a DNS lookup is performed but a soft domain system error (e.g., timeout) occurs, validity must be assumed.

5.2.8 DATA Command: RFC-821 Section 4.1.1

Every receiver-SMTP (not just one that "accepts a message for relaying or for final delivery" [SMTP:1]) MUST insert a "Received:" line at the beginning of a message. In this line, called a "time stamp line" in RFC-821:

- The FROM field SHOULD contain both (1) the name of the source host as presented in the HELO command and (2) a domain literal containing the IP address of the source, determined from the TCP connection.

- The ID field MAY contain an "@" as suggested in RFC-822, but this is not required.

- The FOR field MAY contain a list of <path> entries when multiple RCPT commands have been given.

- An Internet mail program MUST NOT change a Received: line that was previously added to the message header.

DISCUSSION:

Including both the source host and the IP source address in the Received: line may provide enough information for tracking illicit mail sources and eliminate a need to explicitly verify the HELO parameter. Received: lines are primarily intended for humans tracing mail routes, primarily of diagnosis of faults. See also the discussion under 5.3.7.

When the receiver-SMTP makes "final delivery" of a message, then it MUST pass the MAIL FROM: address from the SMTP envelope with the message, for use if an error notification message must be sent later (see Section 5.3.3). There is an analogous requirement when gatewaying from the Internet into a different mail environment; see Section 5.3.7.

DISCUSSION:

Note that the final reply to the DATA command depends only upon the successful transfer and storage of the message. Any problem with the destination address(es) must either (1) have been reported in an SMTP error reply to the RCPT command(s), or (2) be reported in a later error message mailed to the originator.

IMPLEMENTATION:

The MAIL FROM: information may be passed as a parameter or in a Return-Path: line inserted at the beginning of the message.

5.2.9 Command Syntax: RFC-821 Section 4.1.2

The syntax shown in RFC-821 for the MAIL FROM: command omits the case of an empty path: "MAIL FROM: <>" (see RFC-821 Page 15). An empty reverse path MUST be supported.

5.2.10 SMTP Replies: RFC-821 Section 4.2

A receiver-SMTP SHOULD send only the reply codes listed in section 4.2.2 of RFC-821 or in this document. A receiver-SMTP SHOULD use the text shown in examples in RFC-821 whenever appropriate.

A sender-SMTP MUST determine its actions only by the reply code, not by the text (except for 251 and 551 replies); any text, including no text at all, must be acceptable. The space (blank) following the reply code is considered part of the text. Whenever possible, a sender-SMTP SHOULD test only the first digit of the reply code, as specified in Appendix E of RFC-821.

DISCUSSION:
Interoperability problems have arisen with SMTP systems using reply codes that are not listed explicitly in RFC-821 Section 4.3 but are legal according to the theory of reply codes explained in Appendix E.

5.2.11 Transparency: RFC-821 Section 4.5.2

Implementors MUST be sure that their mail systems always add and delete periods to ensure message transparency.

5.2.12 WKS Use in MX Processing: RFC-974, p. 5

RFC-974 [SMTP:3] recommended that the domain system be queried for WKS ("Well-Known Service") records, to verify that each proposed mail target does support SMTP. Later experience has shown that WKS is not widely supported, so the WKS step in MX processing SHOULD NOT be used.
The following are notes on RFC-822, organized by section of that document.

5.2.13 RFC-822 Message Specification: RFC-822 Section 4

The syntax shown for the Return-path line omits the possibility of a null return path, which is used to prevent looping of error notifications (see Section 5.3.3). The complete syntax is:

```
return = "Return-path" ":" route-addr
    "Return-path" ":" "<" ">"
```

The set of optional header fields is hereby expanded to include the Content-Type field defined in RFC-1049 [SMTP:7]. This field "allows mail reading systems to automatically identify the type of a structured message body and to process it for display accordingly." [SMTP:7] A User Agent MAY support this field.

5.2.14 RFC-822 Date and Time Specification: RFC-822 Section 5

The syntax for the date is hereby changed to: date = 1*2DIGIT month 2*4DIGIT
All mail software SHOULD use 4-digit years in dates, to ease the transition to the next century.
There is a strong trend towards the use of numeric timezone indicators, and implementations SHOULD use numeric timezones instead of timezone names. However, all implementations MUST accept either notation. If timezone names are used, they MUST be exactly as defined in RFC-822.
The military time zones are specified incorrectly in RFC-822: they count the wrong way from UT (the signs are reversed). As a result, military time zones in RFC-822 headers carry no information.
Finally, note that there is a typo in the definition of "zone" in the syntax summary of Appendix D; the correct definition occurs in Section 3 of RFC-822.

5.2.15 RFC-822 Syntax Change: RFC-822 Section 6.1

The syntactic definition of "mailbox" in RFC-822 is hereby changed to:

```
mailbox =  addr-spec              ; simple address
/ [phrase] route-addr    ; name & addr-spec
```

That is, the phrase preceding a route address is now OPTIONAL.

This change makes the following header field legal, for example:

```
From: <craig@nnsc.nsf.net>
```

5.2.16 RFC-822 Local-part: RFC-822 Section 6.2

The basic mailbox address specification has the form: "local-part@domain". Here "local-part," sometimes called the "left-hand side" of the address, is domain-dependent. A host that is forwarding the message but is not the destination host implied by the right-hand side "domain" MUST NOT interpret or modify the "local-part" of the address.

When mail is to be gatewayed from the Internet mail environment into a foreign mail environment (see Section 5.3.7), routing information for that foreign environment MAY be embedded within the "local-part" of the address. The gateway will then interpret this local part appropriately for the foreign mail environment.

DISCUSSION:

Although source routes are discouraged within the Internet (see Section 5.2.6), there are non-Internet mail environments whose delivery mechanisms do depend upon source routes. Source routes for extra-Internet environments can generally be buried in the "local-part" of the address (see Section 5.2.16) while mail traverses the Internet. When the mail reaches the appropriate Internet mail gateway, the gateway will interpret the local-part and build the necessary address or route for the target mail environment.

For example, an Internet host might send mail to: "a!b!c!user@gateway-domain." The complex local part "a!b!c!user" would be uninterpreted within the Internet domain, but could be parsed and understood by the specified mail gateway.

An embedded source route is sometimes encoded in the "local-part" using "%" as a right-binding routing operator. For example, in: user%domain%relay3%relay2@relay1 the "%" convention implies that the mail is to be routed from "relay1" through "relay2," "relay3," and finally to "user" at "domain." This is commonly known as the "%- hack." It is suggested that "%" have lower precedence than any other routing operator (e.g., "!") hidden in the local-part; for example, "a!b%c" would be interpreted as "(a!b)%c".

Only the target host (in this case, "relay1") is permitted to analyze the local-part "user%domain%relay3%relay2."

5.2.17 Domain Literals: RFC-822 Section 6.2.3

A mailer MUST be able to accept and parse an Internet domain literal whose content ("dtext"; see RFC-822) is a dotted-decimal host address. This satisfies the requirement of Section 2.1 for the case of mail.

An SMTP MUST accept and recognize a domain literal for any of its own IP addresses.

5.2.18 Common Address Formatting Errors: RFC-822 Section 6.1

Errors in formatting or parsing 822 addresses are unfortunately common. This section mentions only the most common errors. A User Agent MUST accept all valid RFC-822 address formats, and MUST NOT generate illegal address syntax.

- A common error is to leave out the semicolon after a group identifier.
- Some systems fail to fully-qualify domain names in messages they generate. The right-hand side of an "@" sign in a header address field MUST be a fully-qualified domain name.

For example, some systems fail to fully-qualify the From: address; this prevents a "reply" command in the user interface from automatically constructing a return address.
DISCUSSION:
Although RFC-822 allows the local use of abbreviated domain names within a domain, the application of RFC-822 in Internet mail does not allow this. The intent is that an Internet host must not send an SMTP message header containing an abbreviated domain name in an address field. This allows the address fields of the header to be passed without alteration across the Internet, as required in Section 5.2.6.

- Some systems mis-parse multiple-hop explicit source routes such as: @relay1,@relay2,@relay3:user@domain.
- Some systems over-qualify domain names by adding a trailing dot to some or all domain names in addresses or message-ids. This violates RFC-822 syntax.

5.2.19 Explicit Source Routes: RFC-822 Section 6.2.7

Internet host software SHOULD NOT create an RFC-822 header containing an address with an explicit source route, but MUST accept such headers for compatibility with earlier systems.
DISCUSSION:
In an understatement, RFC-822 says "The use of explicit source routing is discouraged." Many hosts implemented RFC-822 source routes incorrectly, so the syntax cannot be used unambiguously in practice. Many users feel the syntax is ugly. Explicit source routes are not needed in the mail envelope for delivery; see Section 5.2.6. For all these reasons, explicit source routes using the RFC-822 notations are not to be used in Internet mail headers.

As stated in Section 5.2.16, it is necessary to allow an explicit source route to be buried in the local-part of an address, e.g., using the "%-hack," in order to allow mail to be gatewayed into another environment in which explicit source routing is necessary. The vigilant will observe that there is no way for a User Agent to detect and prevent the use of such implicit source routing when the destination is within the Internet. We can only discourage source routing of any kind within the Internet as unnecessary and undesirable.

5.3 SPECIFIC ISSUES

5.3.1 SMTP Queuing Strategies

The common structure of a host SMTP implementation includes user mailboxes, one or more areas for queuing messages in transit, and one or more daemon processes for sending and receiving mail. The exact structure will vary depending on the needs of the users on the host and the number and size of mailing lists supported by the host. We describe several optimizations that have proved helpful, particularly for mailers supporting high traffic levels.

   Any queuing strategy MUST include:

   ■ Timeouts on all activities. See Section 5.3.2.

   ■ Never sending error messages in response to error messages.

5.3.1.1 Sending Strategy

The general model of a sender-SMTP is one or more processes that periodically attempt to transmit outgoing mail. In a typical system, the program that composes a message has some method for requesting immediate attention for a new piece of outgoing mail, while mail that cannot be transmitted immediately MUST be queued and periodically retried by the sender. A mail queue entry will include not only the message itself but also the envelope information.

The sender MUST delay retrying a particular destination after one attempt has failed. In general, the retry interval SHOULD be at least 30 minutes; however, more sophisticated and variable strategies will be beneficial when the sender-SMTP can determine the reason for non-delivery.

Retries continue until the message is transmitted or the sender gives up; the give-up time generally needs to be at least 4–5 days. The parameters to the retry algorithm MUST be configurable.

A sender SHOULD keep a list of hosts it cannot reach and corresponding timeouts, rather than just retrying queued mail items.

DISCUSSION:

Experience suggests that failures are typically transient (the target system has crashed), favoring a policy of two connection attempts in the first hour the message is in the queue, and then backing off to once every two or three hours.

The sender-SMTP can shorten the queuing delay by cooperation with the receiver-SMTP. In particular, if mail is received from a particular address, it is good evidence that any mail queued for that host can now be sent.

The strategy may be further modified as a result of multiple addresses per host (see Section 5.3.4), to optimize delivery time vs. resource usage.

A sender-SMTP may have a large queue of messages for each unavailable destination host, and if it retried all these messages in every retry cycle, there would be excessive Internet overhead and the daemon would be blocked for a long period. Note that an SMTP can generally determine that a delivery attempt has failed only after a timeout of a minute or more; a one minute timeout per connection will result in a very large delay if it is repeated for dozens or even hundreds of queued messages.

When the same message is to be delivered to several users on the same host, only one copy of the message SHOULD be transmitted. That is, the sender-SMTP should use the command sequence: RCPT, RCPT,... RCPT, DATA instead of the sequence: RCPT, DATA, RCPT, DATA,... RCPT, DATA.

Implementation of this efficiency feature is strongly urged.

Similarly, the sender-SMTP MAY support multiple concurrent outgoing mail transactions to achieve timely delivery. However, some limit SHOULD be imposed to protect the host from devoting all its resources to mail.

The use of the different addresses of a multihomed host is discussed below.

5.3.1.2 Receiving strategy

The receiver-SMTP SHOULD attempt to keep a pending listen on the SMTP port at all times. This will require the support of multiple incoming TCP connections for SMTP. Some limit MAY be imposed.

IMPLEMENTATION:

When the receiver-SMTP receives mail from a particular host address, it could notify the sender-SMTP to retry any mail pending for that host address.

5.3.2 Timeouts in SMTP

There are two approaches to timeouts in the sender-SMTP: (a) limit the time for each SMTP command separately, or (b) limit the time for the entire SMTP dialogue for a single mail message. A sender-SMTP SHOULD use option (a), per-command timeouts. Timeouts SHOULD be easily reconfigurable, preferably without recompiling the SMTP code.

DISCUSSION:

Timeouts are an essential feature of an SMTP implementation. If the timeouts are too long (or worse, there are no timeouts), Internet communication failures or software bugs in receiver-SMTP programs can tie up SMTP processes indefinitely. If the timeouts are too short, resources will be wasted with attempts that time out part way through message delivery.

If option (b) is used, the timeout has to be very large, e.g., an hour, to allow time to expand very large mailing lists. The timeout may also need to increase linearly with the size of the message, to account for the time to transmit a very large message. A large fixed timeout leads to two problems: a failure can still tie up the sender for a very long time, and very large messages may still spuriously time out (which is a wasteful failure!).

Using the recommended option (a), a timer is set for each SMTP command and for each buffer of the data transfer. The latter means that the overall timeout is inherently proportional to the size of the message.

Based on extensive experience with busy mail-relay hosts, the minimum per-command timeout values SHOULD be as follows:

Initial 220 Message: 5 minutes

A Sender-SMTP process needs to distinguish between a failed TCP connection and a delay in receiving the initial 220 greeting message. Many receiver-SMTPs will accept a TCP connection but delay delivery of the 220 message until their system load will permit more mail to be processed.

MAIL Command: 5 minutes

RCPT Command: 5 minutes

A longer timeout would be required if processing of mailing lists and aliases were not deferred until after the message was accepted.

DATA Initiation: 2 minutes

This is while awaiting the "354 Start Input" reply to a DATA command.

Data Block: 3 minutes

This is while awaiting the completion of each TCP SEND call transmitting a chunk of data.

DATA Termination: 10 minutes.

This is while awaiting the "250 OK" reply. When the receiver gets the final period terminating the message data, it typically performs processing to deliver the message to a user mailbox. A spurious timeout at this point would be very wasteful, since the message has been successfully sent.

A receiver-SMTP SHOULD have a timeout of at least 5 minutes while it is awaiting the next command from the sender.

5.3.3 Reliable Mail Receipt

When the receiver-SMTP accepts a piece of mail (by sending a "250 OK" message in response to DATA), it is accepting responsibility for delivering or relaying the message. It must take this responsibility seriously, i.e., it MUST NOT lose the message for frivolous reasons, e.g., because the host later crashes or because of a predictable resource shortage.

If there is a delivery failure after acceptance of a message, the receiver-SMTP MUST formulate and mail a notification message. This notification MUST be sent using a null ("<>") reverse path in the envelope; see Section 3.6 of RFC-821. The recipient of this notification SHOULD be the address from the envelope return path (or the Return-Path: line). However, if this address is null ("<>"), the receiver-SMTP MUST NOT send a notification. If the address is an explicit source route, it SHOULD be stripped down to its final hop.

DISCUSSION:

For example, suppose that an error notification must be sent for a message that arrived with: "MAIL FROM:<@a,@b:user@d>." The notification message should be sent to: "RCPT TO:<user@d>."

Some delivery failures after the message is accepted by SMTP will be unavoidable. For example, it may be impossible for the receiver-SMTP to validate all the delivery addresses in RCPT command(s) due to a "soft" domain system error or because the target is a mailing list (see earlier discussion of RCPT).

To avoid receiving duplicate messages as the result of timeouts, a receiver-SMTP MUST seek to minimize the time required to respond to the final "." that ends a message transfer. See RFC-1047 [SMTP:4] for a discussion of this problem.

5.3.4 Reliable Mail Transmission

To transmit a message, a sender-SMTP determines the IP address of the target host from the destination address in the envelope. Specifically, it maps the string to the right of the "@" sign into an IP address. This mapping or the transfer itself may fail with a soft error, in which case the sender-SMTP will requeue the outgoing mail for a later retry, as required in Section 5.3.1.1.

When it succeeds, the mapping can result in a list of alternative delivery addresses rather than a single address, because of (a) multiple MX records, (b) multihoming, or both. To provide reliable mail transmission, the sender-SMTP MUST be able to try (and retry) each of the addresses in this list in order, until a delivery attempt succeeds. However, there MAY also be a configurable limit on the number of alternate addresses that can be tried. In any case, a host SHOULD try at least two addresses.

The following information is to be used to rank the host addresses:

1. Multiple MX Records—These contain a preference indication that should be used in sorting. If there are multiple destinations with the same preference and there is no clear reason to favor one (e.g., by address preference), then the sender-SMTP SHOULD pick one at random to spread the load across multiple mail exchanges for a specific organization; note that this is a refinement of the procedure in [DNS:3].

2. Multihomed host—The destination host (perhaps taken from the preferred MX record) may be multihomed, in which case the domain name resolver will

return a list of alternative IP addresses. It is the responsibility of the domain name resolver interface (see Section 6.1.3.4 below) to have ordered this list by decreasing preference, and SMTP MUST try them in the order presented.

DISCUSSION:
Although the capability to try multiple alternative addresses is required, there may be circumstances where specific installations want to limit or disable the use of alternative addresses. The question of whether a sender should attempt retries using the different addresses of a multihomed host has been controversial. The main argument for using the multiple addresses is that it maximizes the probability of timely delivery, and indeed sometimes the probability of any delivery; the counter argument is that it may result in unnecessary resource use.
Note that resource use is also strongly determined by the sending strategy discussed in Section 5.3.1.

5.3.5 Domain Name Support

SMTP implementations MUST use the mechanism defined in Section 6.1 for mapping between domain names and IP addresses. This means that every Internet SMTP MUST include support for the Internet DNS.

In particular, a sender-SMTP MUST support the MX record scheme [SMTP:3]. See also Section 7.4 of [DNS:2] for information on domain name support for SMTP.

5.3.6 Mailing Lists and Aliases

An SMTP-capable host SHOULD support both the alias and the list form of address expansion for multiple delivery. When a message is delivered or forwarded to each address of an expanded list form, the return address in the envelope ("MAIL FROM:") MUST be changed to be the address of a person who administers the list, but the message header MUST be left unchanged; in particular, the "From" field of the message is unaffected.

DISCUSSION:
An important mail facility is a mechanism for multi-destination delivery of a single message, by transforming or "expanding" a pseudo-mailbox address into a list of destination mailbox addresses. When a message is sent to such a pseudo-mailbox (sometimes called an "exploder"), copies are forwarded or redistributed to each mailbox in the expanded list. We classify such a pseudo-mailbox as an "alias" or a "list," depending upon the expansion rules:

- Alias—To expand an alias, the recipient mailer simply replaces the pseudo-mailbox address in the envelope with each of the expanded addresses in turn; the rest of the envelope and the message body are left unchanged. The message is then delivered or forwarded to each expanded address.

- List—A mailing list may be said to operate by "redistribution" rather than by "forwarding." To expand a list, the recipient mailer replaces the pseudo-mailbox address in the envelope with each of the expanded addresses in turn. The return address in the envelope is changed so that all error messages generated by the final deliveries will be returned to a list administrator, not to the message originator, who generally has no control over the contents of the list and will typically find error messages annoying.

5.3.7 Mail Gatewaying

Gatewaying mail between different mail environments, i.e., different mail formats and protocols, is complex and does not easily yield to standardization. See for example [SMTP:5a], [SMTP:5b]. However, some general requirements may be given for a gateway between the Internet and another mail environment.

Header fields MAY be rewritten when necessary as messages are gatewayed across mail environment boundaries.

DISCUSSION:

This may involve interpreting the local-part of the destination address, as suggested in Section 5.2.16.

The other mail systems gatewayed to the Internet generally use a subset of RFC-822 headers, but some of them do not have an equivalent to the SMTP envelope. Therefore, when a message leaves the Internet environment, it may be necessary to fold the SMTP envelope information into the message header. A possible solution would be to create new header fields to carry the envelope information (e.g., "X-SMTP-MAIL:" and "X-SMTP-RCPT:"); however, this would require changes in mail programs in the foreign environment.

When forwarding a message into or out of the Internet environment, a gateway MUST prepend a Received: line, but it MUST NOT alter in any way a Received: line that is already in the header.

DISCUSSION:

This requirement is a subset of the general "Received:" line requirement of Section 5.2.8; it is restated here for emphasis.

Received: fields of messages originating from other environments may not conform exactly to RFC822. However, the most important use of Received: lines is for debugging mail faults, and this debugging can be severely hampered by well-meaning gateways that try to "fix" a Received: line.

The gateway is strongly encouraged to indicate the environment and protocol in the "via" clauses of Received field(s) that it supplies.

From the Internet side, the gateway SHOULD accept all valid address formats in SMTP commands and in RFC-822 headers, and all valid RFC-822 messages.

Although a gateway must accept an RFC-822 explicit source route ("@...:" format) in either the RFC-822 header or in the envelope, it MAY or may not act on the source route; see Sections 5.2.6 and 5.2.19.

DISCUSSION:

It is often tempting to restrict the range of addresses accepted at the mail gateway to simplify the translation into addresses for the remote environment. This practice is based on the assumption that mail users have control over the addresses their mailers send to the mail gateway. In practice, however, users have little control over the addresses that are finally sent; their mailers are free to change addresses into any legal RFC-822 format.

The gateway MUST ensure that all header fields of a message that it forwards into the Internet meet the requirements for Internet mail. In particular, all addresses in "From:," "To:," "Cc:," etc., fields must be transformed (if necessary) to satisfy RFC-822 syntax, and they must be effective and useful for sending replies.

The translation algorithm used to convert mail from the Internet protocols to another environment's protocol SHOULD try to ensure that error messages from the foreign mail environment are delivered to the return path from the SMTP envelope, not to the sender listed in the "From:" field of the RFC-822 message.

DISCUSSION:

Internet mail lists usually place the address of the mail list maintainer in the envelope but leave the original message header intact (with the "From:" field containing the original sender). This yields the behavior the average recipient expects: a reply to the header gets sent to the original sender, not to a mail list maintainer; however, errors get sent to the maintainer (who can fix the problem) and not the sender (who probably cannot).

Similarly, when forwarding a message from another environment into the Internet, the gateway SHOULD set the envelope return path in accordance with an error message return address, if any, supplied by the foreign environment.

5.3.8 Maximum Message Size

Mailer software MUST be able to send and receive messages of at least 64K bytes in length (including header), and a much larger maximum size is highly desirable.

DISCUSSION:

Although SMTP does not define the maximum size of a message, many systems impose implementation limits.

The current de facto minimum limit in the Internet is 64K bytes. However, electronic mail is used for a variety of purposes that create much larger messages. For example, mail is often used instead of FTP for transmitting ASCII files, and in particular to transmit entire documents. As a result, messages can be 1 megabyte or even larger. We note that the present document together with its lower-layer companion contains 0.5 megabytes.

Feature	Section	Must	Should	May	Should Not	Must Not	Footnote
Fully-qualified domain names in header	5.2.18	x					
Create explicit src route in header	5.2.19				x		
Accept explicit src route in header	5.2.19	x					
Send/recv at least 64KB messages	5.3.8	x					

6. SUPPORT SERVICES

6.1 DOMAIN NAME TRANSLATION

6.1.1 INTRODUCTION

Every host MUST implement a resolver for the Domain Name System (DNS), and it MUST implement a mechanism using this DNS resolver to convert host names to IP addresses and vice-versa [DNS:1, DNS:2].

In addition to the DNS, a host MAY also implement a host name translation mechanism that searches a local Internet host table. See Section 6.1.3.8 for more information on this option.

DISCUSSION:

Internet host name translation was originally performed by searching local copies of a table of all hosts. This table became too large to update and distribute in a timely manner and too large to fit into many hosts, so the DNS was invented.

The DNS creates a distributed database used primarily for the translation between host names and host addresses. Implementation of DNS software is required. The DNS consists of two logically distinct parts: name servers and resolvers (although implementations often combine these two logical parts in the interest of efficiency) [DNS:2]. Domain name servers store authoritative data about certain sections of the database and answer queries about the data. Domain resolvers query domain name servers for data on behalf of user processes. Every host therefore needs a DNS resolver; some host machines will also need to run domain name servers. Because no name server has complete information, in general it is necessary to obtain information from more than one name server to resolve a query.

6.1.2 PROTOCOL WALK-THROUGH

An implementor must study references [DNS:1] and [DNS:2] carefully. They provide a thorough description of the theory, protocol, and implementation of the domain name system, and reflect several years of experience.

6.1.2.1 Resource Records with Zero TTL: RFC-1035 Section 3.2.1

All DNS name servers and resolvers MUST properly handle RRs with a zero TTL:
return the RR to the client but do not cache it.
DISCUSSION:
Zero TTL values are interpreted to mean that the RR can only be used for the transaction in progress, and should not be cached; they are useful for extremely volatile data.

6.1.2.2 QCLASS Values: RFC-1035 Section 3.2.5

A query with "QCLASS=*" SHOULD NOT be used unless the requestor is seeking
data from more than one class. In particular, if the requestor is only interested in
Internet data types, QCLASS=IN MUST be used.

6.1.2.3 Unused Fields: RFC-1035 Section 4.1.1

Unused fields in a query or response message MUST be zero.

6.1.2.4 Compression: RFC-1035 Section 4.1.4

Name servers MUST use compression in responses.
   DISCUSSION:
   Compression is essential to avoid overflowing UDP datagrams; see Section 6.1.3.2.

6.1.2.5 Misusing Configuration Info: RFC-1035 Section 6.1.2

Recursive name servers and full-service resolvers generally have some configuration
information containing hints about the location of root or local name servers. An
implementation MUST NOT include any of these hints in a response.
DISCUSSION:
Many implementors have found it convenient to store these hints as if they were
cached data, but some neglected to ensure that this "cached data" was not included in
responses. This has caused serious problems in the Internet when the hints were obsolete or incorrect.

6.1.3 SPECIFIC ISSUES

6.1.3.1 Resolver Implementation

A name resolver SHOULD be able to multiplex concurrent requests if the host supports
concurrent processes.
In implementing a DNS resolver, one of two different models MAY optionally be
chosen: a full-service resolver, or a stub resolver.
   (A)Full-Service Resolver—A full-service resolver is a complete implementation of
   the resolver service, and is capable of dealing with communication failures, failure
   of individual name servers, location of the proper name server for a given name,
   etc. It must satisfy the following requirements:

   ■ The resolver MUST implement a local caching function to avoid repeated
     remote access for identical requests, and MUST time out information in the
     cache.

- The resolver SHOULD be configurable with start-up information pointing to multiple root name servers and multiple name servers for the local domain. This insures that the resolver will be able to access the whole name space in normal cases, and will be able to access local domain information should the local network become disconnected from the rest of the Internet.

(B) Stub Resolver—A "stub resolver" relies on the services of a recursive name server on the connected network or a "nearby" network. This scheme allows the host to pass on the burden of the resolver function to a name server on another host. This model is often essential for less capable hosts, such as PCs, and is also recommended when the host is one of several workstations on a local network, because it allows all of the workstations to share the cache of the recursive name server and hence reduce the number of domain requests exported by the local network. At a minimum, the stub resolver MUST be capable of directing its requests to redundant recursive name servers. Note that recursive name servers are allowed to restrict the sources of requests that they will honor, so the host administrator must verify that the service will be provided. Stub resolvers MAY implement caching if they choose, but if so, MUST timeout cached information.

6.1.3.2 Transport Protocols

DNS resolvers and recursive servers MUST support UDP, and SHOULD support TCP, for sending (non-zone-transfer) queries. Specifically, a DNS resolver or server that is sending a non-zone-transfer query MUST send a UDP query first. If the Answer section of the response is truncated and if the requester supports TCP, it SHOULD try the query again using TCP.

DNS servers MUST be able to service UDP queries and SHOULD be able to service TCP queries. A name server MAY limit the resources it devotes to TCP queries, but it SHOULD NOT refuse to service a TCP query just because it would have succeeded with UDP.

Truncated responses MUST NOT be saved (cached) and later used in such a way that the fact that they are truncated is lost.

DISCUSSION:

UDP is preferred over TCP for queries because UDP queries have much lower overhead, both in packet count and in connection state. The use of UDP is essential for heavily-loaded servers, especially the root servers. UDP also offers additional robustness, since a resolver can attempt several UDP queries to different servers for the cost of a single TCP query.

It is possible for a DNS response to be truncated, although this is a very rare occurrence in the present Internet DNS. Practically speaking, truncation cannot be predicted, since it is data-dependent. The dependencies include the number of RRs in the answer, the size of each RR, and the savings in space realized by the name compression algorithm. As a rule of thumb, truncation in NS and MX lists should not occur for answers containing 15 or fewer RRs.

Whether it is possible to use a truncated answer depends on the application. A mailer must not use a truncated MX response, since this could lead to mail loops. Responsible practices can make UDP suffice in the vast majority of cases. Name servers must use compression in responses. Resolvers must differentiate truncation of the Additional section of a response (which only loses extra information) from truncation of the Answer section (which for MX records renders the response unusable by mailers). Database administrators should list only a reasonable number of primary names in lists of name servers, MX alternatives, etc.

However, it is also clear that some new DNS record types defined in the future will contain information exceeding the 512 byte limit that applies to UDP, and hence will require TCP. Thus, resolvers and name servers should implement TCP services as a backup to UDP today, with the knowledge that they will require the TCP service in the future.

By private agreement, name servers and resolvers MAY arrange to use TCP for all traffic between themselves. TCP MUST be used for zone transfers.

A DNS server MUST have sufficient internal concurrency that it can continue to process UDP queries while awaiting a response or performing a zone transfer on an open TCP connection [DNS:2].

A server MAY support a UDP query that is delivered using an IP broadcast or multi-cast address. However, the Recursion Desired bit MUST NOT be set in a query that is multicast, and MUST be ignored by name servers receiving queries via a broadcast or multicast address. A host that sends broadcast or multicast DNS queries SHOULD send them only as occasional probes, caching the IP address(es) it obtains from the response(s) so it can normally send unicast queries.

DISCUSSION:

Broadcast or (especially) IP multicast can provide a way to locate nearby name servers without knowing their IP addresses in advance. However, general broadcasting of recursive queries can result in excessive and unnecessary load on both network and servers.

6.1.3.3 Efficient Resource Usage

The following requirements on servers and resolvers are very important to the health of the Internet as a whole, particularly when DNS services are invoked repeatedly by higher level automatic servers, such as mailers.

1. The resolver MUST implement retransmission controls to insure that it does not waste communication bandwidth, and MUST impose finite bounds on the resources consumed to respond to a single request. See [DNS:2] pages 43-44 for specific recommendations.

2. After a query has been retransmitted several times without a response, an implementation MUST give up and return a soft error to the application.

3. All DNS name servers and resolvers SHOULD cache temporary failures, with a timeout period of the order of minutes.

DISCUSSION:

This will prevent applications that immediately retry soft failures (in violation of Section 2.2 of this document) from generating excessive DNS traffic.

4. All DNS name servers and resolvers SHOULD cache negative responses that indicate the specified name, or data of the specified type, does not exist, as described in [DNS:2].

5. When a DNS server or resolver retries a UDP query, the retry interval SHOULD be constrained by an exponential backoff algorithm, and SHOULD also have upper and lower bounds.

IMPLEMENTATION:

A measured RTT and variance (if available) should be used to calculate an initial retransmission interval. If this information is not available, a default of no less than 5 seconds should be used. Implementations may limit the retransmission interval, but this limit must exceed twice the Internet maximum segment lifetime plus service delay at the name server.

6. When a resolver or server receives a Source Quench for a query it has issued, it SHOULD take steps to reduce the rate of querying that server in the near future. A server MAY ignore a Source Quench that it receives as the result of sending a response datagram.

IMPLEMENTATION:

One recommended action to reduce the rate is to send the next query attempt to an alternate server, if there is one available. Another is to back off the retry interval for the same server.

6.1.3.4 Multihomed Hosts

When the host name-to-address function encounters a host with multiple addresses, it SHOULD rank or sort the addresses using knowledge of the immediately connected network number(s) and any other applicable performance or history information.

DISCUSSION:

The different addresses of a multihomed host generally imply different Internet paths, and some paths may be preferable to others in performance, reliability, or administrative restrictions. There is no general way for the domain system to determine the best path. A recommended approach is to base this decision on local configuration information set by the system administrator.

IMPLEMENTATION:

The following scheme has been used successfully:

(a)Incorporate into the host configuration data a Network-Preference List, that is simply a list of networks in preferred order. This list may be empty if there is no preference.

(b)When a host name is mapped into a list of IP addresses, these addresses should be sorted by network number, into the same order as the corresponding networks in the Network-Preference List. IP addresses whose networks do not appear in the Network-Preference List should be placed at the end of the list.

6.1.3.5 Extensibility

DNS software MUST support all well-known, class-independent formats [DNS:2], and SHOULD be written to minimize the trauma associated with the introduction of new well-known types and local experimentation with non-standard types.
DISCUSSION:
The data types and classes used by the DNS are extensible, and thus new types will be added and old types deleted or redefined. Introduction of new data types ought to be dependent only upon the rules for compression of domain names inside DNS messages, and the translation between printable (i.e., master file) and internal formats for Resource Records (RRs).
Compression relies on knowledge of the format of data inside a particular RR. Hence compression must only be used for the contents of well-known, class-independent RRs, and must never be used for class-specific RRs or RR types that are not well-known. The owner name of an RR is always eligible for compression.
A name server may acquire, via zone transfer, RRs that the server doesn't know how to convert to printable format. A resolver can receive similar information as the result of queries. For proper operation, this data must be preserved, and hence the implication is that DNS software cannot use textual formats for internal storage.
The DNS defines domain name syntax very generally—a string of labels each containing up to 63 8-bit octets, separated by dots, and with a maximum total of 255 octets. Particular applications of the DNS are permitted to further constrain the syntax of the domain names they use, although the DNS deployment has led to some applications allowing more general names. In particular, Section 2.1 of this document liberalizes slightly the syntax of a legal Internet host name that was defined in RFC-952 [DNS:4].

6.1.3.6 Status of RR Types

Name servers MUST be able to load all RR types except MD and MF from configuration files. The MD and MF types are obsolete and MUST NOT be implemented; in particular, name servers MUST NOT load these types from configuration files.
DISCUSSION:
The RR types MB, MG, MR, NULL, MINFO and RP are considered experimental, and applications that use the DNS cannot expect these RR types to be supported by most domains. Furthermore these types are subject to redefinition.
The TXT and WKS RR types have not been widely used by Internet sites; as a result, an application cannot rely on the existence of a TXT or WKS RR in most domains.

6.1.3.7 Robustness

DNS software may need to operate in environments where the root servers or other servers are unavailable due to network connectivity or other problems. In this situation, DNS name servers and resolvers MUST continue to provide service for the reachable part of the name space, while giving temporary failures for the rest.

Search lists often contain the name of the local host's parent domain or other ancestor domains. Search lists are often per-user or per-process. It SHOULD be possible for an administrator to disable a DNS search-list facility. Administrative denial may be warranted in some cases, to prevent abuse of the DNS. There is danger that a search-list mechanism will generate excessive queries to the root servers while testing whether user input is a complete domain name, lacking a final period to mark it as complete. A search-list mechanism MUST have one of, and SHOULD have both of, the following two provisions to prevent this:

(a) The local resolver/name server can implement caching of negative responses (see Section 6.1.3.3).

(b) The search list expander can require two or more interior dots in a generated domain name before it tries using the name in a query to non-local domain servers, such as the root.

DISCUSSION:

The intent of this requirement is to avoid excessive delay for the user as the search list is tested, and more importantly to prevent excessive traffic to the root and other high-level servers. For example, if the user supplied a name "X" and the search list contained the root as a component, a query would have to consult a root server before the next search list alternative could be tried. The resulting load seen by the root servers and gateways near the root would be multiplied by the number of hosts in the Internet. The negative caching alternative limits the effect to the first time a name is used. The interior dot rule is simpler to implement but can prevent easy use of some top-level names.

6.1.5 DOMAIN NAME SYSTEM REQUIREMENTS SUMMARY

Feature	Section	Must	Should	May	Should Not	Must Not	Footnote
GENERAL ISSUES							
Implement DNS name-to-address conversion	6.1.1	x					
Implement DNS address-to-name conversion	6.1.1	x					
Support conversions using host table	6.1.1			x			
Properly handle RR with zero TTL	6.1.2.1	x					
Use QCLASS=* unnecessarily	6.1.2.2		x				

continues

6.1.5 DOMAIN NAME SYSTEM REQUIREMENTS SUMMARY (Continued)

Feature	Section	Must	Should	May	Should Not	Must Not	Footnote
Use QCLASS=IN for Internet class	6.1.2.2	x					
Unused fields zero	6.1.2.3	x					
Use compression in responses	6.1.2.4	x					
Include config info in responses	6.1.2.5					x	
Support all well-known, class-indep. Types	6.1.3.5	x					
Easily expand type list	6.1.3.5		x				
Load all RR types (except MD and MF)	6.1.3.6	x					
Load MD or MF type	6.1.3.6					x	
Operate when root servers, etc. unavailable	6.1.3.7	x					
RESOLVER ISSUES:							
Resolver support multiple concurrent requests	6.1.3.1		x				
Full-service resolver:	6.1.3.1			x			
Local caching	6.1.3.1	x					
Information in local cache times out	6.1.3.1	x					
Configurable with starting info	6.1.3.1		x				
Stub resolver:	6.1.3.1			x			
Use redundant recursive name servers	6.1.3.1	x					
Local caching	6.1.3.1			x			
Information in local cache times out	6.1.3.1	x					
Support for remote multi-homed hosts:							
Sort multiple addresses by preference list	6.1.3.4		x				

TRANSPORT

Feature	Section	Must	Should Not	May Not	Should	Must	Footnote
Try TCP if UDP answers are truncated	6.1.3.2			x			
Name server limit TCP query resources	6.1.3.2				x		
Punish unnecessary TCP query	6.1.3.2					x	
Use truncated data as if it were not	6.1.3.2						x
Private agreement to use only TCP	6.1.3.2				x		
Use TCP for zone transfers	6.1.3.2	x					
TCP usage not block UDP queries	6.1.3.2	x					
Support broadcast or multicast queries	6.1.3.2				x		
RD bit set in query	6.1.3.2					x	
RD bit ignored by server is b'cast/m'cast	6.1.3.2	x					
Send only as occasional probe for addr's	6.1.3.2			x			
RESOURCE USAGE:							
Transmission controls, per [DNS:2]	6.1.3.3	x					
Finite bounds per request	6.1.3.3	x					
Failure after retries => soft error	6.1.3.3	x					
Cache temporary failures	6.1.3.3			x			
Cache negative responses	6.1.3.3			x			
Retries use exponential backoff	6.1.3.3			x			
Upper, lower bounds	6.1.3.3			x			
Client handle Source Quench	6.1.3.3			x			
Server ignore Source Quench	6.1.3.3				x		
USER INTERFACE:							
All programs have access to DNS interface	6.1.4.2	x					

continues

6.1.5 DOMAIN NAME SYSTEM REQUIREMENTS SUMMARY (Continued)

Feature	Section	Must	Should	May	Should Not	Must Not	Footnote
Able to request all info for given name	6.1.4.2	x					
Returns complete info or error	6.1.4.2	x					
Special interfaces	6.1.4.2			x			
Name<->Address translation	6.1.4.2	x					
Abbreviation Facilities:	6.1.4.3			x			
Convention for complete names	6.1.4.3	x					
Conversion exactly once	6.1.4.3	x					
Conversion in proper context	6.1.4.3	x					
Search list:	6.1.4.3			x			
Administrator can disable	6.1.4.3		x				
Prevention of excessive root queries	6.1.4.3	x					
Both methods	6.1.4.3		x				

1. Unless there is private agreement between particular resolver and particular server.

6.2 HOST INITIALIZATION

6.2.1 INTRODUCTION

This section discusses the initialization of host software across a connected network, or more generally across an Internet path. This is necessary for a diskless host, and may optionally be used for a host with disk drives. For a diskless host, the initialization process is called "network booting" and is controlled by a bootstrap program located in a boot ROM.

To initialize a diskless host across the network, there are two distinct phases:

1. Configure the IP layer. Diskless machines often have no permanent storage in which to store network configuration information, so that sufficient configuration information must be obtained dynamically to support the loading phase that follows. This information must include at least the IP addresses of the host and of the boot server. To support booting across a gateway, the address mask and a list of default gateways are also required.

2. Load the host system code. During the loading phase, an appropriate file transfer protocol is used to copy the system code across the network from the boot server. A host with a disk may perform the first step, dynamic configuration. This is important for microcomputers, whose floppy disks allow network configuration information to be mistakenly duplicated on more than one host. Also, installation of new hosts is much simpler if they automatically obtain their configuration information from a central server, saving administrator time and decreasing the probability of mistakes.

6.2.2 REQUIREMENTS

6.2.2.1 Dynamic Configuration

A number of protocol provisions have been made for dynamic configuration.

- ICMP Information Request/Reply messages—This obsolete message pair was designed to allow a host to find the number of the network it is on. Unfortunately, it was useful only if the host already knew the host number part of its IP address, information that hosts requiring dynamic configuration seldom had.

- Reverse Address Resolution Protocol (RARP) [BOOT:4]—RARP is a link-layer protocol for a broadcast medium that allows a host to find its IP address given its link layer address. Unfortunately, RARP does not work across IP gateways and therefore requires a RARP server on every network. In addition, RARP does not provide any other configuration information.

- ICMP Address Mask Request/Reply messages—These ICMP messages allow a host to learn the address mask for a particular network interface.

- BOOTP Protocol [BOOT:2]—This protocol allows a host to determine the IP addresses of the local host and the boot server, the name of an appropriate boot file, and optionally the address mask and list of default gateways. To locate a BOOTP server, the host broadcasts a BOOTP request using UDP. Ad hoc gateway extensions have been used to transmit the BOOTP broadcast through gateways, and in the future the IP Multicasting facility will provide a standard mechanism for this purpose.

The suggested approach to dynamic configuration is to use the BOOTP protocol with the extensions defined in "BOOTP Vendor Information Extensions" RFC-1084 [BOOT:3]. RFC-1084 defines some important general (not vendor-specific) extensions. In particular, these extensions allow the address mask to be supplied in BOOTP; we RECOMMEND that the address mask be supplied in this manner.
DISCUSSION:
Historically, subnetting was defined long after IP, and so a separate mechanism (ICMP Address Mask messages) was designed to supply the address mask to a host. However, the IP address mask and the corresponding IP address conceptually form a pair, and for operational simplicity they ought to be defined at the same time and by the same mechanism, whether a configuration file or a dynamic mechanism like BOOTP.
Note that BOOTP is not sufficiently general to specify the configurations of all

interfaces of a multihomed host. A multihomed host must either use BOOTP separately for each interface, or configure one interface using BOOTP to perform the loading, and perform the complete initialization from a file later.

Application layer configuration information is expected to be obtained from files after loading of the system code.

6.2.2.2 Loading Phase

A suggested approach for the loading phase is to use TFTP [BOOT:1] between the IP addresses established by BOOTP.

   TFTP to a broadcast address SHOULD NOT be used, for reasons explained in Section 4.2.3.4.

6.3 REMOTE MANAGEMENT

6.3.1 INTRODUCTION

The Internet community has recently put considerable effort into the development of network management protocols. The result has been a two-pronged approach [MGT:1, MGT:6]: the Simple Network Management Protocol (SNMP) [MGT:4] and the Common Management Information Protocol over TCP (CMOT) [MGT:5].

In order to be managed using SNMP or CMOT, a host will need to implement an appropriate management agent. An Internet host SHOULD include an agent for either SNMP or CMOT.

Both SNMP and CMOT operate on a Management Information Base (MIB) that defines a collection of management values. By reading and setting these values, a remote application may query and change the state of the managed system.

A standard MIB [MGT:3] has been defined for use by both management protocols, using data types defined by the Structure of Management Information (SMI) defined in [MGT:2]. Additional MIB variables can be introduced under the "enterprises" and "experimental" subtrees of the MIB naming space [MGT:2].

Every protocol module in the host SHOULD implement the relevant MIB variables. A host SHOULD implement the MIB variables as defined in the most recent standard MIB, and MAY implement other MIB variables when appropriate and useful.

6.3.2 PROTOCOL WALK-THROUGH

The MIB is intended to cover both hosts and gateways, although there may be detailed differences in MIB application to the two cases. This section contains the appropriate interpretation of the MIB for hosts. It is likely that later versions of the MIB will include more entries for host management.

A managed host must implement the following groups of MIB object definitions: System, Interfaces, Address Translation, IP, ICMP, TCP, and UDP.

The following specific interpretations apply to hosts:

- ipInHdrErrors—Note that the error "time-to-live exceeded" can occur in a host only when it is forwarding a source-routed datagram.

- ipOutNoRoutes—This object counts datagrams discarded because no route can be found. This may happen in a host if all the default gateways in the host's configuration are down.

- ipFragOKs, ipFragFails, ipFragCreates—A host that does not implement intentional fragmentation (see "Fragmentation" section of [INTRO:1]) MUST return the value zero for these three objects.

- icmpOutRedirects—For a host, this object MUST always be zero, since hosts do not send Redirects.

- icmpOutAddrMaskReps—For a host, this object MUST always be zero, unless the host is an authoritative source of address mask information.

- ipAddrTable—For a host, the "IP Address Table" object is effectively a table of logical interfaces.

- ipRoutingTable—For a host, the "IP Routing Table" object is effectively a combination of the host's Routing Cache and the static route table described in "Routing Outbound Datagrams" section of [INTRO:1].

Within each ipRouteEntry, ipRouteMetric1...4 normally will have no meaning for a host and SHOULD always be -1, while ipRouteType will normally have the value "remote."

If destinations on the connected network do not appear in the Route Cache (see "Routing Outbound Datagrams section of [INTRO:1]), there will be no entries with ipRouteType of "direct."

DISCUSSION:

The current MIB does not include Type-of-Service in an ipRouteEntry, but a future revision is expected to make this addition. We also expect the MIB to be expanded to allow the remote management of applications (e.g., the ability to partially reconfigure mail systems). Network service applications such as mail systems should therefore be written with the "hooks" for remote management.

6.3.3 MANAGEMENT REQUIREMENTS SUMMARY

Feature	Section	Must	Should	May	Should Not	Must Not	Footnote
Support SNMP or CMOT agent	6.3.1		x				
Implement specified objects in standard MIB	6.3.1		x				

7. REFERENCES

This section lists the primary references with which every implementer must be thoroughly familiar. It also lists some secondary references that are suggested additional reading.

INTRODUCTORY REFERENCES:

[INTRO:1] "Requirements for Internet Hosts — Communication Layers," ETF Host Requirements Working Group, R. Braden, Ed., RFC-1122, October 1989.

[INTRO:2] "DDN Protocol Handbook," NIC-50004, NIC-50005, NIC-50006, (three volumes), SRI International, December 1985.

[INTRO:3] "Official Internet Protocols," J. Reynolds and J. Postel, RFC-1011, May 1987.

This document is republished periodically with new RFC numbers; the latest version must be used.

[INTRO:4] "Protocol Document Order Information," O. Jacobsen and J. Postel, RFC-980, March 1986.

[INTRO:5] "Assigned Numbers," J. Reynolds and J. Postel, RFC-1010, May 1987.

This document is republished periodically with new RFC numbers; the latest version must be used.

TELNET REFERENCES:

[TELNET:1] "Telnet Protocol Specification," J. Postel and J. Reynolds, RFC-854, May 1983.

[TELNET:2] "Telnet Option Specification," J. Postel and J. Reynolds, RFC-855, May 1983.

[TELNET:3] "Telnet Binary Transmission," J. Postel and J. Reynolds, RFC-856, May 1983.

[TELNET:4] "Telnet Echo Option," J. Postel and J. Reynolds, RFC-857, May 1983.

[TELNET:5] "Telnet Suppress Go Ahead Option," J. Postel and J. Reynolds, RFC-858, May 1983.

[TELNET:6] "Telnet Status Option," J. Postel and J. Reynolds, RFC-859, May 1983.

[TELNET:7] "Telnet Timing Mark Option," J. Postel and J. Reynolds, RFC-860, May 1983.

[TELNET:8] "Telnet Extended Options List," J. Postel and J. Reynolds, RFC-861, May 1983.

[TELNET:9] "Telnet End-Of-Record Option," J. Postel, RFC-855, December 1983.

[TELNET:10] "Telnet Terminal-Type Option," J. VanBokkelen, RFC-1091, February 1989. This document supercedes RFC-930.

[TELNET:11] "Telnet Window Size Option," D. Waitzman, RFC-1073, October 1988.

[TELNET:12] "Telnet Linemode Option," D. Borman, RFC-1116, August 1989.

[TELNET:13] "Telnet Terminal Speed Option," C. Hedrick, RFC-1079, December 1988.

[TELNET:14] "Telnet Remote Flow Control Option," C. Hedrick, RFC-1080, November 1988.

SECONDARY TELNET REFERENCES:

[TELNET:15] "Telnet Protocol," MIL-STD-1782, U.S. Department of Defense, May 1984. This document is intended to describe the same protocol as RFC-854. In case of conflict, RFC-854 takes precedence, and the present document takes precedence over both.

[TELNET:16] "SUPDUP Protocol," M. Crispin, RFC-734, October 1977.

[TELNET:17] "Telnet SUPDUP Option," M. Crispin, RFC-736, October 1977.

[TELNET:18] "Data Entry Terminal Option," J. Day, RFC-732, June 1977.

[TELNET:19] "TELNET Data Entry Terminal option—DODIIS Implementation," A. Yasuda and T. Thompson, RFC-1043, February 1988.

FTP REFERENCES:

[FTP:1] "File Transfer Protocol," J. Postel and J. Reynolds, RFC-959, October 1985.

[FTP:2] "Document File Format Standards," J. Postel, RFC-678, December 1974.

[FTP:3] "File Transfer Protocol," MIL-STD-1780, U.S. Department of Defense, May 1984. This document is based on an earlier version of the FTP specification (RFC-765) and is obsolete.

TFTP REFERENCES:

[TFTP:1] "The TFTP Protocol Revision 2," K. Sollins, RFC-783, June 1981.

MAIL REFERENCES:

[SMTP:1] "Simple Mail Transfer Protocol," J. Postel, RFC-821, August 1982.

[SMTP:2] "Standard For The Format of ARPA Internet Text Messages," D. Crocker, RFC-822, August 1982. This document obsoleted an earlier specification, RFC-733.

[SMTP:3] "Mail Routing and the Domain System," C. Partridge, RFC-974, January 1986. This RFC describes the use of MX records, a mandatory extension to the mail delivery process.

[SMTP:4] "Duplicate Messages and SMTP," C. Partridge, RFC-1047, February 1988.

[SMTP:5a] "Mapping between X.400 and RFC 822," S. Kille, RFC-987, June 1986.

[SMTP:5b] "Addendum to RFC-987," S. Kille, RFC-???, September 1987.

The two preceding RFC's define a proposed standard for gatewaying mail between the Internet and the X.400 environments.

[SMTP:6] "Simple Mail Transfer Protocol," MIL-STD-1781, U.S. Department of Defense, May 1984. This specification is intended to describe the same protocol as does RFC-821. However, MIL-STD-1781 is incomplete; in particular, it does not include MX records [SMTP:3].

[SMTP:7] "A Content-Type Field for Internet Messages," M. Sirbu, RFC-1049, March 1988.

DOMAIN NAME SYSTEM REFERENCES:

[DNS:1] "Domain Names—Concepts and Facilities," P. Mockapetris, RFC-1034, November 1987. This document and the following one obsolete RFC-882, RFC-883, and RFC-973.

[DNS:2] "Domain Names—Implementation and Specification," RFC-1035, P. Mockapetris, November 1987.

[DNS:3] "Mail Routing and the Domain System," C. Partridge, RFC-974, January 1986.

[DNS:4] "DoD Internet Host Table Specification," K. Harrenstein, RFC-952, M. Stahl, E. Feinler, October 1985.

SECONDARY DNS REFERENCES:

[DNS:5] "Hostname Server," K. Harrenstein, M. Stahl, E. Feinler, RFC-953, October 1985.

[DNS:6] "Domain Administrators Guide," M. Stahl, RFC-1032, November 1987.

[DNS:7] "Domain Administrators Operations Guide," M. Lottor, RFC-1033, November 1987.

[DNS:8] "The Domain Name System Handbook," Vol. 4 of Internet Protocol Handbook, NIC 50007, SRI Network Information Center, August 1989.

SYSTEM INITIALIZATION REFERENCES:

[BOOT:1] "Bootstrap Loading Using TFTP," R. Finlayson, RFC-906, June 1984.

[BOOT:2] "Bootstrap Protocol (BOOTP)," W. Croft and J. Gilmore, RFC-951, September 1985.

[BOOT:3] "BOOTP Vendor Information Extensions," J. Reynolds, RFC-1084, December 1988. Note: this RFC revised and obsoleted RFC-1048.

[BOOT:4] "A Reverse Address Resolution Protocol," R. Finlayson, T. Mann, J. Mogul, and M. Theimer, RFC-903, June 1984.

MANAGEMENT REFERENCES:

[MGT:1] "IAB Recommendations for the Development of Internet Network Management Standards," V. Cerf, RFC-1052, April 1988.

[MGT:2] "Structure and Identification of Management Information for TCP/IP-based internets," M. Rose and K. McCloghrie, RFC-1065, August 1988.

[MGT:3] "Management Information Base for Network Management of TCP/IP-based internets," M. Rose and K. McCloghrie, RFC-1066, August 1988.

[MGT:4] "A Simple Network Management Protocol," J. Case, M. Fedor, M. Schoffstall, and C. Davin, RFC-1098, April 1989.

[MGT:5] "The Common Management Information Services and Protocol over TCP/IP," U. Warrier and L. Besaw, RFC-1095, April 1989.

[MGT:6] "Report of the Second Ad Hoc Network Management Review Group," V. Cerf, RFC-1109, August 1989.

Security Considerations

There are many security issues in the application and support programs of host software, but a full discussion is beyond the scope of this RFC. Security-related issues are mentioned in sections concerning TFTP (Sections 4.2.1, 4.2.3.4, 4.2.3.5), the SMTP VRFY and EXPN commands (Section 5.2.3), the SMTP HELO command (5.2.5), and the SMTP DATA command (Section 5.2.8).

Author's Address

Robert Braden
USC/Information Sciences Institute
4676 Admiralty Way
Marina del Rey, CA 90292-6695
Phone: (213) 822 1511
EMail: Braden@ISI.EDU

Open Publication License

OPEN PUBLICATION LICENSE Draft v0.4, 8 June 1999

I. REQUIREMENTS ON BOTH UNMODIFIED AND MODIFIED VERSIONS

The Open Publication works may be reproduced and distributed in whole or in part, in any medium physical or electronic, provided that the terms of this license are adhered to, and that this license or an incorporation of it by reference (with any options elected by the author(s) and/or publisher) is displayed in the reproduction. Proper form for an incorporation by reference is as follows: Copyright (c) by <author's name or designee>. This material may be distributed only subject to the terms and conditions set forth in the Open Publication License, vX.Y or later (the latest version is presently available at http://www.opencontent.org/openpub/). The reference must be immediately followed with any options elected by the author(s) and/or publisher of the document (see section VI). Commercial redistribution of Open Publication-licensed material is permitted. Any publication in standard (paper) book form shall require the citation of the original publisher and author. The publisher and author's names shall appear on all outer surfaces of the book. On all outer surfaces of the book the original publisher's name shall be as large as the title of the work and cited as possessive with respect to the title.

II. COPYRIGHT

The copyright to each Open Publication is owned by its author(s) or designee.

III. SCOPE OF LICENSE

The following license terms apply to all Open Publication works, unless otherwise explicitly stated in the document. Mere aggregation of Open Publication works or a portion of an Open Publication work with other works or programs on the same media shall not cause this license to apply to those other works. The aggregate work shall contain a notice specifying the inclusion of the Open Publication material and appropriate copyright notice. SEVERABILITY. If any part of this license is found to be unenforceable in any jurisdiction, the remaining portions of the license remain in force. NO WARRANTY. Open Publication works are licensed and provided "as is" without warranty of any kind, express or implied, including, but not limited to, the implied warranties of merchantability and fitness for a particular purpose or a warranty of non-infringement.

IV. REQUIREMENTS ON MODIFIED WORKS All modified versions of documents covered by this license, including translations, anthologies, compilations and partial documents, must meet the following requirements:

1) The modified version must be labeled as such. 2) The person making the modifications must be identified and the modifications dated. 3) Acknowledgement of the original author and publisher if applicable must be retained according to normal academic citation practices. 4) The location of the original unmodified document must be identified. 5) The original author's (or authors') name(s) may not be used to assert or imply endorsement of the resulting document without the original author's (or authors') permission.

V. GOOD-PRACTICE RECOMMENDATIONS

In addition to the requirements of this license, it is requested from and strongly recommended of redistributors that: 1) If you are distributing Open Publication works on hardcopy or CD-ROM, you provide email notification to the authors of your intent to redistribute at least thirty days before your manuscript or media freeze, to give the authors time to provide updated documents. This notification should describe modifications, if any, made to the document. 2) All substantive modifications (including deletions) be either clearly marked up in the document or else described in an attachment to the document. Finally, while it is not mandatory under this license, it is considered good form to offer a free copy of any hardcopy and CD-ROM expression of an Open Publication-licensed work to its author(s).

VI. LICENSE OPTIONS

The author(s) and/or publisher of an Open Publication-licensed document may elect certain options by appending language to the reference to or copy of the license. These options are considered part of the license instance and must be included with the license (or its incorporation by reference) in derived works. A. To prohibit distribution of substantively modified versions without the explicit permission of the author(s). "Substantive modification" is defined as a change to the semantic content of the document, and excludes mere changes in format or typographical corrections. To accomplish this, add the phrase `Distribution of substantively modified versions of this document is prohibited without the explicit permission of the copyright holder.' to the license reference or copy. B. To prohibit any publication of this work or derivative works in whole or in part in standard (paper) book form for commercial purposes is prohibited unless prior permission is obtained from the copyright holder. To accomplish this, add the phrase 'Distribution of the work or derivative of the work in any standard (paper) book form is prohibited unless prior permission is obtained from the copyright holder.' to the license reference or copy.

OPEN PUBLICATION POLICY APPENDIX:

(This is not considered part of the license.) Open Publication works are available in source format via the Open Publication home page at http://works.opencontent.org/. Open Publication authors who want to include their own license on Open Publication works may do so, as long as their terms are not more restrictive than the Open Publication license. If you have questions about the Open Publication License, please contact TBD, and/or the Open Publication Authors' List at opal@opencontent.org, via email.

Index

J-K-L

Advanced Information on Networking Technologies

New Riders Books Offer Advice and Experience

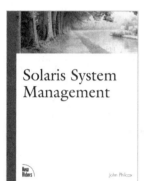

LANDMARK

We know how important it is to have access to detailed, solution-oriented information on core technologies. *Landmark* books contain the essential information you need to solve technical problems. Written by experts and subjected to rigorous peer and technical reviews, our *Landmark* books are hard-core resources for practitioners like you.

ESSENTIAL REFERENCE

The *Essential Reference* series from New Riders provides answers when you know what you want to do but need to know how to do it. Each title skips extraneous material and assumes a strong base of knowledge. These are indispensable books for the practitioner who wants to find specific features of a technology quickly and efficiently. Avoiding fluff and basic material, these books present solutions in an innovative, clean format—and at a great value.

MCSE CERTIFICATION

New Riders offers a complete line of test preparation materials to help you achieve your certification. With books like the *MCSE Training Guide*, and software like the acclaimed *MCSE Complete* and the revolutionary *ExamGear*, New Riders offers comprehensive products built by experienced professionals who have passed the exams and instructed hundreds of candidates.

Books for Networking Professionals

Microsoft Technologies

Inside Windows 2000 Server

By William Boswell
1st Edition
1515 pages, $49.99
ISBN: 1-56205-929-7

Taking the author-driven, no-nonsense approach we pioneered with our *Landmark* books, New Riders proudly offers something unique for Windows 2000 administrators—an interesting, discriminating book on Windows 2000 Server written by someone who can anticipate your situation and give you workarounds that won't leave a system unstable or sluggish.

Windows 2000 Active Directory

By Ed Brovick, Doug Hauger, and William Wade III
1st Edition
416 pages, $29.99
ISBN: 0-7357-0870-3

Written by three of Microsoft's key premium partners, with high-level access to people, information, and resources, this book offers a concise, focused, and informative *Landmark* format, filled with case studies and real-world experience for Windows 2000's most anticipated and most complex feature—the Active Directory.

Windows 2000 Essential Reference

By Steven Tate, et al.
1st Edition
670 pages, $35.00
ISBN: 0-7357-0869-X

Architected to be the most navigable, useful and value-packed reference for Windows 2000, this book uses a creative "telescoping" design that you can adapt to your style of learning. The authors give you answers based on their hands-on experience with Windows 2000 and apply their formidable credentials toward giving you the answers you won't find anywhere else.

Windows 2000 Routing and Remote Access Service

By Kackie Charles
1st Edition
400 pages, $34.99
ISBN: 0-7357-0951-3

Ideal for system administrators looking to create cost-effective and secure remote access across the network. Author Kackie Charles uses concrete examples to demonstrate how to smoothly integrate Windows 2000 routing with your existing routing infrastructure, and connect users to the network while maximizing available bandwidth. Featured coverage includes new authentication models, routing protocols, configuration of the Windows 2000 router, design issues, security, and troubleshooting.

Windows 2000 Deployment & Desktop Management

By Jeffrey A. Ferris
1st Edition
408 pages, $34.99
ISBN: 0-7357-0975-0

More than a simple overview of new features and tools, this solutions-driven book is a thorough reference to deploying Windows 2000 Professional to corporate workstations. The expert real-world advice and detailed exercises make this a one-stop, easy-to-use resource for any system administrator, integrator, engineer, or other IT professional planning rollout of Windows 2000 clients.

Windows 2000 User Management

By Lori Sanders
1st Edition
240 pages, $34.99
ISBN: 1-56205-886-X

With the dawn of Windows 2000, it has become even more difficult to draw a clear line between managing the user and managing the user's environment and desktop. This book, written by a noted trainer and consultant, provides a comprehensive, practical guide to managing users and their desktop environments with Windows 2000.

Windows 2000 DNS

By Herman Knief, Jeffrey Graham, Andrew Daniels, and Roger Abell
2nd Edition
480 pages, $39.99
ISBN: 0-7357-0973-4

Focusing on such key topics as designing and securing DNS services, planning for interoperation, and installing and using DHCP and WINS services, *Windows 2000 DNS* is a comprehensive guide to the newest iteration of Microsoft's DNS. The authors provide you with real-world advice, best practices, and strategies you will need to design and administer DNS for optimal performance.

Windows 2000 Professional

By Jerry Honeycutt
1st Edition
330 pages, $34.99
ISBN: 0-7357-0950-5

Windows 2000 Professional explores the power available to the Windows workstation user on the corporate network and Internet. The book is aimed directly at the power user who values the security, stability, and networking capabilities of NT alongside the ease and familiarity of the Windows 9X user interface. This book covers both user and administration topics, with a dose of networking content added for connectivity.

Planning for Windows 2000

By Eric K. Cone,
Jon Boggs, and Sergio Perez
1st Edition
448 pages, $29.99
ISBN: 0-7357-0048-6

Are you ready for Windows 2000? This book explains the steps involved in preparing your Windows NT-based heterogeneous network for Windows 2000. Rollout procedures are presented in detail as the authors draw from their own experiences and scenarios to explain an otherwise tangled series of procedures. *Planning for Windows 2000* is an indispensable companion to anyone considering migration.

Windows 2000 Professional Reference

By Karanjit Siyan, Ph.D.
3rd Edition
1848 pages, $75.00
ISBN: 0-7357-0952-1

Windows 2000 Professional Reference is the benchmark of references available for Windows 2000. Although other titles take you through the setup and implementation phase of the product, no other book provides the user with detailed answers to day-to-day administration problems and tasks. Solid content shows administrators how to manage, troubleshoot, and fix problems that are specific to heterogeneous Windows networks, as well as Internet features and functionality.

Windows 2000 Security

By Roberta Bragg
1st Edition
500 pages, $39.99
ISBN: 0-7357-0991-2

No single authoritative reference on security exists for serious network system administrators. The primary directive of this title is to assist the Windows networking professional in understanding and implementing Windows 2000 security in his organization. Included are Best Practices sections, which make recommendations for settings and security practices.

Windows NT/2000 Network Security

By Eugene Schultz
1st Edition
440 pages, $45.00
ISBN 1-57870-253-4

Windows NT/2000 Network Security provides a framework that will promote genuine understanding, of the Windows security model and associated capabilities. The goal is to acquaint readers with the major types of Windows security exposures when used in both peer-to-peer and client-server settings. This book teaches readers the specific security controls and settings that address each exposure, and shows them how to evaluate tradeoffs to determine which control (if any) to apply.

Windows NT/2000 Thin Client Solutions

By Todd Mathers
2nd Edition
840 pages, $45.00
ISBN: 1-57870-239-9

A practical and comprehensive reference to MetaFrame 1.8 and Terminal Server Edition, this book should be the first source for answers to the tough questions on the TSE/MetaFrame platform. Building on the quality of the previous edition, additional coverage of installation of Terminal Services and MetaFrame on a Windows 2000 Server, as well as chapters on TSE management, remote access, and application integration, are included.

Windows 2000 Active Directory Design & Deployment

By Gary Olsen
1st Edition
648 pages, $45.00
ISBN: 1-57870-242-9

This book focuses on the design of a Windows 2000 Active Directory environment, and how to develop an effective design and migration plan. The reader is lead through the process of developing a design plan by reviewing each pertinent issue, and then provided expert advice on how to evaluate each issue as it applies to the reader's particular environment. Practical examples illustrate all of these issues.

Windows 2000 Virtual Private Networking

By Thaddeus Fortenberry
1st Edition
350 pages, $45.00
ISBN 1-57870-246-1

Because of the ongoing push for a distributed workforce, administrators must support laptop users, home LAN environments, complex branch offices, and more—all within a secure and effective network design. The way an administrator implements VPNs in Windows 2000 is different than that of any other operating system. In addition to discussions about Windows 2000 tunneling, new VPN features that can affect Active Directory replication and Network Address Translation are also covered.

Windows 2000 and Mainframe Integration

By William Zack
1st Edition
390 pages, $40.00
ISBN:1-57870-200-3

Windows 2000 and Mainframe Integration provides mainframe computing professionals with the practical know-how to build and integrate Windows 2000 technologies into their current environment.

Windows 2000 Server: Planning and Migration

By Sean Deuby
1st Edition
480 pages, $40.00
ISBN:1-57870-023-X

Windows 2000 Server: Planning and Migration can quickly save the NT professional thousands of dollars and hundreds of hours. This title includes authoritative information on key features of Windows 2000 and offers recommendations on how to best position your NT network for Windows 2000.

Windows 2000 Quality of Service

By David Iseminger
1st Edition
264 pages, $45.00
ISBN:1-57870-115-5

As the traffic on networks continues to increase, the strain on network infrastructure and available resources has also grown. *Windows 2000 Quality of Service* teaches network engineers and administrators to how to define traffic control patterns and utilize bandwidth on their networks.

Windows NT Power Toolkit

By Stu Sjouwerman and Ed Tittel
1st Edition
848 pages, $49.99
ISBN: 0-7357-0922-X

A unique offering from New Riders, this book covers the analysis, tuning, optimization, automation, enhancement, maintenance, and troubleshooting of both Windows NT Server 4.0 and Windows NT Workstation 4.0. *Windows NT Power Toolkit* includes comprehensive coverage of all service packs and security updates, IE5 upgrade issues, recent product additions, third-party tools and utilities.

Windows NT Terminal Server and Citrix MetaFrame

By Ted Harwood
1st Edition
46 pages, $29.99
ISBN: 1-56205-944-0

This technical reference details all aspects of planning, installing, administering, and troubleshooting Microsoft Terminal Server and Citrix MetaFrame systems. MetaFrame greatly enhances the usability of NT as a thin-client solution, but the heterogeneous networking issues involved in its integration will be a significant source of information pain. *Windows NT Terminal Server and Citrix Metaframe* is one of only two books available on this technology.

Windows NT/2000 Native API Reference
By Gary Nebbett
1st Edition
528 pages, $50.00
ISBN: 1-57870-199-6

This book is the first complete reference to the API functions native to Windows NT and covers the set of services that are offered by the Windows NT to both kernel- and user-mode programs. Coverage consists of documentation of the 210 routines included in the NT Native API, and the functions that will be added in Windows 2000. Routines that are either not directly accessible via the Win32 API or offer substantial additional functionality are described in especially great detail. Services offered by the NT kernel— mainly the support for debugging user mode applications—are also included.

Windows NT Device Driver Development
By Peter Viscarola and W. Anthony Mason
1st Edition
704 pages, $50.00
ISBN: 1-57870-058-2

This title begins with an introduction to the general Windows NT operating system concepts relevant to drivers, then progresses to more detailed information about the operating system, such as interrupt management, synchronization issues, the I/O Subsystem, standard kernel mode drivers, and more.

DCE/RPC over SMB: Samba and Windows NT Domain Internals
By Luke Leighton
1st Edition
312 pages, $45.00
ISBN: 1-57870-150-3

Security people, system and network administrators, and those writing tools for them all need to be familiar with the packets flowing across their networks. Authored by a key member of the Samba team, this book describes how Microsoft has taken DCE/RPC and implemented it over SMB and TCP/IP.

Delphi COM Programming
By Eric Harmon
1st Edition
500 pages, $45.00
ISBN: 1-57870-221-6

Delphi COM Programming is for all Delphi 3, 4, and 5 programmers. After providing readers with an understanding of the COM framework, it offers a practical exploration of COM to enable Delphi developers to program component-based applications. Typical real-world scenarios, such as Windows Shell programming, automating Microsoft Agent, and creating and using ActiveX controls, are explored. Discussions of each topic are illustrated with detailed examples.

Windows NT Applications: Measuring and Optimizing Performance
By Paul Hinsberg
1st Edition
288 pages, $40.00
ISBN: 1-57870-176-7

This book offers developers crucial insight into the underlying structure of Windows NT, as well as the methodology and tools for measuring and ultimately optimizing code performance.

Applying COM+
By Gregory Brill
1st Edition
450 pages, $49.99
ISBN: 0-7357-0978-5

By pulling a number of disparate services into one unified technology, COM+ holds the promise of greater efficiency and more diverse capabilities for developers who are creating applications—either enterprise or commercial software—to run on a Windows 2000 system. *Applying COM+* covers the features of the new tool, as well as how to implement them in a real case study. Features are demonstrated in all three of the major languages used in the Windows environment: C++, VB, and VJ++.

Exchange & Outlook: Constructing Collaborative Solutions
By Joel Semeniuk and Duncan MacKenzie
1st Edition
576 pages, $40.00
ISBN: 1-57870-252-6

The authors of this book are responsible for building custom messaging applications for some of the biggest Fortune 100 companies in the world. They share their expertise to help administrators and designers use Microsoft technology to establish a base for their messaging system and to lay out the tools that can be used to help build those collaborative solutions. Actual planning and design solutions are included along with typically workflow/collaborative solutions.

Windows Script Host
By Tim Hill
1st Edition
448 pages, $35.00
ISBN: 1-57870-139-2

Windows Script Host is one of the first books published about this powerful tool. The text focuses on system scripting and the VBScript language, using objects, server scriptlets, and ready-to-use script solutions.

Windows NT Shell Scripting
By Tim Hill
1st Edition
400 pages, $32.00
ISBN: 1-57870-047-7

A complete reference for Windows NT scripting, this book guides you through a high-level introduction to the Shell language itself and the Shell commands that are useful for controlling or managing different components of a network.

Win32 Perl Programming: The Standard Extensions
By Dave Roth
1st Edition
640 pages, $40.00
ISBN:1-57870-067-1

Discover numerous proven examples and practical uses of Perl in solving everyday Win32 problems. This is the only book available with comprehensive coverage of Win32 extensions, where most of the Perl functionality resides in Windows settings.

Windows NT Automated Deployment and Customization
By Richard Puckett
1st Edition
300 pages, $32.00
ISBN: 1-57870-045-0

This title offers time-saving advice that helps you install, update and configure software on each of your clients, without having to visit each client. Learn how to control all clients remotely for tasks, such as security and legal software use. Reference material on native NT tools, registry edits, and third-party tools is included.

Windows NT/2000 ADSI Scripting for System Administration
By Thomas Eck
1st Edition
700 pages, $45.00
ISBN: 1-57870-219-4

Active Directory Scripting Interfaces (ADSI) allow administrators to automate administrative tasks across their Windows networks. This title fills a gap in the current ADSI documentation by including coverage of its interaction with LDAP and provides administrators with proven code samples that they can adopt to effectively configure and manage user accounts and other usually time-consuming tasks.

SMS 2 Administration
By Darshan Doshi and Mike Lubanski
1st Edition
448 pages, $39.99
ISBN: 0-7357-0082-6

SMS 2 Administra-tion offers comprehensive coverage of how to design, deploy, and manage SMS 2.0 in an enterprise environment. This book follows the evolution of a software management system from the initial design through the implementation life cycle, to day-to-day management and usage of the system. Packed with case studies and examples pulled from the author's extensive experience, this book makes this complex product seem almost simple.

Internet Information Services Administration
By Kelli Adam
1st Edition
192 pages, $29.99
ISBN: 0-7357-0022-2

Administrators who know IIS from previous versions need this book to show them in concrete detail how to configure the new protocols, authenticate users with the new Certificate Server, and implement and manage the new e-commerce features that are part of IIS 5. This book gives you all of that: a quick read that provides real-world solutions, and doubles as a portable reference.

SQL Server System Administration
By Sean Baird and Chris Miller, et al.
1st Edition
352 pages, $29.99
ISBN: 1-56205-955-6

Assuming that the reader is familiar with the fundamentals of database administration and has worked with SQL Server in some capacity, this book focuses on the topics of interest to most administrators: keeping data consistently available to users. Unlike other SQL Server books that have little relevance to the serious SQL Server DBA, *SQL Server System Administration* provides a hands-on approach that administrators won't find elsewhere.

SQL Server 7 Essential Reference
By Sharon Dooley
1st Edition
400 pages, $35.00
ISBN: 0-7357-0864-9

SQL Server 7 Essential Reference is a comprehensive reference of advanced how-tos and techniques for developing with SQL Server. In particular, the book addresses advanced development techniques used in large application efforts with multiple users developing Web applications for intranets, extranets, or the Internet. Each section includes details on how each component is developed and then integrated into a real-life application.

Open Source

MySQL
By Paul DuBois
1st Edition
800 pages, $49.99
ISBN: 0-7357-0921-1

MySQL teaches readers how to use the tools provided by the MySQL distribution, covering installation, setup, daily use, security, optimization, maintenance, and troubleshooting. It also discusses important third-party tools, such as the Perl DBI and Apache/PHP interfaces that provide access to MySQL.

Web Application Development with PHP 4.0

By Till Gerken, et al.
1st Edition
416 pages, $39.99
ISBN: 0-7357-0997-1

Web Application Development with PHP 4.0 explains PHP's advanced syntax including classes, recursive functions, and variables. The authors present software development methodologies and coding conventions, which are a must-know for industry quality products and make software development faster and more productive. Included is coverage on Web applications and insight into user and session management, e-commerce systems, XML applications, and WDDX.

PHP Functions Essential Reference

By Landon Bradshaw, Till Gerken, Graeme Merrall, and Tobias Ratschiller
1st Edition
500 pages, $35.00
ISBN: 0-7357-0970-X
February 2001

This carefully crafted title covers the latest developments through PHP 4.0, including coverage of Zend. These authors share their knowledge not only of the development of PHP, but also how they use it daily to create dynamic Web sites. Covered as well is instruction on using PHP alongside MySQL.

Python Essential Reference

By David Beazley
1st Edition
352 pages, $34.95
ISBN: 0-7357-0901-7

Avoiding the dry and academic approach, the goal of *Python Essential Reference* is to concisely describe the Python programming language and its large library of standard modules, collectively known as the Python programming environment. This informal reference covers Python's lexical conventions, datatypes, control flow, functions, statements, classes, and execution model—a truly essential reference for any Python programmer!

GNU Autoconf, Automake, and Libtool

By Gary V. Vaughan, et al.
1st Edition
400 pages, $40.00
ISBN: 1-57870-190-2

This book is the first of its kind, authored by Open Source community luminaries and current maintainers of the tools, teaching developers how to boost their productivity and the portability of their applications using GNU Autoconf, Automake, and Libtool.

Linux/UNIX

Linux System Administration

By M Carling, James T. Dennis, and Stephen Degler
1st Edition
368 pages, $29.99
ISBN: 1-56205-934-3

Today's overworked sysadmins are looking for ways to keep their networks running smoothly and achieve enhanced performance. Users are always looking for more storage, more services, and more Speed. *Linux System Administration* guides the reader in the many intricacies of maintaining a secure, stable system.

Linux Firewalls

By Robert Ziegler
1st Edition
496 pages, $39.99
ISBN: 0-7357-0900-9

This book details security steps that a small, non–enterprise business user might take to protect his system. These steps include packet-level firewall filtering, IP masquerading, proxies, tcp wrappers, system integrity checking, and system security monitoring with an overall emphasis on filtering and protection. The goal of *Linux Firewalls* is to help people get their Internet security measures in place quickly, without the need to become experts in security or firewalls.

Linux Essential Reference

By Ed Petron
1st Edition
368 pages, $24.95
ISBN: 0-7357-0852-5

This title is all about getting things done by providing structured organization to the plethora of available Linux information. Providing clear and concise instructions on how to perform important administration and management tasks, as well as how to use some of the more powerful commands and more advanced topics, the scope of *Linux Essential Reference* includes the best way to implement the most frequently used commands, manage shell scripting, administer your own system, and utilize effective security.

UnixWare 7 System Administration

By Gene Henriksen and Melissa Henriksen
1st Edition
560 pages, $40.00
ISBN: 1-57870-080-9

In great technical detail, this title presents the latest version of SCO UnixWare and is the definitive operating system resource for SCO engineers and administrators. SCO troubleshooting notes and tips are integrated throughout the text, as are tips specifically designed for those who are familiar with other UNIX variants.

Developing Linux Applications with GTK+ and GDK

By Eric Harlow
1st Edition
512 pages, $34.99
ISBN: 0-7357-0021-4

This handbook is for developers who are moving to the Linux platform, and those using the GTK+ library, including Glib and GDK using C. All the applications and code the author developed for this book have been released under the GPL.

KDE Application Development

By Uwe Thiem
1st Edition
190 pages, $39.99
ISBN: 1-57870-201-1

KDE Application Development offers a head start on KDE and Qt. The book covers the essential widgets available in KDE and Qt, and offers a strong start without the "first try" annoyances which sometimes make strong developers and programmers give up.

GTK+/Gnome Application Development

By Havoc Pennington
1st Edition
528 pages, $39.99
ISBN: 0-7357-0078-8

More than one million Linux users are also application developers. *GTK+/Gnome Application Development* provides the experienced programmer with the knowledge to develop X Windows applications with the popular GTK+ toolkit. It contains reference information for more experienced users who are already familiar with usage, but require function prototypes and detailed descriptions.

Grokking the GIMP

By Carey Bunks
1st Edition
342 pages, $45.00
ISBN: 0-7357-0924-6

Grokking the GIMP is a technical reference that covers the intricacies of the GIMP's functionality. The material gives the reader the ability to get up to speed quickly and start creating great graphics using the GIMP. Included as a bonus are step-by-step cookbook features used entirely for advanced effects.

GIMP Essential Reference

By Alex Harford
1st Edition
400 pages, $24.95
ISBN: 0-7357-0911-4

As the use of the Linux OS gains steam, so does the use of the GIMP. Many Photoshop users are starting to use the GIMP, recognized for its power and versatility. Taking this into consideration, GIMP Essential Reference has shortcuts exclusively for Photoshop users and puts the power of this program into the palm of the reader's hand.

Solaris Advanced System Administrator's Guide

By Janice Winsor
2nd Edition
587 pages, $39.99
ISBN: 1-57870-039-6

This officially authorized tutorial provides indispensable tips, advice, and quick-reference tables to help you add system components, improve service access, and automate routine tasks. this book also includes updated information on Solaris 2.6 topics.

Solaris System Administrator's Guide

By Janice Winsor
2nd Edition
324 pages, $34.99
ISBN: 1-57870-040-X

Designed to work as both a practical tutorial and quick reference, this book provides UNIX administrators complete, detailed descriptions of the most frequently performed tasks for Solaris. Learn how to employ the features of Solaris to meet these needs of your users, and get tips on how to make administration easier.

Networking

Cisco Router Configuration &Troubleshooting

By Mark Tripod
2nd Edition
330 pages, $39.99
ISBN: 0-7357-0999-8

A reference for the network and system administrator who finds himself having to configure and maintain existing Cisco routers, as well as get new hardware up and running. By providing advice and preferred practices, instead of just rehashing Cisco documentation, this book gives networking professionals information they can start using today.

Understanding Directory Services

By Beth Sheresh and Doug Sheresh
1st Edition
390 pages, $39.99
ISBN: 0-7357-0910-6

Understanding Directory Services provides the reader with a thorough knowledge of the fundamentals of directory services: what Directory Services are, how they are designed, and what functionality they can provide to an IT infrastructure. This book provides a framework to the exploding market of directory services by placing the technology in context and helping people understand what directories can, and can't, do for their networks.

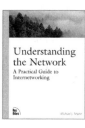

Understanding the Network: A Practical Guide to Internetworking

By Michael Martin
1st Edition
690 pages, $39.99
ISBN: 0-7357-0977-7

Understanding the Network addresses the audience in practical terminology, and describes the most essential information and tools required to build high-availability networks in a step-by-step implementation format. Each chapter could be read as a standalone, but the book builds progressively toward a summary of the essential concepts needed to put together a wide-area network.

Understanding Data Communications

By Gilbert Held
6th Edition
620 pages, $39.99
ISBN: 0-7357-0036-2

Gil Held's book is ideal for those who want to get up to speed on technological advances as well as those who want a primer on networking concepts. This book is intended to explain how data communications actually work. It contains updated coverage on hot topics like thin client technology, x2 and 56Kbps modems, voice digitization, and wireless data transmission. Whatever your needs, this title puts perspective and expertise in your hands.

LDAP: Programming Directory Enabled Applications

By Tim Howes and Mark Smith
1st Edition
480 pages, $44.99
ISBN: 1-57870-000-0

This overview of the LDAP standard discusses its creation and history with the Internet Engineering Task Force, as well as the original RFC standard. LDAP also covers compliance trends, implementation, data packet handling in C++, client/server responsibilities and more.

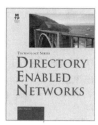

Directory Enabled Networks

By John Strassner
1st Edition
752 pages, $50.00
ISBN: 1-57870-140-6

Directory Enabled Networks is a comprehensive resource on the design and use of DEN. This book provides practical examples side-by-side with a detailed introduction to the theory of building a new class of network-enabled applications that will solve networking problems. DEN is a critical tool for network architects, administrators, and application developers.

Gigabit Ethernet Networking

By David Cunningham
and
Bill Lane
1st Edition
560 pages, $50.00
ISBN: 1-57870-062-0

Gigabit Ethernet is the next step for speed on the majority of installed networks. Explore how this technology will allow high-bandwidth applications, such as the integration of telephone and data services, real-time applications, thin client applications, such as Windows NT Terminal Server, and corporate teleconferencing.

Supporting Service Level Agreements on IP Networks

By Dinesh Verma
1st Edition
270 pages, $50.00
ISBN: 1-57870-146-5

An essential resource for network engineers and architects, *Supporting Service Level Agreements on IP Networks* will help you build a core network capable of supporting a range of service. Learn how to create SLA solutions using off-the-shelf components in both best-effort and DiffServ/IntServ networks. Learn how to verify the performance of your SLA, as either a customer or network services provider, and use SLAs to support IPv6 networks.

Local Area High Speed Networks

By Dr. Sidnie Feit
1st Edition
655 pages, $50.00
ISBN: 1-57870-113-9

There is a great deal of change happening in the technology being used for local area networks. As Web intranets have driven bandwidth needs through the ceiling, inexpensive Ethernet NICs and switches have come into the market. As a result, many network professionals are interested in evaluating these new technologies for implementation. This book provides real-world implementation expertise for these technologies, including traces, so that users can realistically compare and decide how to use them.

Wide Area High Speed Networks

By Dr. Sidnie Feit
1st Edition
624 pages, $50.00
ISBN: 1-57870-114-7

Networking is in a transitional phase between long-standing conventional wide area services and new technologies and services. This book presents current and emerging wide area technologies and services, makes them understandable, and puts them into perspective so that their merits and disadvantages are clear.

Differentiated Services for the Internet

By Kalevi Kilkki
1st Edition
400 pages, $50.00
ISBN: 1-57870-132-5

This book offers network architects, engineers, and managers of packet networks critical insight into the continuing development of Differentiated Services. It addresses the particular needs of a network environment as well as issues that must be considered in its implementation. Coverage allows networkers to implement DiffServ on a variety of networking technologies, including ATM, and to solve common problems related to TCP, UDP, and other networking protocols.

Quality of Service in IP Networks

By Grenville Armitage
1st Edition
310 pages, $50.00
ISBN: 1-57870-189-9

Quality of Service in IP Networks presents a clear understanding of the architectural issues surrounding delivering QoS in an IP network, and positions the emerging technologies within a framework of solutions. The motivation for QoS is explained with reference to emerging real-time applications, such as Voice/Video over IP, VPN services, and supporting Service Level Agreements.

Designing Addressing Architectures for Routing and Switching

By Howard Berkowitz
1st Edition
500 pages, $45.00
ISBN: 1-57870-059-0

One of the greatest challenges for a network design professional is making the users, servers, files, printers, and other resources visible on their network. This title equips the network engineer or architect with a systematic methodology for planning the wide area and local area network "streets" on which users and servers live.

Understanding and Deploying LDAP Directory Services

By Tim Howes, Mark Smith, and Gordon Good
1st Edition
850 pages, $50.00
ISBN: 1-57870-070-1

This comprehensive tutorial provides the reader with a thorough treatment of LDAP directory services. Minimal knowledge of general networking and administration is assumed, making the material accessible to intermediate and advanced readers alike. The text is full of practical implementation advice and real-world deployment examples to help the reader choose the path that makes the most sense for his specific organization.

Switched, Fast, and Gigabit Ethernet
By Sean Riley and
Robert Breyer
3rd Edition
615 pages, $50.00
ISBN: 1-57870-073-6

Switched, Fast, and Gigabit Ethernet, Third Edition is the one and only solution needed to understand and fully implement this entire range of Ethernet innovations. Acting both as an overview of current technologies and hardware requirements as well as a hands-on, comprehensive tutorial for deploying and managing switched, fast, and gigabit ethernet networks, this guide covers the most prominent present and future challenges network administrators face.

The DHCP Handbook
By Ralph Droms
and Ted Lemon
1st Edition
535 pages, $55.00
ISBN: 1-57870-137-6

The DHCP Handbook is an authoritative overview and expert guide to the setup and management of a DHCP server. This title discusses how DHCP was developed and its interaction with other protocols. Learn how DHCP operates, its use in different environments, and the interaction between DHCP servers and clients. Network hardware, inter-server communication, security, SNMP, and IP mobility are also discussed. Also, included in the book are several appendices that provide a rich resource for networking professionals working with DHCP.

Wireless LANs: Implementing Interoperable Networks
By Jim Geier
1st Edition
432 pages, $40.00
ISBN: 1-57870-081-7

Wireless LANs covers how and why to migrate from propri-etary solutions to the 802.11 standard, and explains how to realize significant cost savings through wireless LAN imp-lementation for data collection systems.

Designing Routing and Switching Architectures for Enterprise Networks
By Howard Berkowitz
1st Edition
992 pages, $55.00
ISBN: 1-57870-060-4

This title provides a fundamental under-standing of how switches and routers operate, enabling the reader to use them effectively to build networks. The book walks the network designer through all aspects of requirements, analysis, and deployment strategies, strengthens read-ers' professional abilities, and helps them develop skills necessary to advance in their profession.

Network Performance Baselining

By Daniel Nassar
1st Edition
736 pages, $50.00
ISBN: 1-57870-240-2

Network Performance Baselining focuses on the real-world implementation of network baselining principles and shows not only how to measure and rate a network's performance, but also how to improve the network performance. This book includes chapters that give a real "how-to" approach for standard baseline methodologies along with actual steps and processes to perform network baseline measurements. In addition, the proper way to document and build a baseline report will be provided.

The Economics of Electronic Commerce

By Soon-Yong Choi, Andrew Whinston, Dale Stahl
1st Edition
656 pages, $49.99
ISBN: 1-57870-014-0

This is the first electronic commerce title to focus on traditional topics of economics applied to the electronic commerce arena. While all other electronic commerce titles take a "how-to" approach, this focuses on what it means from an economic perspective.

Intrusion Detection

By Rebecca Gurley Bace
1st Edition
340 pages, $50.00
ISBN: 1-57870-185-6

Intrusion detection is a critical new area of technology within network security. This comprehensive guide to the field of intrusion detection covers the foundations of intrusion detection and system audit. *Intrusion Detection* provides a wealth of information, ranging from design considerations to how to evaluate and choose the optimal commercial intrusion detection products for a particular networking environment.

Understanding Public-Key Infrastructure

By Carlisle Adams and Steve Lloyd
1st Edition
300 pages, $50.00
ISBN: 1-57870-166-X

This book is a tutorial on, and a guide to the deployment of, Public-Key Infrastructures. It covers a broad range of material related to PKIs, including certification, operational considerations and standardization efforts, as well as deployment issues and considerations. Emphasis is placed on explaining the interrelated fields within the topic area, to assist those who will be responsible for making deployment decisions and architecting a PKI within an organization.

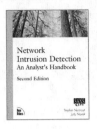

Network Intrusion Detection: An Analyst's Handbook

By Stephen Northcutt and Judy Novak
2nd Edition
480 pages, $45.00
ISBN: 0-7357-1008-2

Get answers and solutions from someone who has been in the trenches. Author Stephen Northcutt, original developer of the Shadow intrusion detection system and former Director of the United States Navy's Information System Security Office, gives his expertise to intrusion detection specialists, security analysts, and consultants responsible for setting up and maintaining an effective defense against network security attacks.

Domino System Administration

By Rob Kirkland
1st Edition
860 pages, $49.99
ISBN: 1-56205-948-3

Need a concise, practical explanation about the new features of Domino, and how to make some of the advanced stuff really work? *Domino System Administration* is the first book on Domino that attacks the technology at the professional level, with practical, hands-on assistance to get Domino 5 running in your organization.

Lotus Notes & Domino Essential Reference

By Dave Hatter, and Tim Bankes
1st Edition
675 pages, $45.00
ISBN: 0-7357-0007-9

If you need something to facilitate your creative and technical abilities—something to perfect your Lotus Notes and Domino programming skills—this is the book for you. This title includes all of the objects, classes, functions, and methods found if you work with Lotus Notes and Domino. It shows the object hierarchy and the overlying relationship between each one, organized the way the language is designed.

Software Architecture and Engineering

Designing Flexible Object-Oriented Systems with UML

By Charles Richter
1st Edition
416 pages, $40.00
ISBN: 1-57870-098-1

Designing Flexible Object-Oriented Systems with UML details the UML, which is a notation system for designing object-oriented programs. The book follows the same sequence that a development project might employ, starting with requirements of the problem using UML case diagrams and activity diagrams. The reader is shown ways to improve the design as the author moves through the transformation of the initial diagrams into class diagrams and interaction diagrams.

Constructing Superior Software

By Paul Clements, et al.
1st Edition
285 pages, $40.00
ISBN: 1-57870-147-3

Published in cooperation with the Software Quality Institute at the University of Texas, Austin, this title presents a set of fundamental engineering strategies for achieving a successful software solution, with practical advice to ensure that the development project is moving in the right direction. Software designers and development managers can improve the development speed and quality of their software, and improve the processes used in development.

A UML Pattern Language

By Paul Evitts
1st Edition
260 pages, $40.00
ISBN: 1-57870-118-X

While other books focus only on the UML notation system, this book integrates key UML modeling concepts and illustrates their use through patterns. It provides an integrated, practical, step-by-step discussion of UML and patterns, with real-world examples to illustrate proven software modeling techniques.

Other Books By New Riders Press

Directory Enabled Networks
1-57870-140-6 • $50.00 US
Differentiated Services for the Internet
1-57870-132-5 • $50.00 US
Policy-Based Networking: Architecture and
Algorithms
1-57870-226-7 • $50.00 US
Networking Quality of Service and Windows
Operating Systems
1-57870-206-2 • $50.00 US
Quality of Service on IP Networks
1-57870-189-9 • $50.00 US
Designing Addressing Architectures for
Routing and Switching
1-57870-059-0 • $45.00 US
Understanding & Deploying LDAP Directory
Services
1-57870-070-1 • $50.00 US
Switched, Fast and Gigabit Ethernet, Third
Edition
1-57870-073-6 • $50.00 US
Wireless LANs: Implementing Interoperable
Networks
1-57870-081-7 • $40.00 US
Wide Area High Speed Networks
1-57870-114-7 • $50.00 US
The DHCP Handbook
1-57870-137-6 • $55.00 US
Designing Routing and Switching
Architectures for Enterprise Networks
1-57870-060-4 • $55.00 US
Local Area High Speed Networks
1-57870-113-9 • $50.00 US
Network Performance Baselining
1-57870-240-2 • $50.00 US
Economics of Electronic Commerce
1-57870-014-0 • $49.99 US

SECURITY

Intrusion Detection
1-57870-185-6 • $50.00 US
Understanding Public-Key Infrastructure
1-57870-166-X • $50.00 US
Network Intrusion Detection: An Analyst's
Handbook, 2E
0-7357-1008-2 • $45.00 US
Linux Firewalls
0-7357-0900-9 • $39.99 US
Intrusion Signatures and Analysis
0-7357-1063-5 • $39.99 US

LOTUS NOTES/DOMINO

Domino System Administration
1-56205-948-3 • $49.99 US
Lotus Notes & Domino Essential Reference
0-7357-0007-9 • $45.00 US

PROFESSIONAL CERTIFICATION

TRAINING GUIDES

MCSE Training Guide: Networking
Essentials, 2nd Ed.
1-56205-919-X • $49.99 US
MCSE Training Guide: Windows NT Server
4, 2nd Ed.
1-56205-916-5 • $49.99 US
MCSE Training Guide: Windows NT
Workstation 4, 2nd Ed.
1-56205-918-1 • $49.99 US
MCSE Training Guide: Windows NT Server 4
Enterprise, 2nd Ed.
1-56205-917-3 • $49.99 US
MCSE Training Guide: Core Exams Bundle,
2nd Ed.
1-56205-926-2 • $149.99 US
MCSE Training Guide: TCP/IP, 2nd Ed.
1-56205-920-3 • $49.99 US
MCSE Training Guide: IIS 4, 2nd Ed.
0-7357-0865-7 • $49.99 US
MCSE Training Guide: SQL Server 7
Administration
0-7357-0003-6 • $49.99 US
MCSE Training Guide: SQL Server 7
Database Design
0-7357-0004-4 • $49.99 US
MCSD Training Guide: Visual Basic 6 Exams
0-7357-0002-8 • $69.99 US
MCSD Training Guide: Solution
Architectures
0-7357-0026-5 • $49.99 US
MCSD Training Guide: 4-in-1 Bundle
0-7357-0912-2 • $149.99 US
A+ Certification Training Guide, Second
Edition
0-7357-0907-6 • $49.99 US
A+ Certification Training Guide, Third
Edition
0-7357-1088-0 • $49.99 US
Available April 2001
Network+ Certification Guide
0-7357-0077-X • $49.99 US
Solaris 2.6 Administrator Certification
Training Guide, Part I
1-57870-085-X • $40.00 US
Solaris 2.6 Administrator Certification
Training Guide,
Part II
1-57870-086-8 • $40.00 US
Solaris 7 Administrator Certification Training
Guide, Part I and II
1-57870-249-6 • $49.99 US

MCSE Training Guide: Windows 2000
Professional
0-7357-0965-3 • $49.99 US
MCSE Training Guide: Windows 2000 Server
0-7357-0968-8 • $49.99 US
MCSE Training Guide: Windows 2000
Network Infrastructure
0-7357-0966-1 • $49.99 US
MCSE Training Guide: Windows 2000
Network Security Design
0-73570-984X • $49.99 US
MCSE Training Guide: Windows 2000
Network Infrastructure Design
0-73570-982-3 • $49.99 US
MCSE Training Guide: Windows 2000
Directory Svcs. Infrastructure
0-7357-0976-9 • $49.99 US
MCSE Training Guide: Windows 2000
Directory Services Design
0-7357-0983-1 • $49.99 US
MCSE Training Guide: Windows 2000
Accelerated Exam
0-7357-0979-3 • $69.99 US
MCSE Training Guide: Windows 2000 Core
Exams Bundle
0-7357-0988-2 • $149.99 US

FAST TRACKS

CLP Fast Track: Lotus Notes/Domino 5
Application Development
0-73570-877-0 • $39.99 US
CLP Fast Track: Lotus Notes/Domino 5
System Administration
0-7357-0878-9 • $39.99 US
Network+ Fast Track
0-7357-0904-1 • $29.99 US
A+ Fast Track
0-7357-0028-1 • $34.99 US
MCSD Fast Track: Visual Basic 6,
Exam #70-175
0-7357-0019-2 • $19.99 US
MCSD FastTrack: Visual Basic 6,
Exam #70-175
0-7357-0018-4 • $19.99 US

SOFTWARE ARCHITECTURE & ENGINEERING

Designing for the User with OVID
1-57870-101-5 • $40.00 US
Designing Flexible Object-Oriented Systems
with UML
1-57870-098-1 • $40.00 US
Constructing Superior Software
1-57870-147-3 • $40.00 US
A UML Pattern Language
1-57870-118-X • $45.00 US

 # How to Contact Us

Visit Our Web Site

`www.newriders.com`

On our Web site you'll find information about our other books, authors, tables of contents, indexes, and book errata. You will also find information about book registration and how to purchase our books.

Email Us

Contact us at this address:

`nrfeedback@newriders.com`

- If you have comments or questions about this book
- To report errors that you have found in this book
- If you have a book proposal to submit or are interested in writing for New Riders
- If you would like to have an author kit sent to you
- If you are an expert in a computer topic or technology and are interested in being a technical editor who reviews manuscripts for technical accuracy
- To find a distributor in your area, please contact our international department at this address.

`nrmedia@newriders.com`

- For instructors from educational institutions who want to preview New Riders books for classroom use. Email should include your name, title, school, department, address, phone number, office days/hours, text in use, and enrollment, along with your request for desk/examination copies and/or additional information.
- For members of the media who are interested in reviewing copies of New Riders books. Send your name, mailing address, and email address, along with the name of the publication or Web site you work for.

Bulk Purchases/Corporate Sales

If you are interested in buying 10 or more copies of a title or want to set up an account for your company to purchase directly from the publisher at a substantial discount, contact us at 800-382-3419 or email your contact information to corpsales@pearsontechgroup.com. A sales representative will contact you with more information.

Write to Us

New Riders Publishing
201 W. 103rd St.
Indianapolis, IN 46290-1097

Call Us

Toll-free (800) 571-5840 + 9 + 7477
If outside U.S. (317) 581-3500. Ask for New Riders.

Fax Us

(317) 581-4663

Solutions from experts you know and trust.

www.informit.com